D1008743

THE CHURCH AND POLITICS IN CHILE

THE CHURCH
AND POLITICS IN CHILE

Challenges to Modern Catholicism

BRIAN H. SMITH

Princeton University Press   Princeton, New Jersey

FOR THE CHRISTIAN COMMUNITIES OF

Centro Bellarmino AND *Cerro Navia*

WHO TAUGHT ME SO MUCH ABOUT THE
REALITY OF THE CHILEAN CHURCH

Contents

Tables

Preface

This book would have been impossible without the advice, criticism, encouragement, technical assistance, and support of many colleagues, friends, and family. At the risk of omitting some acknowledgments, there are several persons and groups to whom I owe a special debt of gratitude and want to mention by name.

Fr. Renato Poblete, S.J., from the very beginning offered invaluable assistance. He introduced me to all the Chilean bishops. Without this personal touch I would not have been able to conduct interviews with leaders at various levels of the Chilean Church so smoothly. Renato also gave me copies of surveys from Centro de Opinión Pública which he had helped Eduardo Hamuy prepare. The contributions of both these men enabled me to include in the book large amounts of empirical data on public opinion in Santiago collected between 1958 and 1973.

Juan Linz and Al Stepan provided such intellectual stimulation for creating the research design and the questionnaire that I was clearly drawn far beyond what I believed possible. From the start they wanted me to write a book and so guided my dissertation at Yale in that direction. Al's analytical originality and Juan's breadth of knowledge and insights into institutional change were constant sources of new ideas as each chapter went through draft after draft. Rocio Linz and Nancy Stepan also gave me strong encouragement on countless occasions during this study, and to each of them as well I am most grateful.

The field research and writing of the dissertation were made financially possible by a Foreign Area Fellowship grant from the Social Science Research Council and by the Society of Jesus (of which I was a member until 1979). The conclusions, opinions, and other statements in the book are my own, however, and do not necessarily reflect attitudes of the SSRC or the Jesuits.

While in Chile, I received other types of very crucial assistance from many different persons, organizations, and communities. Individually or corporately they made contributions which I never could have generated on my own.

The Chilean bishops, priests, nuns, and lay leaders whom I interviewed throughout the country were most cooperative and patient as I subjected them to the rather long questionnaire. The warmth with which so many of these persons received me will forever be remembered and deeply appreciated.

The men and women at Centro Bellarmino with whom I lived and worked for eleven months in 1975 gave me needed suggestions and constructive criticisms. They treated me as a colleague, and with typical Chilean hospitality incorporated me into their *equipo* and into their respective families as well.

The members of the Christian community of Cerro Navia in Pudahuel, Santiago, where I served as a priest, shared their joys, struggles, and faith with me so candidly that I shall always remember my days among them as some of the happiest of my entire life. My knowledge of the Chilean Church became far more than intellectual due to the human experiences I was privileged to share with these deeply committed men and women.

The representatives of the Ford Foundation both in Santiago and New York facilitated my research in countless ways known only to themselves. I could not have completed what I did without the help of Nita and Frank Manitzas, Richard Dye, Gary Horlick, Patricia Nagel, and Pauline Bell. To them and to several others at the Foundation I am most grateful.

Several friends and colleagues participated in the gathering of data or in critiquing various parts of early versions of the manuscript. Among those who were most generous to me with their time and advice are: Fr. Sergio Torres, Sr. Katherine Gilfeather, M.M., José Zalaquett, Tom Sanders, Arturo Gaete, S.J., Patricio Cariola, S.J., Santiago Larraín, Julio Jiménez, S.J., David Apter, José Luis Rodríguez, Tom Quigley, Rev. William Wipfler, Kay Baxter, Eugene Culhane, S.J., Renato Hevia, S.J., Patricia Van Dorp, Carmen Galilea, Josefina Puga, Cristián Vives, Alex Wilde, Fred Turner, Ralph Della Cava, Cornelia Butler Flora, Claude Pomerleau, C.S.C., Mike Dodson, Tom Bruneau, Richard Alan White, Robinson Cárdenas, Freddy Fortoul, José Van der Rest, S.J., Margarita Bennett, Georgette Dorn, Everette Larson, Jonathan Hartlyn, Jonathan Turner, and Michael Fleet.

Others both here in the United States and abroad gave me information on the various sources of financial and personnel support to the Chilean Church since 1960. I am very grateful particularly to Fr. José Kuhl of Mutual Pax Chile, Msgr. Roland Bordelon and Ms. Edith F. Hubler of Catholic Relief Services, Frances Neason in the Secretariat for Latin America of the U.S. Catholic Conference, Sr. Ann Gormly, S.N.D., U.S. Catholic Mission Council, Marcel Duchateau of Coopération Internationale pour le Développement Socio-Economique (CIDSE), Msgr. Emil Stehle of Adveniat, Msgr. Leo Schwarz of Misereor, Dr. Georg Specht and Karl Ammann of Deutscher Caritasverband, and Jim O'Brien and Sal Pinzino formerly of the Inter-American Foundation.

The final version of the manuscript as a dissertation was read entirely by Daniel Levine, Margaret Crahan, and Paul Sigmund. Sections of it were also read by Arturo and Samuel Valenzuela, and by Raimundo Valenzuela, the Methodist bishop of Chile. All of these persons gave me additional content and stylistic suggestions, some of which I have included in the book.

Many persons helped me with preparing the book manuscript. Without their generous assistance, I never could have finished the opus. I want to think especially Elly Terlingen, Mara Ferris, Mary Miller, Gina Sandomato, Robert Polk, Elizabeth Collins, Ruth Miller, Mia Saunders, and Debra DiFiore. I would also like to thank Marilyn Campbell for her most constructive suggestions in editing the final manuscript.

Finally, the encouragement and understanding I received from fellow Jesuits when I was a member of the Society of Jesus (especially at the Woodstock Theological Center at Georgetown University) made it possible for me to persevere for several years in completing the dissertation version of the manuscript. To my own relatives and extended family for their moral support as I went through the agony of writing, I owe a debt of deep appreciation—the Beaulieus, the Gormans, the Gaffneys, the McPhersons, and the Dunns.

To my wife, Mary Kaye, I owe very special thanks. Her common sense, humor, and love as I made the final revisions of this manuscript were invaluable.

PART I

Ideological and Institutional Dynamics of the Roman Catholic Church

1 Changes and Challenges in Post-Vatican II Catholicism

Classical theories on the role of religion in Western society elaborated in late nineteenth and early twentieth centuries by Spencer, Durkheim, Marx, Weber, and Malinowski all concluded that religion, while sometimes a revolutionary element, is normally a conservative force in the process of social change.[1] The Roman Catholic Church at the time these theories were being articulated provided much evidence to justify their conclusion. Since the sixteenth century, the Church had fought against the erosion of its spiritual and temporal power precipitated by the Reformation, the Enlightenment, the French and Industrial Revolutions, Marxism, and the emergence of the secular nation-state. Catholicism opposed values underlying these movements such as individualism, freedom of conscience, democracy, human rights, and revolutionary change as being antithetical to its own belief system. In turn, those identified with these modern currents of thought sought to reduce the Church's influence in the secular realm in order to promote their objectives. In the post-Reformation period, therefore, the Church strengthened its vertical hierarchical structures in order to preserve orthodoxy, and established closer alliances with conservative social and political forces.[2]

In recent years, however, the Roman Church has announced a series of official changes affecting both its stance toward secular developments as well as the style of performing its pastoral mission in the modern world. The Second Vatican Council (1962–1965) committed the Church

[1] In his comparative study of major world religions, Max Weber discovered only one instance in which he believed religion played an important and prolonged role in acting as a contributing agent for social and economic change. In seventeenth-century Europe, the Calvinist virtues of industry, self-denial, and thrift exercised within the context of one's occupational calling (as a means of gaining assurance of salvation) reinforced the rational and efficient dynamics underlying emerging capitalism. Calvinism, according to Weber, provided the urban commercial classes of Holland and England with ascetic and moral resources to challenge the established landed gentry and monarchy. *The Protestant Ethic and the Spirit of Capitalism,* pp. 121–22.

[2] Yves Congar, O.P., "The Historical Development of Authority in the Church: Points for Christian Reflection," pp. 119–56; and François Houtart and André Rousseau, *The Church and Revolution,* pp. 27–111.

to an active role in the promotion of justice, human rights, and freedom, urging all Catholics to share the "joys and hopes, the griefs and anxieties of the men of this age, especially those who are in any way afflicted."[3] An international synod of bishops meeting in Rome in 1971 made even more explicit the connection between religious faith and social justice, arguing the "action on behalf of justice and participation in the transformation of the world" are "constitutive dimensions of the preaching of the Gospel."[4]

Traditional Catholic social principles, once an obstacle to change in emerging capitalist economies, when they were identified with corporatist ideologies, now appear to be more compatible with various socialist models of development. Recent papal encyclicals have reformulated Catholic values of corporate solidarity, the primacy of the common good, and the principle of subsidiarity to legitimize major structural innovations such as restriction on economic competition, state planning and ownership of crucial resources, worker participation in management, and guaranteed price supports for raw materials on the international market.[5]

A much less polemical tone in judgments of Marxism has emerged in recent statements of popes recognizing various "levels of expression" in its ideology and permitting Catholic cooperation in movements based on false philosophical teachings "for the attainment of some practical end which was formerly deemed inopportune."[6] Communism and Catholicism continue to differ in their fundamental conceptions about human nature and social relationships, but since the 1960s there have been initiatives taken on both sides for authentic dialogue.[7]

There has also been a decline in official Church reliance on organized political support and partisan alliances. Vatican II officially set aside the longstanding Catholic tradition of the desirability of the union between

[3] "Pastoral Constitution on the Church in the Modern World," nos. 1, 26, 27, in *The Documents of Vatican II,* ed. Walter M. Abbott, S.J., pp. 199–200, 225–27.

[4] "Justice in the World," no. 6, in *The Gospel of Peace and Justice: Catholic Social Teaching Since Pope John,* ed. Joseph Gremillion, p. 514.

[5] Pope John XXIII, "Mater et Magistra," nos. 82–103; "Pacem in Terris," nos. 60–66; and Pope Paul VI, "Populorum Progressio," nos. 23, 24, 33, 44, 49, 56–61, in ibid., pp. 161–65, 214–16, 394, 397, 402, 404–6.

[6] Pope John XXIII, "Pacem in Terris," nos. 159–60; and Pope Paul VI, "Octogesima Adveniens," nos. 31–2, in ibid., pp. 235–36, 499–500.

[7] Beginning the the mid-1960s, a series of Christian-Marxist dialogues were held in Eastern Europe centered in Prague between Christian theologians and Marxist philosophers. After the Soviet invasion of Czechoslovakia in August 1968, these conversations were cut off, but there is recent evidence that there is renewed interest on both sides to revive them. Some of the most interesting results from these earlier encounters have been published in the works of Roger Garaudy, Giulio Gerardi, Quentin Lauer, Thomas Ogletree, Paul Oestreicher, and Helmut Gollwitzer. (See bibliography for specific references.)

Church and state, stating that the Church "does not lodge her hope in privileges conferred by civil authority." The Council stressed, however, the responsibility of the Church to "pass moral judgments, even on matters touching the political order, whenever basic personal rights or the salvation of souls make such judgments necessary."[8] Many bishops in Latin America, Asia, and Africa since the end of the Council have exercised this prophetic role vigorously, denouncing political disappearances, torture, economic exploitation, and racism perpetrated by authoritarian regimes in their countries.

The endorsement of a more independent and prophetic role for the Church in secular society has been accompanied by greater differentiation and decentralization of its internal structures of control. Vatican II acknowledged the legitimacy of religious liberty, the sacredness of conscience, collegiality in the exercise of episcopal authority, and voice for the laity in pastoral responsibilities.[9] Since the close of the Council, various episcopal conferences around the world have begun to implement these values, thus making national churches more sensitive to rank-and-file demands and problems.

Hence, since the mid-1960s, major transformations in official Catholic positions have provided the opportunity for greater integration of religious and secular values and have shifted the moral weight of the Church away from legitimizing the status quo toward an increased promotion of equity and freedom. These pronouncements not only call for a new style of religious mission, but also influence the social, economic, and political choices of the Church's membership, who constitute approximately one-sixth of the world's population. Linking action for justice with attainment of religious salvation could generate powerful motivational forces influencing the social, economic, and political choice of the Church's formal membership. Its transnational capacities rival those of its major secular counterparts—the United Nations, the multinational corporations, and the Communist Party—in its ability to move personnel and resources across national borders to develop or strengthen its local affiliates in areas where they are weak or under attack. Its commitment to protect human rights and the interests of the powerless is needed now more than ever to promote a moral framework and vision in contemporary international society.

The profile of the Church, therefore, is quite different than the one

[8] "Pastoral Constitution on the Church in the Modern World," no. 76, in *Documents of Vatican II,* ed. Abbott, pp. 287–89.

[9] "Declaration on Religious Freedom," no. 12; "Pastoral Constitution on the Church in the Modern World," no. 16; "Dogmatic Constitution on the Church," nos. 22–3; "Declaration on the Apostolate of the Laity," nos. 10, 23–8; in ibid., pp. 692–93, 213–14; 42–47; 500–506; 510–16.

that characterized it when classical theories on religion and social change were elaborated over fifty years ago. Catholic values and structures are no longer seen to be as hostile to the modern world as they once were, and there is evidence that the Church could become an important conduit for change if new official directives are put into action throughout its international network.

ISSUES FACING THE POST-VATICAN II CHURCH

As exciting as are the consequences that could result from these announced changes for both Church and world, the nature and purpose of the Church raise questions about how effectively these new orientations can be realized. It is the oldest institution in the West and has traditionally absorbed changes cautiously and slowly. Furthermore, its primary religious mission for centuries has been carried out in conflict with some major secular values and movements in the modern world. How quickly and consistently can its multilayered and long-established bureaucracy respond to the challenges of Vatican II and other official pronouncements? Will new social commitments, although officially endorsed as now integral to the pastoral mission of the Church, be given the same priority as religious concerns by leaders at different levels of the institution? Can values of freedom and participation be reconciled with hierarchical patterns of authority? These are hard questions that must be answered before an adequate assessment can be made of the impact announced changes can have on the Church's values and structures.

The voluntary nature of allegiances and varying degrees of commitment among its members also present serious problems for effectively reshaping the attitudes and choices of Catholics. The Church's formal membership of nearly 700 million baptized is multifaceted with a wide spectrum of loyalties ranging from saints, regular participants, irregularly practicing, and nominal members—all of whom differ in identification with the Church and in obedience to its teachings. How readily are Catholics accepting the social thrust of recent Church documents? Are there wide differences of interpretation as well as commitment among different social classes of Catholics? Is the Church capable of generating support for these values among members whose present social and economic interests are most threatened by them? All of these questions are related to the fundamental problem of developing adequate motivational resources throughout the Church to effect a new integration of religious and social commitments at a time when traditional disciplinary methods are being deemphasized.

Aside from these problems that relate to the extent and impact of announced changes inside the Church, it also faces difficult challenges in reorienting its posture in society at large. The organizational outreach of the Church is considerable, giving it unique capacities for transmitting values and resources but also setting parameters on its choices. Restructuring its bases for pastoral and social action throughout the world will be affected by the social and political forces that prevail in each national context. How will the transnational operations of the Church in its efforts to act as a catalyst for change intersect with preoccupations of national sovereignty and security in various nation-states? Can it effectively disengage itself from traditional structural alliances with governments or conservative forces in several parts of the world? What are the political conditions as well as consequences for both Church and society of attempts to use its resources to change the distribution of power among social groups? Can the Church be an effective prophetic force in authoritarian regimes or Marxist-dominated societies without serious curtailment of its freedom? These are some of the crucial questions that must be faced by leaders of the Church at the national and international levels if they are resolutely committed to promoting equity and justice in various nations of the contemporary world.

Each of these series of questions facing the post-Vatican II Church pertains to such traditional strengths as its longevity, diverse membership, and institutional outreach. Yet these very strengths also involve inherent difficulties for realizing changes that are effective and at the same time in continuity with its historical mission. Deeper theoretical problems are also involved in these questions which relate to the larger issue of how change occurs in a complex traditional organization.

The Church is a multilayered organization whose traditional religious mission affects the range of development permissible within it. It is committed to the preservation and transmission of certain truths which, for it, cannot change. Its structured relationships between leaders and followers, although flexible, cannot be radically altered without serious repercussions for orthodoxy and institutional continuity. Certain action patterns acceptable in secular institutions—e.g., decision-making by consensus, reliance on democratic procedures—if overemphasized in the Church could weaken hierarchical authority and threaten core dogmas. These characteristics related to performing its religious mission place definite limits, therefore, on the extent of change acceptable in the norms, structures, and behavior within the Church.

Its new commitments to social justice are consequently hortatory in nature and formulated in general categories meant to be in continuity with basic religious values. They legitimize some alternatives that as of yet have not been developed sufficiently to predict the practical consequences for traditional priorities. In some cases there may be lags in implementation due to bureaucratic inertia or to the lack of new educational processes to internalize them among the members. In other instances they may be interpreted and specified by lower elites and by rank-and-file members in ways not intended by the top leadership. This could challenge or undermine official beliefs or practices.

It remains to be seen to what extent new value orientations can be institutionalized in the Church effectively enough to precipitate major changes in attitudes and behavior of Catholics but without causing serious disruptions of traditional religious priorities. If the Church's commitment to new norms remains unfocused and unenforced, their influence on attitudes and behavior of both elites and various types of members will be erratic and diffuse. Conversely, if decentralization of responsibility and greater emphases on social action lead to consequences perceived by leaders as threatening to the integrity and purpose of the institution, serious conflicts and internal divisions could emerge, as well as a pullback at the top from the pursuit of some of the objectives endorsed in recent papal, conciliar, and episcopal documents. The resolution of this basic predicament will determine how the Church continues to fulfill its traditional religious mission in an age of transition, and will also determine its consistency as a force for social justice.

The Church also faces serious theoretical challenges as it attempts to carry out a new role in secular society. Rome and regional episcopal bodies can legitimize a politically and economically progressive stance for the universal Church, but each national subunit encounters particular opportunities as well as dilemmas in its own national context.

The symbolic moral authority of the Church will be shaped by how its messages relate to the dominant values in each country. If its new social emphases are compatible with the ideology underlying public policies, it could offer supportive reinforcement for the humanistic concerns of that society. The more specifically the leaders of a national church articulate these new norms, the more focused the Church's moral impact will be. The greater will be the danger, however, of associating the Church with very contingent economic or political policies that are beyond its competence. Moreover, in systems whose public norms do not legitimate equity, distributive justice, and participation, the prophetic voice of church leaders could have minimal impact. It could also precipitate serious ideological conflicts with the state that might result in restrictions on the Church's religious activities.

The institutional impact of the Church in each society will depend upon the new alliances it forges with other organizations in its environment. These interactions can both enhance and limit its capacities to influence that society. The closer it associates with secular institutions espousing similar economic or political goals, the more resources it can draw upon, the more allies it has in pursuing its objectives, and the more carriers it has for its own social messages. Yet, the closer religious and secular institutional alliances are forced, the greater will be the divisiveness of religion in pluralistic societies, and the more compromised the Church becomes, thus threatening its independence and moral credibility.

Overlapping memberships that Catholics have in other institutions provide perhaps the most important conduit for Church teachings into civil society. If the pattern of behavior required by their secular commitments or interests, however, is in contradiction to that demanded by the Church, serious crosspressures result. This could lead to alienation of laity from the Church or to their marginalization in other organizations. Either situation diminishes the Church's capacity to influence the larger social system through its membership.

Hence, there are internal predicaments for a complex organization such as the Roman Church when it attempts to modernize while preserving very traditional beliefs and structures. Simultaneously it faces added dilemmas as it attempts through its various national subunits to perform a progressive function in economic and political development without undermining its perennial and primary religious mission.

In order to assess the range of possibilities for resolving some of these predicaments, more probing of the normative, structural, and behavioral dynamics of change within the Church and their relationships with various social systems needs to be done. Most of the literature to date has tended to focus on only one level or aspect of analysis. Major religious works published over the past decade have concentrated on the doctrinal innovations of papal, conciliar, or episcopal statements since the mid-1960s, or have elaborated various models for how the Church could or should act as a result of some new developments in theology.[10] As important as these contributions are, they frequently fail to come to terms with the organizational weight of the institution, to what extent structures are actually evolving, and where there are practical limits on their flexibility. They also lack sufficient empirical methodology to determine if and how Catholic attitudes and behavior are changing in different national contexts.[11]

Studies by political scientists and sociologists on the institutional aspects of the Church and their relationships with wider social forces often

[10] The works of Hans Küng, Karl Rahner, Richard McBrien, and Avery Dulles are notable in this respect.

[11] To date there is no coordinated survey research throughout the Church measuring changes in religious attitudes and behavior over time, or testing for correlations between religious values and practices and social and political choices. An important contribution in this direction has been done in the United States by Andrew Greeley, a priest and sociologist at the National Opinion Research Center in Chicago.

tend to be so narrow in their focus that the results do not lend themselves to comparative analysis. Social scientists also frequently are not sensitive to the religious mission of the Church and how this affects the methods it adopts in confronting social and political problems.[12]

What is needed is a more comprehensive analysis of the Church as a complex religious organization, bringing to bear the methodology of various disciplines. In so doing, one must analyze developments across various levels of the institution and simultaneously their interactions with social forces in different political systems. Critical moral, institutional, and socializing dimensions of the Church that need more careful analysis are: (1) the ways in which its religious norms can be linked with humanistic secular values; (2) the layered nature of its elite system and how greater decentralization of responsibility is affecting authority flows; (3) class differences in religious identification and how these affect the internalization of new moral norms by Catholics; (4) the type and the effects of resource transfers from international church structures to national subunits.

In addition to analyzing the crucial factors determining the consistency and extent of changes possible across levels of its internal organization, more attention must be focused on the interactions between sectors of the Church and social forces at different moments of development and in various contexts. The most important issues that to date have not received sufficient emphasis in the literature are the following: (1) conditions that facilitate the extrication of the Church from traditional political alliances with the state and conservative groups; (2) the development of new roles and structures in the Church that reinforce processes of change in environments open to contributions from religious institutions; (3) factors leading to cooperation as well as conflict between the Church and social forces managing development in contexts where religious and secular goals are in opposition (e.g., in Marxist societies); (4) strategies available to the Church in societies dominated by authoritarian regimes.

In dealing with such sweeping and wide-ranging issues it is necessary to select a framework of analysis that will be manageable and that will also offer significant comparative understanding for other contexts. One solution to this problem would be to select a particular national church that has had to face a number of these internal and external challenges

---

[12] Some recent and very useful contributions to the study of organizational aspects of the Catholic Church that avoid aspects of these dangers have been done by Luigi Einaudi et al., Ivan Vallier, Francis X. Murphy, Thomas Bruneau, Ralph Della Cava, Margaret Crahan, Michael Dodson, John Coleman, Daniel Levine, and Alexander Wilde.

in a short period of time and whose experience can highlight a range of options available to the other churches in comparable situations.

CHILEAN RELIGIOPOLITICAL AND PASTORAL DEVELOPMENTS, 1920–1980

The development of religiopolitical relations in Chile over the past several decades offers a possible, as yet unexplored, field for examining the resolution of various practical and theoretical questions facing the post-Vatican II Church. In a relatively short period of time, Chile has experimented with a wide range of approaches to solve some of its chronic economic and political problems, and the predominantly Catholic cultural heritage of the country coupled with pastoral innovations in the Church has made Catholicism an important factor in shaping some of these experiments.

Chilean society's gamut of change in the twentieth century began with the rise of the liberal state in the 1920s and the emergence of new industrial working and middle classes in the 1930s. The country established Communist and Socialist parties in this period, and in the late 1930s a Popular Front government was in power for a brief period. Since the early 1960s, however, Chile has undergone dramatic economic and political transformations, experiencing three successive and very distinct models of economic and political development: (1) a reform Christian Democratic administration (1964–1970); (2) a Marxist-Socialist coalition government (1970–1973); and (3) an authoritarian military regime (1973–).

Throughout this period of development, the Chilean Catholic Church has faced several of the challenges confronting Catholicism in modern Western society: how to extricate itself from structural dependence on the state and a close association with the upper-class elites; where to develop mechanisms of religious and social control to influence changes in a rapidly developing democratic society; whether to oppose or to cooperate with a freely elected Marxist government; how to exercise a prophetic role on behalf of human rights under an authoritarian regime.

The manner in which Church leaders both in Chile and at the international level have dealt with each of these issues offers rich learning experiences for the Church in other areas of the third world which are struggling with economic and social problems and with the choice of democratic versus authoritarian methods to solve them. The Chilean Church's relationships with Marxism also offer a valuable comparative perspective for Western European societies where the possibility and extent of Christian Marxist cooperation is an issue of growing concern.

In the area of religious development, the Chilean Church has gone quite far in implementing new pastoral emphases of Vatican II—decentralization of parish structures, development of small neighborhood worship communities, promotion of religious women and the laity into positions of leadership, experimentation with new processes of evangelization among the working classes. These developments are all opening up new choices and have made Chilean Catholicism a good context for studying the impact of a wide variety of changes in the post-Vatican II Church.

METHOD AND PROCEDURE

My method for analyzing interrelationships between developments in Church and society in Chile utilizes a combination of three different approaches: (1) study of major currents of change over time that appear in various historical documents and opinion surveys; (2) in-depth structured interviews with Chilean religious elites that I conducted in 1975; and (3) personal experience as a participant-observer in Chile in 1972 as a student and in 1975 as an assistant pastor in a working-class neighborhood.

There is a wealth of historical and empirical evidence on developments in the Chilean Church over the past several decades. While in Chile, I had access to documents, correspondence, books, and periodicals in various Church archives and libraries not available in the United States. On the basis of these, I was able to establish the nature and time sequences of major normative shifts in official Church positions and relate these to major social and political developments.

Since 1958, the Episcopal Conference of Chile and Centro Bellarmino, a Jesuit-sponsored research institute, have done evaluations of various religious and social programs in the Church, as well as surveys of elite opinion and of religious practice in various parts of the country. The opinion research firm, Centro de Opinión Pública, also conducted public opinion surveys in the capital city of Santiago at regular intervals between 1958 and 1973. I had access to all of this empirical data and did secondary analysis of several of the surveys, examining correlations between social class, religious practice, and political choice to determine the extent of attitudinal and behavioral developments among various groups of rank-and-file Catholics during these years.

During my eleven months of field research in Chile in 1975, I also conducted extensive interviews with leaders at various levels of the Church in different parts of the country. I prepared and pretested a questionnaire with the aid of North American social scientists at Yale University and with Chilean social scientists at Centro Bellarmino in

Santiago where I worked as a research associate. The instrument contained fifty closed and open-ended questions designed to probe the patterns of consensus, as well as divergences, across leadership levels regarding the structural and behavioral implications of the new doctrinal and pastoral emphases since Vatican II. Interspersed with the questions on religious change were ones pertaining to the Church's relationship with the Frei, Allende, and Pinochet governments in order to assess the impact of religiopolitical developments under three very different regimes on attitudes of elites at various levels of responsibility in the Church.

I interviewed all thirty active Chilean bishops who exercise official legitimating authority in the Church, spending an average of two to three hours of formal questioning with each of them. While travelling throughout the country, I also interviewed forty-one parish priests in the provinces, selected to represent a diversity of geographical location and parish social composition. In the capital city of Santiago, I constructed a random stratified sample of thirty-one priests using ecclesiastical directories and census information. I interviewed a total of seventy-two priests from eighteen of the twenty-three dioceses who were directly responsible for the administration of subdiocesan parochial units, and who share to a lesser extent in the hierarchy's mission as official representatives of the Church. In order to compare the attitudes of bishops and priests with those having no formal authority but who have more contact with the base communities, I included in my sample thirty-three nuns from seven dioceses in different socio-economic areas, and a stratified sample of fifty-one lay leaders at the neighborhood level, mainly from Santiago.

The experience of living in Chile in 1972 while the Popular Unity government was in power, and again in 1975 under the military junta, gave me a personal vantage point from which to measure social and religious changes over time not easily captured in written documents or survey data. I was a student at the Instituto de Ciencias Políticas of the Catholic University of Santiago for seven weeks in the Chilean winter of 1972. In 1975, I worked for nine months with a team of nuns and lay leaders in promoting clusters of small Christian communities in the neighborhood of Cerro Navia in the county of Las Barrancas in Santiago. Of all my sources of information, this experience gave me the most sensitivity for the human dimensions involved in the formation of a new Church.

I use all of these materials and experiences in addressing major questions facing Catholicism in a period of transition. In each of the remaining chapters, I deal with a separate theoretical issue or challenge facing the universal Church, using a different historical period in the Chilean

Church's experience over the past half-century to illustrate a range of possible options for confronting it. Rather than summary findings at the end of the book, each chapter contains substantive conclusions pertaining to the special set of questions it raises.

Chapter 2 discusses the basic components of the complex transnational character of the Church central to an understanding of its adaptive capacities: the graduated binding force of its system of norms, authority flows across the layered structure of its administrative framework, the varied character of its membership, and resource transactions from center to periphery units. I analyze the theoretical and practical dimensions of these factors in historical perspective, and use empirical data from the Chilean Church to identify the strengths and limitations they provide for religious and social development once the Church is set in motion by change.

Chapters 3 through 6 focus on the possibility of extricating the Church from alliances with reactionary forces and of identifying it with major currents of social and economic change in a democratic society. I deal with the conditions for, and the extent of, the disassociation of the Chilean Church from the state and the Conservative Party in the 1920s and the 1930s, the development of new structures within the Church in the 1940s and 1950s and their linkages with the Christian Democratic Party, and the impact of shifts in the official legitimizing position of the Church on attutides and behavior of Catholics in the 1960s. I assess the cost-benefit factors of forging ideological and structural linkages between Catholicism and reform political movements.

Chapters 7 and 8 address the question of whether a rapprochement is possible between the Church and Marxism in a society undergoing a transition to socialism. Major encounters between Catholicism and Marxism, both at the external public policy level and within the Church itself during the Popular Unity government in Chile in the early 1970s, will serve as the loci for exploring the different dimensions of this issue. I analyze the evolution of changes in official Church and Marxist positions and strategies, using official documents, my interviews with clerical and lay elites active in the Catholic left, changing correlations between religious practice, social class, and political choice, and evaluations of contemporary Church leaders, to determine the significant breakthroughs as well as dilemmas that arose for the Church and for Marxists during the Allende administration. On the basis of the learning experience in Chile, I make some projections as to what strategies are transferable to other contemporary societies where Christian-Marxist cooperation and synthesis are still open questions.

Chapter 9 explores the relations between Church and state during the first seven years of the Pinochet regime in Chile to estimate the degree in which a post-Vatican II Church can act as an effective check against re-pression in an authoritarian society. I shall present documentary and empirical data on the ideological and structural capacities of the Chil-ean Church's efforts to blunt repressive policies of the government, as well as on the similarities and differences that exist among bishops, priests, nuns, and lay leaders as to what strategies the Church should employ in performing its contemporary pastoral and social mission. I offer some comparative analysis of the Church's stance toward authori-tarian regimes in other historical and contemporary contexts in order to underscore the similarities as well as the uniqueness of the Chilean case and what it forbodes for the future performance of the Church's pro-phetic mission.

2   The Church as a Complex Religious Organization

Since 1960, major changes have occurred at the official level of the Roman Catholic Church. The successive papacies of John XXIII, Paul VI, and John Paul II, the convocation of the first ecumenical council in nearly a century, and several international meetings of bishops, all have produced a series of documents signalling a new direction for the Church.

Unlike the First Vatican Council (1869–1870) which was preoccupied with protecting the Church's authority and property against rising tides of nationalism, anticlericalism, and revolutionary ferment sweeping through mid-nineteenth century Europe, Vatican II (1962–1965) met in the context of a very different world. Neither the spiritual nor temporal power of the Church of the 1960s was under such widespread attack as a century before. In Europe, the greater part of its landed interests and political privileges had diminished, and the old culture and social order of which it was a part had changed drastically. In the third world, the breakup of the colonial empires left it facing complex and chaotic problems of development. In the United States it was functioning comfortably in a pluralistic society, with a Catholic having achieved the presidency. The Church, therefore, no longer needed to be so much on the defensive; she now had to relate her mission to a world not openly hostile to religion but less convinced of its public importance.

Long before Vatican II, social encyclicals of Pope Leo XIII and Pope Pius XI—*Rerum Novarum* (1891) and *Quadragesimo Anno* (1931)—attempted to address the issues of injustice resulting from industrialization. Christian lay movements and parties in Germany, Italy, and France in the late nineteenth and early twentieth centuries established links with working-class organizations and secular reformists. These were forerunners of Christian Democratic parties that emerged in the post-World War II era. During the reign of Pius XII (1939–1958) the Church came to view democracy much more positively, especially in the light of its experiences under Nazism and fascism. Significant reforms were also inaugurated in the Church's liturgical life, placing more importance on biblical studies and the training of lay leaders in the 1940s and 1950s. All of these developments preceded Vatican II and, in fact, were influential in shaping the attitudes of the participants of the Council which began in Rome in 1962.[1]

The style of the documents of Vatican II dealing with the internal life of the Church, therefore, were scriptural and nondogmatic in tone. The Council Fathers avoided rigid definitions and scholastic distinctions that had characterized the heavily juridical focus of the previous two ecumenical councils, Trent (1545–1563) and Vatican I.[2] Authority was to be exercised more collegially among the hierarchy: a permanent international Synod of Bishops was to meet at regular intervals with the pope, and episcopal conferences would provide for greater communication and collaboration among bishops at the regional and national levels.[3] Bishops were to engage in more regular discussions with their priests, religious were to "enter more vigorously into the external work of the apostolate" in each diocese, and pastors were to invite lay men and women to a "more direct form of cooperation in the apostolate of the hierarchy." The deaconate for married men was to be restored, and pastoral councils composed of priests, religious, and laity were desirable in each diocese to advise the bishop.[4]

Furthermore, condemnations of modern secular values and movements, such as freedom of conscience, religious toleration, liberalism, communism, and socialism, articulated by the nineteenth-century Church were conspicuously absent in Vatican II's treatment of the mission of the Church in today's world. The Council Fathers recognized the sanctity of conscience as the "secret core and sanctuary" of persons, and supported the "right to religious freedom." They also acknowledged how richly the Church has profited from the progress of science and human development which has purified religion by distinguishing what is transcendent from what is magical and superstitious.[5]

In turn, the Council declared that the Church wants to make a significant contribution back to the world by providing everyday human activity with a deeper meaning, and by promoting the dignity and rights of all people and the common interests of humanity. They emphasized that the Church's unique transnational character enables it to perform

[1] For a good summary of the factors of change both in the world and in the Church that gave rise to the convocation of the Second Vatican Council, see Thomas F. O'Dea, *The Catholic Crisis.*
[2] "Dogmatic Constitution on the Church," nos. 1, 9, 18, in *Documents of Vatican II,* ed. Walter M. Abbott, S.J., pp. 15, 25–26, 37.
[3] "Decree on the Bishops' Pastoral Office in the Church," nos. 5, 37, in ibid., pp. 399–400, 425–26.
[4] Nos. 16, 27, 33, in ibid., pp. 408, 416, 420; "Dogmatic Constitution on the Church," nos. 29, 33, 37, in ibid., pp. 56, 60, 64.
[5] "Declaration on Religious Freedom," no. 2, in ibid., p. 678; and "Pastoral Constitution on the Church in the Modern World," nos. 7, 16, 40, 44, in ibid., pp. 205, 213, 239, 246.

this service. It is bound to no culture or political and economic system and by its "universality can be a very close bond between human communities and nations." They declared that the Church "does not lodge her hope in privileges conferred by civil authority" and "stands ready to renounce certain legitimately acquired rights" to make the "sincerity of her witness" more credible to all peoples.[6] The role, therefore, of the Church in modern society is to act as a catalytic and prophetic force, using moral rather than temporal power to promote justice at national and international levels.

The Council Fathers urged closer cooperation among "believers and unbelievers . . . to work for the rightful betterment of this world in which all alike live." Catholics in particular were encouraged to bring their faith to bear on secular commitments involving justice, and to integrate their "humane, domestic, professional, social and technical enterprises into one vital synthesis with religious values . . ."[7]

These new normative emphases by the Second Vatican Council have been reinforced in other official documents of the Church since the 1960s. Pope John's two major encyclicals on the social order, *Mater et Magistra* (1961) and *Pacem in Terris* (1963), along with *Populorum Progressio* (1967) of Pope Paul, provided a more structural and global analysis of the causes of chronic injustice than previous social encyclicals. They all stressed the need for major organizational changes at the national and international levels to achieve a more equitable distribution of wealth. They placed the moral weight of the Church behind such necessary processes to accomplish this as tax and land reform, social insurance, technical cooperation, disarmament, international price regulations, a world fund for development, and guarantees for social, economic, and political rights.[8] While disavowing a desire "to interfere in any way in the politics of States," the Church in these encyclicals did not hesitate to offer the world "what she possesses as her characteristic attribute: a global vision . . . of the human race."[9]

Various international meetings of bishops in the late 1960s and 1970s echoed conciliar and papal commitments to a prophetic stance on behalf of justice. The Second General Synod of Bishops, meeting in Rome

---

[6] "Pastoral Constitution on the Church in the Modern World," nos. 40–42, 76, in ibid., pp. 239–42, 288.

[7] Nos. 21, 43, in ibid., pp. 219, 243.

[8] Pope John XXIII, "Mater et Magistra," nos. 131–40, 163–65, in *Gospel of Peace and Justice,* ed. Joseph Gremillon, pp. 172–73, 179; "Pacem et Terris," nos. 11–27, in ibid., pp. 203–6; Pope Paul VI, "Populorum Progressio," nos. 24, 51, 61, in ibid., pp. 394, 403, 405, 406.

[9] Pope Paul VI, "Populorum Progressio," no. 13, in ibid., p. 391. Pope John Paul II reiterated several of these themes in his first social encyclical, *Redemptor Hominis* (1979). See Pope John Paul II, *The Redeemer of Man.*

in 1971, asserted that "the promotion of justice was a constitutive dimension of preaching the Gospel," and defended the "right, indeed the duty" of the Church to "denounce instances of injustice when the fundamental rights of man and his very salvation demand it . . ."[10]

In 1968 at Medellín, Colombia, 150 bishops representing all countries of the continent condemned the "institutionalized violence" of the status quo, placing responsibility squarely on the shoulders of those with the "greater share of wealth and power" who "jealously retain their privileges thus provoking 'explosive revolutions of despair.' " They committed the Church to act as a "catalyst in the temporal realm in an authentic attitude of service." As pastors they dedicated themselves "to educate the Christian conscience" in matters of social responsibilities, "to denounce everything which, opposing justice, destroys peace," "to defend the rights of the poor and oppressed," and "to encourage and favor efforts of the people to create and develop their own grass-roots organizations for the consolidation of their rights."[11]

In 1979 (in a follow-up to the Medellín meeting) 187 Latin American bishops at Puebla, Mexico reaffirmed this prophetic and activist role for the Church as it confronts oppressive states. They denounced authoritarian regimes on their continent which use illegitimate concepts of national security to justify "assassinations, disappearances, arbitrary imprisonment, acts of terrorism, kidnappings and acts of torture." They committed the resources of the Church to those suffering such violations, offering its own services to such persons "where public authorities and social organizations are absent or missing."[12]

It is clear that as a result of changes in secular society and in the Church itself, the institution has officially legitimized greater differentiation of religious roles and responsibilities; expanded dominant religious goals to incorporate a greater concern for justice and human rights; encouraged more freedom and voluntary commitments among members, and envisioned a more positive and dynamic interaction between Church and world. The Church has now committed itself to act as a "global pastor," giving "normative support for universal human values" in modern international society.[13]

---

[10] "Justice in the World," nos. 6, 36, in *Gospel of Peace and Justice,* ed. Gremillon, pp. 514, 521.

[11] Latin American Episcopal Council (CELAM), "Peace," nos. 16, 17, 20, 21, 27; "Justice," no. 22; in *The Church in the Present-Day Transformation of Latin America in the Light of the Council,* 2:67, 78–81.

[12] CELAM, "Evangelization in Latin America's Present and Future," nos. 1262, 1286, in *Puebla and Beyond: Documentation and Commentary,* ed. John Eagleson and Philip Scharper, pp. 279, 281.

[13] Ivan Vallier, "The Roman Catholic Church: A Transnational Actor," pp. 499–500.

As yet, however, it is not certain how consistently and uniformly these new commitments can be realized in an institution as traditional and complex as the Church. To assess its capacity to respond to these new challenges from the top, we must analyze several factors determining how they will be integrated with past priorities and implemented at lower levels of the institution.

FOUR CRITICAL VARIABLES AND RELATED CHALLENGES

Of all the possible characteristics that could be examined, I believe that four are the most significant for assessing the capacity of a complex organization to implement change—the degree of flexibility in its normative values, the arrangements of its elite roles and structures, the socialization and motivational processes it employs in incorporating members, and the resources it can generate to support its mission. The flexibility of an institution's values will indicate where new syntheses are possible and what gradation of importance exists among old and new symbols. The arrangement of its leadership roles and structures will determine how rapidly new goals can be operationalized without serious disruptions, and will affect the degree of leeway that exists for program expansion. The type of socialization processes to which members are exposed and the effectiveness of sanctions and rewards will determine the degree to which participants work toward the achievement of new official objectives. The origin and extent of its resource base will determine to what degree an organization can generate the necessary support for sustaining itself in a time of transition and for meeting its new commitments with coherence and autonomy.[14]

Since it is the Roman Catholic Church that is the focus of our analysis we must take into account its particular arrangement of normative, structural, and behavioral components in order to reach an accurate assessment of its capacities for implementing change. It is committed both to spiritual and temporal goals and its normative system must reflect a proportionate balance between these two different priorities, the former more perduring and transcendent and the latter subject to change and development. Its authority flows and elite structures are hierarchically orchestrated. Formal power is concentrated at the top of the institution in order to preserve and transmit certain unchanging religious doctrines. Its organizational network, however, is multilayered and not all decisions are made at the top by those invested with formal authority. Its membership patterns are universal rather than exclusive in scope due to

[14] Although the literature on change within complex organizations is vast, my own thinking process in this area has been most influenced by the writings and lectures of David Apter. See especially his *Choice and the Politics of Allocation*.

a fundamental religious commitment to offer the means of salvation to all types of people. This means, however, that association with the Church is varied, and uneven allegiances exist among different sectors of its formal membership. It is also both a subsystem within each national society as well as an international organization. This enables it to generate and transmit resources throughout the entire globe.

Each of these unique characteristics affecting the arrangement of its normative combinations, leadership roles and organizational structures, membership commitments, and available sources of institutional support have provided the Church with considerable resiliency throughout its 2,000-year history. All, however, place restrictions on its adaptive capacities, and present a number of predicaments for the Church during this recent period of announced change.

The first major predicament involves the integration of new social commitments into the Church's moral and religious system without detracting from what is essential to its mission. In the performance of its role as "global pastor," it must articulate principles in terms that are sufficiently clear and forceful in contemporary society without, however, identifying them too closely with contingent ideologies or movements that will compromise its transcendent purpose. To speak and act effectively, the Church cannot avoid making some very specific judgments on controversial social and economic problems or using its institutional weight to favor some causes and oppose others in the context of secular developments. Yet, it has also recently stated that it is prepared to surrender all vestiges of political power, privileges, and alliances in order to disengage itself from partisan entanglements that long have vitiated its moral credibility and damaged the performance of its universal religious mission. Whether it can balance these two opposing tendencies of greater involvement in secular problems and greater neutrality in partisan disputes, while still exerting significant influence, is a question yet to be answered.

A second major predicament which the Church faces in this age of transition is the challenge of implementing values of collegiality and pluralism without undermining hierarchical authority. Throughout most of its history there has been a certain amount of diversity and flexibility in the layered organizational framework of the Church due to some separation of functions and different levels of responsibility. Now, however, there is normative legitimacy for greater decentralization and sharing of decision-making with leaders at the local level of the institution. Leaders at the top of the Church must balance this increased sharing of responsibility among lower clergy, religious, and laity with maintenance of effective episcopal authority necessary for decisions on issues not subject to change by popular consensus.

A third fundamental challenge confronting the Church is to develop widespread acceptance for its new social emphases and still allow a range of responses to its teachings among different types of Catholics. If it tolerates a diversity of responses to its new social principles as it does in degrees of ritual practice, these teachings may be ignored by large numbers of laity who still frequent the sacraments but whose class interests prevent them from heeding the Church on political and economic issues. If, however, Church leaders demand rigid compliance and impose penalties (including excommunication) for infractions of these social norms, many Catholics may disassociate themselves entirely from the institution, thus detracting from its traditional religious commitment to a church-type rather than sectarian pattern of incorporation.

Finally, the transnational structures of the Church provide important institutional support for its subunits located in a variety of political systems throughout the world, but these also can create tensions with governments preoccupied with sovereignty. Precisely at a time when there is need for institutions such as the Church to bridge cultural boundaries and localized concerns on behalf of the common moral interests of humanity, there are also stronger criticisms of institutions which attempt to affect change beyond their own borders—the CIA, multinational corporations, communist parties, human rights groups. The resolution of the dilemma of rooting itself as a loyal institution in each national context while maintaining strong support linkages with its center and transnational affiliates has been a perennial difficulty for the Church. As it now attempts to serve as a catalytic and prophetic force for justice and human rights, this tension will become even more problematic.

The remainder of this chapter will, therefore, focus on each of the four essential components of the Church: (1) the graduated binding force and specificity of religious and moral norms; (2) the hierarchical nature of authority flows across a layered administrative network; (3) the diversified allegiance patterns among its membership; and (4) the transnational support linkages among center and periphery units. I will show how these historically have both provided the institution with flexibility and placed limitations on its adaptive capacities. I will highlight the particular problems these variables present for the Church now that it is attempting to carry out internal changes, using illustrations from my survey and other data from the contemporary Chilean Church. On the basis of some of the advances as well as tensions or contradictions that are emerging inside the Chilean Church, I will indicate how these also shape its capacities to come to terms with several problems involved in social and political development that are the focus of the following chapters.

VARIABLE NO. 1:
GRADUATED BINDING FORCE AND SPECIFICITY
OF CHURCH NORMS

As the Church attempts to address the moral dimensions of complex social and economic problems, it runs the risk of either speaking in generalities that are not useful for public policy-making or being so specific as to lose credibility by too close an identification with contingent or partisan solutions. Since the Church first began in the late nineteenth century to speak to the ethical issues involved in modern economic development, it has resolved this dilemma by employing different grades of specificity and binding force in its normative pronouncements. It also recognizes different areas of competence for clerics and laity in applying its social principles.

The core dogmas of Catholicism which bind all members are very few, specific, and pertain to the area of religious belief only—e.g., the existence of the Trinity, the divinity of Jesus, the Immaculate Conception of Mary, her Assumption into heaven, and the infallibility of the pope on those very few occasions when he makes it clear he is speaking *ex cathedra* (twice in the past century).[15] In the area of morality, however, there has never been a teaching that has been given the same official weight.

In regard to personal morality, the Church has been very specific in its guidelines, especially in the realm of sexual mores. Its positions are authoritative—i.e., to be taken very seriously, but not absolutely, by all the faithful. No pope, however, has ever invoked infallibility for his pronouncements in this area, even on the issue of birth control. In the realm of social morality, moreover, Church statements (always authoritative, and never infallible) are basically explications of natural law principles. These are theoretically knowable by all reasonable persons regardless of religious belief, but which the Church feels need interpretation, application, and reinforcement in various political and economic contexts.[16]

Church pronouncements on social justice are far more general in formulation than definitions of religious dogma or authoritative teachings on personal morality. Popes have articulated basic values and affirmed ethical principles to be kept in mind by Catholics in approaching social and economic issues, but they seldom specify solutions. The reason is

[15] In 1854 Pope Pius IX made it binding on all Catholics to believe in Mary's freedom from sin from the moment of her conception. In 1950 Pope Pius XII used equally binding language in affirming Mary's reception into heaven, body and soul, after her death. These are the only two instances in more than one hundred years when any pope has presumed to be infallible and so stated explicitly in the language of his pronouncements.

[16] Jean-Yves Calvez, S.J. and Jacques Perrin, S.J., *The Church and Social Justice: The Social Teachings of the Popes From Leo XIII to Pius XII, 1878–1958*, pp. 58–74.

that the Church is aware that it has no competence to provide technical answers to complex problems pertaining to societal development. It has traditionally recognized that honest differences can and do exist among groups of Catholics over the choice of the best practical means to realize the Church's values and principles in their own particular circumstances.[17]

During the fifty-year period from the 1870s to the mid-1920s, however, the Church did adopt specifically partisan strategies to promote its social principles and interests in secular society. Catholic political parties in various countries of Western Europe were supported by the Vatican as a defense against strongly anticlerical regimes and newly emerging leftist parties of Marxist inspiration. It discarded this approach when growing involvement by priests in parties and parliamentary politics compromised the religious mission of the Church, and also made it more vulnerable to attack by authoritarian governments that emerged in Europe in the post-World War I era. Since the mid-1920s, the Vatican has forbidden priests to engage in partisan political activities and no longer formally endorses parties.[18]

Over the past half-century, papal social pronouncements have time and again made a clear distinction between the role of clerics and laity in promoting Catholic social doctrine. The Church has also employed other structures and organizational resources besides political parties to act as carriers for its principles in secular society. The role of the hierarchy and of priests has been to teach and interpret the general norms of social morality, while the laity have been commissioned to make the specific applications of them in the social and political organizations to which they belong.[19] To enable the laity to perform this mission, Catholic Action organizations were formally established in several Western European nations after World War I. These grew out of movements of socially concerned Catholics that originated in Germany, Italy, France, and Belgium during the late nineteenth century. By the 1920s, these were officially endorsed by the Vatican under the title of Catholic Ac-

---

[17] Pope Pius XI, "Divini Redemptoris" (1937), no. 33, in *Social Wellsprings 2: Eighteen Encyclicals of Social Reconstruction by Pope Pius XI*, ed. Joseph Husslein, S.J., p. 355; Church Fathers of Vatican II, "Pastoral Constitution on the Church in the Modern World," no. 43, in *Documents of Vatican II*, ed. Abbott, p. 243; Pope Paul VI, "Octogesima Adveniens," no. 50, in *Gospel of Justice and Peace*, ed. Gremillon, pp. 510–11.

[18] Joseph N. Moody, ed., *Church and Society: Catholic Social and Political Thought and Movements, 1789–1950*, pp. 167–71, 446–74, 477–86. See also Anthony Rhodes, *The Vatican in the Age of Dictators, 1922–1945*, pp. 14–15, 31–32, 103–11, 143, 162–65. Pope John Paul II's 1980 prohibition of priests holding elective office, forcing Fr. Robert Drinan, S.J., to leave the United States Congress, was not a new policy but a reiteration of an old one.

[19] Pope Paul VI, "Populorum Progressio," no. 81, in *Gospel of Peace and Justice*, ed. Gremillon, p. 411.

tion and also spread to other parts of the Catholic world. Their purpose was to develop cadres of lay men and women imbued with a knowledge of the Church's social teaching and committed to finding adequate strategies to carry out these principles in the secular world.[20]

The underlying assumptions of this perspective have been that spiritual and temporal responsibilities of the Church are to be divided between clerics and laity respectively, and that the official Church, as represented by the pope, bishops, and priests, is to maintain a distance from partisan political movements. The goal of this strategy has been to create buffer or intermediate structures between the Church and secular structures capable both of specifying and implementing Catholic social values and of keeping the institutional Church free of too close an identification with political parties.[21]

Since the late 1960s, new challenges have arisen for the Church in maintaining these distinctions. The model developed in a European context fifty years ago does not solve problems facing the Church in many third-world countries of the present. Growing oppression by authoritarian regimes, the suppression of political parties and labor unions, and the lack of other social organizations mediating between the individual and the state are all common characteristics of many developing countries in Asia, Africa, and Latin America. In several of these nations, the Church is the only institution able to speak and act on behalf of the poor. Furthermore, general moral pronouncements by Church leaders on the need for change have frequently gone unheeded by those holding a monopoly of power, and Catholic lay organizations have not been adequately developed to make an impact on the social system. In light of the urgency in these countries, there has been pressure on the hierarchy to speak out more specifically against abuses of power and for clerics to become more directly involved in many of the political and economic problems of the oppressed.

A new style of exercising its role as global pastor has begun to emerge in the third-world Church, and especially in Latin America. The Medellín conference in 1968 did commit the official Church to a much more prophetic role of denunciation of very specific injustices and en-

---

[20] Jacques Maritain, "Catholic Action and Political Action," in *Scholasticism and Politics,* pp. 185–211; Gianfranco Poggi, *Catholic Action in Italy: The Sociology of a Sponsored Organization;* William Bosworth, *Catholicism and Crisis in Modern France,* pp. 97–155; and Moody, ed., *Church and Society,* pp. 161–74, 294–98, 407–34.

[21] The core of leadership of Christian Democratic parties in Italy, Germany, and France in post-World War II Europe emerged from Catholic Action circles in these respective countries. Thus, while no longer formally endorsing parties, the Church maintains close informal alliances and sympathies with certain parties due to the training these elites have received in religious movements and the ongoing association they maintain with the Church. Michael P. Fogarty, *Christian Democracy in Western Europe, 1820–1953.*

dorsed more active engagement by clerics in social action. Traditional assumptions underlying the Church's past performance of its social mission were not explicitly rejected by these bishops. The tone and emphasis of their pronouncements, however, clearly opened up new directions for implementing Catholic moral values in the context of societies experiencing chronic injustice and oppression. Distinctions between clergy and laity, and between spiritual and temporal responsibilities, were not reiterated at Medellín. A commitment to use the Church's resources and organizational structures on behalf of the poor was made. Openness to collaboration with all persons of good will was evident, and endorsements of organizations of specifically Christian inspiration to mediate between official Church and secular institutions were conspicuously absent.

After Medellín, this prophetic and activist role of the Latin American Church became more prominent. Many bishops attempted to disassociate the Church from its traditional identification with the established order, and issued very pointed criticisms against repressive authoritarian governments.[22] Movements of socially committed priests arose in several countries, who in some cases acted more forthrightly than their bishops in speaking out against specific injustices suffered by workers and peasants.[23] Nuns and lay leaders responsible for the formation of small base communities began to employ techniques based upon Paulo Freire's method of consciousness-raising (*concientización*) to heighten the political awareness of their communities and to further a closer integration between religious faith and social commitment.[24]

New religious formulations also began to appear in Latin America in the late 1960s. Theologians stressed collective aspects of sin as manifested in unjust structures and in the domination of one class by another. For them, salvation involves more than personal immortality. It is associated with struggle for liberation from historical patterns of oppression in this world. Christian love requires solidarity with the poor and con-

---

[22] José Marins, Teolide M. Trevisan and Carolee Chanona, *Praxis de los Padres de América Latina: documentos de las Conferencias Episcopales de Medellín a Puebla, 1968–1978.*

[23] ONIS in Peru, Golconda in Colombia and the Movement of Priests for the Third World in Argentina all arose in the late 1960s and were examples of a growing activist commitment by lower clergy in the face of chronic social injustices. For information on the strategies employed by these groups in their respective countries, see Manuel Alzate, *Libertad religiosa en Colombia;* Jeffrey L. Klaiber, S.J., *Religion and Revolution in Peru, 1824–1976;* Michael Dodson, "The Christian Left in Latin American Politics," pp. 45–68. See theses done by Dodson, Mooney, and Macaulay cited in bibliography.

[24] The method involves small-group discussion by poor people who reflect together on the causes of their oppression, and who take some constructive action to change social structure. For a description of Freire's principles and approach, see his works cited in the bibliography.

frontation with the rich, including class conflict. Distinctions between sacred and profane spheres of action are eliminated in this new theological framework, as are lines between religious and political responsibility. God's grace is revealed in historical movements aiming at greater freedom and equality, and the function of the Church is to articulate from *within* these movements the deeper religious meaning that they have.[25]

In the light of these new developments in Latin America, however, questions arose at the official level of the Church about the proper relationship between its spiritual and temporal missions and between its religious and social norms. Pope Paul VI warned against tendencies within small base communities that make them "fall victim to some political option . . . and then to a system, even a party."[26] Some of the Latin American hierarchy themselves became wary of certain of the practical consequences of liberation theology methods. A document sent by the Latin American Episcopal Conference (CELAM) to the Third Synod of Bishops held in Rome in October 1974 acknowledged the "aspirations for liberation" throughout the continent, but placed a heavy emphasis on the spiritual aspects of this phenomenon. The statement warned against a "superficial politicization of the faith" and the "temptation to violence" which the bishops claimed were becoming increasingly appealing to younger people of the Latin American Church.[27]

In my interviews with Chilean religious elites in 1975, therefore, I constructed questions to find out whether traditional concerns about overspecification of social norms and too close an identification of the Church with particular social and political processes were major preoccupations for bishops, priests, nuns, and lay leaders. I also wanted to probe the extent to which the new developments flowing from Medellín and the theology of liberation have come to guide the pastoral decisions of ecclesiastical leaders in that country.

In regard to the first issue, Tables 2.1 and 2.2 indicate that some clear differences of opinion exist among Church leaders in Chile. One-half of the bishops felt that priority normally should be given both by themselves and their priests to preaching moral virtues and teaching social justice from a doctrinal perspective. Close to two-thirds or more of the

---

[25] The literature to date on the theology of liberation originating in Latin America in the post-Medellín period is vast. Some of the most important works (available in English translation) are those of Gustavo Gutiérrez, Juan Luis Segundo, Ignacio Ellacuría, José Míguez Bonino, Enrique Dussel, Hugo Assmann, and José Porfirio Miranda. See bibliography for specific references.

[26] Pope Paul VI, *On Evangelization in the Modern World* (*Evangelii Nuntiandi*), no. 58, p. 41.

[27] Bishop Eduardo Pironio, "Relación sobre la evangelización del mundo de este tiempo en América Latina," pp. 107–15.

Table 2.1

"Which of the following positions do you think more fitting for priests when they confront social problems?" (1975)

	Bishops (N = 30)		Priests (N = 72)		Nuns (N = 33)		Laity (N = 51)		Totals (N = 186)	
1. Avoid getting involved with social problems							2.0% (1)		.5% (1)	
2. Preach Christian morality and its virtues	16.7% (5)	53.4	6.9% (5)		9.1% (3)		17.6 (9)		11.8 (22)	
3. Teach social justice from a doctrinal perspective	36.7 (11)		26.4 (19)		15.2 (5)		9.8 (5)		21.5 (40)	
4. Energetically denounce, but *in general*, situations of injustice	3.3 (1)	43.3	18.1 (13)	63.9	18.2 (6)	72.7	15.7 (8)	66.7	15.1 (28)	62.9
5. Give a witness of solidarity with the oppressed, denouncing every form of repression or injustice *specifically*	40.0 (12)		45.8 (33)		54.5 (18)		51.0 (26)		47.8 (89)	
6. Other (personal witness of his life)	3.3 (1)		1.4 (1)						1.1 (2)	
7. No answer			1.4 (1)		3.0 (1)		3.9 (2)		2.2 (4)	

Table 2.2

"What stance toward social problems is more fitting for a bishop?"
(1975)

	Bishops (N = 30)	Priests (N = 72)	Nuns (N = 33)	Laity (N = 51)	Totals (N = 186)
1. Avoid getting involved with social problems					
2. Preach Christian morality and its virtues	13.3% (4)	4.2% (3)		9.8% (5)	6.5% (12)
3. Teach social justice from a doctrinal perspective	36.7 (11)	22.2 (16)	6.1% (2)	5.9 (3)	17.2 (32)
4. Energetically denounce, but *in general*, situations of injustice	10.0 (3)	16.7 (12)	24.2 (8)	19.6 (10)	17.7 (33)
5. Give a witness of solidarity with the oppressed, denouncing every form of repression or injustice *specifically*	40.0 (12)	45.8 (33)	45.5 (15)	47.1 (24)	45.2 (84)
6. Other (personal witness of his life)			3.0 (1)		.5 (1)
7. No answer		11.1 (8)	21.2 (7)	17.6 (9)	12.9 (24)

Grouped totals (rows 2–3): Bishops 50.0

Grouped totals (rows 4–5): Bishops 62.5 · Priests 69.7 · Nuns 66.7 · Totals 62.9

priests, nuns, and lay leaders, however, preferred much more energetic denunciation of situations of injustice by priests and bishops. Over two-fifths of these local leaders felt that both priests and bishops should give a witness of solidarity with the oppressed, denouncing every form of repression or injustice specifically.

Various reasons were expressed by the bishops to justify their positions. Some said that if denunciation was the only strategy used by Church leaders it would be insufficient. Others felt that consultation at every level of the Church should occur first before explicit public denunciations are made by clerics:

> Give a testimony of solidarity with the oppressed denouncing every form of repression and injustice specifically—but with prudence and not necessarily using denunciation in every instance. A priest should prophetically study the issue with his own community, with his fellow priests, and with his bishop. The same strategy holds true for the bishop's responsibility—solidarity and denunciation—but in communion with the pope and the other bishops and with his pastoral team. A bishop is not isolated.[28]

Still others, however, analyzed this problem in terms of the traditional framework of the Church's responsibility to articulate moral principles and values, while not becoming too closely associated with political strategies or conflicting situations. Two comments of bishops highlight this concern:

> The word denunciation bothers me. It has political implications. It seems to me denunciation is part of our mission, but in the perspective of our wider mission—living and preaching the Gospel and helping the people in their material needs.[29]

> A doctrine can be condemned, but not a person. A public denunciation does not accomplish anything except where a principle is at stake . . .[30]

The hierarchy has a greater distance from the experience of the local church than do the leaders directly responsible for it. Bishops have a broader perspective on overall consequences of pastoral strategies and maintain closer contact with Rome. They also value the importance of consultation and collegial decision-making before committing the official Church to public confrontations. Priests, nuns, and lay leaders involved in the pain and suffering of their relatively homogeneous communities, on the other hand, prefer a more decisive and denunciatory

[28] Interview no. 001, 11 April 1975.
[29] Interview no. 028, 29 October 1975.
[30] Interview no. 007, 29 April 1975.

position in the face of social problems without regard to what this might entail for the wider Church community and its institutions.[31]

A similar division of opinion among church elites also occurred over the question of whether or not a theology-of-liberation approach was a valid method of making more concrete the Church's responsibility as global pastor. Close to two-thirds of the bishops whom I interviewed indicated that this new style did not represent a valid image of the faith of the Latin American people. Nearly one-half of the priests and nuns, and two-fifths of the lay leaders, however, were fairly comfortable with this new pastoral orientation, although recognizing that many people could not comprehend its implications.

Several bishops were negative in their assessments of this trend since they believed that the theology of liberation is insufficiently spiritual. One prelate summarized this position as follows:

> If the theology of liberation means liberation from sin and selfishness, I have no difficulty in accepting it. But if theology of liberation begins with liberation from oppressive structures, or if it is understood as a socializing theology, I do not accept it. I accept the language of St. Paul—liberation from sin and liberation of the spirit. What value is there in speaking of social justice if one is not internally free?[32]

Another bishop stated that this theology really did not represent what poor people actually felt and believed, and stressed the importance of maintaining clear distinctions between sacred and secular issues in pastoral work among them:

> The theology of liberation is not for the simple people. The sacred is something absolute with these people, and they do not associate it with temporal or with social problems. Theology of liberation is for intellectuals and not for the common people.[33]

The views of many who were in closer daily contact with the poor than the hierarchy were far more positive in judging this method than the bishops. One priest in a poor parish in Santiago affirmed that this new religious style has increased the Church's credibility in the eyes of the poor:

> The theology of liberation is a valid reflection of the people's faith. It has attracted many people who were alienated from the Church for its

---

[31] These findings parallel those from a 1969 survey of priests' attitudes in Chile conducted by Renato Poblete, S.J. of Centro Bellarmino in Santiago. Close to two-thirds of the priests chose a form of denunciation as the most effective strategy in face of social injustice. Poblete et al., *El sacerdote chileno: estudio sociológico*, p. 109.

[32] Interview no. 009, 5 May 1975.

[33] Interview no. 016, 22 August 1975.

Table 2.3

Validity of the Theology of Liberation

"Do you feel that the theology of liberation offers a valid image of the Catholic faith of the Latin American people?"
(1975)

	Bishops (N = 24)	Priests (N = 69)	Nuns (N = 33)	Laity (N = 50)	Totals (N = 176)
1. Yes	16.7% (4)	34.8% (24) ⎫ 46.4	36.4% (12) ⎫ 48.5	36.0% (18) ⎫ 40.0	32.9% (58)
2. Yes, but only for an elite or a sector of the people	20.8 (5)	11.6 (8) ⎭	12.1 (4) ⎭	4.0 (2) ⎭	10.8 (19)
3. No	45.8 (11) ⎫ 62.5	30.4 (21)	18.2 (6)	20.0 (10)	27.3 (48)
4. In the sense of liberation from sin, yes; in a political or social sense, no	16.7 (4) ⎭	17.4 (12)	9.1 (3)	2.0 (1)	11.4 (20)
5. Don't know, no answer		5.8 (4)	24.2 (8)	38.0 (19)	17.6 (31)

NOTE: Not asked = 10

being preoccupied with spiritual affairs and the afterlife, while neglecting the problems of the whole person.[34]

A housewife in a working-class family expressed a similar opinion:

> I think the theology of liberation is the only approach that is down to
> earth and which is at the level of popular communities. It deals realis-
> tically with our situation and problems.[35]

A nun involved in both educational and pastoral work in a working-
class neighborhood in the capital city stressed the importance of awak-
ening in the people an awareness of themselves as agents for social
change, which is the basis of the liberation theology perspective:

> It is indispensable because the task of the Church is to serve the world,
> and the world of today is struggling for the development of poor peo-
> ple so that they be agents of their own history. In that task the Church
> should support the original spirit of the Gospel and make Christ in-
> carnate in today's world.[36]

The Chilean hierarchy, like Rome, has continued to be preoccupied
primarily with the Church's religious mission and are fearful that too
close an identification between sacred and secular activities in pastoral
programs could lead to a politicization of faith. Priests, and particularly
nuns and lay leaders, however, who more closely identify with concrete
struggles of their communities are not as concerned with maintaining
distinctions between spiritual and temporal responsibilities of the
Church. A majority of them believe that a closer integration between
religious values and social commitment makes the Church more credible
among marginal sectors of the population.

Thus, although Medellín and the theology of liberation presented
new perspectives and alternate action strategies for specifying the
Church's role as global pastor, very different judgments as to the implementation of this new orientation exist among contemporary religious
leaders. Two distinct solutions for solving the traditional predicament of
making Church social values effective without identifying the institution
with contingent movements coexist within the leadership of the Church.

What one might expect is that in a context of significant transformation of social and economic structures, and rapid mobilization of the
poor to support them, different opinions are likely to emerge among
leaders across levels of the Church as to how closely the institution
should identify with such policies. Conversely, the definition of the
Church's prophetic mission when it is confronted with repressive author-

[34] Interview no. 089, 19 July 1975.
[35] Interview no. 110, 8 October 1975.
[36] Interview no. 182, 10 September 1975.

itarian regimes will probably vary according to the position and responsibility of religious elites. At the basis of such disagreements are not only political judgments but differing views over how to solve perennial problems that face the Church in the performance of its religious and moral mission.

How different opinions among Church elites over the specification of its norms can help explain the Church's official stance toward political forces will be highlighted in Chapter 8 which focuses on relations between the Chilean bishops and Christians for Socialism during the Allende years. Such differences also underlay contrasting views between the hierarchy and local Church leaders over the choice of strategies to alleviate the violation of human rights by the Pinochet regime in 1975. This will be spelled out in Chapter 9.

VARIABLE NO. 2:
HIERARCHICAL AUTHORITY FLOWS ACROSS A LAYERED
ADMINISTRATIVE ORGANIZATION

A fundamental organizational characteristic of the Roman Catholic Church is the hierarchical nature of its authority system. Supreme teaching and governing authority is located in the pope. Assisting him, and acting in his name, are over 2,200 officials (mostly clerics) in the Roman Curia. These cardinals, bishops, and priests administer nine congregations, three tribunals, four secretariats, and twenty-six commissions, councils, and other offices which coordinate Church administration at the highest level. There are also apostolic nuncios or delegates (most of whom are bishops) representing the sovereign state of the Holy See to over one hundred different countries. They carry out Vatican diplomatic policy throughout the world, but have no jurisdictional authority over the respective national churches in countries where they are located.

Over 2,600 other cardinals, archbishops, and bishops share in official teaching authority with and under the pope for the whole Church, and also exercise jurisdictional power over the nearly 2,500 ecclesiastical territorial units—archdioceses, dioceses, abbacies, vicariates, prefectures apostolic—that cover the entire globe. Over 400,000 priests participate to a lesser degree in the authority of the hierarchy and carry out sacramental and teaching functions in parochial and other subdiocesan structures under cardinals, archbishops, or bishops.

In addition to this vertically orchestrated and centrally coordinated chain of clerical authority in the Church, there are ninety-five societies of religious men and 210 congregations of sisters, with a combined total of over one million members. Some of these are constituted as religious orders or congregations of pontifical right and are under the direct juris-diction of the Holy See, while others are subject to the supervision of bishops in their respective dioceses. Religious who are not priests do not participate in formal teaching, sacramental or jurisdictional authority, nor are they required to undergo the same theological and pastoral training as clerics, but they are commissioned to carry out a whole series of religious, educational, welfare, or administrative activities at the dioc-esan or parochial levels of the Church. While not sharing in formal ec-clesiastical power, numerically they constitute the vast majority of de facto leaders for a whole range of important Church activities around the world, and are often in closer contact with the everyday concerns and needs of the faithful than are bishops and priests.

Finally, the Church has developed a whole series of programs for the laity—youth groups, apostolic movements, labor unions, professional or-ganizations. These are officially sponsored by the Church but are ad-ministered by lay men and women with a certain independence from the hierarchy so as to extend the Church's influence into secular society, without formally and officially involving the Church in issues which are beyond clerical competence.[37]

Authority flows in the Church, therefore, are hierarchical with vary-ing degrees of participation in jurisdictional power shared among car-dinals, bishops, and priests under the pope. Command decisions are fil-tered across a whole complex of territorial units and Church-sponsored organizations carrying out religious and social functions at separate levels of the institution. Some of these structures, such as dioceses and parishes, are administered directly by those who participate in formal ecclesiastical authority, but the vast number of schools, hospitals, chari-table organizations, communications media, and apostolic programs that the Church maintains throughout the world are under the supervi-sion of religious and lay personnel. While subject to the hierarchy on issues pertaining to faith and morals they do not exercise canonical powers nor share the same degree of responsibility for the pastoral care of the Church.

On the great majority of issues pertaining to the day-to-day adminis-tration of the Church which do not touch directly upon doctrinal points, uniformity of perspective and behavior is not required. This provides

---

[37] *Annuario Pontificio per l'anno 1976* (Citta del Vaticano: Typografica Poliglotta Va-ticana, 1976), pp. 969–70, 975–1070, 1094–12; Felician A. Foy, O.F.M., ed., *1977 Catholic Almanac* (Huntington, Ind.: Our Sunday Visitor, Inc., 1976), pp. 184–90, 224–26, 444–45; T. Lincoln Bouscaren, S.J. et al., *Canon Law: A Text and Commentary*, pp. 152–229, 286–311, 342–86.

local Church leaders with a relative degree of adaptability. Each level of Church leadership is primarily concerned with fulfilling religious or social tasks adequately for its area of responsibility within broad official guidelines, but without waiting for specific approval from the top.

In a strict juridical sense, the chain of command in the Church involves only three vertically related levels—pope, bishops, priests. The curial officials in Rome, the papal nuncios, regional or national episcopal bodies, religious orders and congregations, and apostolic lay organizations all act in advisory or outreach capacities and do not share in formal canonical decision-making authority. On issues of critical doctrinal or disciplinary concern messages from the top of the institution can be communicated and executed rather expeditiously. These are relatively few in number, however, and the simple three-step formal authority structure would become overloaded if it were set into motion on every decision. Hence, much discretion is left to all local leaders to carry on the routine affairs of the Church.

Moreover, differences in the exercise of authority and responsibility, in the size of the units administered, in the kinds of training and competence required, and in the degree of exposure to various types of problems all give rise to very distinctive perceptions across the layers of ecclesiastical leadership and administration. Different leaders represent the Church to different publics, and the salience of issues impinge on the consciousness of elites unevenly depending upon their location in the hierarchical network of the organization.

Local leaders can act publicly in the Church's name, but do not always reflect the judgments of the pope or bishops as to what is necessary for promoting the interests of the whole Church. So long as their choices and actions do not challenge any of the central beliefs or characteristics of the Church, they are considered within the boundaries of orthodoxy and permissible behavior.

Throughout the history of the Church there have arisen tensions across these levels of the Church's leadership, at times encouraging innovations and in other instances causing crises of authority or even schisms. Reform movements led by saints and religious orders in the Middle Ages provided creative energies for renewal of the papacy and offered constructive criticisms of ecclesiastical bureaucracy.[38] Other movements have arisen from time to time, however, which have challenged the very principle of hierarchical authority. Spiritualist sects opposing visible ecclesiastical structures emerged in the second century and reappeared later in the Middle Ages.[39] Conciliarist tendencies, ar-

[38] Karl Bihlmeyer, *Church History,* rev. Hermann Tüchle, 2:126–33, 213–21, 286–303, 361–75; 3:83–98.
[39] Ibid., 1:146–55, 163–66; 2:303–8.

guing that full ecclesiastical power rests in the faithful, challenged papal supremacy in the early fifteenth century.[40] The Reformation in the sixteenth century was the most severe challenge to the authority and unity of the institution, and ultimately led to a major split in Christendom. All of these movements arose from the ranks of the lower clergy, religious, or laity and met with severe resistance by Rome and the hierarchy, who countered them by reemphasizing the principle of hierarchical authority as a protection for Church unity and the immutability of core dogmas.

From the late seventeenth to the early nineteenth century a series of national church movements presented serious threats to Catholic unity.[41] Vertical lines of authority were strengthened even more, and Rome and the hierarchy assumed more control in ecclesiastical administration. While this defensive strategy provided a protection against internal and external divisive forces, it reinforced very juridical concepts of the Church. It placed great emphasis on legal and disciplinary procedures, and led to an almost complete identification of the institution with the pope and bishops.[42]

The Second Vatican Council in the mid-1960s (when threats to ecclesiastical unity and authority had subsided) tried to revive some of the communitarian aspects of the early Church, open up once again greater local initiative and pluralism, and encourage less authoritarian methods in exercising authority. While there was no basic change in the definition of the nature or locus of ecclesiastical authority by Vatican II, the Council stressed a new style of administration, urging closer collegial ties between pope and bishops, among bishops themselves, and between bishops and priests at the local level. The unique contributions of religious and laity were also recognized, and bishops were urged by the Council to incorporate them more into the direct pastoral mission of the Church. A major goal of Vatican II was to restore a more creative balance between vertical control and local initiative across the layered administrative network of the institution. Consultative bodies were introduced at various levels to achieve this, along with a more widespread sharing of pastoral responsibilities with religious and laity. The documents of the Council, however, did not adopt principles of democratic government as being applicable in the Church, and traditional Catholic emphases on unity and hierarchical authority were reaffirmed.[43]

[40] Ibid., 2:379–88.

[41] These occurred most notably in France, Germany, and Austria and were stimulated by a desire of some bishops and clergy in these countries to limit Rome's financial control over their respective Churches. They also served the political purposes of monarchs desirous of subjecting the Church to the State. Ibid., 3:230–36, 276–84.

[42] Yves Congar, O.P., "Historical Development of Authority," pp. 144–50.

[43] "Dogmatic Constitution on the Church," nos. 9, 13, 22, in *Documents of Vatican II*, ed. Abbott, pp. 25–26, 32, 43.

Since the close of the Council, tensions have reemerged in the Church over the extent of permissible pluralism and the scope of ecclesiastical authority. Some national churches (e.g., in Holland) have moved rapidly to develop structures of participation based upon democratic procedures and assumptions, and this has brought them into conflict with Rome. Moral theologians and priests in several countries of Western Europe and North America have publicly disagreed with official Church teaching on birth control. Some have questioned interpretations of papal infallibility, stressing, as does Hans Küng, the indefectibility of the Church as a whole rather than of the pontiff alone. Traditionalist movements led by dissident clerics such as Archbishop Marcel Lefebvre of France, have refused to accept many of the liturgical reforms and social teachings of the Council and the pope over the past twenty years.[44]

Some problems with hierarchical authority, which in other eras have precipitated serious internal crises, seem to be reappearing. It is not yet clear whether these current conflicts are the result of unavoidable disruptions involved in a period of change, or stem from deeper divisions over the definition of religious authority itself. If the former is the case, these incidents may be transitory and unimportant for assessing overall change in the Church. If the latter, however, is at the base of the disagreements, then the divisions are much more serious and rooted in deeper conflicts that have arisen at other periods of Church history. If such is the case, these could lead to a pullback once again into defensive rigid positions by the hierarchy regarding issues of pluralism and local initiative.

To date no systematic survey research has been done to measure attitudes of leaders at different levels of the institution on the range of acceptable pluralism, on the styles of exercising discipline, on the nature of ecclesiastical authority, and on the validity of more participatory procedures in decision-making. Since the Chilean Church has perhaps gone the farthest of all national Catholic churches in decentralizing its structures and incorporating religious and laity into positions of pastoral leadership at the local level,[45] I included several questions in my inter-

---

[44] For a summary and discussion of the major disruptions that have occurred in the Catholic Church since 1965, see Peter Hebblethwaite, *The Runaway Church: Post Conciliar Growth or Decline.*

[45] Since the 1960s the Chilean hierarchy have taken coordinated action to implement the directives of the Second Vatican Council. Small base communities have been established at the neighborhood level in most of the twenty-four dioceses in the country for the purpose of promoting more effective worship services, catechetical and Bible study programs, leadership training, and social welfare services. Almost one-half of the more than 5,000 women religious in the country have left their traditional work in formal education and have now become actively involved in the promotion of these base communities, concentrating their efforts primarily in low-income areas where there is a scarcity of priests. Eighty of the 760 parishes throughout

views to test for differences across the layered network of Church leadership on the nature and function of authority flows in the post-Vatican II Church. The results of the responses surfaced some very definite similarities among all respondents, as well as striking divergences of opinion.

Regarding attitudes toward the impact of greater pluralism of pastoral styles and religious options in the Church since Vatican II, three-fifths or more of all Chilean bishops, priests, nuns, and lay leaders interviewed felt that pluralism in general was a healthy phenomenon, and in some cases had actually increased respect for the Church. Less than 10 percent of the respondents as a whole believed that greater freedom has actually caused damage to ecclesiastical authority. What is very significant is that over two-fifths of the bishops themselves indicated that pluralism and a less authoritarian style of exercising authority have increased the Church's influence among the people of today. One bishop, in elaborating on this question, remarked:

> In no way has pluralism diminished the influence of the Church. A bishop now lives in less ceremony but closer to the people. Pluralism is a treasure for the Church; differences among persons and a variety of perspectives are very good. There is no conflict among pastoral programs.[46]

This comfortableness with greater diversity among the hierarchy was confirmed by their responses to another question dealing with disagreements between themselves and lower clergy. I asked twenty-three of the thirty bishops what strategies they normally employed when differences of opinion arose over pastoral strategies or clerical life styles. Eight-seven percent of them indicated that their first step to resolve disagreements with priests would be to appeal to friendship and fraternal ties. When asked what they would do if this line of approach failed, nearly 90 per-

---

the country by 1975 were under the exclusive jurisdiction of nuns who function as pastors, and who can perform many priestly functions except celebrate Mass and hear confessions. Katherine Ann Gilfeather, M.M., "Women and Ministry," pp. 191–94.

More than one hundred men have been ordained deacons throughout the country and are preaching, baptizing, officiating at weddings, and carrying out several priestly tasks except celebrating the Eucharist and granting absolution. In addition, throughout the country there are about 10,000 mothers trained to teach religion to their children (*mamás catechistas*). They receive two years of intense Bible instruction in small training groups of women in their respective neighborhoods and subsequently prepare their children for the reception of the sacraments. There are approximately 20,000 committed lay men and women participating in small communities, and carrying on the day-to-day religious and social activities of the *comunidades de base*. Poblete, "Formas ministeriales en la iglesia de Chile," pp. 36–38; ¿"Por qué el diaconado?" *Iglesia de Santiago* (Santiago) August 1975, pp. 29–30; and Interview with Bishop Carlos Camus, Secretary of the Chilean Episcopal Conference, Santiago, 23 September 1975.

[46] Interview no. 016, 22 August 1975.

cent of them responded that they would try again appealing to friendship, a sense of loyalty to the Church, or employing informal methods such as consultation with others, more conversation, or patience. No bishop responded that he would resort to threats or disciplinary action as a first recourse, and only two bishops (9.1 percent) said that they would use this strategy if other means had failed.

A few bishops frankly admitted that changing a priest's assignment does not solve problems of conflict if the priest chooses to remain committed to his views. Some others, however, acknowledged that a range of differing perspectives is by necessity built into the layered nature of ecclesiastical administration, and can provide important advantages for the Church as a whole. One bishop stated the case as follows:

> A priest is closer to the people and offers an important perspective on their problems. A bishop, however, has a more global sense of problems for the whole diocese. Rome also has an even more universal perspective for the whole Church. All of these perspectives are good for the Church.[47]

What is clear from these general responses and specific remarks is that leaders at all levels of the Chilean Church accept greater flexibility and informality in the post-Vatican II era. Bishops rarely use authoritarian methods in governing, are open to listening to, and learning from, various opinions of leaders at the local level, and recognize a diversity of judgments among the leadership as being a healthy phenomenon for the vitality of the institution. In fact, compared to other contemporary national hierarchies, the Chilean bishops are clearly among the most progressive in the style in which they exercise pastoral leadership.

There are, however, some striking differences of opinion among Chilean religious elites as to the definition of episcopal authority. I presented four distinct descriptions of authority to all respondents ranging from authoritarian, centralist, consensual, to democratic. The first model dominated canonical manuals from the Council of Trent after the Reformation to the mid-twentieth century; the second is closer to the model presented in Vatican II; and the third and fourth are more characteristic of many Protestant churches, as well as secular democratic governments. The purpose of the question was to ascertain whether or not greater differentiation of functions and more personal styles of exercising authority were precipitating major differences among leaders at various levels of responsibility over the nature of ecclesiastical authority itself. The results in Table 2.4 dramatically illustrate that sharp differences of opinion do exist in the Chilean Church over the definition of authority. Seventy percent of the bishops and priests chose the model associated with

[47] Interview no. 007, 29 April 1975.

Table 2.4

Perceptions of the Nature of Authority

"With which of the following descriptions of episcopal authority are you in most agreement?"
(1975)

	Bishops (N = 27)	Priests (N = 72)	Nuns (N = 33)	Laity (N = 51)	Totals (N = 183)
1. The hierarchy is the authority imposed on the Church by the Lord; because of this, the bishops should be obeyed even when Catholics are not much in agreement with what they say	3.7% (1)	2.8% (2)	3.0% (1)	7.8% (4)	4.4% (8)
2. The thing the Lord asks is an active obedience by Catholics; the faithful should offer their opinions to the hierarchy, and afterwards the bishops should make the decisions and the laity obey them	70.4 (19)	70.8 (51)	45.5 (15)	25.5 (13)	53.6 (98)
3. Dialogue is the modern form of expressing authority within the Church; there should be discussions with Church authorities until an agreement is reached	22.2 (6)	15.3 (11)	33.3 (11)	21.6 (11)	21.2 (39)
4. The essential part of the Church should be the base Christian communities with an autonomous life; these groups should participate in the important decisions of the diocese through their representatives	3.7 (1)	9.7 (7)	18.2 (6)	43.1 (22)	19.7 (36)
5. No answer		1.4 (1)		2.0 (1)	1.1 (2)

Nuns bracket: 33.3 and 18.2 → 51.5; 64.7

Note: Not asked = 3

Vatican II's new emphasis, but a majority of the nuns and nearly two-thirds of the lay leaders preferred a more dialogical or democratic definition.

Women religious and lay leaders are the ones most responsible for the formation and guidance of clusters of small base communities at the neighborhood level, frequently numbering less than one hundred full-time members. These function along the lines of participatory democracies, and rely on the formation of consensus in reaching important decisions on pastoral and social strategies. Furthermore, religious orders have traditionally included structures of consultation, and these have been extended since Vatican II. Many sisters live in smaller communities now, and have moved faster than men's orders or diocesan clergy in adopting democratic processes for decision-making and selection of superiors. The long civil tradition of electoral and multiparty politics that prevailed in Chile until 1973 helps explain why the laity would come to view as normative participatory processes emerging in the Church now that it has decentralized.

Bishops and priests, however, are responsible for administering larger diocesan and parochial units where more centralized leadership is required.[48] Perhaps even more important, both bishops and priests participate in the exercise of formal ecclesiastical authority and their function, as well as their extensive theological and seminary training (not required of nuns or lay elites), make them more conscious of the importance of hierarchical authority.

While it is not surprising that perceptions on accidental issues relating to pastoral emphases should vary according to position and responsibility, such dramatic divisions between higher and lower levels of Church leaders on the very nature of religious authority illustrate grounds of serious latent conflict. These could become overt and critical when decisions made by episcopal leaders do not meet the expectations of leaders at the local level quickly becoming accustomed to a democratic Church in fact as well as in principle.[49]

[48] The vast majority of dioceses in Chile (twenty-one out of twenty-four) are administered by one bishop without the assistance of an auxiliary. The average size of a diocese is 31,503 sq. km. and includes 423,792 residents. Even excluding Santiago where one-third of the national population lives, the other twenty-three dioceses include an average of 280,261 people. Parishes are usually served by two or three priests responsible for 13,400 people in an average area of 995 sq. km. *Guia de la Iglesia en Chile, 1976* (Santiago: Ediciones Mundo, 1976), p. 506.

[49] Another question in my survey confirmed the democratic preference for ecclesiastical decision-making which characterizes nuns and lay leaders. When asked how bishops should be selected, nearly two-thirds (63.3 percent) of the hierarchy expressed support for the present system—appointment by the pope from a list presented by the national episcopal conference. Several mentioned that more widespread participation by priests, nuns, and laity would not necessarily be good since

On theoretical grounds, one would hypothesize that when the Church faces a major religiopolitical challenge that does not involve large numbers of its leadership elites or does not precipitate serious differences of judgment among them, its institutional response will be more consistent and its impact on secular development more uniform. One would also expect, however, that when different levels of its leadership respond to public issues in very divergent ways, and by so doing precipitate serious crises of authority within the Church, the reinforcing effect of the Church on secular change could be diffused or short-circuited. In such situations bishops are more likely to take defensive reactions to protect the principle of hierarchical authority, and in so doing rule out a particular political option for some Catholics. Finally, one could expect that when differences of judgment exist across leadership levels of the Church on crucial religious or secular issues, but remain latent due to some crisis situation that necessitates formal unity of Church leaders in public, then authority flows in the short run may appear to be smooth and give the Church a certain amount of consistency. This, however, could mean that overt conflicts among religious elites will emerge once the crisis situation subsides.

An exploration of the first hypothesis will be developed in Chapter 3 dealing with the formal extrication of the Chilean Church from the state and the Conservative Party in the 1920s and 1930s. An analysis of the second hypothesis will be examined in Chapter 8 which focuses on attempts at Christian-Marxist synthesis within the Church under the Allende government. The third hypothesis will be developed in the context of pastoral and social developments of the Chilean Church under the current military junta, which is the subject of Chapter 9.

VARIABLE NO. 3:
DIVERSIFIED NATURE OF CHURCH MEMBERSHIP

A major emphasis in Roman Catholic teaching has always been that religious salvation is offered to all. Unlike sectarian movements that believe that redemption is for the few and thus make rigid demands on their members, the Catholic Church has recognized throughout history that not everyone can or will respond to its evangelization efforts in the same way. There have always been movements within the Church that

---

many dioceses do not have a large selection of candidates from which to choose, and people at the local level do not know priests from other dioceses who would be good candidates. No bishop thought that election was an apt method of selecting prelates since it could easily lead to factionalism in the Church. The great majority of local leaders wanted more consultation, and two-fifths of the nuns and lay leaders even preferred election of bishops by priests and base communities.

have encouraged deep religious commitment, such as monasticism which arose in the first centuries of Christianity, the mendicant orders of the Middle Ages, and lay Catholic Action organizations of modern times. These movements, however, have never become the norm for ordinary Catholics, and those who practice irregularly or who are Catholic in name only far outnumber the devout. The Church has accepted various degrees of affiliation among its baptized—saints, regular participants, occasional communicants, rarely practicing, and nominal members with only cultural or familial ties to Catholicism.

A consequence of this universal religious claim and orientation is that the Church has constructed a large organizational network to provide continuity and universality for its mission. It has made efforts to adopt its institutional framework to every type of society in order to maintain the structural capacities to preach the Gospel and celebrate the sacraments in all cultures and for all social classes in each national context. Moreover, only for very grave reasons is anyone formally excommunicated from the Catholic Church. It has traditionally opposed elitist orientations that tend to be exclusive or entirely isolated from the broad mainstream of Catholicism.[50]

The fact that it has allowed differing religious commitments in its ranks has meant that there have been varying degrees of contact with the institutional Church among Catholics. While the rate of Sunday observance is high in a few traditionally Catholic countries such as Ireland and Poland (ranging from 80 to 90 percent of all baptized), the normal pattern in the majority of nominally Catholic cultures is dramatically lower, averaging 37 percent in Italy, 19 percent in France, and between 5 and 20 percent throughout Latin America. Consequently, the number of Catholics exposed regularly to the messages and socialization process of the Church, and who can be counted on to carry out its teachings in their lives as citizens, has always been relatively low compared to overall Church membership.

In addition, since the Church's membership is broadly representative, social class is an important influence on the style and purpose of religious practice among various groups of Catholics. Weber observed that in all major religions of the world, variations in social status and income have had a significant impact on the meaning and goals of religious practice among different classes of their membership. He concluded that persons with high social and economic privilege historically have assigned to their religious faith the function of legitimizing their own particular life style as well as the societal structures that preserve it. Lower

---

[50] Basic distinctions between churches and sects were first delineated by Ernst Troeltsch and Max Weber. Troeltsch, *The Social Teachings of the Christian Churches*, 1:331–43, and Weber, *The Sociology of Religion*, pp. 60–79.

classes, on the other hand, have sought from religion a release from suffering, and their piety has tended to be highly devotional, susceptible to magic and superstition, and oriented toward salvation in the next world. It is not normally characterized, however, by a belief that rational ethical action can make a substantial change in the existing order.[51] According to Weber, neither rich nor poor are susceptible to prophetic elements in religions that emphasize the necessity to change rather than to accept established social structures and distributions of political power.

Empirical studies on correlations between religious practice and political preferences have confirmed Weber's basic insights into the normally conservative social implications of religious belief and practice. Although there are different rates of ritual participation among social classes, survey research since World War II in Western Europe has shown that, within all classes, those who are the most religious have been less likely to support candidates of radical parties than those who do not practice or have no religious faith.[52]

Hence, the option to minister to the religious needs of different social classes and to allow various levels of commitment among members has traditionally made large religious organizations, such as the Roman Church, conservative forces in secular society. Church statements and pronouncements, even when they have encouraged social and economic reforms, have not in the past been sufficient evidence in themselves to predict how the members of an institutionalized Church were likely to act. In fact, there has traditionally been a wide gap between official Church teachings on public moral issues and the attitudes and behavior of large numbers of the laity.

These characteristics traditionally associated with church-type religious communities now present a major dilemma for an institution such as the Roman Catholic Church to carry out its recently announced goal of acting as a catalytic force for change in secular society. It cannot become sectarian, thus betraying its religious mission to all types of persons and groups. To realize its new goals effectively it must generate stronger commitments to its socially progressive teachings among broad sectors of its membership and overcome apathy among rich and poor alike to its ethical demands for structural change in society.

The contemporary Latin American Church offers an important testing area to verify whether or not Catholicism can develop strategies to

---

[51] Weber, *The Sociology of Religion*, pp. 101–8.

[52] Charles Glock and Rodney Stark, *Religion and Society in Tension*, pp. 201–14; Vincent E. McHale, "Religion and Electoral Politics in France: Some Recent Observations," pp. 292–311; and Laurence E. Hazelrigg, "Religious and Class Basis of Political Conflict in Italy," pp. 496–511.

resolve this dilemma. In order to revitalize religious commitments among all social groups, the bishops at Medellín urged the decentralization of parish structures into small base neighborhood communities. These were to be socially homogeneous groupings, "whose size allows for personal fraternal contact" among membership. Such cells were to provide more effective religious evangelization among all social classes, and to offer social services to the larger society. Alongside these new local structures of spiritual and social formation, "basic teams" of elites were to be established among professional, business, and cultural leaders throughout the continent to instill a greater sense of social responsibility among upper-income groups.[53]

Both of these strategies were designed to improve the socialization mechanisms of the Church so as to generate deeper loyalties among the laity and promote a greater integration of religious faith and social commitment among rich and poor alike. The bishops warned, however, that new local programs and small groups were not to become separated from larger parochial, diocesan, and national structures.[54] Hence, while the Latin American bishops have committed themselves to adopt some sectarian characteristics into their efforts to revitalize Latin American Catholicism, they have not abandoned the traditional church model of religious incorporation.

The contemporary Chilean Church provides a useful setting for examining how successfully and consistently sectarian tendencies can be combined with a traditional church pattern of development. The Chilean Church for several decades had one of the most well organized Catholic Action programs in all of Latin America. After Medellín the bishops committed themselves to the formation of small neighborhood base communities in every part of the country, combining religious worship, Bible study, catechetical and leadership training, and service to the social needs of the larger community in which they were located.

Given these attempts in the Chilean Church to implement the guidelines of Medellín, in my 1975 surveys I probed the extent to which opinions across leadership levels of the Church are in agreement over the compatibility of Church and sectarian orientations. I wanted to see whether or not tensions were emerging which could affect the overall

[53] Latin American Episcopal Conference (CELAM), "Joint Pastoral Planning," no. 10, and "Pastoral Concern for Elites," no. 14, in *The Church and the Present-Day Transformation of Latin America*, 2:226, 133.

[54] Ibid. See also, "Pastoral Care of the Masses," no. 3, p. 133. This concern was reiterated at Puebla as well. "Evangelization in Latin America's Present and Future," nos. 617–57, in *Puebla and Beyond*, ed. Eagleson and Scharper, pp. 210–14.

consistency of the Church's impact on secular society. I designed questions to measure leadership attitudes on preferable models of religious development and strategies for stimulating more commitment among those with little formal contact with the institution.

I asked all the respondents whether they preferred the traditional church model of universal scope of membership and adaptation to all types of societies or a model closer to a sectarian movement that would be smaller in membership and more critical of social structures. Very few of the respondents as a whole (13.4 percent) showed sympathies for the church model historically associated with Roman Catholicism. Nearly two-thirds of the priests, however, and well over three-fourths of the nuns and lay leaders chose without hesitation the sectarian pattern, emphasizing smaller and more committed numbers of faithful and frequent criticism by the Church of established social structures and values.

Less than one-fourth of the bishops identified with the traditional universalist-adaptive model, but only one-third were comfortable with an exclusive emphasis on a sectarian orientation. A plurality of the hierarchy (43.4 percent) refused to accept either definition as totally valid, and wanted to combine tendencies from both, following the direction indicated by Medellín. Moreover, among those bishops, priests, nuns, and lay leaders who did select the smaller model, an overwhelming majority of 70 percent or more in each group wanted these small base communities to include as part of their religious commitment an effort to transform political and social structures rather than withdraw from the world to concentrate on exclusively spiritual concerns.[55]

Various bishops commented on these questions, giving reasons for their choices. Some tended to emphasize the importance that the Church never lose its all-embracing scope, saying that "the Church is for the salvation of all people; it is a net in which the good and the bad are included."[56] Others stressed the necessity for compassion in the Church and a capacity to understand human weakness: "Mercy toward all is essential."[57]

Many bishops expressed uneasiness with having to select one of the

[55] Several of the bishops who wanted to combine both models (and who therefore did not respond to the question in Table 2.6 asked only of those who chose the sectarian tendency), mentioned explicitly that they wanted to include a concern for social problems in the development of small base communities. This further confirms the findings in Table 2.6 that the type of sectarian emphases that the hierarchy find desirable are ones that take social commitment very seriously rather than ones that withdraw from the world as some of the classic Christian sects have done.

[56] Interview no. 004, 24 April 1975.

[57] Interview no. 011, 21 June 1975.

Table 2.5
Models of Church Development
"With which of the two models or tendencies in the Church are you more in agreement?"
(1975)

	Bishops (N = 30)	Priests (N = 72)	Nuns (N = 33)	Laity (N = 51)	Totals (N = 186)
1. The tendency that emphasizes the universal character of the Church as an institution to which all people can belong, although differing in depth of commitment and fulfillment of religious obligation. This model also insists upon the necessity that the Church adapt to all types of societies in order to be able to preach the Gospel and celebrate the sacraments	23.3% (7)	18.1% (13)	3.0% (1)	7.8% (4)	13.4% (25)
2. The tendency which emphasizes the importance of every Christian making a profound commitment to the Gospel and the Church, even if this implies that the Church will only include a minority of the people. This model also stresses the necessity that the Church frequently and prophetically critique the values and structures of secular society	33.3 (10)	62.5 (45)	87.9 (29)	78.5 (40)	66.7 (124)
3. Both of these tendencies	43.3 (13)	19.4 (14)	6.1 (2)	7.8 (4)	17.7 (33)
4. No answer			3.0 (1)	5.9 (3)	2.2 (4)

Table 2.6
Social-Activist or Spiritual Sect
"If you have selected the second model, can you tell me with which of the two groups proposing this option you are in more agreement."
(1975)

	Bishops (N = 10)	Priests (N = 45)	Nuns (N = 29)	Laity (N = 40)	Totals (N = 124)
1. With those who say that Christian communities give prophetic witness in the world by the quality and depth of their religious practice but should not try or hope to make significant changes in the social, economic, or political structures	20.0% (2)	24.4% (11)	10.4% (3)	5.0% (2)	14.5% (18)
2. With those who say that Christian communities should make a necessary part of their faith a commitment to the social, economic, and political transformation of the world	70.0 (7)	75.6 (34)	82.8 (24)	92.5 (37)	82.3 (102)
3. Both of these; depends on the situation	10.0 (1)		3.4 (1)		1.6 (2)
4. No answer			3.4 (1)	2.5 (1)	1.6 (2)

two models presented, and several commented why they preferred aspects of both tendencies:

> The Church has to develop both levels at the same time. It has to give light to the masses—Christ Himself also offered something to the masses, but He also selected a small group of apostles. A sophisticated group which rejects the faith of the people is not correct.[58]

> I prefer the second model more, but not a purist Church. There are different ways of belonging to the Church and diverse degrees of commitment among the people.[59]

> Temperamentally I agree with the first—but actually with the second model.[60]

This basic difference in pastoral orientation between bishops and local leaders was also highlighted by a strong divergence of opinion about the validity of the popular piety of the majority of urban workers and peasants (two-thirds of the population). The bishops were unanimous in asserting that the correct theological posture for the Church to take regarding the religious style of the masses was to accept their devotional practices as the only expressions possible for many of them.[61] Less than two-fifths of the priests, nuns, and lay leaders, however, were willing to accept these practices as theologically valid, and many were critical of the superstitious aspects of popular religiosity. Over 40 percent preferred not to work with existing forms of popular faith (as do the bishops), but wanted to create new structures and communal expressions to replace them.

The bishops are responsible for the pastoral care of larger and more diversified areas of territory than priests, nuns, and lay leaders who concentrate their efforts on the formation of committed Christians in

---

[58] Interview no. 016, 22 August 1975.
[59] Interview no. 018, 2 September 1975.
[60] Interview no. 022, 16 September 1975.
[61] The spirituality of most low-income Chileans (like the poor in other Latin American countries) is a mixture of magic, syncretism, and private devotion to the saints. It is not that the Church lost the working classes in Latin America with the emergence of industrialization and urbanization—it never institutionally penetrated the culture of the poor. The Church throughout the continent has never had sufficient numbers of priests and religious to complete the work of evangelization once baptism was conferred. The piety, therefore, of the Chilean poor has developed traditions which are relatively independent of formal Church structures and remain for the most part unaffected by changes in official Church emphasis. Their religiosity has tended to be nourished by private devotions, seasonal pilgrimages to religious shrines and, in areas of the far North, fiestas of religious dances. Enrique Dussel, *Historia de la iglesia en América Latina,* 2nd rev. ed. (Barcelona: Editorial Nova Terra, 1972), pp. 84–88; Phillip Berryman, "Popular Catholicism in Latin America," pp. 284–301; José M. Arevas, S.J., "Religiosidad popular: en torno a un encuentro," pp. 47–49.

smaller more homogeneous neighborhoods. The hierarchy feel a moral responsibility for protecting whatever religious aspirations that exist among many who are unable or unwilling to make strong commitments to the Church, and they are hesitant to allow the destruction of practices by which popular faith has been nourished for centuries.

In addition to the decidedly different pastoral approaches of bishops and local leaders, empirical studies on religious practice indicate that ritual participation in Chile (as in the rest of Latin America) continues to be weak. Survey research done at various intervals in Chile have indicated that Sunday Mass attendance remained basically unchanged between 1940 and 1974: an average of 12 to 15 percent of all baptized participated in weekly Mass, the vast majority of whom were women and young people under twenty-one years of age. Furthermore, among the working classes the rate was much lower—ranging from 4 to 8 percent—while upper income groups averaged between 20 and 25 percent.[62] Hence, the deepening of new lay commitments will be a slow process given the lack of regular contact that most Chilean Catholics have with the institutional Church.

One would expect that on issues which coincide with the political interests of large numbers of the laity, or when conditions in society give rise to crisis support for the Church, there could be widespread acquiescence to Church teaching on social questions. On sensitive issues affecting the distribution of wealth and power in a society, there are likely to be dramatically divergent responses to the Church's position across social classes, thus limiting the impact of its economically progressive norms. Moreover, one could also expect that when the hierarchy believes sectarian tendencies in the Church are progressing too far, they are likely to react defensively on behalf of formal Church unity regardless of the political fallout.

Reactions among different social strata of Catholics to the public statements of the Chilean bishops prior to the 1964 election address the first hypothesis. Opinions of Catholics about the hierarchy's support for many of Allende's goals and opposition to several of the military junta's policies provide evidence for testing the second hypothesis. The official response of the bishops to Christians for Socialism in 1973 and the Chilean Society for the Defense of Tradition, Family and Property in 1976 offer a basis to explore the third.

[62] Alberto Hurtado, S.J., ¿Es Chile un país católico? pp. 80–87. In 1958, the Chilean episcopal conference established within its general secretariat the Oficina de Sociología Religiosa (OSORE) which has been conducting on-site studies of Mass attendance in various dioceses throughout the country since that time. Their careful research throughout the 1960s and early 1970s confirmed the same pattern discovered by Hurtado in 1940: only a little over 10 percent of Chilean Catholics as a whole fulfilled their obligations to attend Mass every Sunday.

VARIABLE NO. 4:
RESOURCE TRANSACTIONS AMONG CENTER
AND PERIPHERY UNITS

A final component of the Church which provides it with unique potential for influence is its international network. The Church has established an institutional presence in almost all major countries of the world and is coordinated by a central headquarters in Rome. It is simultaneously, therefore, both a transnational actor and a conglomeration of subunits operating in a variety of national systems.

Consequently, the Roman Church is one of the few organizations in the world that can transmit ideological and material resources to every corner of the globe and also command supranational loyalties from its members. These characteristics also make it suspect to regimes preoccupied with issues of national sovereignty or committed to preserving absolute control over their internal development. Hence, the Church is faced with the problem of managing activities and objectives with transnational dimensions while simultaneously maintaining credibility as an indigenous institution in each society.

Throughout the history of the Church, the Vatican has had to negotiate with governments to assure freedom for national churches to pursue their religious mission and maintain close contact with Rome. For centuries this was achieved through union of Church and state in each Western country, which allowed rulers a major role in the selection of bishops. In return they gave official public recognition to Catholicism (including monetary support), and promulgated, in their respective countries, Vatican decrees on faith and morals.

This arrangement periodically gave rise to serious conflicts between Church and state. Popes and kings clashed over the temporal power of the Church throughout the Middle Ages. During the rise of the modern nation-state, several monarchs considered the Church a threat to national autonomy and unity, and made efforts to sever connections between Rome and local churches in their countries.[63] Communist governments in post-World War II Eastern Europe severely curtailed religious activities in their countries. In some instances (e.g., in Poland) they promoted a national clergy independent of Rome to break the influence of the Church's ideology and international linkages, both of which represented threats to national priorities.[64]

[63] Bihlmeyer, *Church History*, 2:148–66, 254–75, 345–75; 3:230–36, 266–70, 276–84. In eighteenth- and nineteenth-century France, Germany, and Austria this stimulated national church movements such as Gallicanism, Febronianism, and Josephinism. The Jesuits were expelled from several European nations in the same era, accused of being foreign agents meddling in the internal political affairs of sovereign states.

[64] Vallier, "The Roman Catholic Church," pp. 486–87, 491–94. Erich Weingartner, ed., *Church Within Socialism: Church and State in East European Republics.*

There has always been latent ground for conflict between Church and state due to the former's ability to command supranational loyalties and carry on transnational activities. This conflict has become overt when sectors of the Church have tried to influence the course of political development in particular societies, when currents of nationalism have been running high, or when the ideology or goals of the Church and the state have been at odds. The long, close identification of Church and state in many countries, along with the considerable political and economic power that ecclesiastical leaders wielded in many areas, exacerbated these conflicts when they have arisen.

The major trend in Church-state relations in Western societies since 1870 (when the Vatican lost the papal states) has been towards a differentiation of religious and political structures. In return for the surrender of temporal privileges and official state support, governments have signed concordats with the Vatican guaranteeing the Church's right to carry on religious activities free from state interference. The Vatican has also gained much greater control in the selection of bishops and over the internal religious development of national churches. This trend has strengthened the organizational network of the Church, both between Rome and peripheral units as well as among national churches themselves.[65]

This has produced important consequences for national Church development in many parts of the world. Since World War II the Vatican has appointed many bishops in Asia, Africa, and Latin America with progressive social views. Since the 1950s, several national churches in Europe and North America have substantially increased the flow of personnel to third-world countries that have been unable to recruit vocations to the priesthood and religious life at a rate sufficient to keep pace with increases in population. Many of these missionaries have concentrated their efforts among urban and rural working-class sectors and have brought with them new ideas and skills to meet their needs.[66]

Catholic organizations such as Catholic Relief Services in the United States and Misereor and Adveniat in West Germany over the past fifteen years have channeled considerable financial and material resources to churches in third-world countries. This aid has supported many new religious and social programs, including lay leadership and training, basic educational and literacy projects, nutrition and health programs,

[65] Vallier, "The Roman Catholic Church," pp. 485–90; and Francis X. Murphy, C.S.S.R., "Vatican Politics: Structure and Function," pp. 542–59.

[66] During the late 1950s and the 1960s the training of mission personnel emphasized skills related to problems of housing, public health, group leadership, credit unions and cooperatives, and community small industries. John J. Considine, M.M., *The Missionary's Role in Socio-Economic Betterment.*

construction of buildings, disaster relief, labor organizations, and centers for research and social action.

While the increased transfer of resources across national borders has enhanced the Church's capacity to promote structural change, tensions between Church and state have emerged over issues of internal security and national development. Governments in Asia, Africa, and Latin America have expelled foreign priests for allegedly abetting radical social or political movements, and for publicly avowing ideological views contrary to national objectives. Some governments have placed restrictions on Church activities, and many military regimes maintain close surveillance over Church programs and foreign-born personnel which provide humanitarian services to persecuted enemies of the state.[67]

Thus, the perennial problem that has always faced the Church in attempting to carry out transnational operations through subnational units in various parts of the world is reemerging. Formerly, the major source of conflict was with governments which considered the Church to be a major obstacle to change. The bulk of criticism in recent years, however, is originating from regimes that believe the institution is too committed to progressive social and economic policies.

Internal criticisms have arisen within the Church claiming that negative consequences have occurred due to the influx of large amounts of foreign personnel into third-world churches. Arguments have been made that foreign clergy impose their values on the people whom they serve in these areas or that their very availability prevents Church leaders in these countries from seeking more creative solutions to staffing problems through better use of indigenous clerical and lay personnel.[68] Some have also charged that foreign economic resources have caused divisions between foreign and native-born personnel, and that in some cases foreign donors have manipulated financial grants to control church strategies for political purposes in third-world countries.[69]

Thus far there has been little systematic study done on the amount of transfers throughout the international network of the Church nor on the opinion of religious leaders in host countries on the impact of foreign assistance in their churches. Such empirical data is important for determining how vulnerable to attack a local church will be in conflict situa-

[67] "The Bolivian Government's Plan of Action Against the Church," *Latinamerica Press* (Lima), 15 May 1975, pp. 3–4; Robert Youngblood, "Church Opposition to Martial Law in the Philippines," pp. 505–20; *Journal of Current Social Issues* 15 (Summer 1978); Brian H. Smith, "Churches and Human Rights in Latin America: Recent Trends in the Subcontinent," pp. 89–128.

[68] Ivan Illich, "The Seamy Side of Charity," pp. 89–91.

[69] David E. Mutchler, *The Church as a Political Factor in Latin America: With Particular Reference to Colombia and Chile,* chaps. 1 and 17.

Table 2.7
Nationality of Clergy in Chile, 1945–1973

Year	Chilean Priests		Foreign Priests		Totals	Catholics Per Priest
1945	1,098	(60.7%)	711	(39.3%)	1,809	2,681
1960	1,159	(49.5%)	1,183	(50.5%)	2,342	2,901
1965	1,140	(48.6%)	1,207	(51.4%)	2,347	3,006
1973	1,289	(51.7%)	1,202	(48.3%)	2,491	3,251

SOURCES: Oficina Nacional de Estadística de la Acción Católica Chilena, *Estado de la iglesia en Chile;* Poblete and Gino Garrido, *La iglesia en Chile;* Office of Religious Sociology (OSORE) of the Episcopal Conference of Chile.

tions with hostile governments and how independent a national church can be in choosing its own priorities.

In order to measure the institutional autonomy of the Chilean Church in its active involvement in promotion of social change after 1960, I gathered statistical data on foreign priests and international Church money coming into Chile and compared these with numbers of local clergy and internal financial resources available during the same time span. I also asked several questions in my interviews to determine judgments on the cost-benefit factors of outside sources of support.

Table 2.7 indicates that after World War II the proportion of foreign versus Chilean-born priests rose considerably, with the result that throughout the 1960s and early 1970s foreign priests constituted about one-half of the overall number serving in the country. The Chilean Church had to rely on very substantial numbers of foreign priests during a period of significant renovation. Moreover, even with the large influx of foreign clergy, the ratio of priests to baptized Catholics did not keep pace with growing numbers of the Catholic population during this period.

When asked how they would evaluate the performance of foreign priests in Chile, less than 3 percent of the respondents denied the importance of such support. Nearly sixty percent (58.3 percent) of the priests and over one-half (51.5 percent) of the nuns whom I asked, however, voiced criticisms that many foreigners did not adjust well to the Chilean situation or wasted much of their energies. Over two-fifths (44.8 percent) of the bishops also expressed similar judgments.[70]

More than one bishop voiced the opinion that some foreign priests had come to Chile in order to work out frustrations or in order to engage

[70] In response to the exact same question in Poblete's survey of priests in 1969, a total of 71.6 percent of the respondents voiced similar criticisms of foreign clergy— 29.6 percent believed that some wasted their energies, and 46 percent felt that many did not adapt well to the Chilean context. Poblete et al., *El sacerdote chileno,* p. 143.

Table 2.8
Attitudes Concerning Foreign Priests
"With which of the following statements concerning foreign priests are you more in agreement?"
(1975)

	Bishops (N = 29)	Priests (N = 72)	Nuns (N = 33)	Laity (N = 51)	Totals (N = 185)
1. They have provided very effective support for the Chilean Church	55.2% (16)	36.1% (26)	42.4% (14)	54.9% (28)	45.4% (84)
2. In general they provide effective support but there are some who upon arrival in Chile get involved in too many projects and waste their energies	34.5 (10) ⎤ 44.8	38.9 (28) ⎤ 58.3	30.3 (10) ⎤ 51.5	13.7 (7)	29.7 (55) ⎤ 48.1
3. Those who adjust to Chile offer good support but there are many who do not manage to adapt to our situation	10.3 (3) ⎦	19.4 (14) ⎦	21.2 (7) ⎦	19.6 (10)	18.4 (34) ⎦
4. Despite their substantial numbers, their support has been minimal		1.4 (1)		7.9 (4)	2.7 (5)
5. Other		1.4 (1)			.6 (1)
6. No answer		2.8 (2)	6.1 (2)	3.9 (2)	3.2 (6)

NOTE: Not asked = 1

in social and political activism. A number of Chilean priests remarked that tensions existed between themselves and foreign clergy because the latter enjoyed easy access to financial resources from abroad which they did not readily share with local priests.[71]

The financial dependency of the Chilean Church on outside assistance during this period was even more dramatic than its reliance on foreign personnel. In 1964, the Chilean hierarchy inaugurated a form of tithing to replace parish collections (which traditionally have been small due to a very low rate of Sunday observance), asking all Catholic families to contribute 1 percent of their annual income to the Church. This program, known as Contribución a la Iglesia (CALI), generated $2.8 million during its first ten years of operation. In comparison with foreign support between 1960 and 1973, this sum was extremely small and accounted for only 3.1 percent of overall Church income from non-state grants.[72]

The heavy dependence on foreign money to carry on its projects has created some serious internal problems for the Chilean Church. Two-fifths of the priests in my interviews felt that reliance on foreign financial assistance has artificially sustained the Chilean Church and prevented it from confronting its problems realistically. Nearly one-half of the bishops believed that such aid was justified given the meager resources at their disposal but 40 percent indicated that foreign support must be but a temporary measure employed only until the Church develops its own internal resources.

Almost none of these respondents in 1975 complained of attempts to control the Chilean Church by foreign donor agencies.[73] Some of the bishops indicated that grants were given for very specific projects chosen according to priority interests of donors and said that this has limited

---

[71] I examine these tensions further and go into greater detail on the effects of foreign aid in "The Impact of Foreign Church Aid: The Case of Chile," pp. 23–29.

[72] Although there were other internal sources of financing available to the Chilean Church during this period—such as rents from landholdings, interest from investments, revenues collected at seasonal pilgrimages to religious shrines in various dioceses, and salaries paid to priests teaching required religion courses in public schools—my interviews with Chilean religious leaders confirmed that, coupled with CALI, these provided for little more than basic maintenance of existing buildings and living expenses for bishops, priests, and religious. Everything which the Chilean Church sponsored in the areas of religious and social action—leadership and technical training, catechetical programs, housing construction, rural development, labor organizations, education, health and nutrition, radio stations, research—required large amounts of outside support (private and public).

[73] Only 1.1 percent of the priests in Poblete's 1969 survey expressed belief that foreign control was a major problem with international Church assistance. One-third, however, did feel that such aid prevented the Chilean Church from perceiving and facing its problems realistically, and over two-fifths (44.1 percent) indicated that it can produce negative (but unspecified) consequences if it is not used well. Poblete et al., El sacerdote chileno, p. 145.

Table 2.9
Non-State Financial Resources of Chilean Church, 1960–1973
In U.S. Dollars

Year	West European Catholic Church Organizations		North American Catholic Church Organizations		W. German Government	U.S. Government	Chilean Church (CALI)
	W. Germany	Other Countries	U.S.A.	Canada			
1960	$ 196,000		$ 8,700,000				
1961	729,250	$ 38,623	7,200,000				
1962	1,299,000	38,623	6,700,000		$ 115,000	$ 319,333	
1963	462,625	64,145	3,600,000	$ 5,000	185,250	1,319,333	
1964	899,000	38,623	4,800,000	5,000	100,000	408,285	$ 271,367
1965	850,405	45,416	7,800,000	5,000	272,500	304,405	270,916
1966	1,197,482	45,416	5,357,000	3,500	330,000	330,294	269,345
1967	2,390,495	104,240	2,471,000	1,825	182,500	261,000	280,828
1968	1,098,914	68,226	6,050,706	4,716	98,750	200,000	328,390
1969	818,926	128,263	2,044,000	7,122		255,000	354,009
1970	936,106	640,535	1,660,500	8,900	1,434,426	255,000	404,886
1971	784,915	275,200	3,217,862	93,800			302,632
1972	896,693	210,003	3,265,778	15,300			330,703
1973	1,273,994	256,049	4,215,750	62,200	377,358		59,741
Totals	$13,833,805	$1,953,362	$65,882,996	$212,363	$3,095,784	$3,652,650	$2,872,817

Foreign Total	$88,630,960	(96.9%)
Chilean Total	2,872,817	(3.1%)
Grand Total	$91,503,777	(100%)

SOURCES: West German Catholic organizations: Adveniat, Misereor, and Deutscher Caritasverband.
Catholic organizations from other Western European countries: Fastenopfer der Schweizer Katholiken (Switzerland), Entraide et Fraternité (Belgium), Koordinierungstelle für Internationale Entwicklungsförderung (Austria), Catholic Fund for Overseas Development (Great Britain), Comité Catholique contre la Faim et pour le Développement (France), Bisschoppelijke Vastenaktie (Netherlands).
United States Catholic organizations: Catholic Relief Services, and the Secretariat for Latin America of the U.S. Catholic Conference.

The vast majority of these funds represent the dollar value of food supplies provided by the U.S. government Food for Peace Program distributed by Catholic Relief Services.

Canadian Catholic organizations: Canadian Catholic Organization for Development and Peace, and the Canadian Conference of Catholic Bishops.

U.S. Government: United States Agency for International Development.

West German Government: Zentralstelle. This is a program of the West German government that supports social action projects in Latin America but which is administered by Misereor, the development agency of the West German bishops.

Chilean Church: Contribución a la Iglesia (CALI), the 1 percent tithing of annual incomes of Chilean Catholic families. Data for Table 2.9 was provided to me by the above organizations themselves or by CIDSE in Brussels, the coordinating federation to which most of them belong.

Table 2.10

Attitudes on Foreign Sources of Support

"With which of the following statements concerning foreign financial assistance to the Chilean Church are you in most agreement?"

	Bishops (N = 30)	Priests (N = 72)	Nuns (N = 33)	Laity (N = 51)	Totals (N = 186)
1. Foreign help is completely justified since our Church is at present unable to support itself. (It is an act of fraternal solidarity)	46.6% (14)	36.1% (26)	33.3% (11)	31.4% (16)	36.0% (67)
2. Foreign help has artificially maintained our Church in Chile and as a result prevented us from perceiving and confronting our problems realistically	6.7 (2)	40.3 (29)	33.3 (11)	29.4 (15)	30.6 (57)
3. Foreign help is never disinterested; there is always at least an implicit interest of control involved				3.9 (2)	1.1 (2)
4. Other (It is a necessary but temporary measure until we develop our own resources)	40.0 (12)	23.6 (17)	15.2 (5)	11.8 (6)	21.5 (40)
5. Don't know, no answer	6.7 (2)		18.2 (6)	23.5 (12)	10.8 (20)

their own options and flexibility. The remarks of two bishops illustrate this problem:

> Foreign assistance is too restricted and forces me to select certain projects. Misereor gives money only for health, education and food—it excludes pastoral programs. Adveniat supports pastoral programs, but with its own priorities.[74]

> The money from foreign sources is not controlled, but it is restricted. I would prefer to have the use of money at my own free disposal. . . . Almost all the projects supported by foreign money are good, but if all these funds were not given to the bishops they would not have constructed as many buildings as they have. They could have done much better with 40 percent less money.[75]

Another major problem has been that the motivation for generating indigenous sources of support seems to have been diminished by the availability of large amounts of foreign money. Several bishops commented that CALI has not been promoted sufficiently outside large predominantly urban dioceses such as Santiago and Concepción. Aside from the poverty in many of the provinces, the local clergy has not pushed the idea of tithing sufficiently because many have access to foreign money and do not yet see the importance of attempting to put their parishes on a self-supporting basis.

Chilean Catholics themselves in most dioceses have traditionally not supported the Church with money and their response to CALI thus far has been weak. The average number of persons contributing to this program annually between 1964 and 1973 was approximately 53,000 per year, representing less than 5 percent of all Catholic families in the country.[76] The purpose of this 1 percent contribution of annual family income to the Church was not only financial; it was designed to encourage closer identification with the Church on the part of all Catholics. Such has not resulted. The continual availability of foreign financial resources has reduced the motivation to do so on the part of the Chilean laity who have assumed their Church will carry on its good works without their support.[77]

These statistics on foreign sources of personnel and financial support, as well as the judgments by religious leaders of the consequences of such

[74] Interview no. 007, 29 April 1975.
[75] Interview no. 010, 19 June 1975.
[76] Statistics on annual amounts of contributions from CALI, along with the number of contributing families each year, were provided to me by Rev. José Kuhl in Mutual Pax Chile of the Chilean Episcopal Conference.
[77] When I asked in my interviews what success the Chilean Church had after 1964 in establishing a sufficient and widespread base of popular financial support, over four-fifths (83.7 percent) of those polled indicated that there had been little, very little, or no success made in achieving this goal to date (1975).

assistance, lead to mixed conclusions. Substantial numbers of foreign priests have enabled the Chilean Church to serve many who otherwise would have been without the services of priests, especially in rural and urban working-class areas. Furthermore, foreign financial and material assistance gave the Chilean Church a capacity to initiate and continue many religious and social programs (as will be discussed in later chapters) that would have been impossible without outside support.

Such large amounts of assistance, however, have produced some decidedly negative effects. While foreign control as such does not appear to have been a major problem in the opinion of Chilean religious leaders, many of them believe that such help has prevented the Church from confronting its problems more realistically, limited its flexibility, and curtailed the motivation to search for more internal sources of support. Moreover, rank-and-file members were not forced to take responsibility for maintaining their own Church. The value of newly announced goals of the post-Vatican II Church had not by 1973 convinced many average Chilean Catholics to contribute economic support to their implementation.

Although comparable data is not complete for other third-world countries, it is not unreasonable to suspect that Chile is indicative of a dependency trend that characterizes many national Churches in developing areas. In several other Latin American nations in the late 1960s, such as Peru, Venezuela, Bolivia, Guatemala, Nicaragua, Panama, Honduras, and the Dominican Republic, foreign priests constituted 70 percent or more of the total number of clergy.[78] Furthermore, none of these countries have undertaken extensive tithing programs such as the one begun in Chile in 1964, making outside support even more important for the maintenance of their pastoral and social projects than in Chile. While more empirical research is needed on this issue there is strong probability that the Chilean Church is not unique, and, in fact, may be more autonomous than many others.

Many churches in the third world are therefore heavily dependent on foreign donors. This can lead to very different religiopolitical outcomes depending upon the configuration of forces in a developing country. When a government is implementing progressive structural reforms and welcomes reinforcements by religious institutions, foreign support could enable a local national church to contribute significantly to the process. If foreign donors, however, do not approve the policies of a particular government, they may limit their support to local church groups favoring such objectives, thus reducing that church's reinforcement capabilities to secular changes. In situations when a poor church attempts to

[78] "The Priesthood in Latin America," *Pro Mundi Vita* (Brussels) 22 (1968): 15.

check abuses of an authoritarian regime, foreign support could help sustain its resistance but could also increase its vulnerability to criticism and even attack by the State. Each of these three scenarios will be discussed in later chapters analyzing the interactions of the Chilean Church with the three different regimes since 1964—Christian Democratic, Marxist-socialist, and authoritarian military.

CONCLUSIONS

The Roman Catholic Church is not a monolithic institution. There are different levels of obligation in its teachings and a diversity of action choices that can be deduced from many of them. Leadership roles are diversified, giving rise to very different perspectives that change according to levels of responsibility. There are wide-ranging commitments among members depending on the degree of exposure to the socialization processes of the Church and on the intensity of other more pressing interests in their lives.

Fundamental religious commitments do, however, set parameters on the Church's range of flexibililty and adaptability. The transmission of certain immutable doctrines, the belief that salvation is for all people, and the importance of formal religious unity among members have all given rise to institutional characteristics of the Church that are essential to its integrity—specific binding force of a few clearly defined dogmas, hierarchical structures of authority, diverse membership patterns, and transnational organizational linkages. While variations (and even inconsistencies) in the functioning of these components have occurred over time, the history of the Church also indicates that Rome and the hierarchy will firmly resist developments that in principle challenge or underline any of them.

There is now much more flexibility in the Church than before Vatican II and Medellín, but there are sticking points which the hierarchy will insist upon in order to preserve what they consider to be essential to the Church's religious and moral integrity. An understanding of what these core interests are and how disagreements emerge across levels of the Church over them is crucial for an accurate interpretation of the institution's response to internal forces of change as well as social and political challenges.

Moreover, the disagreements or conflicts that have emerged in the Church since Vatican II, although manifestations of classic historical dilemmas that have always existed in the institution, have taken on new dimensions as a result of the Church's greater involvement in secular development. Addressing values of freedom, participation, and equality more positively and showing a greater willingness to use its national and international capacities prophetically in favor of justice and human dignity, the Church has begun to experience both greater internal dilemmas and more tension with secular powers that are unavoidable.

As the Church attempts to reorient its position and use its resources to support progressive developments, the interactions among its normative, structural, and behavioral components, and in turn their relation to corresponding secular forces, will set the parameters for different religiopolitical results. For example, on a crucial public issue where (a) dominant secular values coincide with important religious interests, (b) authority conflicts do not emerge inside the Church, (c) a decision is binding on all Catholics uniformly, and (d) receives legitimizing support from the Vatican, then the decision may be reached to the mutual satisfaction and advantage of both Church and government, thus avoiding a major religiopolitical conflict. This scenario will be explored in Chapter 3, dealing with the formal extrication of the Chilean Church from the state in 1925.

When Church norms offer legitimation to secular values espousing progressive change, when religious and secular roles and structures are mutually reinforcing, when secular and religious choices are moving in the same direction and receive strong support from international Church sources, we could expect the impact of the Church on secular developments to be significant. The underdevelopment of religious socialization processes and weak structural autonomy in terms of personnel and finances, however, could make such reinforcement tenuous and short-term, especially if the social and political context were to undergo serious polarization. An exploration of this scenario will be presented in Chapters 5 and 6 dealing with the Chilean Church's attempts to reinforce social and economic change during the rise and decline of Christian Democracy in Chile.

If there are some serious differences between religious values and structures and those guiding the process of societal change, but sufficient overlapping concerns to prevent prolonged conflicts, then peaceful coexistence and even limited cooperation might occur between religious and secular groups. In such a context, the Church, while not being a major contributor to change, would neither be a significant obstacle to it. This possibility shall be explored in Chapter 7 in describing relations between Church and state at the public policy level during the Popular Unity government of Salvador Allende.

If in such a situation open conflicts emerge across leadership levels within the Church over the compatibility of religious and secular norms and the formal unity of the institution is threatened by polarized responses among its members, then the reaction of ecclesiastical leaders both at the national and international levels could be quite defensive and rule out further accommodations. This hypothesis will be examined in Chapter 8 in analyzing efforts by Chilean Catholics to forge a synthesis of Christian and Marxist values and tactics within the Church between 1970 and 1973.

Finally, in a situation where the Church is a surrogate for other social institutions curtailed by an authoritarian regime, its capacity to act as a consistent opposition force to the state will also be determined by the interaction of its key normative, structural, and behavioral components with secular forces. If it can articulate norms that are sufficiently forceful to delegitimate public authority, maintain authority flows and protect its structures, preserve basic unity among its formal adherents, and maintain autonomous resource bases, then it could be a crucial factor in blunting repression. If however, its leadership or membership is seriously divided or if its resources can be curtailed by the State, its impact on public policy could be limited and the willingness of the hierarchy to risk sustained and open confrontation with the state diminished. These possible interactions between crucial religious and secular forces will be examined in Chapter 9 which deals with Church and state in Chile under the current military regime.

PART II

The Church and Socioeconomic Reform

3 Separation of the Church from Traditional Structural Alliances: Chile, 1920–1935

Until this century the Catholic Church officially opposed the separation of Church and state. From the time of Constantine through the Reformation period, Catholicism was the officially established religion in all of Europe. Close union between spiritual and temporal authority was legitimized in official Church teaching throughout the Middle Ages as part of God's plan.[1] Even after the breakdown of unity in Christendom in the sixteenth century, the Catholic Church continued to espouse the doctrine of union as a protection for itself against the antireligious sentiments and objectives of liberal movements. As late as 1885 Pope Leo XIII in his encyclical, *Immortale Dei,* denounced separationist theory as being primarily an attack on God and the prerogatives of the Church.[2]

In the post-Enlightenment period, the Church thus maintained close tactical alliances in Europe with monarchical governments and aristocratic elites in order to preserve its influence against secular forces bent on drastically curtailing its moral and political power. In so doing, however, Catholicism opened itself to manipulation by reactionary groups and parties which readily used the Church to perpetuate their own legitimacy and position. This made liberal groups even more intent on removing the Church's privileges, and some also espoused restrictions on its freedom in religious activities.[3]

---

[1] The clearest expression of this doctrine was articulated by Pope Boniface VIII in his bull, *Unam Sanctam* (1302). This document stated that both spiritual and temporal authority were in the keeping of the Church, each to be wielded in separate hands like two swords. The first was to be exercised by the pope and bishops, the second by kings and princes but under the direction of clerics. Anne Fremantle, ed., *The Papal Encyclicals in their Historical Context,* pp. 72–74.

[2] Pope Leo XIII, "Immortale Dei" (1885), nos. 9–12, in *Social Wellsprings: Fourteen Epochal Documents by Pope Leo XIII,* ed. Joseph Husslein, S.J., pp. 75–79.

Among Protestant Churches there has always been much more pluralism on this issue than within the Catholic Church. For an excellent summary of the major Protestant positions and how they have evolved historically, see Thomas G. Sanders, *Protestant Concepts of Church and State.*

[3] This pattern was particularly dominant in several nominally Catholic countries, such as France, Spain, Italy, and Portugal, where strong liberal and anticlerical forces had become significant contenders for power by the late nineteenth and early

A similar pattern characterized Latin American religiopolitical relations from the sixteenth to the nineteenth centuries. Prior to independence, the Church was, in effect, an integral part of the colonial government. It relied heavily on imperial protection and finances to carry out its mission of evangelization. After separation from the crown, and as liberal and radical parties began to gain strength in many countries of mid-nineteenth-century Latin America, the Church came to depend very much on conservative parties to protect its established interests.[4]

The result of these close structural alliances in Western Europe and Latin America during this period was that the Church pursued its objectives through political coalitions and short-term elite maneuvers. This strategy diminished the Church's moral credibility among growing numbers of nominal Catholics who supported liberal movements and values. It also reduced the necessity to develop more effective processes in the institution to deepen commitments to Catholic values and objectives among rank-and-file members.

In Latin America, and in many other Catholic countries of Western Europe as well, allegiance to the Church declined considerably in the eighteenth and nineteenth centuries as secular movements gained momentum. Governments used their financial power over the Church and the right to participate in the appointment of Church officials and in the creation of new dioceses to control the institution or use it for their own political purposes. The Church, therefore, remained organizationally dependent, and in many countries (especially in Latin America), structurally underdeveloped.[5]

In the late nineteenth and early twentieth centuries when liberal Republics in many Western countries designed constitutions separating Church and state, this often occurred amidst bitter controversy. Both the Vatican and national hierarchies normally opposed these measures, and clerical issues exacerbated already serious differences between conservative and liberal parties. In some instances, anticlericalism and religious indifference were so strong that not only was the Church separated from the state, but very severe restrictions were imposed on its religious ministries—e.g., in France and Mexico.[6] In both of these nations, and in several others in Europe and Latin America where separation of Church and state occurred amidst severe conflict, religion still is a significant cleavage factor in politics. Practicing Catholics in Western Europe over-

---

twentieth centuries. Joseph N. Moody, ed., *Church and Society*, pts. I, II, and IV passim, and Thomas C. Bruneau, "Church and State in Portugal: Crises of Cross and Sword," pp. 465–68.

[4] J. Lloyd Mecham, *Church and State in Latin America: A History of Politico-Ecclesiastical Relations*, chaps. 5, 6 , 11, 15, and 16 passim.

[5] Ivan Vallier, *Catholicism, Social Control and Modernization in Latin America*, pp. 23–28.

[6] Moody, ed., *Church and Society*, p. 160, and Mecham, *Church and State*, pp. 386–88.

whelmingly support conservative parties or those favorable to the Church, while the nonpracticing are more prone to back radical or Marxist movements.[7]

In some other countries separation of the Church from the state occurred only partially (e.g., in Germany and Venezuela). In these societies, the Church continues to receive public subsidies and thus remains dependent on the state in a very significant way. In still other Western nations (e.g., Ireland, Colombia, Peru, Bolivia, Paraguay, Argentina) no formal disestablishment has yet transpired. Significant legal and financial privileges are still guaranteed to the Church in return for a continuing government role in the selection process of bishops. In these latter countries there has been little threat to the Church's interests, but neither has it been motivated to develop new internal programs of religious or social renewal. It has also remained a predominantly conservative force in society.[8]

The importance of this issue for contemporary religiopolitical relations is clear. If the Church now wishes to play a socially progressive role in encouraging more just distribution of societal resources in favor of the poor, it needs to be free from close linkages with conservative movements controlled by upper-class interests. If it wants to increase its moral credibility among all sectors of society and to coexist peacefully with leftist parties, undue ecclesiastical privileges must be eradicated from the public realm and Catholics must feel comfortable in supporting parties other than those identified with Church interests. If it is to have the necessary independence to criticize repressive governments, it must be financially autonomous and free from state interference in decisions affecting its internal affairs.

The terms in which each national church confronts the extrication problem definitely influences its ability to resolve each of these others. A church's resources, credibility, and freedom to encourage change, to coexist with liberal and leftist parties, and to speak and act prophetically are all affected by how, and to what extent, it first disengages itself from the state and from traditional political associations.[9] In societies where such an extrication has not yet occurred, is only partial, or has been achieved amidst severe antagonisms, the Church's potential to act as an

---

[7] In contemporary European politics religion accounts for even more variance in voting patterns than social class, and strong anticlerical sentiments continue to characterize various radical and leftist parties. Richard Rose and Derek Urwin, "Social Cohesion, Political Parties and Strains in Regimes," pp. 220–21.

[8] Guenter Lewy, *The Catholic Church and Nazi Germany*, p. 4; Moody, ed., *Church and Society*, pp. 723–32, and Mecham, *Church and State*, pp. 88–138, 160–200, 225–51.

[9] For a theoretical analysis of the importance of separation of the Church from state and from conservative alliances as a precondition for its exercising a change-oriented role in modern society, see Vallier, "Extraction, Insulation and Re-entry: Toward a Theory of Religious Change," pp. 9–35.

effective agent for social justice and human dignity for all is reduced.

One of the smoothest official separations of the Church from the state and from the Conservative Party in Western societies occurred in Chile during the 1920s and 1930s. Although drawn up while an anticlerical Liberal Alliance was in power, the Constitution of 1925 which disestablished the Church met with only limited resistance by the hierarchy. It was also ratified with almost no public disagreement. Since 1925 clerical issues have not played a prominent role in politics, nor has there been the same prolonged resentment against the Church by radical and Marxist-inspired parties as has occurred in many other Western democracies.

During this period, and in the years immediately following the ratification of the constitution, the Chilean Catholic Church was able to distance itself from the Conservative Party. Official ecclesiastical documents in the 1920s and early 1930s emphasized that the Church could not be identified with any political movement and that Catholics were free to vote for candidates of their choice.

Given the difficulty extrication caused for both Church and state in many other countries, the Chilean experience provides very important learning experiences for national churches which still have the extrication issue ahead of them. While some scholars have attributed a peaceful resolution of this problem primarily to the religious indifference in Chilean society at the time,[10] the skills of the archbishop of Santiago,[11] or the graceful acceptance of defeat by the Chilean bishops,[12] I would argue that the process was more complex. The fact that all four of the key components of the Church, as described in Chapter 2, functioned in relative harmony with, or were unthreatened by, corresponding secular forces produced an outcome that was mutually acceptable to both Church and society at large. The remainder of this chapter will examine how this was accomplished, and indicate the positive impact such a relatively successful resolution of the challenge had on subsequent religiopolitical developments in Chile.

CONGRUENCE OF DOMINANT RELIGIOUS AND POLITICAL INTERESTS IN CHILE, 1920–1925

Serious ideological conflict between Church leaders and liberals was avoided in Chile in 1925 since many on both sides had come to see that there were common interests in peaceful extrication. At that time

[10] Mecham, *Church and State,* p. 218.

[11] Henry A. Landsberger, "Time, Persons, Doctrine: The Modernization of the Church in Chile," p. 83.

[12] Frederick B. Pike, *Chile and the United States, 1880–1962,* pp. 184–185.

the Church no longer needed to protect its religious interests by continued union with the state and the Conservative Party. Liberal groups also
considered it politically counterproductive to make anticlericalism a
major element in future electoral campaigns.

Many of the Church's privileges had been eroding gradually since the
middle of the nineteenth century, so that by the 1920s there were few
issues over which conflict between itself and secular groups could arise.
Freedom of religion, although not guaranteed by the Constitution of
1833, by the mid-nineteenth century had become a de facto reality. Due
to the large number of foreigners in Chile (particularly British citizens
involved in mining and commerce), laws were modified in 1844 to allow
non-Catholics to contract matrimony. In 1865 all denominations were
given legal permission to worship and establish schools.[13]

Later, when Liberal and Radical parties dominated the government
in the 1870s and 1880s, reform laws were passed subjecting clerics to
public trials and penalties in civil and criminal cases, releasing ceme-
teries from exclusive Church control, making civil marriage compulsory,
and placing all civil records in the hands of the state.[14] Although ecclesiastical leaders resisted all these restrictions on Church privilege, they
became faits accomplis. During the next forty years no major conflicts
occurred between Church and state.

Unlike the situation in Italy, Spain, and Mexico, the Catholic Church
in Chile was not a major landowner, nor did it possess large amounts of
art and treasures. This relative poverty of the institution removed a further possible reason for anticlericalism. It reduced the salience of financial motives among liberals for disestablishing Catholicism so as to
achieve national economic integration.

During the late nineteenth century, however, the Church came to be
identified very closely with the Conservative Party which fought for its
religious prerogatives in Congress. Aside from being tactically unsuc-
cessful, this alliance had very serious negative consequences for the
Church. Clerics became heavily involved in local electoral campaigns
and in some cases Church funds were purportedly used to promote Conservative Party candidates.[15] These factors not only damaged the moral
credibility of the Church but also precipitated serious internal divisions
among Catholics and between bishops and their priests. It was also clear
that the Conservative Party was using the Church to shore up its own

[13] José Guillermo Guerra, *La Constitución de 1925*, p. 39.
[14] Mecham, *Church and State*, p. 211–14.
[15] Guerra, *La Constitución*, pp. 40–41. Priests wielded great influence in municipal
elections in the late nineteenth and early twentieth centuries, and "until shortly after
1925 it was inconceivable that a good priest would not be a member of the Conservative Party." Fidel Araneda Bravo, *El Arzobispo Errázuriz y la evolución política y social
de Chile*, pp. 198–99, 206.

influence, which by the early twentieth century was eroding in the face of newly emerging middle-class parties.

Significant changes were occurring in the social and economic structures of the country in the first two decades of the century. In 1920, when Arturo Alessandri won the presidency by a very narrow margin with the backing of the Radical and Democratic parties and a fraction of socially progressive Liberals, there was a growing sentiment in the populace that serious reforms were necessary. During the period from 1891 and 1920, a strong parliamentary government ruled the country dominated by an alliance of Conservatives and traditional Liberals. It initiated no major economic reforms despite the growth of an industrial proletariat in the mining areas of the North and the emergence of new commercial middle-class sectors in the central urban regions. By 1920, however, Chile was no longer characterized by a small ruling elite and large amorphous, submissive masses; new segments of the population were voicing demands for significant redistribution of power in society.[16]

Alessandri's platform in 1920 included a whole range of measures to effect economic and social reforms, including abolition of the parliamentary system of government, the reestablishment of a strong presidency subject to direct popular election, state control of banks and insurance companies, and a program of social security. Also included in this package was the proposal to effect a separation of Church and state, one of the main objectives of the Radical Party which was a member of Alessandri's coalition.[17]

Alessandri, however, did not have a rigid ideological position regarding religion as did some members of his government. He wanted to remove the possibility of future religious conflicts in society so as to focus public attention on social reform and widen his own coalition's political base of support. Extrication was seen as an important strategy to weaken the Conservative Party which continued to present itself as the staunch and necessary defender of Church interests. If a separation of Church and state could be achieved that guaranteed the fundamental rights and freedoms of the Church, reasoned Alessandri, the Conservative Party could no longer use religion as a strategy to attract Catholic votes and thus forestall social and economic changes. Hence, Alessandri personally took the initiative in proposing terms for a disestablishment of Catholicism, and he offered conditions that respected several of the Church's demands: a legally guaranteed public juridical personality, the rights to own property and to maintain its own system of education,

---

[16] Federico Gil, *The Political System of Chile*, pp. 51–56.
[17] Ibid.

and freedom to manage its internal religious affairs without state interference.[18]

Furthermore, by the early 1920s Archbishop Crescente Errázuriz of Santiago had become concerned about the problem of clerical intervention in politics and the manipulation of the Church by the Conservative Party. In 1922 he wrote a very strong pastoral letter strictly forbidding priests from participating in political rallies, meetings, and banquets, and from acting as agents or representatives of parties. He gave for his reasons the preservation of the independence and impartiality of the priesthood and the necessity of maintaining strict clerical obedience to the hierarchy alone and not to political leaders. He emphasized that the Church desired nothing from any political party and wanted, in turn, complete freedom from political interference in ecclesiastical affairs.[19]

In addition, although several Chilean bishops wrote individual letters in the early 1920s opposing the separation of Church and state, as a matter of principle, they did not use all the means at their disposal to fight it. They mounted no major public campaign of sermons, books, pamphlets, or threats of excommunication against those proposing it after the election of Alessandri in 1920. One major reason was that many in the Church had come to see some very definite advantages of the Church becoming independent of the state, since it then would no longer have to ask congressional approval to set up new dioceses, seminaries, and religious communities.[20]

Thus, when the new constitution was presented to the voters in a special plebiscite in September 1925, the Chilean hierarchy did not strongly oppose it because of its relatively favorable terms of separation and the evident lack of bitter anticlerical sentiment among its proponents. Moreover, immediately after the Constitution of 1925 was ratified, all fourteen of the Chilean bishops issued a conciliatory pastoral letter ac-

[18] There are also indications that Alessandri was looking beyond the issue of immediate short-term tactical advantage over the Conservative Party by achieving a peaceful separation of Church and state in the mid-1920s. In a 1923 letter to Miguel Cruchaga, his ambassador in Brazil, Alessandri stated that an early and amicable resolution of the religious question could clear the way for a united front by the center and right in Chile against the day on which Marxists might become serious contenders for power in the country. Robert Alexander, *Arturo Alessandri: A Biography*, 1:144.

[19] Archbishop Crescente Errázuriz, "Pastoral sobre la iglesia y los partidos políticos," (8 December 1922), in *Obras de Crescente Errázuriz*, ed. Raúl Silva Castro, 3:61–67.

[20] Previous to formal separation of Church and state in Chile in 1925, Congress not only provided salaries for bishops and priests but also had to approve all major internal organizational changes within the Church. At times such approval was not forthcoming, and up until 1925 there were only four dioceses in the country despite both Rome's and the Chilean hierarchy's desire to establish new ecclesiastical territories.

cepting the decision, giving it specific binding force for Catholics, and recognizing that the motive for separation was not one of persecution of the Church. They also recognized that the Church would have greater freedom than under the previous arrangement that gave patronage rights to the state over internal ecclesiastical appointments and over the publication of Vatican directives to Catholics in Chile. They stated that separation of Church and state under conditions guaranteeing the public juridic personality and freedom of the Church was clearly a lesser evil with which the Church could live. They also offered the Church's full cooperation to the state in promoting the common good and social order.[21]

There were, therefore, congruent interests shared by the newly elected liberal regime and Church leaders which could be achieved by a separation of the Church from the state and the Conservative Party. Significant ideological currents in secular society had been moving in this direction with Church acquiescence for some time, and the absence of severe clerical conflicts in politics for almost half a century created an atmosphere in which a solution could be reached. Not only was the Church's public influence not called into question, but its capacity to pursue its primary religious mission with more autonomy was strengthened. Alessandri in turn removed an important ideological weapon of his conservative opponents, thus widening his own potential base of support.[22]

ACCOMMODATING STRATEGIES OF RELIGIOUS AND POLITICAL LEADERS AND CRITICAL INTERVENTION BY THE VATICAN

Two other essential structures of the Church facilitated its self-distancing from traditional alliances in Chile: (1) hierarchical authority flows, and (2) resource transactions between center and periphery units.

---

[21] "Pastoral colectiva de los obispos de Chile sobre la separación de la iglesia y el estado," (20 September 1925), in *Obras,* ed. Silva Castro, 3:117–21.

[22] Such overlapping normative interests as bases for agreement between Church and liberal leaders simply did not exist in late nineteenth-century Germany, Italy, and France, or early twentieth-century Mexico. The Kulturkampf against Catholicism by Bismarck, the issue of political sovereignty for the Vatican inside Italy, laicist determination to eradicate all traces of religion from education in France, and the Church's adamant opposition to the Mexican Revolution all pitted Catholics and liberals against one another in these other countries around the turn of the century. In those nations very little maneuverability existed on either side, since each considered the goals and ideology of the other as threatening to its own fundamental interests. Hence, a common basis for an amicable settlement of the issue of extrication was much more difficult to establish. In the countries where the anticlericals finally gained predominant political power (France and Mexico), they unilaterally imposed upon the Church terms of separation far more unfavorable than those mutually agreed upon in Chile by Church and state in 1925.

Each of these was critical in establishing the terms of agreement and in realizing them effectively. Since both variables functioned in tandem, with the latter reinforcing the former, I shall treat them together.

A major factor contributing to the Church's acceptance of a separation from the state was the interchange among the president of Chile, the pope, the Vatican secretary of state, and the archbishop of Santiago. Negotiations were carried on among these leaders during 1924 and 1925 to explore conditions of extrication acceptable to both sides.

In September 1924 a military coup occurred in Chile when Congress and the executive were deadlocked over reform proposals and after Congress had violated the constitution by voting itself pay increases. The junta remained in power only five months, and was succeeded by another military group very sympathetic to Alessandri's program. They recalled the president in early 1925 to resume leadership of the country and to prepare a new constitution.

During his exile in late 1924, Alessandri travelled to Rome, where he discussed with the Vatican the issue of a separation of Church and state in Chile. By going to Pope Pius XI and his secretary of state, Cardinal Pietro Gasparri, Alessandri hoped to gain Rome's acceptance of extrication first and thus preempt opposition to it from his local bishops. The pope received Alessandri cordially, and encouraged him to confer further with the secretary of state.

Although Gasparri told him that the Vatican was opposed in *principle* to a separation, the cardinal indicated that such a measure could be acceptable to Rome in *practice* if certain conditions were met. Such conditions included a guarantee for the public legal personality of the Church, indemnification for Church properties, the abrogation of the *patronato* (government participation in selecting bishops), no prohibition of religion courses in schools and no recognition for atheism in the new constitution. Alessandri agreed to all of these conditions, and, although no explicit formula was drawn up in these conversations, he promised to respect the mind of the Vatican in any future constitutional reform efforts.[23]

A major reason for the Vatican's willingness to accept a separation of Church and state in Chile in the mid-1920s was its desire to avoid the useless conflict that had recently occurred in several other nominally Catholic countries—France in 1905, Portugal in 1911, Mexico in 1917,

[23] Information on the content of these conversations between Gasparri and Alessandri was provided to me by Archbishop Carlos Oviedo Cavada of Antofagasta and Fr. Julio Jiménez, S.J., of the Catholic University in Santiago, during interviews I conducted with each of them respectively on 26 August 1975 and on 1 February 1975. See also: Arturo Alessandri, *Recuerdos de gobierno,* 2:56–65; Oviedo Cavada, "Carácter de la separación entre la iglesia y el estado en Chile," pp. 50–56; Jiménez, "Don Crescente y la evolución político-religiosa de Chile," pp. 18–28.

and Uruguay in 1919. Rome and the respective national hierarchies in each of these nations had lost the battle to preserve a close association of Church and state. The type of separation that occurred in each of these societies had weakened the local church considerably and had left very bitter feelings on both sides. The Vatican by the 1920s realized that disestablishment efforts were gaining momentum around the world and believed that Catholics could no longer successfully resist them without grave consequences.

After Pius XI, a scholar and diplomat, was elected pope in 1922, Vatican policy shifted to a more flexible stance both on the Church-state question and also on the issue of religiously oriented parties. It moved from a position of opposition to post-World War I secular governments in Europe to one of negotiation to improve the condition of national churches. The Holy See in the 1920s and 1930s signed concordats with these new regimes, including dictatorships in Portugal, Italy, and Germany, even though the conditions required a formal separation of Church and state. It also withdrew its support for Catholic parties in return for legal guarantees of religious freedom for Church ministries and new lay apostolates.[24]

The Vatican also wanted more direct dealings with national churches outside Europe which an abrogation of the *patronato* would effect. Such freedom would give Rome greater control over the organizational development of various periphery units in the institution. In Brazil, for example, after the separation of Church and state in 1891, the Vatican was able to oversee the establishment of many new dioceses and seminaries without government interference, and also exercise a stronger formative role in inaugurating new clerical and lay training programs.[25]

Cardinal Gasparri, in his conversations with Alessandri in 1924, asked only that the separation be worked out with the least possible restriction on the Church's freedom. He also specifically referred to Brazil as a possible model of extrication for Chile. Alessandri's response was that he would design a form of separation as favorable to the Chilean Church as had occurred in Brazil.[26]

When Alessandri returned to Chile in early 1925, he continued his communications with the Vatican through Ramon Subercaseaux, his

[24] Vatican support for the Catholic Popular Party in Italy was withdrawn in 1924, for the French Catholic political movement, Action Française, in 1926, and for the Christian-inspired German Center Party in 1933. In their place Pius XI encouraged the development of nonpolitical lay organizations (Catholic Action) so as to withdraw the official Church from party alliances, minimize conflictive relations with new secular governments, and unite Catholics on a religious and moral basis. Anthony Rhodes, *Vatican in the Age of Dictators,* chaps. 1, 2, 3, 6, 7, 8, 11, and 12 passim.

[25] Bruneau, *The Political Transformation of the Brazilian Catholic Church,* pp. 32–34.

[26] Alessandri, *Recuerdos,* 2:56–57.

ambassador to the Holy See. He also maintained close contact with Archbishop Crescente Errázuriz of Santiago, who while not in favor of the separation, also did not rigorously oppose it.[27] Furthermore, he personally supervised the writing of the parts of the new constitution providing for separation of Church and state.

The final version worked out in a constitutional commission in June 1925 recognized the legal personality of the Roman Catholic Church only, but also provided for the free exercise of all religions and guaranteed their respective rights to own property and erect buildings. It abrogated the government's patronage rights over ecclesiastical appointments and its veto privileges over the promulgation of papal decrees in Chile. It allowed the Church to establish dioceses, seminaries, and religious communities without congressional approval.[28] It exempted from taxation ecclesiastical properties used for religious purposes, and permitted the Church to maintain its own educational system. Finally, the government agreed to pay the Church a sum of 2,500,000 pesos (U.S. $303,125) annually for five years so as to facilitate the transition to private financing of clerical personnel and structures. It did not, however, rule out the future possibility of public support for Church-sponsored educational programs.[29]

---

[27] Aside from seeing separation of Church and state as a means of getting clerics out of party entanglements, Errázuriz was also on good personal terms with Alessandri which further disposed him to a successful resolution of the issue. In 1918 when Alessandri was minister of the interior in the previous Liberal government, he was influential in having President Sanfuentes and the Chilean Senate recommend Errázuriz to Rome for the position of archbishop of Santiago after the See became vacant in June of that year. Errázuriz was seventy-nine years old at the time, a competent historian and canon lawyer, with no previous political involvements, and favored by the Liberals and Radicals for the appointment. The Vatican was at first reluctant due to the priest's age and opposition to his candidacy by many Chilean clergy. Rome consented, however, after President Sanfuentes assured them that Errázuriz was the best person to maintain good relations between the Church and the new Liberal government. Pope Benedict XV thus named Errázuriz archbishop of Santiago on 30 December 1918 where he remained until his death in June 1931. Always a friend of Alessandri during his reign, Errázuriz also received from the president an annual pension of 37,000 pesos (US $4,486) after the separation of Church and state in 1925. Araneda Bravo, *Arzobispo Errázuriz,* pp. 152–56, and interview with Archbishop Carlos Oviedo, Antofagasta, 26 August 1975.

[28] On 18 October 1925 (the very day the new constitution was promulgated) the Vatican created six new dioceses in Chile, increasing their number from four to ten. Interview with Archbishop Carlos Oviedo, Antofagasta, 26 August 1975.

[29] The constitution only terminated state payment of salaries to clerics and support for the upkeep of Church buildings. In fact, during the 1950s the Congress legalized public subsidies for Catholic schools, thus reestablishing a Church-state dependency relationship which would create considerable difficulties for Catholic education at all levels after the military coup in 1973. *Constitution of the Republic of Chile, 1925* (Washington, D.C.: Pan American Union, 1967), art. 10; Julio Chaná Cariola, *Situación jurídica de la iglesia,* pp. 67–69, 81–136; Mecham, *Church and State,* pp. 219–21.

Once Rome was informed of the final terms of the separation, Cardinal Gasparri cabled his approval to Alessandri. He also instructed the papal nuncio in Santiago to tell the Chilean bishops that the Vatican approved the outcome and wanted them to support it. Although not all of the hierarchy were happy with this decision (especially Bishop Gilberto Fuenzalida of Concepción where Masonic and anticlerical groups were strongest), the bishops did not oppose it once Rome had made known its will so clearly.[30] This intervention by the Vatican was the most decisive factor which led to their acquiescence and to their subsequent pastoral letter after the September plebiscite approving the outcome as a lesser of two evils.

Hence, religious and secular roles and structures interacted smoothly throughout the entire process of the separation of Church and state. Neither cluster clashed seriously with the other, and respective leaders through careful negotiation and action strategies made their decisions binding in their own institutions. Neither the hierarchical chain of command nor the transnational linkages of the Church were threatened. In fact, each functioned in tandem to produce a successful resolution of the challenge.[31]

Efforts at recuperation of Church privileges and active encouragement of maintaining an alliance with the Conservative Party went on privately, however, for almost a decade after ratification of the new constitution. Bishop Fuenzalida of Concepción continued to speak publicly in favor of a restoration of Church-state union, and repeatedly stressed the need for a Catholic party. Conservative Party leaders were also desirous of maintaining Catholic support. In the early 1930s conditions were ripe to formalize this alliance once again.

In 1933, two years after the death of Archbishop Errázuriz, the Chilean hierarchy weakened in their determination to maintain a neutral

---

[30] After the Gasparri message was communicated to the Chilean hierarchy, Archbishop Errázuriz told President Alessandri that he himself could not be more papal than the pope nor disobey the Vatican after it had accepted Alessandri's terms. Alessandri, *Recuerdos*, 2:61.

[31] In France and Mexico during the extrication process both of these Church variables were either directly threatened or did not function well. The French Constitution of 1905 gave civic associations, not bishops, supervisory power over financial administration of the Church. Moreover, the French bishops in the late nineteenth century ignored repeated suggestions of Pope Leo XIII that they come to terms with the Liberal Republic, which might have produced more favorable terms of separation at the turn of the century. The Mexican Constitution of 1917 made the state, not the episcopacy, the final arbiter over the geographical distribution of clergy. The Mexican government also restricted international ecclesiastical transfers by forbidding future entry of foreign priests into the country. Amidst such mutual antagonisms and direct attacks on the Church's hierarchical structures and its transnational linkages, accommodation between itself and the state was impossible in both countries. Moody, ed., *Church and Society*, pp. 152–61; Robert E. Quirk, *The Mexican Revolution and the Catholic Church, 1910–1929*, pp. 79–112.

position in party politics. At their annual meeting in November of that year, the bishops decided to announce public support for the Conservative Party. The late 1920s and early 1930s in Chile was a period of serious internal upheaval characterized by economic depression, labor unrest, a series of military coups, a short-lived socialist republic in 1932, and the founding of a heavily Marxist-oriented Socialist Party in early 1933. In such an uncertain context the hierarchy feared the possibility of leftists coming to power and a rekindling of anticlerical sentiment. Upon the urging of Bishop Fuenzalida, the hierarchy concluded that all Catholics should rally behind conservative political forces in Chile—a strategy being followed by Catholics to protect their interests in other nominally Catholic countries of the time, including Italy, Germany, Spain, Portugal, Brazil, Argentina, and Peru.[32]

Bishop Hector Felice, the papal nuncio, however, requested that the Chilean episcopacy await word from the Vatican before announcing this decision, and he asked Rome to send him an advisory opinion on the matter. In a letter dated 1 June 1934, Cardinal Pacelli, then Vatican secretary of state (to become Pope Pius XII in 1939) responded to Felice's petition by strongly reaffirming the position taken by Archbishop Errázuriz twelve years before. Pacelli stated that it was the conviction of the Holy See that "the Church could not bind itself to the activities of a political party without compromising its supernatural character and universality of its mission." He also warned that bishops and priests must not engage in partisan politics.

He further observed that no one political party "even if it should claim to draw its inspiration from Catholic teachings and to be the defender of the rights of the Church can pretend to represent all Catholics." Pacelli stated that the laity are free to support any party that respects the rights of the Church and of citizens in general. Finally, he encouraged the formation of strong Catholic Action programs in Chile to train the laity in the social doctrine of the Church, but demanded that these apostolic structures and their leaders refrain from involvement in "the struggles of political parties, even if these be formed by Catholics."[33]

This response by the Vatican in 1934 to developments in the Chilean Church is understandable in light of the policies it was then effectively pursuing elsewhere. The goals of Pius XI for the Church to attempt

---

[32] Gil, *Political System,* pp. 61–65; Rhodes, *Vatican in the Age of Dictators,* chaps. 3, 8, 11, 12; Bruneau, "Church and State," pp. 468–72; Bruneau, *Political Transformation,* pp. 38–46; Pike, "South America's Multi-faceted Catholicism: Glimpses of Twentieth-Century Argentina, Chile and Peru," pp. 55–60; 64, 69.

[33] "La iglesia y los partidos políticos: documento pontificio dirigido a nuestros obispos," *Boletín de la Acción Católica de Chile* (Santiago) 2 (September 1934): 525–29.

peaceful coexistence with various types of governments, to withdraw from party alliances, and to strengthen its internal religious organization were already being realized in several countries in Western Europe by the mid-1930s. New concordats had been signed by the Holy See with Mussolini (1929), Salazar (1930), and Hitler (1933), extracting from them written legal guarantees for the Church's freedom to pursue its strictly religious mission. Close ties between the Church and anti-fascist clerical-dominated parties in Italy and Germany had also been officially broken by this time, and Catholic Action was being strongly promoted.

Although the Chilean democratic context in the early 1930s was different from that of much of Western Europe during this period, some parallels did in fact exist. Economic collapse associated with failures of laissez faire capitalism, burgeoning social unrest among working classes, the growing attraction of Marxism, and the appearance of a Nazi Party in 1932[34] all made Chile somewhat comparable to several European countries of the era. Its liberal democratic system and its economy were in crisis. Had either the Marxists or Nazis come to power, the Vatican feared that a close alliance between the Chilean Church and the Conservative Party would prove both embarrassing and dangerous. Hence, Rome decided to urge the same strategy for the Church in Chile as it had for its counterparts in Western Europe—withdrawal from party alliances, prohibitions for clerical involvement in parties, and emphasis on religious and social formation of laity.

Upon reception of the Pacelli letter in 1934, the Chilean bishops once again acquiesced to the clear and definitive instruction from the Vatican. They did not publish their private decision reached in 1933 to urge Catholic support for the Conservative Party. Subsequently they announced guidelines for Catholics in electoral politics which incorporated each of the points outlined in the 1934 communiqué from the Holy See.[35]

---

[34] Between 1932 and 1938, Chile had one of the strongest Nazi parties in Latin America, with a membership of about 40,000 at the height of its power in the mid-1930s. It made a conscious effort to attract Catholic voters on the basis of its anticapitalist program, and insisted that its ideology and goals were similar to those outlined by Pope Pius XI in his social encyclical, *Quadragesimo Anno*, in 1931. After an ill-conceived attempt to overthrow the civilian government in September 1938, it was smashed and it never regained its earlier momentum. Pike, *Chile and the United States,* pp. 204–208; Michael Potashnik, "Nacismo: National Socialism in Chile, 1932–1938" (Ph.D. dissertation, University of California at Los Angeles, 1974), pp. 196–99.

[35] "Circular dirigida al clero y a nuestros amados diocesanos sobre la relación de la iglesia con la política," *Boletín de la Acción Católica de Chile* 3 (December 1935): 537–41.

Thus, as with the separation issue in 1925, a decade later the two key variables of transnational linkages and hierarchical authority flows preserved and finalized the official disassociation of the Chilean Church from the Conservative Party. Critical Church interests and policies at the international level precipitated decisive Vatican intervention into national Church decisions. Moreover, by explicitly invoking its higher authority in the chain of command Rome stopped Chilean episcopal efforts to recuperate political privileges from the state and reestablish formal ties to the Conservative Party.

PARTIAL NEUTRALIZATION OF LAY CATHOLIC OPPOSITION
TO EXTRICATION OF THE CHURCH FROM ITS TRADITIONAL
ALLIANCES

Three of the four core elements in Catholicism functioned effectively and in tandem with secular dynamics in the extrication of the Church from its traditional alliances—articulation of social norms, exercise of vertical authority, and linkages with the international Church. For the settlements to be lasting, however, the fourth crucial variable had to be engaged—the attitudinal and behavioral responses of lay Catholics. For the separation of the Church from the state, this variable played no significant role for or against. For the disassociation of the Church from the Conservative Party, it offered no problem for the formal aspects but militated against de facto extrication in electoral politics.

Prior to the constitutional plebiscite in Chile in September 1925 lay Catholics as a group were not involved in the decision. It was managed almost exclusively by clerics in close cooperation with secular leaders. Moreover, there were no channels within the Chilean Church whereby potential lay opposition could be voiced. Catholic Action structures for lay participation were not yet in existence in Chile in 1925. Nor were there influential lay publications that could crystallize conservative Catholic opinion against the position of Rome and the bishops.

A convergence of factors in the political arena prevented lay Catholic opposition to the separation issue from being effectively expressed through the Conservative Party. In the plebiscite voters had to either accept or reject the constitution as a whole and could not veto certain parts. Dominant sectors of the military supported the new charter completely since it guaranteed strong executive powers to intervene in economic affairs and thus initiate needed reforms to avoid further social instability. Rumors also circulated just before the plebiscite that there were again growing divisions in the military that prefigured another coup. Voters went to the polls in an atmosphere of uncertainty and fear.[36]

Radical Party leaders urged their followers to abstain from casting ballots. Although members of Alessandri's coalition in 1920, they opposed the strengthening of the office of the executive in the new constitution because their power was congressional and they supported continued parliamentary supremacy dominant in Chile since 1891. The Radicals also felt that the terms of separation of Church and state were too moderate, since the new constitution did not explicitly prohibit the teaching of religion in public schools nor eliminate state-subsidized chaplains in the armed forces. Communists actively campaigned against the charter because they wanted more restrictions on private property and greater government controls over the economy than were provided for in the document.

Public fears of another military intervention, diverging strategies of other parties, the desire by anticlericals for even more drastic conditions of separation, and the impossibility of voting only for sections of the new constitution all led to a decision by many in the Conservative Party to boycott the plebiscite as well. The result was a turnout of less than 50 percent of eligible voters (43.6 percent), with 128,381 in favor, 6,040 opposed, and 173,923 casting no ballots. All of these factors neutralized any potential lay Catholic opposition to the separation from being mobilized through parties and guaranteed its acceptance by the public as part of the Constitution of 1925.[37]

Although Rome and the bishops finally disassociated the Chilean Church officially from the Conservative Party in the mid-1930s, the party itself continued to proclaim itself as the one closest to Catholic principles and teachings. As we shall see in the next chapter, most Chilean practicing Catholics continued to support this party in electoral campaigns throughout the 1940s and 1950s despite formal Church neutrality in partisan politics.

Moreover, important laity within the Church continued to articulate and defend a political philosophy based upon corporatist and even fascist principles. Prominent Catholic intellectuals in the faculties of his-

[36] Frederick M. Nunn, *Chilean Politics, 1920–1931: The Honorable Mission of the Armed Forces*, pp. 94–99.

[37] In late nineteenth-century France, opposition by prominent laity to a rapprochement with the Liberal Republic was mobilized and channeled through the well-organized Catholic political movement, Action Française, and a series of royalist Catholic journals and newspapers. These proved to be a major obstacle to possible Catholic accommodation with liberals on the separation issue. It was also a reason why the French bishops ignored the pleas of Leo XIII that they be flexible in dealing with the state in the late nineteenth century. Moody, ed., *Church and Society*, p. 153.

tory, law, and philosophy of the Catholic University in Santiago in the 1930s hailed the successes of Catholic authoritarian regimes in Italy, Spain, and Portugal as a bulwark against communism and liberalism. A common theme running through their writings included a distrust of the pragmatism of the United States and the materialism of the Soviet Union. As an alternative to liberal capitalism and Marxist socialism they proposed a type of Catholic corporatism, with a system of guilds (*gremios*), vertically orchestrated by the state to promote a harmony of economic and political interests in society. Such a system of Integralism, they argued, was much more in accord with Church teachings and the traditional Hispanic culture to which Chile was an heir than was liberal democracy.

Although these intellectuals were few in number, their influence in the Catholic University continued for several decades. As I shall describe later in the book, they trained an important generation of leaders for the Right, and also provided intellectual and moral legitimacy for reactionary currents that have remained salient in the Chilean political system.[38] Thus, while the lay attitudinal and behavioral variable did not act as a drawback in separating the Church legally from the state nor officially from the Conservative Party in the 1920s and 1930s, it acted as a check against *de facto* extrication of Catholicism from electoral identification with political conservatism and, in some aspects, reactionary, political philosophy. Statements from the highest Church levels in Chile and in Rome could effect formal institutional extrication but could not (nor were they intended to) move lay Catholics *away* from conservative parties or ideologies, provided such support did not directly implicate the official Church.

[38] The intellectual leader of Integralism from the 1930s through the 1950s was the historian, Jaime Eyzaguírre. Although not active in politics himself, he trained many students at the Catholic University who were to become important political figures, including Jaime Guzmán, the chief legal consultant for the military junta after 1973 for drafting a new constitution for Chile. In an interview on 7 November 1975, in his office in Santiago, Eduardo Frei told me that Eyzaguírre's ideas contained definite elements of fascism and that he influenced many people now important in Chilean politics.

Other prominent Catholic lay figures in this movement included: Jaime Larraín Garcia Moreno, a leader of the Agrarian Labor Party which supported the successful presidential candidacy of ex-dictator, Carlos Ibañez, in 1952; Julio Philippi, active in diplomatic work for the present military regime; and Arturo Fontaine, editor of *El Mercurio* in the mid-1970s, the most prestigious newspaper in Chile.

Information on these Integralist and corporatist currents in Chilean Catholicism that emerged in the 1930s can be found in Pike, *Chile and the United States,* pp. 192, 414–15.

The writings of this group appeared in two important journals of Catholic thought published in Chile successively between 1932 and 1967—*Estudios* (1932–1957), and *Finis Terrae* (1957–1967).

CONCLUSIONS

Accommodation was possible between Church and government in the 1920s due to a long-term pattern of emerging congruence between dominant religious and secular values. In several other nominally Catholic countries such congruence never developed and rigid ideological attitudes and inflexible strategies in both Church and society produced bitter and practically unresolvable conflicts in religiopolitical relations for decades. Furthermore, the general normative agreements between Church and state in Chile were given binding force by very clear and specific declarations—the Constitution of 1925, and the joint letter of all the Chilean bishops in September 1925 accepting the separation of Church and state. These legal and religious documents left no room for various interpretations or differing applications of guidelines by lower clergy or laity.

In addition, some religious leaders in Chile in the 1920s and 1930s realized that core religious interests of the Church (such as its formal unity and the authority of bishops over priests) could be preserved *only* by its formal disassociation from the Conservative Party. This led to firm and very specific positions on this issue as well that carried binding weight throughout the Chilean Church—the pastoral letter of Crescente Errázuriz of 1922 forbidding clerical participation in political parties, and the hierarchy's guidelines of 1935 reaffirming that no party represented the views of all Catholics.

None of these normative agreements or specifically binding statements in Church and government, however, could have been made effective had not authority flows worked well in both institutions. Alessandri's shrewd leadership within his coalition, his delicate negotiations with the Church, and the balance of political forces in society all helped make possible the exercise of his decisive authority as president and thereby win sufficient acceptance for the Constitution of 1925. Within the Church, the process of reaching the decisions to separate from the state and the Conservative Party involved only a small number of leaders, and this factor helped make possible a uniform impact of authority flows among a small core of religious elites responsible for the decision.

The international linkage of the Chilean Church with the Vatican was perhaps the most decisive factor both in facilitating a compromise with the state over the conditions of separation and in neutralizing opposition within the Chilean Church to extrication from its traditional alliance with the Conservative Party. Resource transactions between center and periphery units in the Church can involve more than transfers of personnel and finances. They also include important messages and information in both directions. When the Vatican takes a very clear and strong position on an issue it considers essential for the integrity of the

Church, or for maintaining or enhancing its own control over the direction of a particular national church, its influence can be decisive given the ultimate supremacy of its authority in the institution.

Although the attitudes and behavior of rank-and-file Catholics did not uniformly support either aspect of extrication, there were no structural possibilities for lay dissent within the Church, and contextual factors in the political arena neutralized their opposition there as well. Once Church leadership took a unified position, variegated responses to it by the faithful were not a major obstacle in making the process a legal reality.

Thus, the interaction of norms, structures, and behavior in the Chilean Church in the 1920s and 1930s functioned effectively in relation to one another so as to produce a fairly smooth official extrication of the Church from traditional structural alliances. Each of the major characteristics of the Church constituting its essential dynamics as a complex religious institution—graduated binding force and specificity of norms, hierarchical authority flows across a layered administrative framework, diversified membership allegiances, and transactions among center and periphery units—were significant in producing a positive outcome. Given their harmonious interactions with secular forces as well, no major Church-state conflict occurred. Under such conditions, religiopolitical problems can be resolved not only amicably but in terms relatively beneficial to both Church and society.

The differentiation of religious and political structures in Chile in the 1920s and 1930s, however, was not total. The door was left open for reestablishing future dependency relationships between Church and state in terms of financial support, and significant sectors of the laity continued to justify support for conservative politics on the basis of traditional Catholic social teaching. These lingering ties and unfinished business would later come to have significant impact on the Church and the political system in Chile.

The degree of distancing achieved at the time was, nevertheless, significant, and it established a base line from which new religiopolitical developments could evolve. The emergence of effective progressive forces in the Church that could act as an important reinforcement of major structural changes in society, however, would require additional factors. These will be the focus of the next two chapters.

4 The Incubation of Social Catholicism: Chile, 1935–1958

Official extrication of the Church from traditional alliances is only a starting point. New challenges emerge, however, in shifting ecclesiastical resources to a position of support for movements espousing wider social participation and more equitable distribution of income. The next three chapters will focus on these challenges, using the Chilean experience to analyze the interactions between Church and society that can resolve them. The following questions of theoretical and practical import will be addressed:

(1) How do new combinations of religious values favoring political and economic reforms actually emerge? Under what conditions can they have a significant impact for change at the symbolic level of society?

(2) How does a rearrangement of roles and structures within the Church occur in a way compatible with reform-oriented secular programs? Can secular institutions act as carriers for religious values in society without identifying the Church with a partisan political movement and vice versa?

(3) Given uneven membership allegiances, how can the Church marshal effective support among different classes of its laity for societal changes, and can such commitments be sustained over time?

(4) Do international linkages help or hinder a local church if it attempts to promote greater equity and justice in its own society?

In answering these major theoretical questions I will concentrate on the interactions between the Church and the political system in Chile at three different time periods: 1935–1958, 1958–1964, and 1964–1970. Each of these separate time spans provides a perspective on how secular and religious reform dynamics can evolve and thus produce very distinctive outcomes. By analyzing these developments over time, the important elements accounting for change can be seen more clearly, and we can provide more nuanced and complete answers to issues related to the above questions than much of the previous literature has.[1]

[1] Many scholars to date have concluded that the Church provided powerful support for the Christian Democratic Party (PDC) during its original emergence as a political force in Chile in the 1940s and 1950s, that the Catholic vote solidly supported the PDC in 1964 and 1970, and that religion was a very critical factor in pre-

This chapter will examine the first period, 1935-1958. It was during this era that many new developments began to occur inside the Chilean Church, setting it apart from most other Latin American churches and also preparing the context for the more intense religious changes that characterized the later two time frames, 1958-1964 and 1964-1970.[2] It was also in this period that the Church had to coexist with a Popular Front government in which the Left participated, and that new forms of social Catholicism gave rise to Christian Democracy in Chile.

In Chapter 5, I shall focus on 1958-1964, when the first Christian Democratic administration in Latin America was elected to executive power. During 1964-1970, examined in Chapter 6, significant changes in politics as well as in the Church itself led to the first victory of a Marxist presidential candidate in a free election in Western society.

These three chapters, therefore, cover very critical and quite different religiopolitical developments: (1) the incubation of reform elements within a traditional religious institution; (2) the culmination of the advance of progressive religious forces that coincide with the electoral victory of a major reform political movement; and (3) the decline of a centrist party and the challenge which the emergence of radical political forces presents to a progressive Church.

Where each of these successive phases offers important similarities or contrasts with other Latin American or Western European countries, I shall highlight them in order to broaden our comparative knowledge of the role of religion in modern Western politics. At the end of Chapter 6, on the basis of a comparative longitudinal analysis, I shall address the major theoretical questions raised at the beginning of this chapter regarding the mutileveled challenges involved in religious reinforcement of secular reform.

RELIGIOUS DEVELOPMENTS IN CHILE, 1935-1958

There was a gradual but steady evolution of progressive elements at different levels of the Chilean Church from the mid-1930s to the late 1950s. The Chilean bishops wrote several major pastoral letters urging

---

venting a wider base of support for Allende in both these elections. Those espousing some or all of these conclusions are Petras, Mutchler, Langton and Rapoport, Comblin, Torres, Vanderschueren and Rojas, and Tiago de Chile.

[2] Vallier has indicated that after the separation of Church and state in 1925, the Chilean Church went through a phase of "insulation" from politics for several decades during which it concentrated primarily on deepening and strengthening its pastoral structures and processes of religious influence among the laity. This phase, according to Vallier, prepared the Church to "re-enter" the political arena in the 1960s with new and effective strategies to promote social reform. Ivan Vallier, "Extraction, Insulation, and Re-Entry."

Catholics to take seriously papal social teachings, such as Leo XIII's *Rerum Novarum* (1891) and Pius XI's *Quadragesimo Anno* (1931). They also established Catholic Action programs in the mid-1930s to give the laity a more profound spiritual and social training according to these new Church principles.

In the late 1930s and throughout the 1940s, when various coalition governments included sectors of the Left, the Church's leadership maintained an official posture of neutrality in electoral politics. In fact, in 1938 after the election by a slim plurality of the popular vote of Pedro Aguirre Cerda, the presidential candidate of a Popular Front supported by Radical, Socialist, and Communist parties, it was a public letter by Bishop José Maria Caro of La Serena (named archbishop of Santiago in 1939) that helped solidify the legitimacy of the new government and allay popular fears of communism.[3]

During this period a core of progressive clerical leaders emerged to leadership positions in the Chilean Church, many of whom had been exposed to advanced currents of social Catholicism in European universities. Upon their return from studies abroad, these priests served as chaplains to Catholic Action groups, and taught in Catholic high schools and at the Catholic University. They also formed study circles of professionals to explore the implications of papal encyclicals, established labor organizations of Catholic inspiration, and set up various social welfare and education programs among workers and peasants.[4]

Out of these various institutions arose a generation of young Catholic intellectuals who formed the Falange Nacional party in 1938 to transmit the social teachings of the Church into a secular political program.

[3] Reminding Catholics of their obligation of obedience to duly constituted governments, Caro stated that "the Church would always be respectful of legitimate governments" in Chile and would be willing to cooperate with them in promoting the common good. "Obediencia a los poderes legitimamente constituidos," *Estudios* (Santiago), no. 71 (October 1938), p. 39. These words of the bishop later to become the first cardinal of Chile both reaffirmed the religiopolitical trend established in the previous decade and set a precedent for the bishops' acceptance of Allende's electoral victory thirty-two years later.

[4] Henry A. Landsberger, "Time, Persons, Doctrine," pp. 81–89; Oscar Larson, *La ANEC y la democracia cristiana,* pp. 13–28; Ricardo Boizard B., *La democracia cristiana en Chile* (Santiago: Editorial Orbe, 1963), pp. 149–53, 198–205; Mario Zañartu, S.J., *Desarrollo económico y moral católica,* pp. 7/15–7/16.

The Catholic University of Santiago, founded in 1888, expanded its programs and enrollments considerably while Crescente Errázuriz (a scholar) was archbishop of the capital city during the 1920s. Throughout this decade, the university modernized its course of studies and established several new faculties in the humanities, social sciences, physical sciences, commerce, and law. The student population quadrupled from 500 in 1919 to over 2,000 in 1929. Along with the Catholic University of Lima (founded in 1917), the Catholic University in Santiago since the 1920s has rivalled some of the best national universities in Latin America in quality. Fidel Araneda Bravo, *Arzobispo Errázuriz,* pp. 232–38, and Edward J. Williams, *Latin American Christian Democratic Parties* (Knoxville: University of Tennessee Press, 1967), p. 175.

Members participated in the cabinets of two different administrations in the 1940s, and by early 1957 they had one senator and fourteen deputies in the Congress. In July 1957 the Falange merged with several other small social Christian movements to form the Chilean Christian Democratic Party (PDC), and its first presidential candidate in 1958, Senator Eduardo Frei, ran on a platform of agrarian reform, profit-sharing by workers, and industrial concentration on basic consumer goods rather than luxury goods.[5]

Despite these significant developments within the Church, opinion survey data collected by the Centro de Opinión Pública in Santiago a month before the 1958 September presidential election[6] indicate that religious practice was still strongly correlated with rightist political tendencies and with support for the candidate of the Conservative and Liberal Parties. Table 4.1 shows that those who identified themselves as Catholics were considerably more to the Right than those who were of other faiths or who had no religious identification at all. Furthermore, among Catholics, those who practiced regularly (saying that they attended Mass once a month or more) were far more prone to describe themselves as being on the Right than those who went to Mass occasionally (a few times a year) or who did not practice. Conversely, support for the Left increased steadily as religious practice decreased, and those of other religions or of no religious persuasion were decidedly more to the Left than all types of Catholics.[7]

In examining candidate and party preferences among Catholics in the

---

[5] For a history of the Falange, its programs, and the origins of the PDC, see: Alberto Edwards Vives and Eduardo Frei Montalva, *Historia de los partidos chilenos*, pp. 242–45; Jaime Castillo Velasco, *Los fuentes de la democracia cristiana*.

[6] Centro de Opinión Pública is an opinion research firm in Santiago conducted by Eduardo Hamuy, a Chilean sociologist. It administered random sample surveys based on dwelling units throughout Santiago from 1957 to 1973, and its results on political preference questions just prior to elections were closely correlated with actual voting over the years. Neither this firm nor any other has conducted national surveys of political choice over time in Chile. Since one-third of the Chilean population lives in the capital, however, and since Hamuy's sample of the greater metropolitan area of Santiago included some agricultural sectors, his surveys represent the most comprehensive cross-section of attitudes available. Renato Poblete, S.J., a close collaborator of Hamuy on several of the surveys, graciously made copies available to me in 1975, and I conducted secondary analysis of them with the help of computer technicians at Yale University.

[7] In controlling for class, there are some expected differences. Among those in the lower class, 26.9 percent identified themselves as being on the Right as compared to 36.8 percent of the middle class and 42.7 percent of the upper class. Religious practice, however, among all social classes was definitely correlated with support for the Right. Close to one-third (31.8 percent) of those in the lower class who practiced their faith regularly identified themselves as being on the Right, whereas 24.1 percent of the poor who rarely or never went to Church did so. Among the middle class, 46.7 percent of regular practicing Catholics considered themselves as rightists, whereas only 31.6 percent of those who rarely or never attended Mass chose the Right. In the high-income bracket, 48.5 percent of those who practiced regularly were rightist as compared to 34.4 percent of the least devout.

Table 4.1
Political Tendency and Religion
Greater Santiago, August 1958
(N = 782)

	Catholics			Protestant, Jewish, Other (N = 56)	No Religion (N = 79)
	Regularly Practicing (N = 272)	Occasionally Practicing (N = 228)	Nonpracticing (N = 147)		
Left	19.5% (53)	22.8% (52)	29.3% (43)	44.6% (25)	59.5% (47)
Center	21.3 (58)	20.2 (46)	23.8 (35)	16.2 (9)	16.5 (13)
Right	44.1 (120)	36.0 (82)	29.9 (44)	19.6 (11)	15.2 (12)
Undecided	15.1 (41)	21.0 (48)	17.0 (25)	19.6 (11)	8.8 (7)

SOURCE: Centro de Opinión Pública, Santiago, Chile.

Table 4.2
Political Choice and Religious Practice (Catholics)
Greater Santiago, August 1958
(N = 647)

	Regularly Practicing (N = 272)		Occasionally Practicing (N = 228)		Nonpracticing (N = 147)	
	Candidate	Party	Candidate	Party	Candidate	Party
Allende (Communist-Socialist)	12.9%	7.7%	14.6%	11.8%	22.4%	15.6%
Zamorano (Independent Left)	1.1	—	.9	—	.7	—
Bossay (Radical)	5.9	12.1	6.1	9.2	10.9	15.6
Frei (Christian Democratic)	23.5	23.2	17.1	15.9	16.3	10.9
Alessandri (Conservative, Liberal)	37.1	30.5	32.9	29.4	31.3	21.8
Undecided	19.5	26.5	18.4	33.7	18.4	36.1

SOURCE: Centro de Opinión Pública, Santiago, Chile.

survey, the same general pattern holds. In a close five-man race for the presidency, Jorge Alessandri, candidate of the Conservative and Liberal parties, gained a plurality among all types of Catholics including those who rarely or never attended Mass. Vote for Allende was significantly diminished by degree of religious practice, with almost twice as many nonpracticing Catholics supporting him as those who attended Mass regularly. Furthermore, a plurality of Catholics in every category identified with the two parties of the Right (Conservative and Liberal), including nearly one-third of those who attended Mass regularly (30.5 percent).[8]

Despite significant progressive changes in Chilean Catholicism, an officially neutral position by the Church in partisan politics since the 1930s, and the emergence of a Christian-inspired reform party, religion was still a decidedly conservative factor in electoral politics in the late 1950s. The hierarchy did not endorse any candidate in the 1958 campaign, and Cardinal Caro of Santiago several months before the election publicly reiterated the position that the Church had no party preference. Nevertheless, identification with the Church was a decisive factor in conservative political choice in Santiago in 1958. In a close election in which the conservative candidate won by 33,500 votes out of 1.2 million ballots cast, this was crucial.

Such low support for the Christian Democratic Party by Catholics in Chile in the late 1950s was in direct contrast to the pattern that characterized most Western European countries after World War II. One-half or more of practicing Catholics in several of these countries in the postwar period supported newly formed or reorganized parties of Christian inspiration with moderate reform programs.[9] Table 4.3, for example,

---

[8] The rather high percentage of undecided respondents as to party preference in 1958 can be explained in part by the fact that during the 1950s the personalities of some candidates were stressed more than party affiliation. Ex-dictator Carlos Ibañez won the presidency in 1952 on a populist platform without the backing of any of the traditional parties, and during his six-year term of office he appealed to voters to forget past party labels and to support the local candidates he backed on the basis of personal loyalty to himself as president. In 1958 Jorge Alessandri (son of former president, Arturo Alessandri), although supported by both the Conservative and Liberal parties, continued this personalistic trend during his successful campaign, and promised if elected to form a government based on technical expertise and administrative competence rather than political or ideological orientation. Furthermore, the Chilean Communist Party (PCCh) was outlawed between 1948 and 1958, and those sympathetic to its program were reluctant to identify publicly with it as a movement. For all of these reasons, it is not surprising why in Hamuy's September 1958 survey candidate preference (on the Right and on the Left) was well ahead of party identification. George W. Grayson, *The Chilean Christian Democratic Party: Genesis and Development*, pp. 160–309.

[9] Countries such as Germany, Belgium, Holland, Austria, and Switzerland had Christian parties defending Church interests dating back to the late nineteenth century, and in Italy and Czechoslovakia they appeared just after World War I. Initial attempts to establish a progressive Christian party in France were made in the interwar years that crystallized in the MRP after World War II. All of these movements

Table 4.3

Comparative Political Preferences of Regularly Practicing Catholics in Chile, Germany, Italy and France in the Post-World War II Period

	Chile (1958) (N = 272) Candidate	Germany (1953) (N = 1,106) Party	Italy (1964) (N = 132) Party	France (1952) (N = 572) Party
Left				
Marxist	12.9% (PCCh,PS)	.1% (KPD)	24.0% {(PCI)	1.0% (PCF)
Nonmarxist	1.1 (Ind.)	21.1 (SPD)	{(PSI)	5.0 (SFIO)
Center				
Radical	5.9 (PR)			2.0 (RGR)
Christian Democratic	23.5 (PDC)	50.1 (CDU/Z)	67.0 (DC)	54.0 (MRP)
Right	37.1 (PL,PC)	11.9 (BP,FDP,BHE,DP)	8.0 (PLI,PNM,MSI)	38.0 (PRL,RPF)
Undecided	19.5	16.8	—	—

SOURCES: Data on Germany is from a subsample of Catholics in a survey conducted in West Germany by UNESCO in 1953 and reported in Juan J. Linz, "The Social Bases of West German Politics," p. 189. Data on Italy is from a DOXA survey of 1964 reported in Laurence E. Hazelrigg, "Religious and Class Basis," p. 502. Data on France is from an IFOP survey of 1952 reported in Fogarty, *Christian Democracy*, p. 361. Data on Chile is from a September 1958 survey of Santiago taken by the Centro de Opinión Pública. Due to the large percentage of undecideds on party preference in the Chilean survey, candidate choices are given.

contrasts the political choices of regularly practicing Catholics in Chile in 1958 with their counterparts in Germany, Italy, and France at about the same time.

How can we account for this contrasting pattern given some very important changes within the Chilean Church after 1930 similar to those characterizing its Western European counterparts? I would argue that the general style of social teachings by the bishops, the lack of effective structural carriers to make new Catholic values operative either in Church or society, some serious challenges to episcopal authority by progressives, weak religious socialization processes for large numbers of laity, and the contradictory messages coming from the Vatican all prevented Chilean Catholicism from changing its legitimating role in society before 1958. In addition, despite some movement to the Left after the late 1930s, the political system in Chile was still dominated by powerful conservative forces who continued to use religion and fear of Marxism to block the potential drawing power of reform-oriented movements among Catholics.

DIFFUSE ARTICULATION OF THE CHURCH'S NEW SOCIAL NORMS AND DOMINANCE OF CONSERVATIVE POWER IN POLITICS

Throughout the 1930s and 1940s, the Chilean bishops published four pastoral letters on social problems urging Catholics to take seriously the social doctrine of the Church. Although some specific problems were mentioned (e.g., low wages for workers) rarely did the bishops treat them as symptoms of basic flaws in the economic system requiring structural changes. They emphasized instead the moral evils they believed present in both liberal capitalism and Marxism. They stressed the need for conversion in the individual human heart, rather than major changes in the structure of the economy as a means to eliminate poverty.[10]

---

were the forerunners of, or in direct line with, reform-oriented Christian parties that drew heavily on Catholic Action members for their cadres after the 1920s and became governing or coruling groups in their respective governments in the immediate post-World War II period. All of them also enjoyed very substantial electoral support among all practicing Catholics, although they did not receive official endorsement by the hierarchy. Michael P. Fogarty, *Christian Democracy*, pp. 294–339.

[10] Episcopado Chileno, *La verdadera Y única solución de la cuestión social; El justo salario;* "Deber social de los católicos," pp. 42–46; *Instrucción pastoral acerca a los problemos sociales*. An analysis of these documents can be found in Zañartu, *Desarrollo económico*, chap. 7. Zañartu concludes that all of these episcopal statements remained at a very general moral level of analysis, and mostly reiterated papal teachings without using any intermediary structural concepts of analysis to give them specific applicability to Chile.

Furthermore, although there was some shift in the Chilean political system in the 1930s and 1940s when a coalition of leftist and radical parties controlled the executive branch of government and in the 1950s when President Ibañez articulated populist ideals, the power of the Right continued to be predominant. The Conservative and Liberal parties maintained over 40 percent of the vote and a plurality in Congress and prevented major structural reforms benefiting peasants or workers. No agrarian reform nor increase in property taxes ever was seriously considered, government intervention in the economy favored an expanding bourgeoisie class during the early phase of import-substitution industrialization, and laws restricting union activity remained in force. The general exhortations of the hierarchy for social reform found no resonance in a corresponding normative shift in the political arena that had possibilities of being successful.[11]

The hierarchy did maintain peaceful relations with several governments between 1938 and 1952 that included the participation in varying degrees of Marxist parties. Such official neutrality did not mean that there was complete indifference by the Chilean bishops as to how Catholics should behave politically. On the contrary, an important preoccupation of many of them throughout this period was the growing attraction of Marxism, especially among the working classes. The hierarchy issued strong normative warnings from time to time urging Catholics not to cooperate with Marxist movements.[12]

Moreover, the Conservative and Liberal parties were the only ones who remained adamant opponents of the Left throughout this period. Their image as the protectors of Catholic interests was maintained in public opinion long after the Church had officially disassociated itself from the Right in the 1930s. In fact, a Conservative Party declaration as late as 1961 stated:

> The party holds as its highest ideal a Christian social order, and in economic affairs espouses measures that promote the common good according to principles of justice and charity. It bases its fundamental

---

[11] Federico Gil, *Political System of Chile*, pp. 76–77.

[12] The letters on the social question written by the bishops during this period all contained very strong condemnations of Marxism. Some were written specifically on this problem and forbade all forms of Catholic cooperation with Marxist parties. See, for example, Bishop Alfredo Silva Santiago, *Estudio sobre la manera práctica de combatir el comunismo en Chile* (Santiago: Imprenta Chile, 1937); Episcopado Chileno, "Firmes en la fe: la masonería, el protestantismo y el comunismo, enemigos de los católicos," pp. 1–3. In congressional elections between 1937 and 1953 the Communist and Socialist parties varied in support from 19 to 30 percent of the electorate. Julio Serrano L., ¿Cómo han votado los chilenos, 1937–1961?," *Política y Espíritu* 17 (February–March 1963): 35

doctrine on the teaching of the Church. It understands and supports rights, duties and liberties in a Catholic perspective.[13]

The general and individualistic style of social pronouncements by the hierarchy, the lack of effective political movements for reform in society, and the specific normative condemnations of Marxism by the bishops all contributed to a continued tacit association of Catholic norms with the political Right throughout this period, despite the absence of a formal alliance between the Church and the Conservative Party.

LACK OF EFFECTIVE STRUCTURAL CARRIERS FOR CATHOLIC SOCIAL TEACHINGS AND CHALLENGE TO EPISCOPAL AUTHORITY BY PROGRESSIVES

A second major problem that prevented the specification of new Catholic social norms into change-oriented programs was the lack of well-developed structures to link them with new policies. Neither Catholic Action circles, other social welfare programs sponsored by the Church, nor the reformist Falange Nacional attracted large numbers of adherents during this period. Furthermore, serious crises of authority arose between the hierarchy and the Catholic lay leaders of the Falange which discredited this progressive party in the eyes of many Catholics in the late 1940s precisely at the time when its European counterparts were growing in popularity.

Although almost every diocese in the country had established Catholic Action programs by the late 1930s to train more committed laity (fashioned along the parochial model developed in Italy), these circles of reflection and social action were relatively small in membership and also were primarily focused on middle and upper-class Catholics. The total number of participants in the various branches of Catholic Action in 1936 was 45,761—or approximately 1 percent of the Catholics in the country. Nine years later in 1945 the numbers had grown to 58,071 adults and youths, but this still represented only 1.3 percent of the 4.8 million Catholic population.[14]

In the 1950s efforts were made to establish specialized branches of

---

[13] "Declaración fundamental: programas y estatutos del Partido Conservador," *Acción Conservadora*, Boletín no. 16 (Santiago: Talleres Claret, 1961). This is also cited in German Urzua Valenzuela, *Los partidos políticos de Chile* (Santiago: Editorial Jurídica de Chile, 1968), p. 105.

[14] "Acción Católica de Chile: Marzo de 1936," *Boletín de la Acción Católica de Chile* 4 (July 1936): 224; and Oficina Nacional de Estadística de la Acción Católica Chilena, *Estado de la iglesia en Chile*, p. 411. The total number of subscribers to the *Boletín de la Acción Católica de Chile* in 1942 was 821 persons—less than .024 percent of the national Catholic population.

Catholic Action according to occupation (similar to strategies being followed in Belgium and France), so as to penetrate the culture of the working classes who constituted the vast majority of the population. These, however, were also very small. By 1957, for example, the Juventud Obrera Católica (JOC), under the guidance of French-trained Bishop Manuel Larraín of Talca, was operating in only four of the twenty dioceses, and included 380 leaders and 2,800 militants.[15]

The Asociación Sindical Chilena (ASICH), founded by Alberto Hurtado, S.J., in 1947 to train union leaders with a Christian orientation, reached only a small group of working-class leaders and never affected the vast numbers of those who were unorganized or who participated in the Marxist-dominated labor movement.[16] Despite the attempts of committed chaplains of Catholic Action and the pioneer work of individual clerics such as Larraín, Hurtado, and others, these new structures of the Church were elitist and never directly affected the vast majority of Catholics, especially low-income sectors who constituted over 60 percent of the 5 million Chilean population.[17]

In addition to this narrow base of progressive lay Catholics, throughout 1947 there occurred several strong public differences between leaders of the Falange and some members of the episcopacy. Bishop Augusto Salinas, national episcopal chaplain of Catholic Action, publicly reprimanded the Falange for favoring diplomatic relations with the Soviet

[15] "El Catolicismo en Chile," *Política y Espíritu* 13 (1 May 1958): 19.

[16] Interview with Guillermo Balmaceda, S.J., Concepción, 27 June 1975. Balmaceda knew Hurtado well and worked with him. Despite Hurtado's hard efforts, according to Balmaceda, he was able to train only about 300 labor leaders in ASICH from the time of its founding in 1947 up until his own untimely death in 1952. Hurtado also pioneered many other apostolic and social action projects among the Chilean lower classes between 1936 and 1952. The best presentation and analysis of his life and work has been done by Alejandro Magnet, *El Padre Hurtado.*

[17] Eduardo Frei, who had been active in the late 1920s in the Catholic University student movement and closely associated with members of Catholic Action in the 1930s, told me that in his judgment the structures of Catholic Action never made significant inroads into working-class culture. (Interview with Eduardo Frei, Santiago, 7 November 1975.) Bishop Augusto Salinas, who was the national episcopal chaplain of Catholic Action during the 1940s, confirmed this opinion and said that Catholic programs for workers never made much headway in the unions due to strong Marxist influence in the organizations. (Interview with Bishop Augusto Salinas, Linares, 20 June 1975.)

This lack of a significant Christian trade union movement made Chile very different from most Western European countries where such organizations date back to the late nineteenth century in France, Italy, Germany, Belgium, Holland, and Switzerland. By the early 1950s in Belgium and Holland, Christian trade unions enjoyed a majority of organized workers, and in France and Italy they were significant competitors to Communist-controlled industrial syndicates. In the German-speaking nations (West Germany, Austria, Switzerland), although in a minority, they had very considerable strength, second only to Social Democratic and Liberal unions in working-class membership. In all of these countries, Christian labor organizations among industrial workers provided a very important base of electoral support for

Union while criticizing the authoritarian practices of the Catholic regime of Franco in Spain. He also admonished the party for proposing Catholic participation in labor unions controlled by Marxists, and for claiming that rightist parties were using anticommunism as an excuse for not supporting needed economic reforms. Salinas argued that these political positions undermined Church teaching that Catholics could not cooperate in any way with communism, and that those Catholics who were not doing all in their power to stop Marxism were "enemies of Christ." He also reprimanded the Falange for allegedly attempting to attract young members out of Catholic Action circles into the party, thus tampering with the internal pastoral structures of the Church. The Falange defended itself against these charges and publicly criticized Salinas for his unjust attack against their party.

Once the issue had become public and involved a strong rejection by Catholic laity of the judgment of a bishop on what he considered to be a matter essential to Catholic principle, the hierarchy closed ranks and distanced themselves from the new party. The five bishops of the Episcopal Commission for Catholic Action condemned what they believed to be a public offense by the Falange against "the authority of a member of the hierarchy." Cardinal Caro of Santiago reiterated this censure of the Falange for its lack of respect for the episcopacy, and also criticized the party for its policies regarding the Soviet Union and Spain and for its lack of strong opposition to communism in Chile.[18]

The hierarchy stopped short of forbidding Catholic participation in the Falange, and two bishops (Bishop Manuel Larraín of Talca and

---

Christian Democratic parties in the post-World War II period. Fogarty, *Christian Democracy*, chap. 16.

In Chile, however, the Communists—and later they, along with the Socialists—dominated those industrial unions that emerged in the pre-World War I era (especially in mining areas). The labor movement as a whole in Chile during the 1920s also suffered a series of legal restrictions on its scope of activities. The Labor Code of 1924 (enacted when the Conservatives and Liberals were in control of the Congress) forbade unions in factories employing less than twenty-five workers. Since a majority of those engaged in manufacturing worked in establishments with nine employees or less, the percentage of industrial work force enrolled in unions was small (about 20 percent) up to the time of Allende's presidency. Alan Angell, *Politics and the Labour Movement in Chile*, pp. 12–31, 42–56.

Hence, when Catholic Action organizations and the Falange Nacional emerged in Chile in the 1930s, not only were unions already dominated by the Left but the legal situation made it difficult to initiate new unions competitive to those led by Marxists. Rather than making such an attempt, the Falange encouraged Christian workers to join existing labor organizations dominated by Communists and Socialists and to influence them from within.

[18] All the documents relating to this heated exchange between the hierarchy and the Falange from August to December 1947 are reprinted in *Política y Espíritu* 3 (November–December 1947): 124–71. See also Grayson, *Chilean Christian Democratic Party*, pp. 242–50.

Bishop Roberto Bernadino Berrios of San Felipe), along with Cardinal Caro himself, made it explicit that the bishops were not ordering the dissolution of the party. The public image of the Falange, however, was badly damaged among practicing Catholics.

Once the Falange seemed to be attacking the official leadership of the Church, the bishops reacted predictably to protect a principle that is central to the integrity of the institution—the hierarchical nature of ec-clesiastical authority. The effect, however, on the legitimating role of the Church in the political system was that Catholic values continued to be tacitly identified with the parties of the Right as the only staunch opponents of Marxism in politics.[19]

WEAK ALLEGIANCES TO THE INSTITUTIONAL
CHURCH AND CLASS BIAS OF TRADITIONAL
RELIGIOUS SOCIALIZATION

Throughout the 1930s, 1940s, and 1950s in Chile, allegiances to the Church were very weak among the vast majority of its members, and those who did practice with any regularity were not sufficiently challenged to change their social perspectives or political behavior. Two major studies (in 1940 and 1956) were conducted by priest-sociologists during this period on Catholic attitudes and practices. Both of these surveys of the quality of Chilean religious commitment concluded that the Church was extremely understaffed, was still not present institutionally in many parts of the country, and that the religious beliefs and practices of vast numbers of Catholics were very weak. They also emphasized that the religious and educational apostolates of the Church continued to be oriented toward serving the upper classes, leaving the pastoral and social needs of the more modest sectors of the Catholic population unfulfilled.[20]

[19] The economic and political context of Western Europe after World War II was quite different from Chile and helped to galvanize support for Christian-inspired parties in several countries. The postwar economies of Germany, France, Italy, Belgium, and Holland were in shambles, and the reform and growth-oriented programs of these parties were very compatible with the Marshall Plan strategies for rebuilding economic structures. Moreover, the rightist parties were not a viable political alternative to Marxism since they had been discredited by too close an association with fascism. The Christian Democratic parties all were on good terms with their respective hierarchies and favored by them as the best means for keeping the Left from coming to power. None of these contextual factors characterized Chile after World War II. The economy had been stimulated by the war (9 percent annual industrial growth rate in the 1940s), rightist parties were still viable, and the Falange had shown itself tolerant of the Left and as a result was nearly condemned outright by the hierarchy as a viable political option for Catholics.

[20] Alberto Hurtado, S.J., ¿Es Chile un país católico?; and Humberto Muñoz Ramirez, Sociología religiosa de Chile.

The study by Alberto Hurtado in 1940 was based upon personal observations in travelling all over Chile to organize Catholic Action circles and on a survey by mail of pastors throughout the country. He concluded that in many senses Chile was not a Catholic country: three-fifths of the population were on the margins of the pastoral care of the Church, 50 percent of the marriages in the country were not contracted in the Church, and only 9 percent of the women and 3.5 percent of the men attended weekly Sunday Mass.[21] He also observed that Catholics did not know or practice the social teachings of the Church, and that as a result the Church was badly neglecting the chronic economic and social problems in the country which kept the workers and peasants in a continuous state of misery.

A province-by-province study done sixteen years later by Humberto Muñoz on the strength of Catholicism among the Chilean people reached similar negative conclusions: a parish in which even 20 percent of its members received Communion once a year was rare; various Protestant denominations had increased their membership by 105 percent between 1940 and 1952, and vast territorial areas of the country (e.g., the mining region of the far North and areas of the far South in Aysén and Magallanes) still were mission territories.[22]

Muñoz also observed that in urban areas of the country the concentration of the Church's efforts in terms of religious personnel and educational programs was focused on the upper classes and a small minority of the middle class. It was not at all uncommon in Santiago, for example, to see a working-class parish of forty to fifty thousand people served by only one priest. Furthermore, priests were not preaching the social doctrine of the Church at Mass or in Catholic schools (attended mainly by the rich), and the working classes still had the definite impression that the Church was not concerned with them.[23]

In the rural areas, especially in the Central Valley where Catholicism had its deepest roots from colonial times, the owners of large estates (latifundios) exercised great influence over the Church. They built chapels, arranged for religious missions, and housed the priests in their mansions when they came to celebrate Mass and hear confessions. The faith of the small farmers and peasants was preserved, but ignorance, superstition, and religious passivity perdured. The Church in the minds of the rural poor was closely identified with the latifundia system and the Conservative Party which protected it. The Conservative Party in the rural areas, and also in urban working-class neighborhoods populated by recent mi-

[21] Hurtado, ¿Es Chile un país católico?, pp. 80–87.
[22] Muñoz, Sociología religiosa, pp. 14, 17–19, 44–45.
[23] Ibid., pp. 30–31.

grants from the countryside, continued to attract the vote of those in any way associated with the Church.[24]

The very weak religious allegiances of the populace and the class bias and conservative style of religious ritual for many of those who did identify with the Church were additional determinative factors that led to a strong correlation between religious practice and rightist political choice. It is not surprising, therefore, that no significant mutation of rank-and-file Catholic attitudes and behavior in the direction of social or political reform had occurred before 1958.

AMBIGUOUS IMPACT OF INTERNATIONAL CHURCH LINKAGES

During the period from 1935 to 1958 Vatican pronouncements emphasized the necessity for social change, but they also strongly warned against the danger of communism. Moreover, there was not yet a significant influx of new personnel and money into the Chilean Church from abroad. The impact of these international factors tended, therefore, to be minimal. If anything, they provided greater legitimacy for Catholic conservatives.

The Vatican gave some normative support to changes within the Chilean Church during this period. Pope Pius XI's encyclical, *Ubi Arcano Dei* (1922), encouraged the establishment of Catholic Action circles throughout the world, and the Chilean bishops' founding of Acción Católica Chilena in 1931 was a direct response to this call. Throughout those years the Vatican continued to support Catholic Action, and in 1945 sent warm words of praise to the Chilean Church for its successes with this program.[25]

The social encyclical, *Quadragesimo Anno,* written by Pius XI in 1931, was widely read and studied by members of Catholic Action and provided the moral basis of the platform of the Falange Nacional after its founding in 1938. In addition, a letter by Bishop Dominico Tardini, Secretary of the Congregation of Extraordinary Affairs of the Vatican, sent to the Chilean bishops in 1950 had a calming effect on the Church after the tension between the bishops and the Falange Nacional in 1947. It reiterated the position of the Pacelli letter of 1934 that the Church had no political party and that Catholics were free to support any political can-

---

[24] Federico Gil learned in interviews in Chile during the early 1960s with Conservative Party leaders that they still were using religion as an issue in electoral campaigns in rural areas. They expressed to Gil that they believed 50 to 60 percent of their sympathizers supported the party out of religious convictions. Gil, *Political System of Chile,* pp. 246–48.

[25] José Cardenal Pizzardo, "Mensaje de aliento y orientación de su Eminencia el Cardenal Pizzardo a la Acción Católica Chilena," *Boletín de la Acción Católica de Chile* 13 (April-May-June 1945): 77–78.

didates who respected "religion and the doctrine and rights of the Church." The letter also called for unity among all Catholics and a strong commitment to implementing the social teachings of the popes.[26]

In this same period, however, strong and very specific warnings were issued by the Vatican against the dangers of communism, forbidding any Catholic cooperation with Marxist movements or parties. In 1937 Pius XI categorically condemned communism as being "intrinsically wrong," and stated that "no one who would save Christian civilization may collaborate with it in any undertaking whatsoever."[27] The Russian occupation of Eastern Europe after 1945 and the emergence of the Communist Party as a serious electoral contender in Italy in 1948 caused Pope Pius XII great concern as well, and he issued several strong condemnations of Marxism during the immediate postwar period. This culminated in a decree from the Sacred Congregation of the Vatican's Holy Office in 1949 forbidding under pain of excommunication any direct or indirect cooperation by Catholics with Communist parties.[28]

These pronouncements from Rome, concerned with problems in Europe, had definite repercussions in Chile and clearly bolstered the position of political and religious conservatives. The official organ of the Archdiocese of Santiago, *La Revista Católica*, reiterated this Vatican position in early 1958 and used it as a basis for condemning the repeal of the Law for the Defense of Democracy. This legislation, passed in 1948 and outlawing the Communist Party, was in the process of being repealed in 1958 when the *Revista Católica* stated bluntly that any Catholics who favored such a repeal would be considered public sinners and subject to deprivation of the sacraments. Communists, according to the declaration, had no natural right to vote and positive laws granting them such rights were not genuine law. Finally, the document stated that, although those Catholics who cooperated with communism indirectly were not excommunicated, they were morally culpable and guilty of sin.[29]

---

[26] Bishop Dominico Tardini, "Llamado a la unidad de los católicos chilenos," *Boletín de la Acción Católica Chilena* 18 (1950): 1–2.

[27] Pope Pius XI, "Divini Redemptoris" (1937), no. 58, in *Papal Encyclicals*, ed Anne Fremantle, p. 261.

[28] In responding to the question whether or not a Catholic may be a member of the Communist Party or support it in any way, the Congregation replied negatively. It stated that the party "is materialistic and anti-Christian and its leaders, despite their words that they are not against religion, in both their theory and action show them to be hostile to God, true religion and the Church of Christ." *Acta Apostolicae Sedis* (Rome), 41 (1949): 334.
The Vatican reaffirmed this position ten years later when it also forbade Catholics to vote for any candidates who, although not Communists themselves, are in some way collaborators of the party or who favor communism. *L'Osservatore Romano* (Rome), 13–14 April 1959.

[29] Alejandro Huneus Cox, "Consultas sobre la cooperación al comunismo," *Revista Católica* (Santiago), no. 980 (January-April 1958), p. 1963.

The Conservative Party took advantage of Vatican condemnations of communism, using these as a means to discredit the Falange Nacional in the eyes of Catholics. Since the Falange Nacional had opposed the Law for the Defense of Democracy in Chile in 1948 and favored its repeal in 1958, leaders of the Conservative Party were quick and frequent to declare that this movement was implicitly condemned by the official Church.[30]

Furthermore, Chilean Catholic Integralists who had emerged during the 1930s also utilized various papal pronouncements of the 1930s, 1940s, and 1950s to justify their reactionary political positions. *Quadragesimo Anno* (1931) and some subsequent papal allocutions on the social question implicitly endorsed a corporatist type of alternative to liberal capitalism and Marxism. Some fascist-leaning Chilean Catholics relied heavily on these papal documents to legitimize authoritarian models for Chilean economic and social development.

Jorge Iván Hübner Gallo, a devout Catholic professor of legal and social sciences at the University of Chile, published a book in 1959 with an official imprimatur of the Archdiocese of Santiago. In it he denounced liberal democracy and called for government by those with most competence to rule for the common good. He endorsed a corporatist state for Chile similar to that in Spain, justifying his position on statements by the Vatican and claiming that the Catholic corporatist state had been upheld as a model fourteen times by Popes Pius XI and Pius XII between 1931 and 1956.[31]

Finally, during this era the massive influx of outside ecclesiastical aid into Chile—which occurred during the 1960s—had not yet begun. The Chilean Church in the 1950s began to experience serious economic difficulties in covering the rising costs of its educational system due to spiralling inflation (which reached 71 percent in 1954) and weak allegiance of

[30] "Fragmento del discurso que pronunció el Sr. Sergio Fernandez en la reunión del Directorio General del P. Conservador," *El Diario Ilustrado* (Santiago), 22 March 1948. Reprinted in *Política y Espíritu* 3 (March-April 1948): 40–42.

[31] "Only a government that is authoritarian, honest, impersonal and efficient, and which does not represent the majority but the better people in society, can inculcate true respect in the masses. This is the only regime that can implant the principles of order, hierarchy and discipline into social life, all of which are indispensable for the attainment of the common good and national progress." Jorge Iván Hübner Gallo, *Los católicos y la política,* pp. 95–96. Although it is true that Pope Pius XII during and after World War II stressed the importance of reestablishing democratic structures in Europe and other parts of the world in the wake of fascism, it is also clear that the social ideology underlying such papal documents as *Quadragesimo Anno* (1931) was very close to corporatism in style and language. Public order, strong central government, hierarchically orchestrated organizations (*gremios*) for social participation, nonconflictual partnerships between labor and capital, and aversion both for liberal capitalism and Marxist socialism all were primary values and goals stressed in the social pronouncements of Pius XI and Pius XII.

its nominal members. In the absence of internal and external Church sources of income (and no clear prohibition of public aid to the Church in the 1925 Constitution), a series of laws were passed by the Chilean Congress (dominated by the Right) in the 1950s which permitted the state to provide money for Catholic schools, varying in percentage according to whether or not these schools charged formal tuition.[32] In later chapters we shall see how these measures, which reinstated a critical dependency relationship between Church and state, at times have created problems for its autonomy to implement change and limited its capacity to attract voluntary lay contributions for its new programs.

International Church linkages promoted diverse currents within the Chilean Church in the late 1930s, 1940s, and 1950s. Vatican statements had a formative influence on the attitude and behavior of a small circle of liberal clerics and laity in Chile and provided them with encouragement. Other Vatican positions, however, strongly endorsed anticommunism and, at least implicitly, forms of corporatism. These commitments of Rome provided the Right in Chile with important legitimizing resources to oppose any type of significant change or reform. Finally, the lack of international financial support induced the reestablishment of dependency ties between Church and state in the absence of autonomous sources of financing for religious schools. Given the religiopolitical context of the country throughout this period, the conservative strains of international Catholic thought had far more importance and impact in Chile than the emerging progressive currents in the universal Church.

CONCLUSIONS

The conclusion in some of the literature that progressive currents were steadily gaining momentum in the Chilean Church in the 1930s, 1940s, and 1950s and that these acted to bolster the rise of Christian Democracy is wrong. The close correlation in 1958 between Catholic religious practice and support for conservative parties, in fact, is quite understandable given the dynamics that characterized both the Church and the political system.

[32] Under laws passed by the Chilean Congress in 1951, 1952, 1957, and 1958, the state was empowered to provide subsidies to private primary, secondary, and vocational schools. According to these arrangements (which still are in effect today), for each student enrolled in a private institution that charges no fixed tuition the government pays the school a sum equivalent to 50 percent of the estimated cost necessary to educate that same student in a public institution. Private schools that charge tuition receive an amount equal to 25 percent of the public cost. The remainder of the expenses of private education are met through a system of voluntary payments by parents or students. Louis A. Brahm M., Patricio Cariola, S.J., and Juan José Silva U., *Educación particular en Chile: antecedentes y dilemas*, pp. 60–62.

The articulation of new social norms by the bishops was general and personalistic with no well-developed structural carriers either in Church or in society to concretize their progressive content. There were also very weak allegiances to the Church among vast numbers of Catholics, and those who did practice in any regular fashion were exposed mainly to very traditional pastoral and social emphases. There was no strong stimulus from Chilean secular society acting to promote change within the Chilean Church, nor outlet in society to channel social Catholicism into effective change-oriented programs. Conservative forces maintained a solid plurality in Congress and continued to block major changes in economic structures in Chile during this period. Marxist parties averaged over 20 percent of the vote between 1938 and 1957 and proposed radical economic reforms, but they lacked sufficient political power in various coalition governments with the Radical Party to push them through.

In such a stalemate, conservative forces in the Church, both in the hierarchy and among upper-class laity, feared the possibility of an eventual breakthrough by Marxists and staunchly opposed any reform tendencies that could weaken united Catholic opposition to communism. This factor, coupled with the challenge to espiscopal authority which the progressive Falange Nacional seemed to present in 1947, prevented an effective reform-oriented Catholic movement from gaining significant ground during this period.

Finally, the messages coming from the Vatican were cautious and ambiguous: promote social change, do everything to stop communism, and construct a type of corporatism as the best alternative to liberal capitalism and Marxist socialism. Such messages, in the religiopolitical situation that characterized Chile between 1935 and 1958, had the effect of giving greater legitimacy to dominant conservative forces.

Despite the absence of major Church-state confrontations and the maintenance of correct relations between the Church and various coalition governments that included leftist parties from 1938 to 1952, the Church was not as "insulated" from secular concerns, as Vallier has indicated. It provided major moral and political opposition to Marxist parties and tacitly acted to bolster the dominance of conservative movements.

Furthermore, Chile in the postwar years was politically very different from Western Europe. In countries such as France, Italy, Belgium, Holland, and Germany, reform parties of Christian inspiration filled a gap left by the Right after the war, had a substantial base of support among Christian labor organizations, and enjoyed significant Catholic electoral support. The Right in Chile, however, did not collapse after the war, continued to attract the support of the plurality of churchgoers as the best way to stop Marxism, and the Falange Nacional lacked a significant trade union base to challenge the Right or the Left.

Social Catholicism in Chile between 1935 and 1958, however, was the most significant movement of its kind in Latin America. This was due to the socially progressive orientation of Catholic Action programs, the small but committed nucleus of lay leaders these structures trained over time, and the perdurance of a reformist party of Christian inspiration in competitive multiparty politics throughout this entire period. These factors made Chile unique on the continent during this era.[33] Such conditions, coupled with the continued officially neutral position of the Church in partisan politics after the mid-1930s, laid important groundwork for major advances by the Chilean Christian Democratic Party in the 1960s.

The dynamics of all the major variables in the Chilean Church—articulation of norms, arrangement of authority roles and structures, strength of membership allegiances, and the functioning of linkages with the international Church—changed dramatically after 1958. So did their corresponding normative, structural, and behavioral components in Chilean politics. The resulting impact of new religiopolitical interactions in the early 1960s contributed to a decidedly different electoral outcome in 1964 than occurred in 1958.

[33] Although Catholic Action movements were begun in Argentina and Peru in the 1930s, Integralist and profascist tendencies dominated them for several decades, similar to the situation in Spain and Portugal. In Colombia Catholic Action was somewhat more progressive but the vast majority of clerics and laity remained quite conservative and unaffected by it. Moreover, the Church in all of these countries remained officially linked with the state and publicly sided with conservative political parties. Frederick B. Pike, "South America's Multifaceted Catholicism," pp. 57–60, 65–66. John J. Kennedy, "The Legal Status of the Church in Latin America," in *Church and Social Change,* ed. Henry A. Landsberger, pp. 164–65; Alexander Wilde, "The Contemporary Church: The Political and the Pastoral," pp. 209–10.

In Brazil, new lay organizations did have a progressive thrust when they arose in the 1920s but by the mid-1930s took a turn to the Right in their social and political orientation. The Brazilian hierarchy pursued a policy of recuperation of lost privileges in the Vargas era (1930–1945), identified the Church closely with the corporatist values and strategies of his regime and actively discouraged the formation of progressive lay political movements. Thomas C. Bruneau, *Political Transformation,* pp. 45–46.

The only Latin American Church somewhat comparable to that of Chile in the 1930s and 1940s was in Venezuela. The Venezuelan Church had been separated from the state in the nineteenth century amidst strong anticlerical sentiment and was too weakened to pursue a recuperation strategy under the various dictators who ruled the country throughout the early part of this century. It did establish, however, socially progressive Catholic Action organizations in the mid-1930s. These provided the backbone of leadership for a reformist Christian Democratic Party—COPEI—founded in 1946 and later a serious contender for power at the end of the ten-year dictatorship of Pérez Jiménez in 1958. Daniel H. Levine, *Conflict and Political Change in Venezuela,* pp. 30–33.

5 The Rise of Christian Reformism: Chile, 1958–1964

Between 1958 and 1964 there were dramatic shifts in the Chilean political system. During this six-year period there was growing dissatisfaction among salary and wage earners with the economic policies of the Alessandri government. These imposed cuts in public expenditures, provided incentives for private domestic and foreign investors, and prevented wage increases from keeping pace with inflation. Such policies pleased industrialists and financiers, but damaged the purchasing power of middle and low income sectors. As a result opposition parties on the Left and Center made considerable electoral gains in the 1961 congressional and 1963 municipal elections. The Communists and Socialists (united since 1956 in an electoral coalition known as Frente de Acción Popular, or FRAP), increased their share of the electorate from 10.7 percent of the vote in 1957 to 22.1 percent in 1961, and to 23.5 percent in 1963. The Christian Democrats (PDC) jumped from 9.4 percent in 1957 to 15.4 percent in 1961, and finally to 22 percent in 1963, becoming in that year the largest single party in Chile.[1]

The electoral power of the Right declined in this period. The Conservative and Liberal parties formed a governing coalition with the Radicals in 1962 but this disintegrated in March 1964 when the FRAP candidate won a surprising upset in a by-election in the agricultural province of Curicó, a traditional stronghold of the Radical Party. As a result, the Radicals withdrew from the government, and the Conservatives and Liberals decided to back Eduardo Frei of the PDC in order to prevent a Marxist victory in the September presidential election.

Although the Radical Party entered a candidate (Julio Durán) in the presidential campaign, there were only two major contenders: Salvador Allende of the FRAP and Christian Democrat, Eduardo Frei, who had the unsolicited backing of Conservatives and Liberals. Despite differences in style and degree, the platforms of Allende and Frei were similar. Both stressed the need for agrarian reform, more governmental controls of industry, and greater state ownership of natural resources.[2] Frei won

---

[1] Barbara Stallings, *Class Conflict and Economic Development in Chile, 1958–1973*, pp. 80–90.

[2] For a discussion of the presidential campaign, see Ernst Halperin, *Nationalism and Communism in Chile;* and Federico Gil, *Political System of Chile*, pp. 298–304.

the election with an overwhelming 55.7 percent of the vote, while Allende gained 38.6 percent and Durán 4.9 percent (with .8 percent of the ballots null or void). Frei thus became the first Christian Democrat to win executive power in Latin America.

When we examine the correlations between religious practice and political preference, we discover some very dramatic differences between 1958 and 1964. According to surveys conducted in Santiago one month before the 1964 election by the Centro de Opinión Pública, among Catholics of every category of religious practice there was a significant shift away from the Right, a substantial gain for the Center and a slight increase for the Left. Whereas in 1958 a plurality of *all* types of Catholics identified with the Right, six years later those who attended Mass regularly or occasionally were decidedly more in the Center and a plurality of nonpracticing Catholics defined themselves as leftists.

This shift in political tendency among Catholics was translated into overwhelming support for Eduardo Frei and into almost a total collapse of Catholic identification with the Conservative and Liberal parties. Mass attendance was very highly correlated with preference for Frei, and nearly three-fourths of those practicing regularly chose Frei and less than 10 percent Allende. Degree of ritual participation was also strongly associated with support for Christian Democracy, since nearly three-fifths of regularly practicing Catholics identified with the PDC.[3] Frei, however, ran well ahead of his party in all three categories of Catholics, an indication both of his broad personal appeal and of the fact that many Conservatives supported him as the best way to defeat Allende. Thus, in a rather brief span of time, religiopolitical contours in Chile came to resemble more closely patterns prevalent in contemporary Western European countries where DC parties compete for power in a

[3] When we control for gender, we find that the correlation between religious practice and candidate choice still remains significant. Catholic women were somewhat more favorable to Frei than were Catholic men, but not significantly—63.2 percent as compared to 59.6 percent. Among both groups, those who said they regularly attended Mass were decidedly stronger Frei supporters than the nonpracticing—71.2 percent of the women and 86.2 percent of the men who attended Mass once a month or more chose Frei. Fifty-two percent of both men and women who never attended Mass, however, also preferred Frei.

When we control for class in the survey, we find that Frei won handily in each major category. Over three-fifths of those who identified themselves as being in the upper class (63.6 percent), and 61.4 percent in the middle class chose Frei, but so did over one half in the lower class (52.4 percent). Within each social class, frequency of religious practice was a significant factor assisting Frei, with over 70 percent of every group who attended Mass once a month or more supporting him—75 percent in the upper class, 79.1 percent in the middle class, and 70.1 percent in the lower class.

Hence, religious practice among men and women and in all social groups was significantly correlated with support for Christian Democracy, but it was not the only factor accounting for Frei's victory. A strong majority preferred Frei regardless of degree of affiliation with the Church. Religion was a help to Frei, but it was far from the only determinative factor and he would have won without it.

Table 5.1
Political Tendency and Religious Practice (Catholics)
Greater Santiago, August 1958 and 1964

	Regularly Practicing		Occasionally Practicing		Nonpracticing	
	1958 (N = 272)	1964 (N = 235)	1958 (N = 228)	1964 (N = 337)	1958 (N = 147)	1964 (N = 361)
Left	19.5% (53)	23.4% (55)	22.8% (52)	26.1% (88)	29.3% (43)	34.1% (123)
Center	21.3 (58)	37.9 (89)	20.2 (46)	27.6 (93)	23.8 (35)	31.0 (112)
Right	44.1 (120)	22.6 (53)	36.0 (82)	25.2 (85)	29.9 (44)	13.9 (50)
Undecided	15.1 (41)	16.1 (38)	21.0 (48)	21.1 (71)	17.0 (25)	21.0 (76)

SOURCE: Centro de Opinión Pública, Santiago, Chile.

Table 5.2
Political Choice and Religious Practice (Catholics)
Greater Santiago, August 1964
(N = 933)

	Regularly Practicing (N = 235)		Occasionally Practicing (N = 337)		Nonpracticing (N = 361)	
	Candidate	Party	Candidate	Party	Candidate	Party
Allende (FRAP)	9.8%	6.8%	18.1%	11.3%	25.2%	16.6%
Durán (Radical)	2.1	6.4	1.8	4.2	5.0	11.9
Frei (PDC)	74.9	57.9	62.9	50.7	52.4	40.7
(Conservative-Liberal)	—	7.7	—	4.2	—	3.3
Undecided	13.2	21.2	17.2	29.6	17.4	27.5

SOURCE: Centro de Opinión Pública, Santiago, Chile.

multiparty system. Practicing Catholics shifted their support from reactionary political movements to the centrist position of a Christian reform party, while continuing to show strong antipathy to the Left.

How can we account for such significant changes in the role of Chilean Catholicism in the political system in such a short period of time? I would argue that a new synthesis of religious and secular reformist values, the expansion of progressive social programs in the Church closely linked to a successful centrist party, the shift of lay Catholic attitudes after the failure of a conservative administration, and important new resources from the international Church all acted in concert to provide a powerful stimulus for progressive religiopolitical change. There was, in addition, considerable crisis support for social and economic changes out of fear of communism, and this also tended to make Catholics appear more in favor of major structural reforms in society than actually was the case.

NEW SYNTHESIS OF RELIGIOUS AND SECULAR REFORMIST VALUES

In 1962 the Chilean hierarchy published two pastoral letters on social problems that received widespread attention in the media both in Chile and in several foreign countries for their orginality of style and prophetic call for major structural reforms. The first document was issued in April, and it focused on the problems of production and working conditions in the agrarian sector.[4] The second one, published in September, analyzed a range of economic challenges facing the country and the corresponding social and political responsibilities Catholics had in relation to these.[5]

Both letters drew heavily on existing empirical studies of secular experts that described chronic structural inequities in the Chilean political economy. Both also specified very concrete changes that were necessary if a moral and religious commitment to justice were to become a reality. In this way, they were very different from previous Chilean episcopal pronouncements that had primarily emphasized general principles and individualistic solutions without coming to grips with structural causes of problems nor the necessary economic and political measures to resolve them.

The letter on agrarian problems, for example, denounced the underutilization of productive land, absentee landlordism in the countryside, and the lack of technical assistance and training for small landholders.

---

[4] Episcopado Chileno, "La iglesia y el campesinado chileno," pp. 185–94A.
[5] Episcopado Chileno, "El deber social y político en la hora presente," pp. 577–87.

The document spelled out some solutions to these problems: the establishment of the Institute of Agrarian Reform with teams in each region of the countryside; the expropriation of large landed estates and subsequent distribution of these properties to those who work them; vigorous government action in promoting cooperatives, technical training and education, and credit institutions; higher taxes on land; price regulations; and a system of social security for workers.[6]

The second document on the social and political responsibilities of Catholics quoted extensively from public and private studies of agriculture, education, housing, industrial production, and distribution of income to substantiate the case for basic structural reforms instead of traditional charitable projects to help the poor. The bishops called for authentic agrarian, tax, and industrial reforms, and administrative reorganization in government. They also endorsed strategies to increase national wealth— greater efforts in raising worker productivity, more investment by industrialists in basic consumer goods rather than luxury items, and a cessation of the export of capital. Finally, they called for a "genuine spirituality of economic development" among all Chileans, and emphasized that "love of neighbor also involves a serious responsibility for economic development."[7]

The synthesis of religious motives and technical expertise encouraged by the hierarchy to produce equitable development coincided very closely with the ideology of the Christian Democratic Party. Eduardo Frei promised major structural changes that would have similar far-reaching effects on the political economy to those being proposed by Allende, but he constantly stated that his administration would employ democratic rather than authoritarian means to implement change. His would be a "Revolution in Liberty," combining technical expertise, democratic procedures, and Christian humanistic values.[8] The close fit

---

[6] "La iglesia y el campesinado chileno," nos. 24, 33, 42, 48, 50–56, pp. 188–89, 192–94.

[7] "El deber social y política en la hora presente," nos. 6, 12–17, pp. 578, 580–81.
Other important pronouncements of clerical leaders occurred during this period calling for profound normative and structural changes in the country. In 1961 a group of thirteen pastors in the diocese of San Felipe wrote a public letter to the bishops and the president calling for major agrarian reforms. The editors of the Jesuit monthly magazine, Mensaje, devoted two issues of the journal in 1962 and 1963 to the need for structural reforms endorsed by the hierarchy. They spoke of the necessity of a thorough revolution channelled in a Christian framework, and called upon Christians not to oppose revolution but to encourage and "Christianize" it. Science and technology, they said, were definitely needed resources combined with humanistic values as a basis for "integral human development." Mensaje 10 (August 1961): 362; "Revolución en América Latina: visión cristiana," Mensaje 11 (December 1962): 589–748; "Reformas revolucionarias en América Latina," Mensaje 12 (October 1963): 480–686.

[8] Gil, Political System of Chile, p. 303.

between the new Church statements and the program of the Christian Democratic Party in 1964 was very striking, and each position reinforced the other.

The bishops also expressed another major concern in their September 1962 pastoral that not only reinforced Frei but clearly hurt Allende—the dangers inherent in Marxism and the possible evils that could result if Marxists gained power in Chile. Although the hierarchy devoted one paragraph of their letter to the abuses of liberal capitalism, six long sections focused on the errors of Marxism, the reasons for its growth, and the illegitimacy of any type of cooperation between Christians and Marxists.

They reiterated papal condemnations of Marxism, and stated emphatically that "communism is diametrically opposed to Christianity." They emphasized that "in a communist regime the workers have no rights, except those the state wishes to allow them," and that in such countries there is no opportunity for a "legitimate strike" nor for "free unions." The bishops also warned the Catholic populace that if communism was victorious in Chile Christians could expect "persecution, tears and bloodshed."[9]

In such a clear-cut race between Frei and Allende, by calling both for reform and a strong rejection of Marxism, the official voice of the Church clearly implied that there was only one acceptable choice for Catholics in the 1964 election. Technically, the bishops did not endorse a candidate or party. Given the context, they did not have to do so. Their message was clear—it espoused reformism and condemned the only viable alternative.[10]

CONGRUENT DEVELOPMENT OF NEW RELIGIOUS AND SECULAR STRUCTURES AIMED AT SOCIETAL REFORM

A major factor which both accounted for the evolution of a new style in Church statements and provided the impetus for the development of institutional carriers for these new social norms was the emer-

[9] "El deber social y política en la hora presente," nos. 20–22, pp. 582–83.

[10] Renato Poblete, S.J. of Centro Bellarmino, who has been a close advisor to the Episcopal Conference for twenty years, told me that the first draft of the pastoral letter of 1962 on the social and political duty of Catholics did not contain a strong condemnation of communism. It was added later to gain support of all the bishops for the document. There was not complete harmony among the hierarchy in this period, and a conservative minority (led by Bishop Alfredo Silva Santiago, rector of the Catholic University of Santiago, and Archbishop Alfredo Cifuentes of La Serena) were not sympathetic to the Falange Nacional or its successor, the PDC. These bishops were strong anti-Marxists and wanted a reiteration of the evils of communism in the pastoral letter. (Interview with Renato Poblete, S.J., Santiago, 16 November 1975.)

gence of a generation of bishops and clerics who came into leadership positions in the late 1950s and early 1960s. These men developed new roles and structures in the institution which corresponded to roles and structures developing in society (particularly in the Christian Democratic Party), thus placing the institutional weight of the Church behind secular change. Authority flows across the layered hierarchical organization operated efficiently and smoothly among this new generation of bishops and clerics since all shared the same vision and goals for Church and society.

Between 1955 and 1964, fourteen of the twenty-eight bishops in the country retired or died and their replacements tended to be social progressives. Seven of the new bishops as young priests had been chaplains of Catholic Action programs. All of them had received their education in the same high schools and university circles which formed the leaders of the Christian Democratic Party in the 1930s and 1940s. Many of the new bishops and leaders of the PDC also had close friendship or family ties.

The leadership of the Episcopal Conference after 1958 fell to Archbishop Raúl Silva Henríquez and Bishop Manuel Larraín. Silva, before being consecrated a bishop in 1959, had been director of Cáritas-Chile, a Church-sponsored social welfare program, and was well known for his administrative ability and concern for the poor. He was appointed archbishop of Santiago in 1961 by Pope John XXIII and was elected president of the Episcopal Conference in the same year. Larraín long had actively promoted Catholic Action programs, was sympathetic to the ideology and goals of the Falange and the PDC, and also acted as the intellectual leader of the episcopacy during this era. In the late 1950s and early 1960s, these two men provided vigorous leadership in the Episcopal Conference for a more active commitment by the Church to social reform.[11]

In addition, a new generation of men were coming to positions of responsibility in the lower clergy. Throughout the 1950s, the major seminary in Santiago (one of the two in the country), under the direction of Rev. Emilio Tagle (to become archbishop of Valparaíso in 1961), turned out priests with a sensitivity to problems of the poor. Tagle had been chaplain for the Social Action Department of Catholic Action in Santiago, and was also pastor of a very poor parish in La Florida, before becoming rector of the seminary in 1950. During his eight-year term as

---

[11] For an excellent description of the background, attitudes, social and pastoral priorities, and key personalities among the Chilean bishops during the 1960s, see Thomas G. Sanders, "The Chilean Episcopate: An Institution in Transition," *American Universities Field Staff Reports,* West Coast South America Series no. 15 (August 1968): 1–30.

rector, the whole tone of the seminary changed, and great emphasis was placed on exposing the students to the needs of the poor through part-time service in working-class parishes. When they graduated from the seminary, they carried this formative experience with them and either went to work in poor areas or stressed social responsibility in their sermons in middle and upper-class parishes. They too, like the bishops, shared many of the social values of the newly emerging PDC.[12]

Thus, many in authority roles in the administrative network of the Church in the late 1950s and early 1960s had a different formative experience than their predecessors, and this made them more open to social change and the Church's responsibility to promote it actively. This congruence of leadership between the Church and the PDC helps explain why new concerns in official documents of the Church coincided with and reinforced those of Christian Democracy. It also helped to prevent a major clash between hierarchy and party as had occurred in 1947 between the bishops and the Falange Nacional.

This generation of clerics worked hard to develop structures in the Church to act as carriers of its new socially progressive teachings and to dramatize the Church's institutional commitment to change. The Episcopal Conference introduced several major innovations during these years to make the pastoral work of the Church more effective and link it more closely with the social concerns of the faithful, especially the poor.

The Office of Religious Sociology (OSORE) was established in 1958 in the Secretariat of the Episcopal Conference to conduct empirical studies of religious attitudes, practices, and needs throughout the country and to evaluate existing pastoral programs. Two major dioceses in the country—Santiago and Talca—inaugurated decentralization processes in 1962, creating zones and deaneries to vitalize local structures of the Church and bring them closer to the people. An Office of Technical Planning (OTP) was also begun by the Episcopal Conference, staffed by clerical and lay experts to advise the bishops on long-range pastoral planning.[13]

In addition to publishing their monthly journal, *Mensaje*, the Jesuits established clusters of study and action programs in the late 1950s in Santiago affiliated with Centro Bellarmino. These involved socioreligious research, a graduate school of social studies (ILADES), institutes of Social Communication and Christian Humanism, and a center to

---

[12] Eduardo Frei told me that undoubtedly many of the lower clergy of this new generation were very sympathetic to Christian Democracy during his presidential campaign of 1964. He also felt, however, that these clerics successfully maintained the independence of the Church from identification with the party as such. (Interview with Eduardo Frei, Santiago, 7 November 1975.)

[13] Interview with Renato Poblete, S.J., Santiago, 16 November 1975.

elaborate models of economic development (DESAL). This center also sponsored a network of organizations among the urban poor, called Popular Promotion (which the Frei government later attempted to incorporate into the government), to assist unorganized shantytown dwellers to articulate their social needs to public authorities.[14]

During this period a whole series of new Church-sponsored action projects emerged and existing social programs were expanded. These included labor unions and educational and technical training programs for peasants, land reform projects on Church-owned estates, low-income housing construction cooperatives, and courses in the social doctrine of the Church for business leaders.[15] These projects reached people with very little contact with the Church's ritual activities. They also dramatized to all sectors of the populace that the institutional weight of the Church was being placed behind secular reforms, and that the Church was making a commitment in deed as well as in word to development.

Many of these study and action projects acted as laboratories for new socioeconomic programs being proposed in the platform of the Christian Democratic Party. In fact, many of the lay leaders and technical experts who helped design and administer them for the Church were very close to the PDC. Several of them later came to hold leadership positions in the party or in Frei's administration after the election.[16]

In addition to these new technical programs sponsored by the Church, the traditional structures of Catholic Action—especially among students—expanded significantly in the late 1950s and early 1960s. Young priests committed to social change became chaplains to the newly founded University Catholic Action (AUC) established in 1955, and after 1958 both the membership and the scope of activities of this program grew rapidly. Significant numbers of middle and upper-class youth both at the University of Chile and the Catholic University of Santiago joined AUC in these years. In fact, the AUC and other Catho-

---

[14] For a description and analysis of these projects sponsored by Centro Bellarmino in the early 1960s, see Sanders, *Catholic Innovation in a Changing Latin America*, pp. 2/1–2/21. The Popular Promotion program by early 1964 had set up neighborhood committees, mothers' centers, and youth organizations in 115 of the 215 working-class shantytowns in Santiago and in fifteen other cities of the provinces. Mario Zañartu, S.J., *Desarrollo económico*, pp. 7/32–7/33.

[15] Zañartu, *Desarrollo económico*, pp. 7/27–7/40.

[16] Sanders observes that several Catholic laymen who participated regularly in seminars and discussions at Centro Bellarmino, and who also published articles in *Mensaje*, later were to hold important cabinet positions in Frei's government: Jacques Chonchol (minister of agriculture), William Thayer (minister of labor), Gabriel Valdés (foreign minister), Sergio Ossa (minister of public works), and Radomiro Tomic (ambassador to Washington and successor to Frei as presidential candidate of the PDC in 1970). Sanders, *Catholic Innovation in a Changing Latin America*, p. 2/7.

lic Action groups similar to it (Juventud Obrera Católica and Juventud Estudiantil Católica) were the only effective competitors to the Juventud Comunista among Chilean youth in this period.[17] The focus of these organizations included spiritual guidance, discussion of strategies for economic and social reform, and service work in factories, coal mines, and rural and urban working-class areas. All of these activities had a profound impact on the values and attitudes of young people, and led them to conclude that a new political strategy was needed to effect structural reforms in society. Many of those in AUC in fact became active in new student political organizations being set up in the universities by the PDC in the early 1960s. The great majority of those who later were leaders in Christian Democratic clubs also had been activists in AUC and maintained close ties to it.[18]

Hence, it is clear that there was a decided congruence, and even overlap, between roles and structures of the Church and those of the Christian Democratic Party in the early 1960s. At the same time that the Chuch was developing new organizations and strengthening its structural linkages with hitherto neglected sectors of the population (peasants, workers, students), the PDC was also moving among the same groups and drawing its local cadres of leaders from Church-related programs. Many of those working in new Church-sponsored programs were recruited into the structures of the party.[19]

In this phenomenon of overlapping associational relationships between branches of Catholic Action and structures of the PDC, the Chilean case in this period came to resemble the pattern that has dominated several Western Europe countries for decades. Lay men and women trained in Catholic apostolic and social action programs provided ready recruits for Christian Democracy. In so doing, unofficial but powerful structural alliances were established between Church and party.[20]

[17] Interview with Eduardo Palma, member of the Christian Democratic Party and professor at the Institute of Political Science of the Catholic University of Santiago, 28 November 1975.

[18] Interview with José Vial, S.J., former chaplain of AUC, conducted in November 1974 by Josefina Puga and Carmen Galilea of Centro Bellarmino.

[19] Giles Wayland-Smith in interviews conducted with 166 activists of the PDC from three different counties of Santiago in 1965–1966 found that over two-fifths (42 percent) of them had formerly been active in various Church-sponsored programs, especially Catholic Action. Three-fifths of them also indicated that they read some Church documents or publications (such as pastoral letters of the Chilean bishops and *Mensaje*), and over two-thirds (68 percent) said they at least occasionally discussed the social doctrine of the Church with their friends or other party members. Wayland-Smith, *Christian Democratic Party,* pp. 5/26–5/29.

[20] After World War II, both the MRP in France and the DC in Italy drew heavily from the ranks of Catholic Action and other Catholic lay organizations for their respective leaders during their rise to power. William Bosworth, *Catholicism and Crisis,* pp. 249–51, and Gianfranco Poggi, *Catholic Action,* p. 27.

A SHIFT IN CATHOLIC ATTITUDES AND STRONG CRISIS SUPPORT FOR THE CHURCH

There was no significant increase in religious practice among Catholics during this period. On-site surveys conducted in churches on Sunday mornings in several dioceses throughout the country indicated that average Sunday observance was approximately 12 percent, and in working-class areas it was less than half this rate. Furthermore, women and children constituted the vast majority of those who participated in weekly Mass.[21]

While allegiance ties to the Church as expressed in traditional forms of ritual participation remained very weak, the Church made new efforts to reach nonpracticing Catholics of every social class in 1963. The newly-formed Office of Technical Planning (OTP) set up to assist the Episcopal Conference elaborated the beginnings of a Pastoral Plan by the early 1960s. It included the suggestion that religious missions be conducted by teams of clerics, religious, and laity at the neighborhood level in each parish.[22] As a result, Santiago and several other dioceses conducted the Great Mission of evangelization for several months in 1963.

This program consisted in broadcasting brief fifteen-minute religious programs, followed up by small group discussions in local neighborhoods, factories, and social clubs on the meaning and implication of these radio messages.[23] General catechetical instructions were given by the organizing teams, along with analysis of the social teaching of the Church and the recent pastoral letters of the Chilean hierarchy—including their strong condemnations of Marxism. In such a way, many of those with little or no formal contact with the Church of Sundays were reached in a short period of time and exposed to its new social message.

There is evidence from the Hamuy surveys conducted in Greater Santiago during August 1964 that, despite continued low rates of ritual practice, changes in the Church's religious and social focus were having an impact on Catholic attitudes. When asked if the Church favored social changes, nearly two-thirds (64.8 percent) or all those interviewed said yes, including three-fourths (76.6 percent) of those who said they practiced regularly. Two-thirds (67.6 percent) of the entire sample also expressed belief that social change was necessary, with almost the same

[21] Source: Office of Religious Sociology (OSORE), Secretariat of the Chilean Episcopal Conference, Santiago.

[22] A copy of this first Pastoral Plan of the Chilean hierarchy has been translated into English. See "Pastoral Plan of the Chilean Episcopate," *Pro Mundi Vita*, no. 1 (1964), pp. 1–18.

[23] "Nuestra misión general de 1963," *Boletín Informativo Arquidiocesano* (Santiago) 1 (December 1962): 1–4.

percentage of the most devout Catholics (67.3 percent) agreeing. The vast majority, regardless of their rate of ritual participation, knew about the Church's position and seemed to support it.[24]

Six years before, the public legitimating role of the Church was clearly conservative, and this paralleled significant correlations between religious practice and rightist tendencies and choices. By 1964, however, a plurality of Catholics shifted to the center of the political spectrum, and their attitudes also seemed to show very definite support for major structural changes in the economy. They knew the Church's public position was behind such changes, and their varying degrees of association with it was not an obstacle to endorsing such policies, many of which closely paralleled those of the PDC.

The Hamuy surveys, however, also revealed some other significant attitudinal characteristics which perhaps played an even more significant role in marshalling Catholic support for the PDC than a desire for social reforms. When asked if the religious beliefs of a candidate were important factors in giving him support, close to three-fifths (58.2 percent) of nonpracticing Catholics said they did *not* consider religion in making their selection of a candidate. The majority (53.2 percent) of those who said they practiced regularly, however, said such a factor *was* significant and that they did take it into account.

This attitudinal factor was particularly important in the 1964 campaign since 85.7 percent of the total respondents in Hamuy's survey (and 88.1 percent of those Catholics who practiced regularly) indicated that they believed Eduardo Frei was the candidate of the Catholics. Although Frei did not explicitly identify himself as the candidate of the Church, his long association with Catholic Action programs, the ideology of his party, and the very close affinity between his platform and the proposals outlined in recent Chilean episcopal documents all helped to shape his image as the preferred candidate of Catholics in contrast to Allende, the Marxist. The fact that a majority of practicing Catholics did consider religion an important factor in choosing a candidate clearly worked in Frei's favor.

The negative corollary of the religious factor in the 1964 campaign, which worked in Frei's favor, was the fear of communism. This significantly detracted from Allende's potential support. Two questions in Hamuy's August 1964 survey were particularly revealing in regard to the significance of such anxiety in the minds of voters, especially on the part of the most devout Catholics:

---

[24] Regarding one specific measure to effect change—namely, greater public control of industry, which both the FRAP and the PDC espoused in various degrees—the overwhelming number of total respondents (83.5 percent) wanted greater government regulation or ownership. Intensity of religious practice was *not* significantly correlated with the responses. All types of Catholics favored more controls.

Table 5.3

Is Communism a Real Danger in Chile?

"*Do you feel that communism is a real danger in Chile, or do you believe that anticommunist propaganda is a means to avoid the reforms the country needs?*"

Greater Santiago, August 1964

	Catholics (N = 933)			
	Regularly Practicing (N = 235)	Occasionally Practicing (N = 337)	Nonpracticing (N = 361)	Total Sample (N = 1,095)
Communism is a real danger	74.0% (174)	62.0% (209)	55.7% (201)	58.8% (644)
No, the issue is a means to avoid needed reforms	11.5 (27)	22.0 (74)	26.9 (97)	24.4 (267)
Undecided	14.5 (34)	16.0 (54)	17.4 (63)	16.8 (184)

SOURCE: Centro de Opinión Pública, Santiago, Chile.

Table 5.4

Would Allende Be a Dictator?

"*Do you believe that Allende, as the candidate of communism, would, if elected, install a dictatorship in order to implement his program?*"

Greater Santiago, August 1964

	Catholics			
	Regularly Practicing (N = 235)	Occasionally Practicing (N = 337)	Nonpracticing (N = 361)	Total Sample (N = 1,095)
Yes	55.7% (131)	49.6% (167)	43.8% (158)	46.4% (508)
No	28.9 (68)	33.8 (114)	40.7 (147)	38.1 (417)
Undecided	15.4 (36)	16.6 (56)	15.5 (56)	15.5 (170)

SOURCE: Centro de Opinión Pública, Santiago, Chile.

(1) Do you feel that communism is a real danger in Chile, or do you believe that anticommunist propaganda is a means to avoid the reforms the country needs?

(2) Do you believe that Allende as the candidate of communism would, if elected, install a dictatorship in order to implement his program?

As Table 5.3 dramatically illustrates, fear of communism was a major concern for a large majority of Chileans in Santiago a month before the 1964 election. Nearly three-fifths (58.8 percent) of *all* the respondents in Hamuy's survey indicated that communism was a real danger and not merely an instrument of propaganda manipulated by the Right to avoid major reforms. Furthermore, nearly three-fourths (74 percent) of regularly practicing Catholics felt this way, indicating that the strong warnings against Marxism by the bishops were well known and accepted by the most devout.

The responses to the second question regarding the probability that Allende would use dictatorial methods in order to implement his program are also extremely revealing. Nearly one-half (46.4 percent) of *all* respondents expressed the fear that he would turn into a dictator if elected. Intensity of religious practice was very clearly correlated with fear of dire consequences following upon an Allende victory, but even among nonpracticing Catholics over two-fifths (43.8 percent) believed Allende would not respect democratic processes as president.

Controlling for social class, similar patterns of fear existed even among the poor. Over one-half (54.5 percent) of those who identified themselves as being in the upper class believed Allende would use dictatorial means once in office, and almost the same proportion in the middle class (51.5 percent) shared that view. What is surprising, however, is that just over two-fifths (41 percent) of those in the lower class believed this. About the same percentage of workers (40.8 percent) disagreed, and almost one-fifth (18.2 percent) were undecided.

Throughout the presidential campaign the PDC emphasized that Allende was only a pawn who, once elected, would be manipulated by the communists in order to set up a dictatorship of the proletariat. Allende vigorously denied this, and frequently throughout the campaign made efforts to establish his independence from communism.[25] Nevertheless, the preceding tables and data graphically illustrate the preponderance of such fears of communism and of a possible dictatorship which cut across all classes. This was very damaging for Allende's candidacy and

---

[25] Gil, *Political System of Chile,* p. 299; Frank Bonilla and Myron Glazer, *Student Politics in Chile,* p. 209; Miles D. Wolpin, *Cuban Foreign Policy and Chilean Politics,* pp. 195–204.

diminished his appeal among many Chileans irrespective of their degree of affiliation with the Church. The leftist parties were not able to offset these fears even among their own natural constituency.

Nevertheless, it is also true that those residents of Santiago who maintained fairly regular contacts with the Church were more prone to harbor such fears than nonpracticing Catholics. The strong condemnations of Marxism in the 1962 bishops' letter in which they warned of "persecution, tears and bloodshed" for the Church if a communist should win clearly reinforced such fears and also made it almost impossible for a devout Catholic to support Allende in good conscience.[26]

In such a clear-cut and polarized campaign as 1964, support for basic structural changes and fear of communism were mixed together to produce a powerful motivational impact on Catholic opinion—even among those with little or no regular contact with the Church. As we shall see in the next chapter, however, such crisis support would be short-lived since it masked divisions that still existed among Catholics regarding the content and pace of social reform.

NEW CHANGE-ORIENTED RESOURCES FROM THE
INTERNATIONAL CHURCH

International Church influences in Chile after 1958 produced a powerful stimulus for change. New emphases in papal encyclicals, Vatican appointments of several progressive Chilean bishops, the beginning of the Second Vatican Council, and the influx of large amounts of foreign Church personnel and resources all reinforced new developments occurring in the Chilean Church.

In November 1958, John XXIII was elected to the papacy at the age of seventy-seven. Although he reigned for less than five years, he began major transformations in Catholicism. He convoked the first international meeting of all Catholic bishops in nearly one hundred years. He wrote major letters on the social question. Pope John was responsible for a small but significant "opening to the Left" which would lead to important Christian-Marxist dialogue in several parts of the world after his death. He also urged Catholics in Western Europe and North America to commit a significant percentage of their personnel and resources to churches in developing countries.[27]

[26] Here again the pattern of Chilean Catholic attitudes and behavior in the early 1960s paralleled what has been true of Western European politics for a century: strong public condemnations by the hierarchy of Marxism, ingrained fears among Catholics of possible disastrous consequences for Church and society in the eventuality of a Marxist electoral victory, and very significant negative correlations between intensity of religious practice and support for the Left.
[27] For an analysis of Pope John XXIII's impact on Church and international society, see E.E.Y. Hales, *Pope John and His Revolution.*

Some of the solutions to economic problems mentioned in Pope John's encyclical letter of 1961, *Mater et Magistra,* which empahsized the necessity of specific structural changes in stagnant economies, were included by the Chilean bishops a year later in their two pastoral letters on social problems in Chile—commodity price supports, social insurance, cooperative farming, tax reforms, agrarian reform, technical training of workers.[28] Moreover, corporatist language and style was conspicuously absent in Pope John's writings. He emphasized technical competence and democratic reform rather than authority and order as means to promote effective development. This new orientation in papal teaching clearly reinforced similar currents of thought emerging in Chilean episcopal statements.

Another major influence exercised by the Vatican in the Chilean Church in the late 1950s and early 1960s was the Holy See's appointment of several young progressive priests to the episcopacy. As mentioned previously, there was a 50 percent turnover rate in the Chilean hierarchy (fourteen of twenty-eight) between 1955 and 1964. A progressive papal nuncio during the late 1950s, Sebastian Baggio, recommended many of these new prelates, and the Vatican confirmed his choice of men who represented reform elements in the lower clergy.[29]

Participation in Rome at the Second Vatican Council for all Catholic bishops (1962–1965) also was a major formative influence on the Chilean hierarchy. There the Chilean bishops were exposed to progressive currents of European theology, and, in turn, gained the respect of other bishops for being well-prepared and for exercising decisive leadership in the Council.[30] Their cohesiveness and ability to work in unison at the Council for progressive changes in the universal Church reinforced determination to carry out reforms in their own home dioceses in Chile—e.g., decentralization of authority, greater responsibilities for laity, and commitment to social action on behalf of the poor.[31]

Perhaps the most crucial international influence on the Chilean Church after 1958 was the significant flow of personnel and financial and material resources into the country. After Fidel Castro announced his commitment to Marxist-Leninism in the early 1960s, Pope John issued a call for a major new missionary effort in Latin America. He called

[28] Pope John XXIII, "Mater et Magistra," nos. 123–43; 163–65; 222–41, in *Gospel of Peace and Justice,* ed. Joseph Gremillion, pp. 170–74, 179, 190–94.

[29] "Chile," *Pro Mundi Vita,* no. 49 (1974), p. 25.

[30] Rocco Caporale, in his interviews with seventy-three cardinals and bishops from thirty-nine different countries during the Council, found that the Chilean bishops were frequently identified as the leading episcopate in Latin America by other prelates. They had a good reputation at the Council for being well-organized, thoroughly prepared by their theological advisors, and for exercising important progressive input into the meetings. Rocco Caporale, *Vatican II: Last of the Councils,* pp. 158–59.

[31] Interview with Renato Poblete, S.J., Santiago, 16 November 1975.

upon bishops and religious superiors in Western Europe and North America to commit 10 percent of their personnel to Latin America by 1970.

Leaders of churches in the North Atlantic region responded quickly to this urgent appeal. In a few years, U.S. Catholic mission personnel in Latin America grew by nearly 65 percent, increasing from 2,126 in 1958 to 3,506 in 1964. U.S. priests and nuns serving in Chile doubled—from 122 in 1958 to 246 in 1964. Western European churches also increased their supply of missionaries in the late 1950s and early 1960s. The result was that the total number of priests in Chile expanded by 27.8 percent between 1950 and 1965, the major factor accounting for the increase being the influx of foreign priests.[32]

The bishops assigned large numbers of these missionaries to urban and rural working-class districts where the Church's staffing problem was most acute. In a short period of time, therefore, the Chilean Church was able to strengthen its presence significantly in hitherto neglected areas, and to initiate new pastoral and social programs among the poor. Such added personnel made possible many of the new projects undertaken by the Church in the eary 1960s, such as the Great Mission of evangelization and various educational and technical training programs mentioned earlier.

Perhaps of greater importance than personnel transfers was the large amount of foreign financial aid sent to Chilean Church projects during this period. Organizations sponsored by the West European and North American bishops provided over $34 million in money, food, clothing, and medicines to Church-affiliated social and pastoral projects in Chile between 1960 and 1964.[33] Almost all of the new programs in the Chilean Church set up to assist the poor were heavily subsidized by foreign church aid—agrarian reform projects on Church lands, low-income housing construction, technical training and basic education for peasants, socioeconomic research and action projects.[34]

[32] Source: U.S. Catholic Mission Council, United States Catholic Conference, Washington, D.C.

As indicated in Chapter 2, the percentage of foreign clergy in Chile expanded from 39.3 percent in 1945 to 51.4 percent in 1965.

[33] Table 2.9 presents the annual amounts given by various Catholic institutions in Western Europe, the United States, and Canada during this period.

[34] Zañartu in his book persents a project-by-project inventory of these Church-sponsored activities as of January 1964, giving in several cases the amounts and sources of foreign sources of funding. *Desarrollo económico*, pp. 7/27–7/36.

A less reliable (and cynical) evaluation of foreign sources of income for various projects supported by the Chilean Church during these years may be found in David E. Mutchler, *Church as a Political Factor*.

For an overview and summary of the work of Catholic Relief Services in Chile between 1957 and 1965, along with a statistical summary of some of the personnel and financial resources supplied by U.S. religious congregations, see Wolpin, *Cuban Foreign Policy*, pp. 267–75.

Some of these new programs—e.g., the Rural Education Institute (IER) and the National Center for Slumdwellers (CENAPO)—also received substantial financial assistance from the Chilean as well as foreign governments.[35] Both Catholic Relief Services in the United States and Misereor in West Germany acted as conduits for very substantial amounts of public aid from their respective governments flowing to Chilean Church projects in these years. A significant amount of direct U.S. government aid was also channeled into Chilean Catholic development programs through USAID assistance that was greatly expanded at the beginning of the Alliance for Progress.[36]

Without this money and material assistance, none of the new social projects begun and carried on by the Chilean Church in the early 1960s would have been possible. The internally generated financial resources of the Chilean Church coming from Sunday collections and stole fees for administration of the sacraments provided barely enough to maintain existing buildings and to pay clerical salaries. A 1 percent tithe on Catholic family income—Contribution to the Church (CALI)—was begun by the bishops in 1964, but during its first year of operation accounted for only $271,367 of additional income (see Table 2.9). In comparison with the $34 million provided by Catholic Relief Services in the United States and Misereor and Adveiat in West Germany between 1960 and 1964, this amount was very insignificant and insufficient to sustain all the new religious and social projects undertaken by the Chilean Church in the early 1960s.

During the previous generation substantial foreign assistance was unavailable to the Chilean Church, and it had to depend largely on upper-class Catholics and the Chilean government (controlled by conservative elements) for financial support for its religious and educational programs. After 1958, with the decline of the power of the Right in Congress and the availability of new sources of foreign money interested in promoting change-oriented programs in Chile (and thus thwarting Marxism), the Church found other donors with a close affinity with her newly emerging reformist ecclesiastical leadership.

[35] Between 1962 and 1964, 60 percent ($1.8 million) of IER's $3 million budget came from various ministries in the Chilean government and 31 percent ($958,000) was supplied by USAID grants. Misereor, CARE, and Catholic Relief Services provided the bulk ($124,000) of the remaining 9 percent. William Thiesenhusen, "Experimental Programs of Land Reform in Chile" (Ph.D. dissertation, University of Wisconsin, 1965), chap. 2, pp. 54–55.
[36] The food shipments of Catholic Relief Services (which constitute the great bulk of CRS aid) are donated by the U.S. government under its Food for Peace program. The West German government's relief program, Zentralstelle, channeled over $400,-000 to Chile through Misereor between 1962 and 1964. USAID sent over $2 million in development assistance to Church-sponsored programs during the same time span. See Table 2.9.

CONCLUSIONS

The conclusions in much of the literature that Catholicism became very closely associated with Christian Democracy in Chile between 1958 and 1964, that the Church provided the PDC with significant legitimacy support and recruits for its cadres, and that practicing Catholics voted overwhelmingly for Frei are all substantially correct. The judgment, however, that the Church played a preponderant role in limiting Allende's base of support must be qualified. Other critical factors were also working against him in 1964, especially the widespread fear of communism among all Chileans regardless of religious practice, and the lack of widespread electoral support for the Left among low-income sectors of the population. While association with the Church clearly reinforced these tendencies or problems, it did not create them.

During this period, Church pronouncements on social and economic issues were much more structural and technical in their analysis and also resonated with ideological shifts in Chilean politics. Structural mechanisms were developed in the Church to operationalize its new social teachings, and these were congruent with reformist political structures. In fact, there was a strong overlap of religious and secular roles involving the Catholic Church and the surging PDC. Moreover, at no time was there an internal crisis of ecclesiastical power, and authority flows operated efficiently and smoothly across the layered administrative framework of the Church.

Although ritual allegiances to the Church remained chronically weak, these were offset by well-planned, short-term evangelization programs for families in their homes. The most significant factor affecting Catholic attitudes, however, was the fear of communism which was translated into cohesive crisis support for the Church's new social position as a means of stopping the electoral advances of the Left. Under such conditions, a consensus among Catholics in all social classes could be forged in a short period of time for Church-endorsed changes and the candidate who most closely articulated them in his platform—Eduardo Frei. This shift of attitudes within the Church from the Right to the Center also corresponded to, and reflected, the general shift of opinion in society at large where conservatives supported the PDC candidate as the best way to block Allende in 1964.

Finally, unlike the previous period when messages from the Vatican were diverse and diffuse and resource transactions with other national churches still underdeveloped, in the post-1958 period social pronouncements from Rome were consistently behind strategies for socioeconomic reform, and at times quite specific in the solutions suggested. These papal statements provided clear and strong support for progressive normative positions by the Chilean hierarchy and could not be manipulated by conservative political forces as in the previous generation. Furthermore, structural ties to an international pool of Church personnel and finances were forged. These in turn acted as conduits of significant change-oriented resources flowing into Chile. Without such assistance, the Chilean Church's new social programs of the early 1960s would not have been possible nor its institutional impact on reformist politics as sustained or forceful.

Thus, in this period the major components of the Church as a complex religious institution—articulation of social norms, authority flows and structures across a layered administrative network, allegiance patterns of members, and international resource linkages—all acted in tandem and in the same change-oriented direction as corresponding secular dynamics. In such a context, Chilean Catholicism acted as a significant reinforcing agent of political reformism in the early 1960s. The convergence of lines between the Church and the PDC, however, was so close (and in some cases identical) that some very serious problems arose for the Church once the political context changed in the late 1960s.

The Apex and Decline of Christian Democracy: Chile, 1964–1970

The literature on the Frei Administration is substantial, and interpretations on the extent of reform vary according to the ideological perspective of the authors. Most critics, however, are in agreement that during the first three years significant advances were made in lowering inflation and unemployment, expanding agrarian reform and unionization, increasing tax collections and public ownership of basic resources, improving services in health, education, and housing, and encouraging wider participation in social and political organizations among the poor.[1]

All of these programs, however, created serious problems for the administration in Congress on both the Right and the Left. Conservatives and Liberals strongly opposed agrarian reform since it attacked the interests of one of their major bases of support—large landholders. The Left, while offering support for breaking up large underutilized estates, opposed the only partial nationalization (51 percent) of foreign-owned copper for being too piecemeal, and the establishment of rival union organizations separate from those already controlled by the Communist and Socialist parties and government sponsorship of new grass-roots organizations for solidifying the power base of the Christian Democrats among urban and rural workers. Since Frei attempted to govern without seeking strategic alliances with other parties, these differences caused him serious difficulty and he had to make compromises in content or timing of several proposals in order to gain congressional approval for his program.[2]

[1] Critical assessments of the policies of the Frei Administration have been done by Petras, Sigmund, Grayson, Francis, Loveman, A. Valenzuela, and Stallings.
[2] Although the PDC gained 42.3 percent of the vote in the 1965 congressional elections (the largest plurality in recent history for any single party), the Christian Democrats had a majority until 1969 only in the Chamber of Deputies (82 of 147). In the Senate, however, they controlled thirteen of forty-five seats, two short of the one-third which, in combination with a majority in the Chamber, could override senatorial amendments to bills originating in the lower house. As a result, the Frei Administration had to make concessions on compensations for expropriated lands and on the rights of reserve retained by owners. It also delayed industrial and business reform proposals so as to win congressional approval for agrarian reform and the "Chileanization" of copper. Paul E. Sigmund, *The Overthrow of Allende and the Politics of Chile, 1964–1976*, pp. 37–38, 48–49, 52.

Furthermore, within the PDC serious divisions arose regarding the pace and style of Frei's reform proposals midway through his term. By 1967 the younger sectors of the party, intellectuals, ideologues, and working-class leaders were criticizing what they considered to be the administration's gradualist approach to change, its bias toward capital and landed interests, its heavy reliance on technocrats over party leaders in government administration, and its emphasis on economic growth more than redistribution. For a brief period in 1967 these groups even gained control of the National Council of the PDC.[3]

Social unrest emerged by mid-1967 among sectors whose expectations for major redistribution of resources and political power had been raised but not totally met. Strikes and illegal land seizures increased significantly. Working-class leaders complained of bureaucratic control of popular organizations, administration appeals for wage restraints, and its proposal of forced savings by workers.[4] In addition, urban guerilla violence in 1967 and 1968 perpetrated by the Revolutionary Left Movement (MIR, founded in 1966), the bloody repression of several workers' demonstrations by riot police in 1967 and 1968 which left several dead, and a revolt of army officers in 1969 seeking higher pay and expressing concern over societal disorder, all were indications of growing political polarization during the last three years of Frei's presidency.

The electoral impact of all of these developments was an erosion of the political base of the PDC in the late 1960s. After gaining 42.3 percent of the vote in the March 1965 congressional elections, party support diminished to 35.6 percent in the national municipal elections of April 1967, and to 29.8 percent in the congressional campaign of March 1969. In contrast, Conservative and Liberal parties (amalgamated into the new National Party in 1966) regained much of their electoral support from an ebb of 12.8 percent in 1965 to 14.3 percent in 1967 to 20 percent in 1969. The Socialists and Communists also made steady gains throughout the period, increasing their combined share of the vote from 22.7 percent in 1965 to 28.1 percent in 1969.

A left-wing sector of the PDC withdrew from the party in May 1969 to form the Movement for Unitary Popular Action (MAPU), and called for unity of all working-class groups to achieve radical solutions to economic and social problems. Later in the year, MAPU joined the Popular

---

[3] For an analysis of these criticisms and their repercussions on party unity, see George Grayson, "Chile's Christian Democratic Party," and Sigmund, *Overthrow of Allende,* pp. 50–54.

[4] Barbara Stallings, *Class Conflict,* pp. 105, 110–13, 247, and Sigmund, *Overthrow of Allende,* pp. 63–70, 85–87. A critique of Frei's policies by the Christian Left is given in Gonzalo Arroyo, S.J. and Sergio Gomez, "Una etapa conflictiva de la reforma agraria," *Mensaje* 17 (October 1969): 475–81; Victor Arroyo B. et al., "¿Promoción o utilización popular?," *Mensaje* 17 (May 1969): 172–74.

Unity coalition, formed by the Communist, Socialist, Radical, Social Democratic, and Independent Popular Action parties, which nominated Salvador Allende as the candidate of the united Left in the 1970 presidential campaign. The National Party, angered over the reform policies of the Frei Administration, refused to back Christian Democracy again and nominated its own candidate—former president Jorge Alessandri. The PDC, hoping to prevent further defections to the Left from the party, chose Radomiro Tomic, who was sympathetic to the view of leftist members of Christian Democracy.[5]

In a very close and hard-fought campaign, Salvador Allende emerged with a plurality of 36.2 percent of the vote in the September 4th election. Jorge Alessandri placed second with 34.9 percent, Radomiro Tomic third with 27.8 percent, while 1.1 percent of the ballots were blank or void. After considerable bargaining among parties, and an attempted provocation of a military coup through the assassination of the chief general of the army by rightist forces, on 24 October the Congress chose Salvador Allende as president.[6] He was sworn into office on 3 November, becoming the first Marxist to win executive power in a free election in the Western Hemisphere.

Throughout these six years of significant reforms amidst growing societal polarization, the official policy of the Church supported socioeconomic change within a constitutional framework. The bishops spoke in favor of democratic procedures and condemned violence. Unlike 1964

[5] The 1970 campaign platforms of Allende and Tomic were similar, both calling for acceleration of agrarian reform, more governmental control of foreign and domestic businesses, and complete nationalization of copper. They differed in degree and style, however, with Allende more vigorously attacking industrial and banking interests and denouncing the reformist policies of Frei. Alessandri, in contrast, offered no major structural proposals. He appealed to a return to social order and a strengthening of public authority, and emphasized nonconflictive methods for solving labor-management problems.

Summaries of the platforms of the respective candidates can be found in *Política y Espíritu*, no. 317 (August 1970), pp. 15–56. For a critical assessment of each, see Joan E. Garces, *1970: la pugna por la presidencia en Chile*, pp. 73–128. Descriptions of the tactics in the electoral campaign itself are summarized by Sigmund, *Overthrow of Allende*, pp. 92–106.

[6] The Chilean Constitution requires the Congress to select the president when no candidate receives an absolute majority at the polls. In Chile's multiparty competitive system, very seldom does any candidate achieve more than 40 percent of the vote, and the Congress traditionally has selected the person with a plurality of electoral support. After the September 1970 election in Chile, there was considerable domestic and foreign pressure on the Congress (including CIA intrigue) not to choose the Marxist candidate despite his plurality at the polls. After the Christian Democrats exacted from the Marxists a willingness to support a statute of democratic guarantees in the Constitution assuring the continuation of the multiparty system, continued freedoms in education, trade unions, and the media, and the independence of the armed forces from political control, they voted in favor of Allende in the Congress, thus assuring his victory. Sigmund, *Overthrow of Allende*, pp. 112–23.

they also maintained a neutral position in the presidential campaign. There were, however, some dramatic shifts in political preference among Catholics in both directions during this six-year period. As Table 6.1 indicates, Catholic support for Christian Democracy substantially declined in 1970, and Tomic gained the same support among nonpracticing Catholics as he did among those who attended Mass regularly. Moreover, Allende increased his base of support significantly among *all* types of Catholics, including the most devout. However, there was also a strong resurgence of Catholic support for the candidate of the Right, especially among those who practiced regularly.

There were similar changes in party alignment among Catholics in 1970 as compared to 1964. Support for the united Left increased significantly among the practicing, up 30 percent among those who attended Mass regularly. Both groups of practicing Catholics, however, reduced their backing for Christian Democracy by one-half or more, and nonpracticing Catholic preference for the PDC declined by about one-third. Moreover, the rightist parties nearly doubled their support among all types of Catholics while a plurality in every category indicated that they were undecided as to party preference. Although the official Church had not withdrawn its support for reform, nor shifted its implicit legitimation to the Right, a plurality of practicing Catholics chose the candidate and party which favored reversing the momentum of the Frei period.

Furthermore, this same correlation between intensity of religious practice and support for the Right held true regardless of differences in gender. In the August 1970 Hamuy survey of Greater Santiago, Alessandri enjoyed a plurality (averaging between 34 percent and 40 percent) among men and women who regularly or occasionally attended Mass. Intensity of religious practice was not correlated with either male or female support for Tomic, and even Allende equalled or surpassed Tomic in every category of Catholic males and females except regularly practicing women, where Tomic gained 29.3 percent and Allende 19.6 percent.[7]

In controlling for class, it is not surprising that workers (skilled, unskilled, independent, and domestic) were more favorable to Allende than middle-income (white collar employees and small business owners) and upper-income (professionals, managers, and large business owners) groups. What is again surprising, however, is that religious practice was a decisive factor helping Alessandri, *not* Tomic, in *every* social class.

---

[7] Only among nonpracticing men and women did Allende gain a plurality—38.8 percent and 30.8 percent respectively. Even among these men and women least exposed to the Church, however, Tomic and Alessandri together gained well *over* two-thirds support—indicating a continued lack of cohesive base for the Left among the least religious in Santiago in 1970.

Table 6.1
Candidate Choice and Religious Practice (Catholics)
Greater Santiago, 1964 and 1970

	Regularly practicing		Occasionally practicing		Nonpracticing	
	1964 (N = 235)	1970 (N = 171)	1964 (N = 337)	1970 (N = 246)	1964 (N = 361)	1970 (N = 119)
Allende	9.8%	22.2%	18.1%	30.5%	25.2%	35.3%
Durán	2.1	—	1.8	—	5.0	—
PDC (Frei '64, Tomic '70)	74.9	28.7	62.9	25.2	52.4	27.7
Alessandri	—	40.4	—	35.4	—	24.4
Undecided	13.2	8.7	17.2	8.9	17.4	12.6

SOURCE: Centro de Opinión Pública, Santiago, Chile.

Table 6.2
Party Preference and Religious Practice (Catholics)
Greater Santiago, 1964 and 1970

	Regularly Practicing		Occasionally Practicing		Nonpracticing	
	1964 (N = 235)	1970 (N = 171)	1964 (N = 337)	1970 (N = 246)	1964 (N = 361)	1970 (N = 119)
Communist, Socialist	6.8%	17.0%	11.3%	21.1%	16.6%	27.7%
Radical	6.4		4.2		11.9	
PDC	57.9	29.2	50.7	22.8	40.7	27.7
Conservative, Liberal (National)	7.7	12.9	4.2	11.4	3.3	7.6
Undecided	21.2	40.9	29.6	44.7	27.5	37.0

SOURCE: Centro de Opinión Pública, Santiago, Chile.

What Table 6.3 also illustrates is that significant support for the Right occurred among nonpracticing Catholics in Santiago of every social class, including nearly one-fifth of the workers. Even when non-Catholics are included and the total subsample of workers in the survey are examined (last column in the right, top section, in Table 6.3), Allende gained just over two-fifths support (43.9 percent) as opposed to a solid one-quarter for Alessandri (24.6 percent) and 23.4 percent for Tomic.

Thus, while religion was an important correlate of conservative political choice in Santiago in 1970, it was not the only variable accounting for support for Alessandri. Even among lower income sectors of the population with little or no contact with the Church, there was a lack of overwhelming identification with the Left as exists in other nominally Catholic countries with long-established Marxist parties.[8]

Hence, although Chilean religiopolitical relationships in 1964 paralleled Western European patterns, by 1970 the Chilean case was substantially different. Religion was no longer a significant factor enhancing the Christian Democratic electoral strength as it continues to be in Europe. Moreover, despite the appearance of a near total collapse in 1964, the Right recaptured substantial support (including that of practicing Catholics) by 1970. The Left, however, also made considerable inroads into the Catholic vote, notwithstanding strong fears of Marxism exhibited just six years before. Finally, overall Chilean working-class support in Santiago in 1970 (even that of blue-collar industrial workers) was not overwhelmingly behind the Left as it is in Western European multiparty democracies.

Most scholars of Chilean politics during this period have not alluded to such changes. In fact, they have assumed the opposite was true regarding the major points documented above.[9] When we examine more

---

[8] Elsewhere I have analyzed the political preferences of the *industrial workers alone* in this 1970 preelection survey by Hamuy, and have found patterns similar to those that characterize *all* the lower income sectors in the sample. Only 42 percent of the industrial workers in Santiago in 1970 favored Allende, and Alessandri enjoyed a solid 25 percent of their support. Brian H. Smith and José Luis Rodríguez, "Comparative Working-Class Political Behavior: Chile, France and Italy," p. 66.

[9] Much of the literature assumes that the close identification between practicing Catholics and Christian Democracy continued through the 1970 election. The works of Petras and Zeitlin, Mutchler, Torres, and Vanderschueren and Rojas all either explicitly or implicitly avow this position without, however, offering the results of survey data to verify their assumptions.

Petras and Zeitlin (on the basis of ecological analysis alone) have, in addition, argued that the great solidarity and cohesiveness in working-class support for the Left made Allende's victory in 1970 possible, but such was not the case. James Petras, "The Working Class and Chilean Socialism," pp. 240–47; Maurice Zeitlin and Petras, "The Working-Class Vote in Chile: Christian Democracy versus Marxism," pp. 16–29. Despite access to Hamuy's survey data, Stallings cites it selectively (leaving out nonworking women and undecideds) to justify the same conclusion. For a

Table 6.3

Candidate Preference and Religious Practice by Class (Types of Catholics compared to total sample) Greater Santiago, August 1970

		Catholics only (N = 533)			Total sample (N = 620)
		Regularly Practicing	Occasionally Practicing	Nonpracticing	
Working Class (skilled and unskilled manual laborers, independent workers, domestic service workers)	Allende	36.4 (12)	40.0 (32)	47.2 (17)	43.9 (75)
	Tomic	27.3 (9)	23.8 (19)	25.0 (9)	23.4 (40)
	Alessandri	27.3 (9)	30.0 (24)	19.4 (7)	24.6 (42)
	Undecided	9.1 (3)	6.3 (5)	8.4 (3)	8.1 (14)
		N = 33	N = 80	N = 36	N = 171
Middle Class (white collar employees, small business owners)	Allende	20.8 (20)	30.6 (33)	31.0 (18)	30.3 (92)
	Tomic	28.1 (27)	26.9 (29)	29.3 (17)	26.6 (81)
	Alessandri	41.7 (40)	30.6 (33)	25.9 (15)	31.9 (97)
	Undecided	9.4 (9)	12.0 (13)	13.8 (8)	11.2 (34)
		N = 96	N = 108	N = 58	N = 304
Upper Class (professionals, managers, large business owners)	Allende	12.2 (5)	17.0 (10)	21.7 (5)	20.0 (29)
	Tomic	31.7 (13)	24.1 (14)	30.4 (7)	25.5 (37)
	Alessandri	48.8 (20)	51.7 (30)	30.4 (7)	45.5 (66)
	Undecided	7.3 (3)	6.9 (4)	17.5 (4)	9.0 (13)
		N = 41	N = 58	N = 23	N = 145

SOURCE: Centro de Opinión Pública, Santiago, Chile.

carefully, however, the multilevelled interrelationships between religious and political dynamics in Chile after 1964, these results become more understandable and even predictable.

A new tone and emphasis in the articulation of the Church's norms, the emergence of greater ideological pluralism in Chilean Catholicism, the "fall-out" effect of too close a structural overlap between the Church and the PDC in the early 1960s, the lack of well-developed socialization mechanisms to generate lasting changes in Catholic attitudes, and the divisive impact of foreign Church linkages in the post-Vatican II era all contributed to a disintegration of Catholic reinforcement for Christian Democracy. Some Catholic support moved to the Left due to some new attitudes in the Church toward Marxism (both in Chile and at the international level) and to a corresponding openness to Catholicism by the Chilean Left. A plurality of practicing Catholics in 1970, however, backed Alessandri as being more viable than Tomic in stopping Allende. There was also a close fit between the values he espoused and the traditional religious orientation that still characterized large numbers of Catholics in the country.

DIFFUSE ARTICULATION OF CATHOLIC SOCIAL MORALITY
AND GREATER NORMATIVE PLURALISM IN CHURCH AND
SOCIETY

The major social pronouncements of the Chilean bishops in the late 1960s continued to support structural changes that promoted a redistribution of social and economic power in favor of the poor. In a major pastoral letter in 1968, the hierarchy reminded the country of some unresolved social problems—the lack of basic necessities for one-third of the populace and the overlooked needs of ethnic minorities, especially the Mapuche Indians. They also denounced specific abuses of economic power that hampered sustained development, such as the exodus of both capital and professionals from the country.[10] Episcopal statements in the months before the 1970 election stressed the need for more equitable sharing of housing, employment, food, and educational opportunities, reiterated continued Church support for agrarian reform, and

more nuanced and accurate view, see James W. Prothro and Patricio E. Chaparro, "Public Opinion and the Movement of the Chilean Government to the Left, 1952–1972," pp. 2–43.

For documentation on the contrasting cohesiveness of Western European working-class support for the Left, where two-thirds or more of the industrial workers in most countries have consistently voted for parties representing various shades of socialism for some time, see the works of Lipset and Rokkan, Hamilton, Rose and Linz.

[10] Episcopado Chileno, "Chile, voluntad de ser," pp. 190–97.

called for a sustained commitment by all Chileans to construct a more just society.[11]

The tone and emphasis in these documents, however, were quite different from those which characterized the two major episcopal letters in 1962. There was no attempt to link Catholic social norms with a reformist analysis as had been done earlier. The bishops rather stressed the Church's contribution to social solidarity and dialogue amidst unavoidable disruptions and conflicts associated with either type of progressive change, reformist or socialist. The bishops also criticized too narrow a focus on technical aspects of development to the detriment of public attention to the values of respect, tolerance, reconciliation, and cooperation.[12]

Not only did the new tone and emphasis in these statements reflect a certain distancing of the hierarchy from the reformist ideology and technocratic style of the PDC,[13] but it also reflected an attempt on the part of the bishops to play a new public role in society at large. As the country became more polarized, and as the popularity of Christian Democracy declined, the hierarchy shifted their position to one of reinforcement for basic democratic procedures. No longer were the bishops primarily concerned about providing legitimacy for reform, since significant structural change was well underway. Rather they placed their moral prestige behind traditional constitutional and electoral processes as the best way to resolve disagreements about the pace and content of change.

The most dramatic example of this new orientation was reflected in an episcopal statement in the wake of a show of force in October 1969 by military officers in Santiago concerned about both their deteriorating salaries and growing social unrest. The bishops denied the legitimacy of a military coup or terrorism, and warned that either would ultimately

[11] Comité Permanente del Episcopado de Chile, "Declaración episcopal sobre la situación actual del país," 12 December 1969, pp. 77–79; "Carta de Mons. José Manuel Santos, Presidente de la Conferencia Episcopal de Chile (CECH), a algunos dirigentes campesinos de Linares," Valdivia, 19 May 1970, in *Documentos del Episcopado: Chile, 1970–1973,* ed. Bishop Carlos Oviedo Cavada (Santiago: Ediciones Mundo, 1974), pp. 10–15; Bishop José Manuel Santos, Presidente de la CECH, "Chile exige el advenimiento de una sociedad más justa," Santiago, 4 September 1970, in ibid., pp. 26–28.

[12] Episcopado Chileno, "Chile, voluntad de ser," nos. 24–28, 37–39, pp. 193–94, and Santos, "Chile exige el advenimiento de una sociedad más justa," p. 27.

[13] During interviews with twenty-three Chilean bishops in 1968, Tom Sanders found that some felt that the Church had become too closely linked with the PDC. One bishop remarked that now " 'the problem is to get the Church detached from a reformist political movement' (obviously Christian Democracy)." Thomas G. Sanders "The Chilean Episcopate," p. 25. In my own interviews with all thirty bishops in 1975 I discovered a similar uneasiness among several with the heavy technical emphasis in their 1962 pastoral letters and such a close identification with the reformist ideology of the PDC.

lead to a "reign of terror" including "political recriminations, forced exiles, flagrant injustices, suppressing of a free press, denial of all possibility of self-defense . . . and executions."[14]

Concomitant with this growing episcopal concern with threats to constitutionalism and peace was the absence in their pronouncements of polemical warnings against leftist parties. The hierarchy did not reiterate condemnations of Marxism of the early 1960s. As the election approached, both the cardinal and the Episcopal Conference issued statements indicating that the Church favored no party or candidate, and that neither bishops, priests, nor deacons could serve any ideology or faction or become activists in any political movement. The cardinal's remarks, made in a television interview six weeks before election day, also stressed the fact that the Church wished to be a home for all Chileans regardless of political persuasion and thereby provide a needed source of unity for the country.[15] By the late 1960s, with the decline in electoral support for the PDC, steady gains by the Left, and the growing sympathy for more radical political solutions by some younger Catholics, the bishops realized that continual close identification of the Church with a staunch anti-Marxist position could be counterproductive—especially given the very real possibility of a leftist victory in 1970.[16]

Some semiofficial Church pronouncements went even further than those of the hierarchy, and even offered some positive support to the Left. The Jesuit monthly magazine, *Mensaje,* by 1967 began to criticize some of the policies of the Frei regime for not going far enough. Several articles also encouraged Christian-Marxist dialogue and cooperation and more radical identification by Christians with the poor, while others stressed the compatibility of religious faith with a revolutionary political commitment

---

[14] Comité Permanente del Episcopado de Chile, "Declaración episcopal sobre la situación actual del país," pp. 77–79.

[15] Cardinal Raúl Silva Henríquez, "Iglesia, sacerdocio y política," in *Documentos,* ed. Oviedo, pp. 23–25, and "Carta de Mons. José Manuel Santos," pp. 10–15.

[16] In the interviews which Tom Sanders conducted with Chilean bishops in 1968, there was evidence that a substantial number had modified their position on Marxism. Sanders asked twenty-one of them whether cooperation or participation in Marxist organizations by Chilean Catholics constituted a problem or was a legitimate expression of Christian political action. *Ten* of the bishops told Sanders they saw no difficulty, and they regarded such cooperation or participation as an acceptable conscientious act by Catholics. *Six* hedged their views, but were open to this phenomenon. Only *four* bishops were opposed, and the military vicar for the armed forces felt he should not express an opinion because of his position. According to Sanders, a reason for the tolerance was their recognition that some Catholics already participated in organizations of Marxist inspiration (unions or parties). Some of the younger bishops indicated that they shared Catholic students' aspirations for cooperation with Marxists. Sanders, "The Chilean Episcopate," pp. 17–18.

—including some aspects of Che Guevara's life and thought.[17]

This openness to the Left was met by corresponding normative overtures by some Chilean Marxists toward Catholics. At the Thirteenth Party Congress in 1965, Senator Luis Corvalán, secretary general of the Chilean Communist Party, spoke favorably of changes occurring within Catholicism, and reminded his comrades that there were in the party "more than just a few militants and . . . many sympathizers who profess religious faith." He also promised that "so long as the Church refrains from interfering in party politics," there would exist "mutually respectful relations between it and the revolutionary government of the future."[18]

The *Program of the Communist Party* drawn up at the Fourteenth Congress in 1969 also recognized a growing radicalization among some Christians and the contribution that some religious believers were making to leftist movements:

> Many believers draw inspiration for rejecting capitalism from their own personal religious sentiments or from the teachings of their churches. There are many among them who are sympathetic to the revolution, and there are also some who are joining its cause. To the extent that these people participate in the struggles of the people, they are seeking contact with popular organizations and with Communists. This experience constitutes the beginnings of dialogue, and also reveals to them the depth of the crisis in the existing regime. It promotes the radicalization of analysis and consciousness and furthers the possibility of enriching the revolutionary movement with new groups.[19]

This mutual openness between some official sectors of Catholicism and the Chilean Communist Party in the late 1960s, along with a neutral position by the hierarchy, was a dramatic change from the early 1960s when the Church leadership condemned Marxism and predicted "persecution, tears and bloodshed" for Catholics in the event of a Marxist victory. It also helped to reduce reluctance among some Catholics to vote for Allende in 1970.

In contrast, however, traditional conservative currents reemerged in the Church during the Frei years. A small but vocal group of upper-middle class Catholics, disgruntled with social and economic changes undermining their influence both in Church and society, founded the Society for the Defense of Tradition, Family and Property (TFP) in the

[17] Manuel Ossa, S.J., "Cristianos y marxistas marchan juntos," *Mensaje* 16 (August 1967): 368–70; Arturo Gaete, S.J., "El largo camino del diálogo cristiano-marxista," pp. 209–19; Gonzalo Arroyo, S.J., "Las 'comunidades rebeldes,' " *Mensaje* 17 (July 1968): 275–80; "El 'Che': reflexiones sobre un diario," *Mensaje* 17 (August 1968): 333–38; and Pablo Fontaine, SS. CC., "El revolucionario cristiano y la fe," pp. 165–72.

[18] Luis Corvalán, "Seguir avanzando con las masas," mimeographed, Informe Central al XIII Congreso del PC, 1965, p. 65.

[19] *Programa del Partido Comunista de Chile* (Santiago: XIV Congreso Nacional de Partido Comunista, 23–29 November 1969), pp. 57–58.

mid-1960s. This movement was the ideological successor to the small group of Catholic Integralists active in Chile in the 1930s and 1940s, and espoused positions associated with traditional Catholicism: authoritarianism, the sacredness of private property, and the necessity for a staunch rejection of all forms of dialogue and cooperation with Marxism. These positions coincided rather closely with the political platform proposed by Alessandri and, in fact, members of the TFP worked in his campaign, placing great emphasis on the dangers that would result from an Allende victory.[20]

Thus, as *Mensaje* provided normative legitimation for Catholics moving to the Left, TFP did the same for Catholic conservatives returning to the Right. Each appealed to Catholic values to justify their potential positions, and both provided moral justifications for abandoning reformism.

The decline of widespread public support for Christian Democracy by 1967 coincided with corresponding political polarization. By 1970 normative divergence reduced the unified moral reinforcement for Christian Democracy provided by the Church six years before, and, in the context of greater ideological pluralism in politics, opened up a trilogy of valid electoral options for Catholics.

STRUCTURAL SHRINKAGE AND FRAGMENTATION IN THE
CHURCH AND THE PDC

Ironically, the very factor that enabled the Church to place its institutional weight behind secular reforms in the early 1960s—the close overlap of religious roles and structures with those of the PDC—led to a dissipation of its institutional resources for influence in the late 1960s. Close structural ties to the PDC precipitated internal fragmentation and authority conflicts within the Church and reduced the consistency of its organizational reinforcement of secular reform programs.

Many Catholic laity active in Catholic Action or social projects sponsored by the Church prior to 1964 (peasant unions, educational programs for workers, housing cooperatives, neighborhood associations) left these organizations once Frei was elected and entered the Christian Democratic administration. Such programs had acted as training and recruiting grounds for Christian Democracy, and they collapsed (or were

[20] The best original source of documentation on the TFP and its ideology can be found in its monthly tabloid, *Fiducia,* which originated in Santiago in 1963 and continued to be published throughout the 1960s. See especially: "Declaración frente a la reforma constitucional y la reforma agraria: en defensa del derecho de propiedad privada," *Fiducia* 3 (February-March 1965): 5–9; Jaime Guzmán E., "El diálogo, la socialización y la paz utilizados como slogans de la revolución," *Fiducia* 3 (May-June 1965): 10–11; Guzmán, "El capitalismo y los católicos de tercera posición," *Fiducia* 3 (October 1965): 4–5.

coopted by the party) after 1964.[21] Thus political concerns replaced religious interests among many students, workers, peasants, and former Catholic Action leaders.

Moreover, the government took over many of the social service functions formerly performed by the Church. It carried out these tasks more effectively and offered higher pay and better career opportunity for Catholic laymen than ecclesiastical organizations. Within a short period of time, therefore, the Church's social action projects begun in the early 1960s shrank dramatically or passed over into government hands, and the institutional support for reformism previously provided by the Church declined.[22]

Another negative consequence that resulted from close identification of religious and political structures was polarization inside Church programs coinciding closely with the splits in the PDC after 1967. As some sectors of the party moved to the Left politically their corresponding affiliates in the Church became more religiously radical. Others, however, withdrew from official Church programs as these became identified with political reformism and created their own conservative religious organizations.

Just as some within the PDC criticized its leadership for gradualism, too much control from the top, and reluctance to attack domestic and foreign capitalists, so also some young people still active in the Church began to find fault with it for similar reasons. In 1967 student leaders formerly active in University Catholic Action launched a campaign against the Catholic University system for what they considered to be its authoritarian structures, its dearth of courses on socioeconomic change, and its classist patterns of student recruitment.[23] Other young Catholics

---

[21] The network of Popular Promotion in urban shantytowns designed and implemented by Roger Vekemans, S.J., of Centro Bellarmino was closely tied to the PDC by the Frei Administration. For an analysis of how this was done, and the conflicts that emerged in both the Church and the Congress over this event, see José Luis Rodríguez, "The 'Poblador' in Chilean Society" (Senior thesis, Lehman College, 1971).

[22] Complaints against the PDC for "draining" Catholics away from Church-sponsored projects after 1964 was a recurring theme empahsized by clerical and religious elites in my interviews in 1975. Several bishops expressed the belief that the Church had made a strategic error in the early 1960s by placing such a great emphasis on constructing a network of social action programs. While admitting that such efforts had strengthened the outreach of the Church for a short period of time, these bishops also recognized that such a tactic led to a neglect of religious programs and a serious loss of committed personnel once these lay leaders were absorbed into the party or the Frei Administration.

[23] In August 1967, students seized various buildings of the Catholic University in Santiago. They demanded major structural reforms in the institution, including student and faculty participation in the selection of the rector and heads of faculties, more scholarships for working-class students, and a greater variety of courses related to social and economic development. After a week of negotiations between them and

publicly criticized a lack of sufficient lay participation in ecclesiastical decision-making, and the Church's failure to make a radical commitment to the poor.[24]

In addition, between 1967 and 1969, twelve of the twenty-three dioceses in the country held synods, where elected representatives of clergy, religious, and laity discussed how to implement the directives of the Second Vatican Council at the local level. These popular assemblies also brought out substantial criticisms from the base (especially from working-class groups) that the Church was authoritarian and predominantly oriented to the middle and upper classes in its ministries.[25]

Many members of all these groups formerly had been active in the Church or in the PDC. Their disenchantment with the party coincided with a growing alienation from the institutional Church as well. Many ceased formally practicing their faith, and some joined new political movements on the Left such as MAPU.

There were others who moved to the Right religiously. Many youths from the upper and middle classes who had been active in the Church's programs of the early 1960s, and who had supported Frei primarily as the most effective alternative to Marxism, later became disillusioned both with Christian Democracy and the religious ideas supporting it. In the late 1960s these groups formed new Catholic organizations, such as the Gremialist Movement among university students and Opus Dei among professional and business sectors. The theological and religious tastes of these new structures were elitist and traditionalistic.[26] Although

academic and ecclesiastical authorities, the cardinal gave assurances that changes would be made and the university reopened. Similar occurrences developed in the branch of the Catholic University in Valparaíso where student demands were also met. Sanders, *Catholic Innovation in a Changing Latin America*, pp. 4/19–4/37; Erica Vexler, "El mañana reclama hoy," *Ercilla* (Santiago), no. 1681 (23 August 1967), pp. 2–5 (edición especial).

[24] In August 1968, 200 people (including six priests) seized the cathedral of Santiago for one day to dramatize their frustration with the slowness of the institutional bureaucracy of the Church to adopt internal reforms and orient more of its pastoral energies toward the poor. Many of them were active in social and religious programs in working-class areas of Santiago. This group became the nucleus of a new movement, called the Young Church, and for the next two years formed small cells for reflection and action among workers and students so as to identify the Church more closely with the struggles of the lower classes. Iglesia Joven, *Documentos: Movimiento Iglesia Joven, 11 Agosto 1968–11 Agosto 1969.*

[25] Sínodo Pastoral, *Iglesia de Santiago: ¿Qué dices de tí misma?;* VI Sínodo Concepción-Arauco, "Proposiciones recopiladas," mimeographed Arzobispado de Concepción, (September 1968); Diócesis de Talca, *Sínodo pastoral: documentos básicos* (Talca: Escuela Tipográfica Salesiana, 1969); Diócesis de Temuco, "Sínodo pastoral de Temuco: acuerdos," mimeographed (Temuco, 1968).

[26] The Gremialist Movement was an attempt after 1967 by conservative professors and students at the Catholic University of Santiago to offset the influence there of the PDC and leftist Catholics. It purportedly was aimed at depoliticizing the univer-

claiming to be nonpartisan, they clearly reflected upper-class interests and espoused a restoration of the pre-Frei status quo in society. While not formally withdrawing from the Church neither were they officially endorsed by the Chilean bishops. Many of them closely identified with the reactionary political position of TFP, and actively supported Alessandri in 1970 as a means of promoting order and respect for private property.

The ecclesiastical polarization precipitated some serious crises of authority. Students and clerics active in the Catholic University reform movement and in the Young Church clashed with the hierarchy over the extent to which democratization should be introduced into the Church and over traditional Catholic teachings on clerical celibacy and birth control.[27] Those in TFP, on the other hand, openly criticized the Church's official support for agrarian reform, and argued publicly that Catholics did not have to obey episcopal pronouncements on this issue.[28]

The hierarchy reacted predictably to all these criticisms which they considered a direct threat to ecclesiastical authority and tradition. In 1968 the bishops criticized tendencies that they considered to be extremist on both the Left and the Right. While agreeing that the Church should be very concerned with the poor, they stated that they would not allow "those who aren't poor or young to become alienated from the Church" since it is open to all. They also emphasized that "a Church separated from its legitimate pastors . . . 'agitated by whirlwinds of doc-

---

sity and called for noninterference by parties in academia. It also espoused a corporatist plan for society whereby political parties would be replaced by vertically orchestrated guilds (*gremios*) which would promote the interests of all occupational groups in such a way as to further the common good as defined by the state. Its social theory was very similar to that espoused by Chilean Catholic Integralists of the 1930s and 1940s, described in Chapters 3 and 4. In fact, Jaime Guzmán, a founder of the Gremialist Movement, was a disciple of Jaime Eyzaguírre, professor of history at the Catholic University and intellectual leader of Chilean Catholic Integralism in the previous generation. Opus Dei is a Catholic apostolic movement that began in 1928 in Spain and spread to various parts of the Catholic world in the post-World War II era. Its purpose is to train cadres of Catholic professionals and technocrats to infiltrate secular institutions and influence them from a traditional Catholic perspective. It is geared to upper-middle class educated Catholics, is authoritarian and male-dominated, highly secretive, and a staunch defender of corporatist values. Norman B. Cooper, *Catholicism and the Franco Regime*, pp. 20–28. Both of these organizations later came to wield significant influence in education and government in Chile after the military coup of 1973.

[27] The reform movement in the Catholic University of Santiago demanded the removal of the conservative rector of the university, Bishop Alfredo Silva Santiago, thus angering some members of the hierarchy as an affront to episcopal authority. The Young Church argued publicly that hierarchical control of the Church by bishops was an outmoded concept. The movement also rejected celibacy for priests and the Church's teaching against artificial methods of birth control.

[28] Patricio Larraín Bustamante, "¿Es lícito a los católicos discordar del proyecto de reforma agraria del Presidente Frei?," *Fiducia* 4 (February-March, 1966): 8.

trines' " is not the Church of Christ. They claimed that they disagreed with some positions defended by students at the Catholic University, as well as "certain articles published in *Mensaje.*" They equally disapproved of "positions taken on the other side of the spectrum" by those who "wrap themselves in the mantle of the Church" while launching "insidious attacks and calumnies against their pastors."[29]

Although no schisms occurred, drainage of personnel, collapse of programs, internal divisions, and crises of authority all seriously weakened the Church's structural capacity to reinforce secular reform movements with the same force as in the early 1960s.[30]

PERSISTENCE OF TRADITIONAL RELIGIOUS ATTITUDES AND
DECLINE OF CRISIS SUPPORT FOR THE CHURCH AND THE PDC

After the collapse of many Church-sponsored social action projects the bishops inaugurated a program of pastoral innovation at the subparochial level as a more effective means of religious evangelization. In 1968 and 1969 they authorized the formation of small base communities in neighborhoods which were to train new cadres of laity as catechists, Bible teachers, and leaders of prayer and nonsacramental worship. Social action was to be included as one aspect of these small, homogeneous units but as an outgrowth, not in place, of spiritual re-

[29] "Declaración de la Conferencia Episcopal al término de su reunión plenaria del 4 del octubre de 1968," mimeographed (Santiago 1968). This statement was never printed in *Mensaje.* In fact, in an editorial in October 1968, the editors made it clear that they did not consider their publication to be an official organ of the Church, but rather an expression of one strand of Catholic opinion: ". . . We have never been, nor do we now pretend to be, an official voice of the Church. . . . We are a small group of Jesuits in close collaboration with some lay persons who together scrutinize the 'signs of the times.' " "Un cumpleaños más," *Mensaje* 17 (October 1968): 466–67. As we shall see in Chapter IX, the editorial board of *Mensaje* changed its position after 1973 when a military government strictly censored all publications except those officially sponsored by the Church.

[30] The only other contemporary Latin American Church closely comparable to Chile in this regard was Brazil. There, emerging progressive Catholicism in the early 1960s fragmented into reformists and radicals when Christian-Marxist cooperation developed. Conservative and wealthy Brazilian Catholics also became staunch critics of both religious change and the reformist policies of the Goulart government. There never was a strong DC party in Brazil to reflect these divisions politically, however, and, in addition, the military coup of 1964 terminated such controversies before they reached the level of religiopolitical tension that characterized Chile in the late 1960s. Emanuel de Kadt, *Catholic Radicals in Brazil,* pp. 102–78. In Western Europe there also were divisions in the Church along progressive-radical-conservative lines after Vatican II, and some ideological splits within DC parties themselves. Long entrenched Christian-Marxist antagonisms, the lingering impact of Stalinism and the Cold War, and the lack of viability of rightist parties in most of these countries kept such controversies, however, from causing significant drainage of Catholic support from Christian Democracy as occurred in Chile.

sponsibilities.[31] These innovations required time and adequately trained personnel to implement, however. By 1970 the majority of Catholics in all social classes still had no regular contacts with the Church, nor systematic exposure to its new social teachings. They continued to express their faith very traditionally and privately—prayer and devotions in the home, occasional participation in processions and pilgrimages in honor of the saints, and attendance at Mass on major feasts.[32]

Survey data on Catholic attitudes in 1971 in Santiago indicated that large numbers of Catholics still preferred a strictly spiritual emphasis in their faith.[33] When respondents were asked to select definitions of the essence of religion (with multiple responses permitted from a selection of categories), four-fifths (80.7 percent) of those who said they attended Mass regularly, and nearly three-fourths (73.6 percent) of the occasional participants, chose strictly spiritual or privatistic answers—it is faith in God; it is a discipline for the passions; it is a solace in difficult moments. Only one in ten practicing Catholics (11.1 percent of the regulars and 12.2 percent of the occasionals) included service to one's neighbor as part of religious responsibilities, and only 6.7 percent of the nonpracticing did so.[34] The social emphases that characterized official Church statements throughout the 1960s had not by 1971 been accepted by the vast number of Catholics as integral parts of religious commitment.

Respondents were also asked to describe the nature of the Church. A plurality of over 40 percent of the regular and occasional observers selected (from a list of prepared categories) institutional or spiritual definitions—the Church is a religious organization made up of priests and faithful; it is the house of God wherein prayer and celebration of the sacraments takes place; it imparts religious salvation. Very few Chilean

[31] Conferencia Episcopal de Chile, *Orientaciones pastorales I* (Santiago: Imprenta Alfonsiana, 1968); *Orientaciones pastorales II* (Santiago: Tipografía San Pablo, 1969).

[32] A survey of Catholics done in 1967 by Centro Bellarmino in conjunction with a marketing research firm in two major urban areas of the country revealed very weak exposure to religious communications media and low rates of participation in Church organizations. Fifty-seven percent of the 842 persons interviewed in Santiago, and 54 percent of the 480 polled in Concepción, said they never, or only rarely, read books or journals of Catholic opinion. Fifty-one percent in Santiago, and 56 percent in Concepción, also indicated that they never, or only rarely, listened to Catholic programs on radio and television. Ninety-one percent in Santiago, and 92 percent in Concepción, did not participate in any Catholic organization or movement. *Estudio de opinión pública sobre la iglesia: Santiago y Concepción*, pp. 139, 141, 146.

[33] One year after the survey taken by Centro de Opinión Pública in Greater Santiago in August 1970, a team of sociologists at Centro Bellarmino used the same sample of respondents to examine religious attitudes. Although the questions were asked in 1971, it is highly unlikely that attitudes would have changed significantly in twelve months, given the long-standing patterns of Chilean religious behavior documented in earlier chapters.

[34] In controlling for class, no significant differences occur. Four-fifths of regular practicing Catholics from every class chose strictly spiritual definitions of religion.

Catholics (10.5 percent of the regulars, 6.1 percent of the occasionals, and 3.4 percent of the nonpracticing) identified with the communitarian categories emphasized in the new pronouncements of Vatican II or in the guidelines of the Chilean hierarchy in the late 1960s. What is more, a sizeable proportion of all types (14 to 18 percent) viewed the Church primarily as a "refuge and solace in difficult moments" or as an "opiate for troubles."[35]

A final empirical verification of this chasm between official Church teaching and attitudinal patterns of Chilean Catholics at the time of Allende's election is seen in response to a question in the same 1971 survey regarding the type of sermon Catholics preferred. Two-thirds of those who said they went to Mass regularly wanted the priest to speak *only* about the life of Jesus and the necessity of Christian love and *never* to speak or issues relating to poverty, injustice, or the necessity to participate in efforts to change social and political structures. Ironically, the ones with fewer contacts with the Church's preaching—those who went to Mass occasionally, rarely or not at all—wanted stronger prophetic words by priests against injustice and poverty or for revolutionary action by Christians.[36]

In the context of the presidential campaign of 1970, these traditional religious attitudes and preferences of most Catholics coincided closely with the image and style of Alessandri. Both Allende and Tomic stressed the necessity of continued societal reforms and the importance of moving beyond the accomplishments of Frei. Alessandri, however, placed greater emphasis on moral virtues of integrity and honesty as a solution to social evils, and he also espoused an end to social disruption and a return to law and order.[37] His appeal was more personalistic than programmatic, and this resonated with the spirituality of most Chilean Catholics in 1970 which tended to be very privatistic and disassociated

[35] Again class differences were not very significant in accounting for variations in responses. A plurality in every class gave institutional and spiritual-oriented answers. Slightly more in the lower income bracket (18.2 percent) identified with the new communitarian emphases than those in the upper bracket (14.6 percent), but these were still a small minority of workers. What is very striking is the fact that more Catholics in *every* category of practice and social class preferred the definition of the Church as an *escape* from the world to the one emphasizing community dimensions and personal commitment. Furthermore, over 30 percent of the practicing Catholics (regular and occasional) and over 50 percent of the nonpracticing remained undecided as to what constituted the nature of the Church.

[36] Once more, class was not a determining factor in discriminating among the responses. Approximately two-thirds of all those in every group who regularly attended Church (63.6 percent in the working class, 65.6 percent in the middle class, and 63.4 percent in the upper class) all preferred sermons that *excluded* references to poverty, injustice, or the necessity to make radical change in societal structures.

[37] Michael J. Francis, *The Allende Victory: An Analysis of the 1970 Chilean Presidential Election*, pp. 33–38, 53.

Table 6.4
What Type of Sermon Do You Prefer? (Catholics)
Greater Santiago, August 1971
(N = 536)

	Regularly Practicing (N = 171)	Occasionally Practicing (N = 246)	Nonpracticing (N = 119)	Total (N = 536)
A priest who preaches against injustice and poverty	30.4% (52)	50.4% (124)	37.8% (45)	41.2% (221)
A priest who goes further and says Christians must make the revolution come about	4.1 (9)	2.8 (7)	26.9 (32)	8.6 (46)
A priest who *never* preaches about these themes and who speaks only on love of neighbor and the life of Jesus	64.3 (110)	45.1 (111)	23.5 (28)	46.5 (249)
Undecided	1.2 (2)	1.7 (4)	11.8 (14)	3.7 (20)

SOURCES: Centro de Opinión Pública, and Centro Bellarmino, Santiago, Chile.

with an active or structural approach to achieving either social justice or religious salvation.

Moreover, this data tends to confirm that many Catholics in the middle and upper classes voted for Frei in 1964 as the only way of stopping Marxism (as discussed in Chapter 5) rather than as a result of a deep and lasting change in attitudes. Once disruption and polarization occurred in the late 1960s amidst the process of social tansformation, their political tactics shifted. The Christian Democratic platform was much further to the Left in 1970 than in 1964, and Tomic endorsed radical structural changes rather close to those espoused by Allende. In such a context, the best alternative for blocking or slowing down the pace of change and for stopping Marxism was to support the candidate of the Right, not the Center. For Catholics who feared Marxism, opposed radical change, and had very privatistic or otherworldly views about the purpose of religion, Alessandri was the more appealing presidential candidate.[38]

[38] The Chilean political context in 1970 differed significantly from the Western European situation in two important ways. First, the DC platform had in a short span of time moved much further to the Left and was very close to the position espoused by the Marxist candidate. Secondly, the Right had reemerged with consid-

Although traditional religious piety may have contributed to some working-class support for the Right, other more critical factors limited Allende's appeal among the Santiago poor. As seen earlier in this Chapter (Table 6.3), one quarter (24.6 percent) of the low-income sectors in Hamuy's 1970 preelection survey chose Alessandri and a little over two-fifths (43.9 percent) backed Allende.[39] Due to a restrictive Labor Code in existence since 1924 forbidding unions in factories with less than twenty-five workers, only 20 percent of Chilean industrial workers were unionized in 1970. The majority of blue-collar laborers were not unionized since over one-half worked in small family-owned factories of ten or less hired hands under the close supervision of owners or managers. Even among the minority of industrial workers who were organized throughout the 1960s, the PDC was becoming more active and challenging some of the Left's traditional overwhelming strength.[40]

Furthermore, urban industrial workers (unionized and nonunionized) in 1970 constituted less than 25 percent of the economically active population (EAP) due to late industrialization (begun during the Depression) and the importation of capital-intensive technology after 1950. A significant and growing proportion of the urban poor in Chile (about 12 percent in 1970) were engaged in independent work (artisans, street vendors, etc.) and personal services.[41] They were not unionized and spent a great deal of their work time in close contact with, or under the supervision of, middle and upper-income clients or employers. The leftist parties previous to Allende's election had not constructed an organizational base among these low-income sectors (social or political), and thus had not monopolized their electoral support.[42]

---

erable respectability and vitality, and was considered by many as having a greater chance to defeat the Marxist candidate than the Christian Democratic choice. In such a context, many Chilean middle and upper-class Catholics (unlike most of their European counterparts) backed the conservative aspirant to the presidency so as to protect their social and economic interests.

[39] This significant support for Alessandri among workers in Hamuy's August 1970 survey is also verified by other opinion data as well. In a random sample of 1,000 adult residents of Santiago in July 1970 taken by the marketing research firm of Salas-Reyes, Ltd., 28.5 percent of workers chose Allessandri, 40.5 percent Allende and 29 percent Tomic, with 2 percent undecided. Smith and Rodríguez, "Comparative Working-Class Political Behavior," p. 66.

[40] Ibid., pp. 78–79, and Alan Angell, *Politics and the Labour Movement*, pp. 42–56.

[41] Between 1960 and 1970 the percentage of the labor force that was self-employed or in personal services increased by 38 percent, whereas the industrial work force grew by only 4 percent. Oficina de Planificación Nacional, *Plan de Economía Nacional, 1971–1976* (Santiago: ODEPLAN, 1971), p. 68.

[42] The only areas of Chile where a proletarian subcultural environment developed which was penetrated by effective Marxist social and political organizations was in the nitrate, coal, and copper mining zones (where about 2 percent of the EAP resides). Even among peasants (who constitute approximately 25 percent of the EAP) the Left has not had widespread support, due to the long-standing influence of large

Personalistic and patronal values have traditionally been very salient among the poor in Santiago and have enhanced the appeal of popular centrist (Frei) and even conservative (Ibañez, Alessandri) candidates among them despite their own economic deprivation. They thus resemble the "Tory," or deferential, workers of England much more than the strongly class-conscious leftist workers of France and Italy in electoral behavior.[43] The Hamuy 1970 preelection survey in Santiago and the one during the 1964 campaign described in Chapter 5 both illustrated a lack of overwhelming support for the Left by the poor in Santiago throughout the 1960s.

Hence, lingering traditional religious attitudes, the perdurance of class interests over religious ideals, and the evaporation of crisis support for the Church and Christian Democracy as the best way to stop Allende, all combined to provide significant Catholic support for the Right in 1970 among the middle and upper classes. While some of these factors contributed to cleavages in the working-class vote as well, far more salient in limiting Allende's base of support among poor Catholics in Santiago was the lack of deep organizational penetration by Marxists of working-class culture in the capital prior to 1970.

DIVISIVE IMPACT OF INTERNATIONAL CHURCH INFLUENCES

In the early 1960s international linkages consistently reinforced progressive changes in the Chilean Church. In the latter part of the decade, however, multiple dynamics in the universal Church stimulated very diverse responses in Chile, and aggravated already growing polarization and authority conflicts.

---

landholders, the absence of legally recognized unions until 1967, and the inroads made by the PDC in the 1960s resulting from the creation of their own labor organizations and farm cooperatives during Frei's land reform program. More extensive treatment of perduring cleavages in Chilean working-class political behavior, as compared to the cohesive working-class support for the Left in most of Western Europe, can be found in Smith and Rodríguez, "Comparative Working-Class Political Behavior," pp. 70–81.

[43] For an analysis of the cleavages in the British working-class vote and the factors accounting for support for the Conservative Party by some manual workers with deferential attitudes, see Robert McKenzie and Allan Silver, *Angels in Marble: Working-Class Conservatives in Urban England;* Eric A. Nordlinger, *The Working-Class Tories: Authority, Deference and Stable Democracy.* Further empirical evidence as to the attraction of Alessandri among the Chilean poor in Santiago in 1970 is presented in the Salas-Reyes, Ltd. survey. In this poll, among those in the lower-income sectors who preferred Alessandri, a large plurality of 39 percent gave very personalistic and patronal, as opposed to class-conscious, reasons for their choice—he was an honest man and independent; he possessed great integrity of character; he was the most experienced candidate; he was likable; he would restore order, security, and tranquility. Smith and Rodríguez, "Comparative Working-Class Political Behavior," p. 91.

One of the most significant changes in Catholicism resulting from the papacy of John XXIII (1958–1963) and the deliberations of Vatican II was a greater tolerance for secular currents of change, including those of explicitly atheistic origin. In *Pacem in Terris* (1963) Pope John recognized that historical movements which philosophically were opposed to religious faith could be carriers of important truths. He also acknowledged that Christians could cooperate with those identified with such movements in order to achieve specific goals related to the common good.[44] Although he did not mention Marxism specifically, he clearly had this in mind, and he personally received Khrushchev's son-in-law cordially at the Vatican in 1963. He also approved the "opening to the Left" in Italian politics whereby the Socialist Party joined in a parliamentary coalition with the Christian Democrats in 1962.

In 1965 Vatican II reinforced this more open attitude toward atheists. These bishops from every corner of the globe officially admitted that some of the major criticisms of the Church by nonbelievers have been valid. They also acknowledged that some causes of atheism have been due to the Church's own failures and lack of credibility, especially regarding carrying out its social teachings.[45]

Pope Paul VI (1963–1978) continued this more tolerant attitude toward Marxism. He became the first pope to receive a Communist foreign minister—Andrei Gromyko in 1966. He also initiated a new Vatican policy of *Ostpolitik,* making diplomatic overtures to countries in the Soviet bloc in order to improve Vatican communications and influence with churches in Eastern Europe.[46] His most significant social encyclical, *Populorum Progressio* (1967), was much closer to socialist, rather than capitalist or corporatist, models of development in its analysis and prescription.[47]

In addition to these significant modifications of Vatican posture toward Marxism in the mid and late 1960s, the meeting of 150 Latin American bishops at Medllín, Colombia in 1968 signalled major social and religious shifts for all of Latin American Catholicism. The documents approved by these prelates representing every major country of South and Central America urged profound commitments to the poor

[44] Pope John XXIII, "Pacem in Terris," nos. 159–60, in *Gospel of Peace and Justice,* ed. Joseph Gremillion, pp. 235–36.

[45] "Pastoral Constitution on the Church in the Modern World," nos. 19–21, in *Documents of Vatican II,* ed. Walter M. Abbott, S.J., pp. 215–20.

[46] For a summary of these initiatives of Paul VI and their political and religious results, see John M. Kramer, "The Vatican's Ostpolitik," pp. 283–308.

[47] In the encyclical, Paul VI stated that "private property does not for anyone constitute an absolute and unconditional right." He also endorsed the expropriation of poorly used land for the common good, and called for greater centralized planning as a means for development. "Populorum Progressio," nos. 23, 24, 33, in *Gospel of Peace and Justice,* ed. Gremillion, pp. 394, 397.

by Catholics in the region. They also committed the institutional Church to an aggressive role in promoting structural change. Finally, they called for greater pastoral innovation in the evangelization efforts of the Church throughout the continent by the formation of small base communities and greater responsibilities for lay men and women.[48]

All of these major normative shifts to the Left in Catholicism at the international level had a considerable legitimizing impact on corresponding developments occurring within Chilean Catholicism. The Chilean bishops quoted extensively from *Populorum Progressio* in 1968, reiterating their staunch support for continued efforts to transform economic and social structures. The Medellín pronouncements also legitimized at a higher level their decision that same year to decentralize Church structures and incorporate lay people into decision-making positions.

Those clergy and laity calling for more radical approaches to reform than espoused by official sectors of the PDC (such as *Mensaje* and the group that formed MAPU) pointed to Vatican II and the statements of Popes John and Paul to justify their own sympathies with Marxist analysis and cooperation with leftist parties. Others who focused on specifically religious reforms (such as the Young Church) cited Medellín as a justification for demanding a more complete identification of the Church with the poor and more radical social commitments by Catholics than had occurred during Christian Democracy.

None of these major changes at other levels of the Church *caused* the greater tolerance for, or shift to, the Left by some sectors in Chilean Catholicism in the late 1960s. These were occurring in response to changes in the Chilean political system and in the local Church itself. There is no doubt, however, that, given the absolute legitimizing position of Rome and the teaching authority of the universal episcopacy, these developments at the international level of the Church further diminished the normative barriers to a leftist option among Catholics in Chile.

Other ideological developments in international Catholicism, however, were used by conservative elements in the Chilean Church to justify their own positions. Strong reactionary elements in the Brazilian Church in the early 1960s had mobilized considerable popular support against the policies of the Goulart government prior to the military coup in 1964. This movement, known as Tradition, Family and Property (TFP), established close linkages with the reactionary movement of the

---

[48] CELAM, "Justice," "Peace," "Pastoral Concern for the Elites," "Lay Movements," "Joint Pastoral Planning," in *The Church in the Present-Day Transformation of Latin America*, 2:55–82, 127–36, 163–70, 221–33.

same name formed in Chile at about the same time. In fact, *Fiducia,* the official publication of the TFP in Chile, drew upon the intellectual capital of its Brazilian counterpart, and from time to time reprinted articles originally published in Brazil vociferously attacking Marxism.[49] *Fiducia* also reproduced materials from reactionary Catholic circles in Argentina, another country where Integralist and neofascist movements have continued to wield important influence in the Church since the 1930s.[50]

Transnational ideological linkages not only bolstered the moral legitimacy of leftist elements in the Chilean Church during the late 1960s, but also shored up the diminishing influence in Church and society of reactionary forces. The post-Vatican II period did not automatically usher in an era of universally accepted progressivism throughout the Catholic Church. Rather, the growth of religious and moral diversity in matters not essential to core doctrines was the most immediate normative impact of the Council. The transnational linkages of the Church were used to transmit various, and sometimes contradictory, messages in the years succeeding the closing of the Council in 1965. Once pluralism was given official legitimation at the highest level of the Church, the traditional Catholic Right as well as the newly-emerging Left in the Church could use currents in international Catholicism to bolster their respective local positions.[51]

Structural linkages with international organizations also aggravated internal weaknesses and divisions within the Chilean Church and limited its autonomy. In the post-Vatican II years in Europe and North America there was a significant exodus from the priesthood and a re-

[49] Plinio Correa de Oliveira, "La libertad de la iglesia en el estado comunista," *Fiducia* 2 (June-July 1964): 5–17. A prominent Catholic lawyer active in TFP in Brazil wrote a book in 1967 severely attacking Eduardo Frei for having directly paved the way for a communist takeover in Chile. This book, published in Spanish by a reactionary Catholic press in Argentina, was given wide circulation by the TFP in Chile. Fabio Vidigal Xavier da Silveira, *Frei, el Kerensky chileno* (Buenos Aires: Ediciones Cruzada, 1967). For an analysis of the linkages between reactionary Catholic movements in Brazil, Argentina and Chile, see "Como opera el integrismo católico fascista contra la iglesia católica en Chile: el rol de Fiducia," *Chile-América* (Rome), no. 16–17–18 (March-April-May 1976), pp. 121–28.

[50] P. Julio Meinville, "El pensamiento del P. Teilhard de Chardin," *Fiducia* 2 (November 1964): 10–11. For a summary of the religious and cultural factors related to the origins and perdurance of Catholic Integralism in Argentina, see Frederick B. Pike, "South America's Multi-faceted Catholicism," pp. 54–60.

[51] Conservative, reactionary, progressive, and radical Catholic currents continued to coexist side by side in many Western countries other than Latin America since the close of the Vatican Council in 1965. These have diverged on social and political issues as well as on matters relating to religious doctrine and discipline, such as papal infallibility, liturgical reform, birth control, clerical celibacy, and exclusion of women from the priesthood. For a description and analysis of these post-Vatican II controversies, see Peter Hebblethwaite, *Runaway Church.*

duction of new clerical and religious vocations, which resulted in a sharp decline in missionaries going to third-world countries. In the late 1960s the number of foreign priests in Chile levelled off and local vocations to the priestly and religious life declined significantly.[52] While this factor led to efforts by bishops to attract laity into leadership positions, in the short term while nonclerical personnel were being recruited and trained the Chilean Church suffered a serious staffing problem. This further limited its capacities to institutionalize religious change and commitments to the poor, begun in large part by the influx of foreign clergy in the early 1960s.

Furthermore, although the flow of foreign money and material into the Chilean Church continued to be substantial during this period (see Table 2.9), some very serious tensions emerged. Religious service organizations in the 1960s provided an efficient delivery system to channel foreign aid to the Chilean poor. This gave the Chilean Church, however, an image of paternalism and political power that angered some religious and secular leaders.

At the Diocesan Synod of Santiago in late 1967 and early 1968 (attended by nearly 500 clerical, religious, and lay representatives) working-class delegates seriously criticized the bureaucratic style of Cáritas-Chile, the Chilean Church-sponsored organization which distributed large amounts of food, clothing, and medicines channeled into the country by international Catholic agencies (especially Catholic Relief Services of the United States). The final documents of the Synod approved by an overwhelming majority of participants reflected these judgments, and observed that Cáritas had created a "powerful and paternalistic image for the Church" and had contributed to "receptive attitudes toward charity among the poor," thus promoting among them a "sense of irresponsibility" that undermined "human dignity."[53]

Others outside the Church also began to criticize severely its financial ties with foreign governments or Church groups favorable to Frei's reforms. A reporter for the Communist daily newspaper, El Siglo, published a book in 1968 arguing that the Church in Chile had been a major conduit of foreign governmental and ecclesiastical money in the mid-1960s (especially from Germany and the United States), given specifically to enhance Christian Democracy and halt the spread of Marxism. Some of the data presented in this book linked several social action programs sponsored by the Chilean Church with CIA money, and also attacked Belgian Jesuit, Roger Vekemans, of Centro Bellarmino, for act-

[52] Renato Poblete, *Crisis sacerdotal.*
[53] Sínodo Pastoral, *Iglesia de Santiago,* 2:59.

ing as an important facilitator in obtaining such funds.[54] Whether such accusations were in fact true, it is certain that heavy foreign subsidies by both governments and Churches in Western Europe favorable to Christian Democracy by the late 1960s had damaged the credibility of the Chilean Church in sectors of the population with leftist sympathies.

Moreover, by the late 1960s there was evidence that some foreign donors used their money as a leverage against leftist Christians in Chile. The most notable example of this occurred in an internal struggle for control between Christians with Marxist sympathies and those committed to reformist approaches in ILADES—a Jesuit-sponsored graduate institute for research and education on development problems and Catholic social doctrine. When professors and students committed to giving Marxist concepts of social analysis a dominant place in the curriculum became a majority in ILADES, others who preferred a concentration on traditional social teachings of the Church complained to the cardinal and to Adveniat, the German Catholic foundation supporting ILADES, which also was unsympathetic to Marxism. Upon learning of Cardinal Silva's unwillingness to continue to act as a sponsor for ILADES given its change in orientation, Adveniat indicated funds would be curtailed. This strengthened the hand of the moderates and the more radical groups had to resign.[55]

Regardless of the internal merits of the arguments on both sides of this dispute, what is clear is that internal conflicts in Chilean Church programs were exacerbated by financial dependency on foreign donors who had their own agendas and used influence to pursue them. Such disputes were not resolved on the basis of local authority configurations, and the capacity for Chilean Church projects to decide autonomously their own goals was significantly diminished.[56]

---

[54] Eduardo Labarca Goddard, *Chile invadido: reportaje a la intromisión extranjera,* pp. 64–67, 75–106, 161–65. David E. Mutchler argues the same position in his book, *The Church as a Political Factor in Latin America.* He is convinced that the C.I.A. was a major indirect source of funds flowing into some Chilean Church projects during the 1960s, especially through Belgian Jesuit Roger Vekemans. Both Goddard and Mutchler have been criticized for distorting evidence and selectively quoting confidential reports and files to which they had access. Until more thorough and substantial research is done on this issue of C.I.A. aid to the Chilean Church during these years, it remains an open question—although evidence indicates that there was a connection. Whether or not the C.I.A. gave Vekemans and others money in the Chilean Church, it is clear that the impact of foreign aid (both religious and secular) to the Chilean Church favored the Christian Democratic Party and hurt the Left. Such foreign linkages solidified the ideological ties between reformist Church programs and PDC structures, and in the early 1960s enabled clerical, religious, and lay personnel to inaugurate programs that opposed Marxism.

[55] Yves Vaillancourt, "La crisis de 'Ilades.' "

[56] In 1967 Ivan Illich made a similar critique of foreign Church support to the Latin American Church in general in "The Seamy Side of Charity."

Table 6.5
Image of the Chilean Church
Santiago and Concepción, 1967
(N = 1,322)

	Santiago (N = 842)	Concepción (N = 480)
Rich	49% (413)	52% (250)
Modest	34 (286)	32 (154)
Poor	11 (93)	12 (57)
Don't know, no answer	6 (50)	4 (19

SOURCE: Centro Bellarmino, *Estudio de opinión pública sobre la iglesia*, p. 62.

Perhaps a more serious problem precipitated by such dependency on foreign aid was the inability of Chilean bishops to convince middle and upper-income laity to support their own Church, given their traditional unwillingness to do so and the availability of ample foreign funds. Although the Chilean bishops embarked upon a program of self-financing for Church programs in the mid-1960s, the response to their appeals netted only $1.9 million between 1965 and 1970. The combined dollar equivalent of foreign Church support from Western Europe and North America during the same period totalled $35.8 million—approximately the same amount given between 1960 and 1964 (see Table 2.9).

In an opinion survey conducted in 1967 by Centro Bellarmino in the two largest urban areas of the country, Santiago and Concepción, only about one in ten respondents thought that the Chilean Church was poor. Approximately one-half of those polled (49 percent in Santiago, and 52 percent in Concepción) stated that the institution was actually rich.[57]

Heavy state subsidies to support Catholic education begun in the 1950s, substantial public support to maintain Catholic social action programs in the 1960s, and massive amounts of foreign aid throughout the decade all had combined to create the impression among many Chileans that their Church was not in need of money. Thus, there was no adequate motivation among Chilean Catholics—especially those financially capable—to respond to the hierarchy's appeal in the mid and late 1960s for support through voluntary tithing of family income.[58]

Such reluctance by wealthier lay people to give significant monetary

[57] Centro Bellarmino, *Estudio de opinión pública sobre la iglesia*, p. 62.
[58] In disaggregating the responses in Table 6.5 by social class, it is clear that those more capable of supporting the Church financially were the most inclined to view the Chilean Church as a rich institution. In Santiago, 50 percent of the upper class and 53 percent of the middle class considered the Church in Chile as well taken care of financially. In Concepción, 57 percent of the upper-income sectors and 55 percent of the middle groups looked upon the institution as wealthy. Ibid., p. 63.

support to ecclesiastical projects aimed at promoting religious and social change further diminished the institution's capacity to make a lasting impact on their attitudes and behavior. This was an additional factor which helps explain both the decline of Catholic support for reformism and a considerable shift to the Right in 1970. Class and other contextual factors marginalized religious and ethical motivations among rank-and-file Catholics in the 1970 campaign who never had made a firm and visible commitment to their Church or its public programs. All of these international normative and structural impacts seriously weakened the Chilean Church's capacity to continue to act as a coherent force for political centrism as it had been in the early 1960s and to effect lasting mutations in Catholic attitudes.

FRAGMENTATION OF SOCIAL CATHOLICISM IN THE LATE 1960s

The conclusion implicit in the literature to date that practicing Catholics in Chile continued to provide strong electoral support for Christian Democracy in 1970 is wrong. Unlike 1964, Mass attendance was not correlated with preference for the Christian Democratic party or candidate. Some important shifts to the Left occurred in the Catholic vote, but traditional correlations between religious practice and conservative political choice reemerged among a plurality of churchgoers. These patterns again set Chile apart from other nominally Catholic countries in Western Europe with comparable religiopolitical configurations.

Furthermore, social scientists who have attributed Allende's victory in 1970 to a cohesive working-class base of support are also wrong. Unlike their counterparts in France and Italy, Chilean industrial workers in Santiago throughout the 1960s exhibited considerable diversity in electoral behavior. It is also clear that only 40 percent of the *whole* working class in Santiago (industrial, independent, personal, and domestic service workers) voted for the Left in 1970, and religion was only one, and not the most determinative, factor in accounting for rightist inroads into the potential base of support for Allende among the poor.

From the preceding analysis of the interactions between religious and secular dynamics during these years, such patterns are understandable. Normative consensus in both Church and society, which in 1964 had coincided to link Catholicism to a centrist reform ideology, broke apart by 1970. Officially articulated religious norms were much more diffuse and general in 1970, while widely diverging interpretations and applications of these norms were made by Catholic elites on the Right and the Left. In such a context, the legitimating power of the Church was not as consistent as in the pre-1964 period, and this also coincided with a reemergence of viability of multiple political ideologies in secular society.

Moreover, normative dialectics in the Church reflected very closely secular ideological debates in the late 1960s precisely because of the very close previous identification of religious structures with those of the PDC. As ideological and structural fragmentation of the party occurred, the same polarization developed within the Church and for similar reasons. Rightist and leftist Catholics became alienated from Christian Democracy, and as they withdrew support for the party their criticisms of the Church increased, thus precipitating serious authority conflicts across the layered administrative network of the institution. All of these splits, disruptions, and loss of personnel were part of the "fall-out" effect of too close a structural overlap between religious and reformist political programs of the early 1960s, and this seriously weakened the Church's institutional capacity to reinforce gradualist change in society.

At the behavioral level, crisis support for the Church and for Christian Democracy among Catholics of all social classes subsided after 1964. Fears of Marxism declined among some progressive Catholics in the lower and middle classes, and wealthier and more conservative Catholics found the rightist candidate and party a more viable political alternative than the PDC to defeat Allende and thus protect their economic interests in 1970. In the absence of such crisis support, very weak allegiances to the Church by rank-and-file Catholics prevented moderately progressive Church positions from mobilizing their support behind the reformist candidate as in 1964. Traditionalistic religious orientations reinforced class interests of Catholics in the middle and upper classes to produce significant support for the Right. Lack of well-developed progressive religious socialization processes, along with an absence of a network of union and leftist party structures, among workers led to considerable cleavages in the lower income electoral behavior as well—including some significant support for the Right.

Finally, the international Church was no longer providing consistent resources for reformist developments in Chile. As international Catholicism experienced disruptions, cleavages, and crises of authority in the immediate post-Vatican II period, these came to reinforce similar divisions emerging in Chilean Catholicism. In some instances these linkages provided important legitimacy for more leftist options among Catholics, while in others they enhanced the resurgence of reactionary forces in the Chilean Church. Dependency relationships also diminished the Church's credibility as well as autonomy to set its own agenda and resolve its problems independently.

Religiopolitical relationships in Chile thus led to a very different outcome in 1970 than in 1964. The major dynamics of each of the four major characteristics of the Church—articulation of norms, authority flows across a layered institutional chain of command, variegated membership patterns, and linkages with the international Church—all were characterized by greater pluralism, tension, and even contradiction. They did not act in concert with one another or with corresponding secular forces as had occurred in 1964. The result was a significant electoral disassociation by Catholics from Christian Democracy, some important gains by the Left among churchgoers, but a considerable resurgence of Catholic identification with the Right.

THE POSSIBILITY FOR RELIGIOUS REINFORCEMENT OF
POLITICAL AND ECONOMIC REFORMS (CHILE, 1935–1970)

After having analyzed the role of religion in Chile during three very distinctive time frames covering thirty-five years of recent history, we are in a position to give more complete answers to the series of questions raised at the beginning of Chapter 4 regarding the conditions under which religion can act as a positive force for political and economic reforms. The Chilean experiences also provide useful comparative insights as to the possibilities of Catholicism acting as a reinforcement for change in other societies as well.

The first set of questions relate to the causes of progressive shifts in religious values and the conditions under which they can contribute legitimation to secular development. The Chilean Church confirms the pattern that characterized Vatican II Catholicism (mentioned in Chapter 2)—namely, new official normative emphases emerged primarily as a defensive reaction to major external challenges, but they also have had resonance with some progressive but minority currents that have existed for some time within the institution itself.

The pronouncements of Vatican II were an attempt to recoup some of the loss of credibility the Church was experiencing in the modern world. They also were the culmination of some progressive movements in theology that had been developing among small elite groups in the Church over a thirty-year period. These needed, however, the proper socioreligious context to replace older theological positions as officially normative for the universal Church.

In Chile, the same socially progressive movements which finally led to Vatican II at the international level also were stirring during the 1930s. Given the configuration of religious and political forces in the country until the late 1950s, these never became dominant either in Church or society, and older, more conservative and corporatist social norms dominated episcopal statements. Once, however, the Church sensed a critical institutional threat to its interests from the Left after 1958 amidst a decline of conservative parties, the conditions were ripe for its articulation of reformist emphases.

Normative shifts in Chilean Catholicism also resonated with the ideology of a rapidly rising reformist movement in politics. There thus emerged a secular counterpart to the Church's new public messages. Such normative overlap provided the conditions for significant legitimation by religious symbols for economic and political change.

Neither in the pre-1958 period nor in the post-1964 periods in Chile did significant consensus for change exist in the Church that corresponded to a secular counterpart of similar consistency and content. Furthermore, in the first period (1935–1958), effective political movements that resonated with progressive social Catholicism had not yet been sufficiently developed. During the last period (1964–1970) these fragmented ideologically, precipitating corresponding value conflicts in the Church itself. In these two periods, therefore, religious norms could not perform the same unified public legitimating role that they played between 1958 and 1964.

Furthermore, during this middle period (1958–1964) there was strong public fear that the major competitor to the Church—Marxism—might gain political power in the wake of weakened political conservatism. Such fears provided a stimulus for apparent widespread acceptance of new Church positions favoring change and for a new Center party. In the other two time frames, such anxiety did not work to the advantage of reform-oriented forces, but instead acted as reinforcement for conservative religious and political groups alike who offered the most viable way for defeating Marxism.

In several other countries of Latin America during this thirty-five year period, currents of progressive Catholicism were not as strong or continuous, nor did they find expression in reform parties opposing a formidable Left in electoral politics. In Brazil, Argentina, Colombia, and Peru the social Catholicism that emerged in the 1930s was more conservative or even corporatist in style, and also never found resonance in viable Christian Democratic parties. Moreover, in each of these countries, the official Church had not yet severed ties with its traditional conservative allies, nor has Marxism ever been a serious contender for power in electoral politics in any of them. Only in Venezuela did religiopolitical conditions come near to matching those of Chile in the post-1958 period, but even here the Left has not been a serious electoral contender nor the Church as potent a social force.

Similar religiopolitical conditions which developed in Chile in the early 1960s, however, have characterized several nominally Catholic countries in Western Europe since World War II. There, after the collapse of a fascist Right in 1945, religious values have continued to provide powerful reinforcement for reformist DC parties amidst perduring fears of significant Marxist movements.

The conditions that seem to be crucial for explaining the emergence of religious norms which can contribute signficant legitimation for social and economic reforms are: (1) an incubation period for progressive social positions inside a Church which eventually become official policy; (2) the resonance between these principles and those of a significant reform party; (3) the emergence of a serious normative competition or perceived political threat to a Church by a radical political force; and (4) the absence, or decline, of conservative movements in Church and politics.

When these conditions are all operative simultaneously, there is a possibility for the Church to resolve the predicament described in Chapter 2—namely, to articulate principles general enough to maintain moral credibility but specific enough to legitimate moderate economic and political changes. The Chilean experience between 1964 and 1970, however, indicates that conditions 3 (perceived leftist threat to the Church) and 4 (nonviability of rightist parties) are reversible. If such occurs, despite the continued saliency of the first two conditions (socially progressive Church positions, and their resonance with those of a significant reform party), the political impact of religious norms are more diverse, breaking to the Left, the Center, and the Right.

The second set of questions raised at the beginning of Chapter 4 pertain to the challenge of placing the institutional weight of the Church behind reformist movements in politics without identifying it with a specific party. The Chilean experience in the various time frames we have analyzed indicates that the resolution of this dilemma is almost impossible, especially for a financially weak and structurally underdeveloped religious institution. The very close, although unofficial, linkages between change-oriented roles and structures of the Chilean Church with those of the Christian Democratic Party developed as a result of related cohorts of reformist religious and political leaders who simultaneously rose to power in their respective organizations. In such a context, the Church designed social programs that coincided with the platform of the PDC and trained personnel who subsequently moved into the party, thus placing the resources of the Church at the disposal of moderate political reformers.

The very close overlap, however, between religious and secular roles and structures, while providing important institutional carriers for Church norms in politics, eventually led to serious personnel drainage from the Church once the party replaced the Church as a more effective channel for societal reform. Furthermore, despite official Church denials, in the mind of the populace the Church became identified almost totally with the PDC, losing a substantial amount of credibility and influence among significant numbers of citizens of different political persuasions (on the Left and the Right) in the late 1960s. Financial subsidies by the state and overlapping recruitment patterns between Church programs and those of the party also provided immediate structural resources for the Church to exercise significant political influence, but in the longer term proved institutionally divisive and debilitating.

Similar overlapping recruitment patterns and generational cohort ties between the Church and Christian Democratic parties have also prevailed in much of Western Europe since World War II, along with significant public subsidies to Church social and educational programs. Thus far, such conditions have prolonged a significant influence for the Church in politics, but in a very partisan fashion, thus diminishing its wider moral credibility. Moreover, additional problems are likely to occur in Europe if Christian-inspired parties suffer greater internal fractionalization, if the Left should increase its electoral base, and if the Right regains political strength. Unless the Church can develop autonomous methods to concretize its progressive social message independent of Christian reform parties, it risks internal politicization and external diminishment of credibility as a force for universal moral values.

A factor that limits the Church's capacity of reaching such a goal is its weak membership commitments in most Western countries—a problem related to the third set of questions raised in Chapter 4. Unless more laity voluntarily identify with the Church than in the past and make its newly announced social goals their own, the Church will not have the autonomous resources and outreach into the world to make its message effective. The Chilean case between 1935 and 1970 indicates, however, that traditional religious attitudes and behavior change very slowly and are very often overshadowed by economic self-interest. Newly announced changes at the official level may effect some progressive elites within the institutions, but unless deeper loyalties are developed among rank-and-file members that are equal to, or stronger than, their class interests, it cannot hope to have very significant and long-term impact on economic and political structures favoring the poor in any society. Such a conversion of heart among the majority of Catholics in the middle and upper classes throughout the Western world is not a likely possibility in the near future.

During moments of crisis for both religion and society, however, when a major threat appears to challenge widely accepted moral and political values, the dominant religious institution in a society may be able to rally significant immediate support for its reform objectives, especially if these are closely linked with a defense of national cultural values. Widespread fear of Marxism in Chile galvanized apparent Catholic support for economic reforms in the early 1960s which was translated into overwhelming support for Christian Democracy. Somewhat comparable situations have arisen from time to time on other Western countries, such as France and Italy in the late 1940s when Marxist parties presented themselves as serious electoral competitors for power.[59] If the crisis subsides, however, or if the context changes—and Chile is an indication that new factors can arise quickly making other than reform movements the most effective instruments for defeating the Left—the Church's ability to parlay popular fears into lasting support for structural reform favoring greater distribution of wealth and power can be substantially weakened.

Given such chronic weaknesses in Churches in most Western countries, the international network of Catholicism can provide important stimuli and resource supports for some change-oriented programs, especially in the third world. This factor pertains to the last set of questions laid out at the beginning of Chapter 4—the cost-benefit impact of international support for Churches trying to promote economic and social justice in their respective societies. The Chilean experience during the early 1960s is a rather dramatic example of how at certain moments progressive resources from international Catholicism can reinforce change in a national Church and empower it to play a more reformist role in its own national context. If major dependency linkages are maintained over time, however, local Church structures may suffer serious internal contradictions and a loss of national credibility. Chile in the late 1960s is a clear example of how such international support can backfire once divisions reemerged at the international level of the Church and in the local political context itself. Changes in international

---

[59] Events in Poland in the late 1970s indicate that Catholicism can act as a significant force for progressive reform in time of crisis in other Western societies as well, even when an authoritarian Marxist government is in power. There the Church has been effective in gaining more equitable economic policies and political participation in large part because it has had a significant secular ally pushing the same policies (labor), and has been able to mobilize crisis support by interweaving religious and nationalist values.

Developments in Iran and the United States in the late 1970s also highlight the galvanizing potential of religion during real or perceived crisis in other contemporary cultures and contexts. In both cases (Islam in Iran, evangelical Christianity in the United States) majorities or significant minorities have perceived secularizing trends as threatening their cultural and religious values, and in each case this has spilled over into very significant political movements (the overthrow of the Shah in Iran, and the targeting of liberal politicians for electoral defeat by the Moral Majority and its political allies in the United States). In neither of these last two situations, however, has support for religious beliefs led to political strategies favoring greater economic equity or pluralism. Crisis support for religion can, and often does, lead to very reactionary or authoritarian social policies depending upon the context and perceived source of the threat.

Catholicism since Vatican II have not been entirely consistent, nor all in the direction of progressive religious and social reform. Conservatives, liberals, and radicals all point to different currents in the international Church to justify their respective religious and political options.

Furthermore, certain ideological preferences for moderate reformist positions which characterize many international Church donor organizations in one context can act as stimuli for change, but in another very different configuration of national political forces can reinforce conflict and divisions in a local Church. The fact that some of these programs, such as Catholic Relief Services of the United States and Misereor of West Germany, act as conduits for public grants from their respective national governments (who also give aid directly to some churches in developing countries) is an additional factor that can diminish the objectivity or credibility of a local Church.

Finally, the very availability of such international resources further delays the necessity of a periphery unit to become sef-supporting. Massive amounts of outside aid can act as surrogates for chronically underdeveloped local support. Ironically, however, their very existence can lull the laity in the receiving Church into a state of prolonged complacency and not force them to take more responsibility for their own religious structures and programs. This problem further aggravates the already weak ties to the institution that many of these nominal Catholics have and reduces the possibility of winning their commitment to the institution's newly announced social goals.

The only feasible resolution to this last predicament related to international transfers would seem to be placing a predetermined time limit on their operations in a particular national context after which more of the laity in the local institution would have to take responsibility for the Church's maintenance. The Chilean case in the late 1960s offers little indication that this can be done easily—especially since it was the Catholics most capable of contributing to the upkeep of the Church who were becoming most disenchanted with its positions favoring sustained economic reforms.

These last four chapters have highlighted both the similarities and differences between the Chilean and other national Churches in responding to such classic religiopolitical challenges as differentiation of ecclesiastical and political structures, the creation of progressive religious and social forces in a traditional religious institution, and reorienting the public role of the Church in Western democratic society behind greater economic and political equity. The successes of Chilean Catholicism in responding to these challenges, along with lingering problems that remained unresolved, have provided some important comparative insights into the range of possibilities for the contemporary

Catholic Church to act as a positive agent for economic and social reform.

The next three chapters deal with two very different, and perhaps more crucial, challenges for the post-Vatican II Church which go beyond the context of reformist societies: the coming to terms with new developments in Marxism, and the exercise of a prophetic public role under authoritarian regimes. Despite contradictions carried over from the previous periods we have examined, the Chilean Church since 1970 has made some very significant advances on both these fronts. These can also provide some rich learning experiences for many other countries where both of these challenges are becoming more crucial both for Church and society.

PART III

Christian-Marxist Rapprochement

7 Church-State Coexistence during the Chilean Popular Unity Government

Thus far we have focused on challenges to modern Catholicism in political situations where the religious mission of the Church is respected and where it is permitted to play a formative role in public policy. Very different problems face the Church in Marxist-dominated political systems. Where the ideology of government calls into question the validity of religion, Catholicism historically has been a significant source of opposition to the regime rather than a positive force contributing to socialist objectives.

Since mid-nineteenth century, both Marxism and Catholicism have ruled out the possibility of long-term coexistence. Marx denied the validity of religion's transcendent claims, and spoke of it as an opium of repressed people that treated only the symptoms, not the cause of pain—economic exploitation. He further argued that religion served the bourgeoisie as an instrument to perpetuate the enslavement of the proletariat because Christian social principles emphasized only passive virtues—"cowardice, self-contempt, abasement, submission, dejection."[1]

Conversely, several Catholic pronouncements on social problems in the same period included severe condemnations of Marxism's atheistic and materialistic premises, and also rejected class struggle, the use of violence, and concentration of power in the hands of the state as fundamentally incompatible with Christianity. As we have seen earlier, papal encyclicals and Vatican decrees in the 1930s and 1940s categorically rejected communism as being "intrinsically wrong," forbade Catholics to "collaborate with it in any undertaking whatsoever," and imposed excommunication on anyone who directly or indirectly assisted Communist parties.[2]

---

[1] Karl Marx, "Contribution to the Critique of Hegel's Philosophy of Right: Introduction," in *Karl Marx: Early Writings,* ed. T. B. Bottomore, pp. 43–59; "The Communism of the Paper, 'Rheinischer Beobachter,' " *On Religion,* by Marx and Engels, p. 84.

[2] Pope Pius XI, "Divini Redemptoris," (1937), no. 60, p. 365; and *Acta Apostolicae Sedis* (Rome) 41 (1949): 334.

For an excellent analysis of the historical and philosophical challenges of nineteenth-century Marxism to which these Church documents were addressed, see Arturo Gaete, S.J., "Socialismo y comunismo: historia de una problemática condenación," pp. 290–302; "Catolicismo social y marxismo en el siglo XIX: un diálogo

Very bitter problems developed for both systems as a result of their mutually exclusive and antagonistic doctrinal positions. Church-state conflicts in the Soviet Union have resulted in restrictions on religious activities. Churches in the Soviet Union and Eastern Europe have been major focal points of opposition to goverments, most recently and dramatically in Poland.[3] In Cuba the Catholic Church acted as a haven for those who rejected socialist objectives in the early 1960s after a Marxist government came to power.[4]

Furthermore, in the Western nations where Marxist movements have not yet come to power, Catholics who identify with their revolutionary program have moved away from the Church. Conversely, those who have maintained significant allegiances to the institution have traditionally shunned Marxist parties, and religious practice has been one of the most critical factors in diminishing support for the Left in Western multiparty democracies.[5]

Since the 1960s, however, there have been indications that both sides see it in their interest to reduce some of the tensions and to limit the areas of disagreement and conflict. Papal encyclicals of Pope John XXIII and Pope Paul VI were less polemical in their treatment of both Marxism and socialism. These and other official Church statements (such as the Vatican II and Medellín documents) have also recognized the possibility of cooperation between believers and nonbelievers in programs promoting the common good of society. In addition, mutual diplomatic overtures between the Vatican and several governments in Eastern Europe since the late 1960s have resulted in some thaw in relations and greater interchange between Rome and the respective Churches of these countries.[6]

---

imposible," pp. 588–602; "Los cristianos y el marxismo: de Pio XI a Pablo VI," pp. 328–41. These three articles have been translated into English and appear in *Latin Americans Discuss Marxism-Socialism*, pp. 16–66.

[3] For an analysis of Church-state political and legal conflicts as well as religious dissent in Eastern Europe and the Soviet Union, see: Gerhard Simon, "The Catholic Church and the Communist State in the Soviet Union and Eastern Europe," pp. 190–221; Barbara Wolfe Jancar, "Religious Dissent in the Soviet Union," pp. 191–230; Albert Boiter, *Religion in the Soviet Union*, Washington Papers no. 78 (Beverly Hills: Sage Publications, 1980).

[4] For a description of the role of the Church in providing a base for counterrevolutionary groups in Cuba in the early 1960s, see: Leslie Dewart, *Christianity and Revolution: The Lesson of Cuba*, pp. 116–73; Margaret E. Crahan, "Salvation Through Christ or Marx: Religion in Revolutionary Cuba," pp. 156–84.

[5] Richard Hamilton has argued that except for the influence of religious practice, "vote for the Left or Marxist parties in Europe would have shown substantial majorities rather than halting (outside of Scandinavia and England) at roughly the 40 percent level." *Affluence and the French Worker in the Fourth Republic* (Princeton: Princeton University Press, 1967), p. 266.

[6] Hansjakob Stehle, *Eastern Politics of the Vatican, 1917–1979*, pp. 314–74; Erich Weingartner, ed., *Church Within Socialism*, pp. 1–6, 51–53; Dennis J. Dunn, *Detente and Papal-Communist Relations, 1962–1978*; John M. Kramer, "The Vatican's Ostpolitik."

Among Marxists in Western Europe in the 1970s there were initiatives that could enhance the prospects for democratic socialism and thus narrow the grounds of conflict with the Church. The original document outlining the principles of Eurocommunism in 1975 committed the French and Italian Communist parties to the construction of a type of socialism that would maintain constitutional procedures and also respect traditional political and civil liberties. The Spanish and British Communist parties subsequently endorsed similar positions regarding the necessity of using democratic procedures to engineer a transition to socialism in Western Europe.[7]

In addition to criticizing statist tendencies in traditional Marxist-Leninist societies, spokespersons of Eurocommunism also took more moderate positions regarding religion. They recognized that there have been some significant shifts in the official position of Catholicism since Vatican II which no longer make it the strong opponent to socialism that it once was. They also acknowledged the emergence within the Church of a minority of Christians committed to political and economic objectives close to their own.[8]

While conceding that fundamental philosophical differences still separate Catholicism and Marxism they expressed belief that coexistence between Eurocommunism and the Church is possible. They therefore committed themselves to respect the freedom of the Church to continue its pastoral mission if they eventually come to power, and solicited Catholic rank and file participation in Communist parties. In making such public commitments and overtures, these Communist party leaders hoped to remove religion as a divisive element in politics and convince Church officials to remain neutral in West European electoral campaigns.

[7] The original text of this joint communiqué by both parties was published in their respective party newspapers, L'Humanité (Paris) and L'Unità (Rome) on 18 November 1975. Leaders of Eurocommunism in the late 1970s also criticized violations of human rights in the Soviet Union and rejected several traditional Marxist-Leninist strategies, such as dictatorship of the proletariat, one-party rule, and violent revolution, as not being useful for achieving socialism outside the Soviet bloc. In place of these, Georges Marchais of the French party (PCF), Enrico Berlinguer of the Italian Communists (PCI), and Santiago Carrillo of the Spanish movement (PCE) all endorsed the formation of broad-based electoral coalitions of wage-earners, multiparty cooperation, the achievement of majority support at the ballot box, and democratic planning as methods more applicable for the construction of socialism in advanced capitalist European societies.

Georges Marchais, "Report to the 22nd Congress of the French Communist Party on Feb. 4, 1976," pp. 182–92; Antonio Tato, La "questione" comunista, 2 vols. (Rome: Editori Riuniti, 1975); Santiago Carrillo, Eurocomunismo y estado. Good treatments in English of Eurocommunism are: Rudolf L. Tökes, ed., Eurocommunism and Détente (New York: New York University Press, 1978); William E. Griffith, ed., The European Left: Italy, France and Spain (Lexington, Mass.: Lexington Books, 1979).

[8] Marchais, "Adresse aux Chrétiens de France," Lyon, June 1976, pp. 25–50; Carrillo, Eurocomunismo, pp. 37–43; Enrico Berlinguer, "Cattolici e comunisti."

In addition to these new official overtures on both sides to enhance their respective interests, there are indications that some Catholics want to go further and forge a synthesis of Christian and Marxist values and strategies. Many theologians in Latin America after 1968 endorsed Marxist strategies or perspectives, such as class conflict and the impossibility of neutrality for the official Church in partisan politics.[9]

Moreover, in the late 1960s, radical priest organizations emerged in Colombia, Argentina, and Peru. In their public statements they used Marxist analysis in condemning dependent capitalist development. Several of their documents recognized the legitimacy of violence, and some of their numbers joined leftist parties or revolutionary movements to effect change.[10]

Movements of Christians for Socialism also arose in the 1970s in Western Europe and in North and South America criticizing the identification of religious symbols with bourgeois ideology, and urging closer structural ties between local Church communities and political movements working for socialism. In their perspective, socialism is the only economic system compatible with Christianity, and they claim churches must become predominantly rooted in the culture of the working classes to achieve their mission authentically.[11]

It is difficult to judge what these recent developments within Catholicism and Marxism bode for the future. Some very important political consequences could result if such trends continue, however. The diminishment of religion's negative impact on support for the Left could enhance the electoral chances of Communist and Socialist parties in countries such as France, Italy, Spain, and Portugal. Conversely, respect by Marxists for constitutional processes and civil liberties as well as the interests of the Church could reduce the possibilities of debilitating religiopolitical conflicts during the future transition to socialism in these or other countries should the Left eventually gain executive power.

If a synthesis of some Marxist and Christian values and strategies can be made within Catholicism itself, as some Christian leftists are propos-

---

[9] Some of the better-known and more widely circulated works in this rapidly growing body of theological literature include the writings of Gutiérrez, Segundo, Míguez Bonino, Dussel, Assmann, Miranda, and Ellacuría.

An excellent analytical survey in English of this literature has been done by Phillip E. Berryman, "Latin American Liberation Theology," pp. 357–95. An expanded version of this article, which includes a survey of the literature up to mid-1975, appears in *Theology in the Americas*, ed. Sergio Torres and John Eagleson, pp. 20–83.

[10] *Social-Activist Priests: Colombia, Argentina.* For additional references on the radical priest movement in Peru, and for other sources on Colombia and Argentina, see Chapter 2, note 23.

[11] Eagleson, ed., *Christians and Socialism: Documentation of the Christians for Socialism Movement in Latin America;* "Option for Struggle II: More Documents of Christians for Socialism," mimeographed (New York: Church Research and Information Projects, 1975); Emidio Campi, ed., "Christians for Socialism," mimeographed (New York: Church Research and Information Projects, 1976).

ing, the style and scope of the Church's mission could be substantially altered. Its religious symbols and legitimating force, the arrangement of its roles and structures, and the behavior of its members would all be significantly affected were the institution as a whole closely linked with socialist objectives. Depending on how far internal alterations could go, the possibility of Catholicism becoming an agent for radical change could be significantly enhanced.

These new developments within both camps toward rapprochement involve, therefore, two related but quite separate issues: (1) coexistence and cooperation at the external policy level, and (2) the assimilation of Marxism within the Church itself. The first involves significant but limited changes on each side so as to reduce the grounds of disagreement and thus allow each to achieve their respective goals without major conflict. The second entails a major reorientation within the Church of how it conceives its religious mission and how closely the performance of the mission can be identified with an active involvement in radical secular change.

The problem of coexistence and limited cooperation with a Marxist government requires some areas of normative compatibility with socialist objectives, authoritative action strategies by Church leaders to operationalize these and avoid institutional conflicts with the state, acquiescence by international Church authorities to coexistence, and the ability of rank-and-file members to make political decisions on other than religious grounds. If corresponding normative, structural, and behavioral flexibility toward the Church occurs on the Marxist side in a society undergoing a transformation to democratic socialism, one could expect the chances for resolving the coexistence-cooperation problem successfully to be good.

The assimilation-synthesis problem involves digestion of Marxism within the Church, and is likely to require more substantial alterations in the basic dynamics of the institution. Here what is necessary is a clear specification of the Church's social norms to legitimate socialism, a close linking of the roles and structures of the Church with secular organizations promoting radical political change, the acceptance of class conflict among different strata of Church members, and the support from the international Church for these alterations.

The challenge demands more than *acquiescence* to secular change and minimization of conflict with the state at the external policy level. It requires a positive *promotion* of socialist political and economic objectives by various sectors of the Church. One, therefore, could expect more serious authority conflicts and strains on formal unity to arise within the institution in confronting the assimilation-synthesis challenge than in resolving the coexistence-cooperation problem.

Undoubtedly, these two aspects of Christian-Marxist rapprochement are empirically interrelated. Efforts by ecclesiastical and political leaders to establish a framework for peaceful coexistence and limited cooperation will act as a positive signal for some Catholics (on the Left and the Right) that close ideological and strategic alliances with Marxism are legitimate. Regardless of what official Church pronouncements and diplomatic overtures to Marxist governments intend for *external* policy issues, they cannot but have fall-out effects *within* the institution. Some lower echelon leaders and rank-and-file members sympathetic to Marxism may feel encouraged to go further and thus try to make the Church a positive agent in the promotion of socialism. Other Catholics might view official attempts at cooperation as the first step toward complete capitulation and could resort to obstructionist tactics.

Conceptually and practically, however, both of these challenges involved in Christian-Marxist rapprochement can be analyzed separately. The Marxists themselves are primarily concerned with achieving a breakthrough at the first level of coexistence-cooperation—namely, removing religion as an obstacle to widening their electoral base and keeping the official Church neutral during a transition to socialism. Advances at this level could occur regardless of what success groups have in making an assimilation or synthesis of Marxist perspectives within the Church itself, or even if some opposition emerges from conservative Catholics.

Moreover, it is likely that the challenges presented by the assimilation-synthesis problem will be much more difficult to work out given the radical changes these entail for traditional religious beliefs and institutional characteristics of the Church. Attempts to digest Marxist values and strategies into the internal dynamics of the institution may very well create far more serious conflicts for Catholicism, require much more time to resolve, and, at least in the short term, be of less political significance.

Thus far there has been no adequate opportunity to test whether or not the coexistence-cooperation challenge can be worked out successfully. A united Left has yet to gain power in any of the countries where Eurocommunism has emerged, and the Socialist government of Mitterrand has so far been careful to avoid conflict with the Church—although it has committed itself to nationalizing private schools. In addition, Catholic reactions to new developments on the Left in Europe have been mixed. The French and Spanish hierarchy have both shown an openness to accepting some elements of Marxism as a method of analysis and to approving some tactical cooperation between Catholics and Marxists. The Italian bishops, however, have continued to remain adamantly opposed to the possibility of coexistence or cooperation with Marxists at any level.[12]

In addition, although there have been some indications of growing Catholic support for the Left in recent years in Western Europe, the vast majority of devout Catholics in Italy, France, and Spain still vote for reformist or conservative candidates.[13] It is not clear how far each side is capable or willing to go in making accommodations to the other in Western Europe should the Left continue to be a serious contender for power.

There also has been no extensive analysis of what may be the consequences for the interior life of the Church when groups within it attempt to take Marxism seriously. In Latin America, where there has been the most effort by Christian groups to make such an assimilation, most of these movements have been preemptively short-circuited by the emergence of authoritarian military regimes committed to the eradication of all forms of Marxism in their respective societies. In Western Europe

[12] In a major statement on Marxism issued in June 1977, the French hierarchy recognized certain elements of truth in Marxism as well as changes in the French Communist Party making it less unacceptable for Catholics. While warning Catholics of the dangers in accepting Marxism as a whole, the bishops did admit the possibility of practical collaboration between Christians and Marxists. Conseil permanent de l'Épiscopat français, "Le marxisme, l'homme et la foi chrétienne," pp. 684–90. The Spanish bishops in a February 1977 declaration emphasized that Catholics could not support parties that proposed models of society in which fundamental rights and liberties would be suppressed, that use violence to achieve their objectives, or that make profit motives and private property absolutes. This left the door open for Spanish Catholics to vote for leftist parties proposing democratic models of socialism. Conseil permanent de la Conférence épiscopale espagnole, "Les chrétiens et la politique," pp. 239–50. Furthermore, a survey of Spanish bishops made by the Episcopal Conference in February 1976, and reported in the weekly magazine *Possible* of Madrid, indicated that all the bishops who responded recognized the legitimacy of Christian collaboration with Marxists in social and political matters. Carrillo, *Eurocomunismo,* p. 40. The Italian Episcopal Conference, however, in a statement before the June 1976 parliamentary elections, affirmed the "incompatibility at the theoretical and practical levels between Christianity and atheistic communism," and declared that this prevents believers from "belonging to, favoring or supporting an authentic Marxist movement even when they do not accept the ideology." Vescovi italiani, "Testimonianza concorde dei Vescovi italiani dovere di coerenza nelle scelte civili," *L'Osservatore Romano,* 26 May 1976, pp. 1–2.

[13] Some of the gains for the Left in recent elections in Italy have been attributed to the moderate position of the PCI on divorce and abortion reform, the presence of committed Catholics on elected lists of the party, and the Church's declining influence in controlling the Catholic vote. It is still unclear, however, whether significant practicing Catholic support for the Left will occur as the Communist Party comes close to sharing power in Western Europe. The vast majority of devout Catholics in Italy, France, and Spain still support moderate or conservative parties. Giacomo Sani, "The PCI on the Threshold," pp. 28–36; "Les elections legislatives des 4 et 11 Mars 1973," *Sondages* (Paris), 35 (1973): 22–26; Juan J. Linz, "Religion and Politics in Spain: From Conflict to Consensus Above Cleavage," pp. 255–77.

such efforts to date have remained at the level of dialogue, or have not had the organizational strength to affect large sectors of the Church.

In several respects, however, Chile between 1970 and 1973 does provide significant experiences for examining some of the possibilities and limits of both challenges of rapprochement. It is the only situation to date in a Western democracy where a Marxist coalition has gained executive power in a competitive election, and for three years the government made serious effects to initiate a transition to democratic socialism. The Church did not officially oppose Allende's election, and a significant minority of Catholics openly supported his campaign program and voted for the Left in 1970. These conditions set the stage for major efforts by groups on both sides after the election to explore concrete possibilities for coexistence and even some cooperation.

Furthermore, mutual attempts towards coexistence stimulated efforts by a well-organized Christians for Socialism movement to forge close ideological and structural links between sectors of Chilean Catholicism and the objectives of the Popular Unity government. In addition, the process of decentralization of Church leadership, the development of neighborhood base communities, and the continued availability of foreign Church resources in working-class areas all gave the Church adaptive capacities to relate closely to the local dynamics involved in the transition to socialism.

In facing the first challenge of coexistence with Marxism, the Chilean Church offers a hopeful prospect for resolving this problem fairly productively for both sides. Although there were some tensions that arose between Church and state toward the end of Allende's administration, the Church officially never became a major source of sustained opposition to the regime. In turn, the government by and large respected the Church's freedom. There were also some important positive contributions from the Catholic side to bolster the government's legitimacy, expand its support, and promote democratic procedures. On the basis of how the challenge of coexistence was faced by the Church and the Marxist government in Chile in the early 1970s, there is reason to believe that in future situations where the same mutual dynamics are operating, similar working relationships can be created between the institutional Church and a Marxist-dominated state.

In regard to the second challenge of assimilating Marxist dynamics *within* the Church, the Chilean experience indicates that the costs can be high and the consequences quite threatening for the fulfillment of the Church's religious mission as it has been traditionally conceived. While not ruling out the possibility of any assimilation and synthesis of Marxist-Christian perspectives in other contexts, the Chilean case highlights some of the major difficulties involved and pitfalls to be avoided.

The next two chapters will focus on each of these challenges. The major dynamics of the Church as developed in previous chapters will again serve as a framework of analysis—the articulation of social norms, authority flows across hierarchically arranged roles and structures, membership commitments and attitudes, and resource transactions with the international Church. By looking at the interaction of these components with one another and in relation to corresponding dynamics in secular society, a comprehensive picture of the implications of both aspects of rapprochement can be presented and oversimplification can be avoided.

NORMATIVE DIMENSIONS OF COEXISTENCE

Initiatives by Church Leaders to Establish Shared Values
with Marxists

As we have seen in Chapter 6, well before the 1970 campaign the Chilean bishops had attempted to distance themselves somewhat from their previous close identification with Christian Democratic ideology. As Allende's election appeared more possible, they ceased issuing warnings against the dangers of Marxism and maintained a neutral position throughout the presidential campaign.

During the first months following Allende's election, several factors stimulated the Chilean hierarchy to search for common ground with the new regime. They had committed themselves to respect the outcome of the electoral process and knew they would lose substantial credibility if they opposed the government at the start. They were well aware that Catholic opinion was divided in the 1970 campaign, and that a significant minority had supported Allende and participated in his coalition. They also wished to avoid if at all possible a major Church-state confrontation which might result in serious restrictions on religious freedom and also precipitate political instability during the transition to the new administration.

In addition, many bishops sympathized with several objectives outlined in the Popular Unity campaign program—expanded housing programs for the poor, greater control on prices, creation of more jobs, and stricter limitations on the activities of foreign companies—and felt that they had to give the government an opportunity to initiate its programs.[14] This general openness was reflected in a statement by

---

[14] In a document prepared for an international Synod of Bishops in Rome in October 1974, the Chilean Episcopal Conference mentioned several of these reasons as justifications for its initial openness to the Allende regime. Secretariado General del Episcopado Chileno, "Sínodo de obispos, 1974: respuesta de la Conferencia Episcopal de Chile."

Cardinal Silva two months after the election, when he told a Cuban journalist:

> The basic reforms contained in the Popular Unity program are supported by the Church. . . . I believe that socialism contains important Christian values, and in many respects is very superior to capitalism—the value it places on work, and the primacy of the person over against capital. I think that other extraordinary values of socialism are its break with the necessity and tyranny of the pursuit of profit and its ability to coordinate all levels of production. I believe that these ideals which it espouses are very close to the Church's preferred goals in the organization of society.[15]

In early 1971, a major development in Rome gave added legitimacy to this initial openness of the Chilean bishops to some of Allende's objectives. In mid-May, on the eightieth anniversary of the publication of *Rerum Novarum*, Pope Paul VI issued an apostolic letter in which he presented a critical but more nuanced assessment of both socialism and Marxism. He recognized that some Christians were attracted by socialism and wanted to promote it. He asked Christians to distinguish carefully among different aspects of socialism in order to protect humanistic values of "liberty, responsibility, and openness to the spiritual" in their political commitments. He also acknowledged that some Christians are interested in "concrete rapprochements" with Marxism since it had undergone a "certain splintering," was no longer a "unitary ideology," and manifested "various levels of expression." Among these different forms of Marxism the Pope mentioned class struggle, the exercise of political and economic power by a single party, the ideology of historical materialism, and a scientific method for analyzing social and political reality. While maintaining a critical attitude toward all four dimensions, he admitted the usefulness of this last component as a "working tool" which helps "decipher . . . the mainsprings of the evolution of society." He warned Christians that it would be dangerous to overlook the connection that links all four elements, or to promote class struggle "while failing to note the kind of totalitarian and violent society to which this process leads." He did not, however, reiterate traditional papal condemnations of Marxism or of all forms of Christian-Marxist collaboration.[16]

This cautious but significant shift in official Vatican policy provided the Chilean hierarchy with new maneuverability in dealing with Marxism in their own context. In fact, shortly after the appearance of the Pope's letter, the Chilean Episcopal Conference issued a major docu-

---

[15] *Última Hora* (Santiago), 12 November 1970.
[16] Pope Paul VI, "Octogesima Adveniens," nos. 31–34, pp. 499–501.

ment entitled, "Gospel, Politics and Various Types of Socialism." It analyzed doctrinal and practical aspects of Marxist socialism and examined
the possibility of Christians collaborating with its current manifestation
in Chile. In some respects the statement followed very closely Pope
Paul's analysis, but was more thorough and also more specific in setting
down parameters for legitimate Christian-Marxist rapprochment at the
external policy level and within the Church itself.

The bishops reiterated the official Church position that Catholics are
not bound to support any specific economic or political system. They
stressed that the laity must work for the establishment of those structures
that best realize humanistic values of liberation, justice, and love which
are endorsed by the Gospel. They also admitted that it is possible to implement such values in socialist systems, provided these avoid concentration of power in the hands of the state:

> ... Actually, there are many forms of socialism. It is conceivable that
> among them there are some that are compatible with the spirit of
> Christianity. These would be the forms of socialism that can duly
> guarantee that the state will not be transformed into an uncontrolla-
> ble and dictatorial force, and that can assure the promotion of the
> values of personal and social liberation which the Gospel of the Risen
> Christ proclaims.[17]

After acknowledging this possibility, however, the bishops recognized
that classical expressions of Marxism have not brought about such forms
of socialism. They observed that Marxist-Leninism, as it has been practiced to date, has led to the concentration of power in the hands of the
State, to absolute rule by a single party, and to the absence of ideological
pluralism and multiparty competition. It has also denied in practice,
they said, basic human freedoms such as liberty of expression and of the
press, the right to dissent and the right to strike. They concluded that
such practices and beliefs of Marxist-Leninism make it guilty of the
same abuses of classical liberal capitalism—the subordination of persons
to the necessities of production, their reduction to the level of means,
and the denial of their dignity and liberty.[18]

Notwithstanding their criticisms of *classical* practices and beliefs of
Marxism, the bishops recognized that the Chilean case could be different and might produce a more democratic form of socialism:

> ... The Chilean case presents unique possibilities which could lead to
> a different evolution of events. This will depend in great part on the
> good sense and democratic maturity of our people, the strength of

---

[17] "Evangelio, política y socialismos," nos. 17, 25, in *Documentos del Episcopado: Chile, 1970–1973*, pp. 67, 71.

[18] Ibid., nos. 36, 46, 49, 52, pp. 76–77, 81–84.

Christians and the openness and critical spirit of Marxists themselves toward their own system . . .[19]

The hierarchy, therefore, did not rule out the possibility of tactical cooperation between Christians and Marxists in their own society. While not explicitly encouraging lay people to support leftist parties and programs, neither did they forbid such an option as they had done nine years before in their 1962 pastoral letter. Rather they reminded believers who chose to do so that they must intensify their religious commitment so as to be able to reevaluate their political option constantly and not allow it to become all-consuming in their life. Each person, they said, must seriously weigh his or her own capacity for overcoming the risks involved and then act accordingly.[20]

Although recognizing the feasibility of coexistence and cooperation with Chilean forms of Marxism at the external policy level, the bishops set down definite limits as to how far an internal assimilation could be made within the Church itself. They recognized "significant incompatibilities between Marxism and Christianity" which made a synthesis at the level of principle impossible. In so doing, they reiterated traditional Catholic criticisms of Marxist doctrines of atheism, exacerbated class conflict and violence, materialism, and economic determinism in explaining the dynamics of societal change.[21]

Furthermore, the hierarchy emphasized the crucial importance that all official representatives of the institutional Church—bishops, priests, deacons, religious, and lay personnel holding positions of pastoral responsibility—must not publicly identify with any party, nor use their moral authority to promote partisan positions. Such neutrality, argued the bishops, not only enables the Church to perform its primary religious mission, but also enables its leaders to serve the moral needs and values of the entire society and offer a "service of unity and dialogue."[22]

After ruling out certain doctrinal and practical linkages of Marxism and Christianity *within* the Church, the bishops concluded their pastoral letter with a positive commitment to cooperate with the newly elected Marxist regime at the *external* policy level of societal change. This collaboration, they said, would consist of two contributions: (1) support for all that was liberating in the process of the transition to socialism, and (2) opposition to anything that would enslave people. These contributions would be realized not only by individual Christians participating in various secular institutions and parties, but also by the bishops themselves

[19] Ibid., no. 54, p. 85.
[20] Ibid., nos. 64, 67, pp. 89–91.
[21] Ibid., nos. 35, 44, 48, 53, pp. 76, 79–82, 84.
[22] Ibid., nos. 69–70, p. 92.

who stood ready to speak out on moral issues as the common good demanded.[23]

In some respects, this document was consistent with officially articulated Chilean Church positions dating back to the 1920s. The letter reiterated previously stated commitments such as the legitimacy of a plurality of political options for Catholics, the importance of political neutrality by the official Church, the danger of clerical involvement in parties, and the incompatibility between Catholicism and Marxism in several key doctrinal and strategic areas.

On other points, however, "Gospel, Politics and Various Types of Socialism" marked an important advance in the position of the Chilean Church and in Christian-Marxist understanding in general. While maintaining a critical stance toward several classical manifestations of Marxist-Leninism, the Chilean bishops became the first national hierarchy in the world to admit publicly and as a body the compatibility of other forms of socialism with Catholic doctrine. They further acknowledged the possibility of achieving democratic socialism in their own society under a Marxist regime. They also acquiesced to Catholic lay cooperation with Marxists at the tactical level of party politics and government administration. Finally, they explicitly committed themselves as leaders of the Church to offer cooperation and constructive criticism to the government in promoting socialist objectives in society at large.

Hence, this pastoral letter was a cautious, but significant, attempt from the Catholic side to expand the normative parameters of shared values with Marxism. While ruling out some combinations of Marxism and Christianity *inside* the Church, it provided a basis for coexistence of Church and state at the external level to collaborate in promoting further structural change within a legal framework.

Two of the four major institutional components of Catholicism operated positively to bring about this new opening to the Left in Chile—general articulation of Catholic social norms, and resource interactions with the international Church. The Chilean hierarchy—as they had done in 1962, and again in 1968—effected a shift in emphasis of their social teaching, but this time in a style more open to socialism. However, their articulation was sufficiently general to avoid explicit

---

[23] Ibid., no. 88, p. 99. The Catholic bishops of Nicaragua issued a similarly nuanced but positive statement on socialism in Nicaragua four months after the downfall of Somoza, encouraging constructive participation in the new society by Christians. La Conferencia Episcopal de Nicaragua, *Compromiso cristiano para una Nicaragua nueva* (Managua: Comisión Justicia y Paz, 1979). For an analysis of the role of Churches during the downfall of Somoza and during the first year of the revolutionary government, see Michael Dodson and Tommie Sue Montgomery, "The Churches in the Nicaraguan Revolution."

identification of the moral weight of the Church with any particular economic model.

In addition, the occasion and legitimacy for this general normative shift was provided by a change in the social teaching of the Vatican which was moving in the same direction. Such a mutation in Rome's public position in early 1971 (cautious and nuanced as it was) reinforced the adaptation toward Marxism and socialism made by the Chilean bishops, which could not have taken place without acquiescence by the pope.

Initiative by the Chilean Left to Expand the Value Parameters of Classical Marxism

Parallel to the shift in official positions of the Chilean Church regarding possibilities for Christian cooperation with some aspects of Marxist socialism, the Popular Unity program made significant adaptations in traditional Marxist doctrines to fit the Chilean context. Such changes expanded the areas of normative compatibility with Catholicism, since the UP explicitly rejected many aspects of Marxist-Leninism condemned by Rome and the Chilean bishops.

The Chilean Left agreed to work within the country's traditional democratic framework in engineering a transition to socialism. They ruled out as inapplicable in the Chilean situation strong centralized state control, single-party rule, dictatorship of the proletariat, and revolutionary violence. Instead, the 1970 program of the Popular Unity coalition and public commitments of its spokespersons following the election emphasized the viability of combining democratic political processes with socialist economic objectives—a mixture of public and private ownership of resources, widespread popular participation in public planning and administration, broad coalitions of wage-earners sharing in effective power, guarantees for political liberties, and a peaceful transition to socialism through legal means.

Their program called for an expanded role by the government in controlling the economy, but also placed limitations on the scope of state intervention. Basic resources and wealth controlled by foreign capital or internal monopolies were to be fully nationalized—large mining enterprises, private banks and insurance firms, foreign trade, distribution enterprises, strategic industrial monopolies, communications and transportation systems. The vast majority of mining, agricultural, industrial, and service enterprises, however, were to remain in private hands, or involve the state as a partner with private capital.[24]

---

[24] "UP Program of Government," *New Chile* (New York: North American Congress of Latin America, 1972), pp. 137–38.

Furthermore, the governmental apparatus as it expanded its activities was also to guarantee pluralism and participation at every level of decision-making—a value stressed in traditional Catholic social teaching, and especially emphasized in the Vatican II and Medellín pronouncements. In such a way, claimed the Popular Unity platform, abuses of public power and tendencies toward statism would be avoided. The goal was the construction of a new "popular state" functioning with expanded respresentative mechanisms and not subject to control by any one party or class. In addition, all wage-earning groups, not just the industrial proletariat, would provide the broad base of government legitimacy and share in effective power—"workers, employees, peasants, shantytown dwellers, housewives, students, professionals, intellectuals, craftsmen, small and middle-sized businessmen."[25]

The Left also committed itself to safeguard all liberties basic to Chile's democratic tradition, including freedom of speech, press, assembly, and union rights, and to "respect . . . all religious ideas and beliefs and guarantees for the exercise of worship." It also promised to honor certain educational freedoms, which particularly interested the Church. While the educational system was to be subjected to more centralized planning and additional subsidies were to be provided for adult education, technical training, and work-study programs in public and private institutions, all affected groups of citizens were to be consulted and invited to participate in this transformation.[26]

Thus, while not explicitly condemning doctrines and practices prevalent within the Soviet bloc, Chilean Communists and Socialists in 1970 clearly distanced themselves from strict observance of Marxist-Leninism. Like their Eurocommunist contemporaries, they sought new normative combinations between Marxist and democratic values so as to develop an alternate model of socialist transformation more suited to the culture and possibilities of their own context.

In fact, shortly after the popular election, Allende made distinctions between his strategy for a transition to socialism in Chile and the path followed in Cuba, the Soviet Union, and Eastern Europe:

> . . . Our socialist goal is in accord with Chilean traditions and historical development. . . . We have not come to power through bullets but by votes, and we will make our revolution accordingly. . . . We will not follow the Cuban, nor the Soviet, nor the Yugoslav model, but a Chilean model. We are forming a unity of six parties with participation of Christians, Marxists, and laicist groups.[27]

[25] Ibid., p. 135.
[26] Ibid., pp. 134–35.
[27] Interview in Santiago with Salvador Allende by Luis Suárez of the journal *Siempre* (Mexico City), 9 October 1970. Reprinted in *El pensamiento de Salvador Allende,* ed. Hugo Latorre Cabal (Mexico, D.F.: Fondo de Cultura Económica, 1974), pp. 22–23.

In his inaugural speech, Allende repeated his commitment to finding a specifically Chilean road to socialism, denying that "one-party rule is a necessity for the transition to socialism" and promising to create mechanisms "respecting pluralism of the great majority."[28]

Hence, in several major doctrinal and strategic areas, the Chilean Left during and subsequent to the 1970 election expanded the core parameters of traditional Marxism. In so doing, its policies and objectives came closer to official Catholic positions than did traditional Marxist-Leninsim, especially on issues such as an expanded but limited role for the state in the economy, allowance for multiparty competition and popular participation, and guarantees for human rights and freedoms.

It was, moreover, in Allende's interest to seek an immediate rapprochement with the Church after the popular election. He had won a very slim plurality of votes, and consequently he sought to neutralize the Church as a possible obstacle to his congressional confirmation. He also wanted to prevent his opponents' using the argument of potential religious persecution as an additional weapon against him.

While not a believer himself, he respected freedom of conscience and recognized in the evolution of Catholic teaching several points of congruence with socialist values. He felt the Church could be a useful ally in forging a larger public consensus for many of his objectives. In an interview with the *New York Times* in early October, he indicated that he foresaw no major conflict with the Church, since the objectives of his coalition, he said, closely paralleled current Church teachings:

> I believe the Church will not be a factor against the Popular Unity government. On the contrary, they are going to be a factor in our favor, because we are going to try to make a reality of Christian thought.[29]

The Communist Party (PCCh) also reaffirmed its position of openness to Christian-Marxist cooperation articulated previously in its 1965 and 1969 party congresses. Luis Corvalán, secretary general of the PCCh, in an interview with a journalist some months after the election, stated that while atheism was still a fundamental philosophical tenet of his party, renunciation of religious faith was not a necessary requirement for membership:

> . . . To enter the Communist Party one must be in agreement with its program and statutes, and also with the essential objective of building a socialist society. It is not required that one renounce his or her reli-

---

[28] Salvador Allende, "Discurso en el Estadio Nacional," 5 November 1970, in *Salvador Allende: su pensamiento político*, p. 22.

[29] Joseph Novitsky, "Allende Sees Chile Finding Her Own Way to Socialism," pp. 1, 24.

gious belief. . . . Of course, Marxism is atheistic in its philosophical doctrine. The Communist Party which is guided by this doctrine, however, does not demand that its members renounce the Catholic faith, or any other faith which they may have . . .[30]

This position of the Chilean Communist Party regarding the compatibility of religious faith and party membership was thus quite different from policies officially or unofficially espoused in Eastern Europe. In those societies, religious belief and practice are still looked upon as drawbacks to sincere participation to socialist objectives and obstacles to advancement inside the Communist Party.

The Left in Chile, as it made these overtures to the Church, was not subject to any pressures or criticisms from Communist parties or regimes in other parts of the world. In fact, as in the Church, some linkages it maintained with the international movement confirmed and legitimized such efforts at the local level for a rapprochement with its traditional foe.

When Fidel Castro visited Chile in late 1971, he spoke with several priests from working-class neighborhoods of Santiago who were sympathetic to socialism. Impressed by his conversations with them and by their dedication to the struggle against injustice, he referred to these talks in his farewell address before leaving the country. He stated that there were "many points of coincidence" between "the purest concepts of Christianity and Marxism," and that such convergence made possible a "strategic alliance between Marxist revolutionaries and Christian revolutionaries."[31]

As on the Catholic side, pragmatic domestic factors as well as some reinforcing international encouragements provided legitimacy for the Chilean Left to effect significant adaptations in Marxist norms. While not surrendering elements central to the Marxist tradition such as athe-

---

[30] Eduardo Labarca Goddard, *Corvalán, 27 horas: el PC Chileno por fuera y por dentro,* p. 207.

At a dinner party hosted by the cardinal in his home for some leaders of the Communist Party in March 1971, Corvalán also stated that he saw no reason why the Church and the Party could not coexist well in Chile. He promised the cardinal that the PCCh would not imitate the policy of Eastern European communist governments of fomenting divisions among Catholics and promoting national Churches independent of Rome. Such separate Churches, he said, proved to be more reactionary than ones linked to the Vatican. The cardinal, on his part, responded that so long as the Communist Party respected the democratic traditions of Chile, he would cooperate with the government. (Arturo Gaete, S.J., of *Mensaje,* is my source of information for this conversation. Gaete was present at the dinner, and helped arrange other meetings and dialogues between Church representatives and leaders of the PCCh during the Popular Unity administration.)

[31] Fidel Castro, "Farewell Speech: Who has Learned the Most?," National Stadium, Santiago, 2 December 1971, in *Fidel in Chile: A Symbolic Meeting Between Two Historical Processes* (New York: International Publishers, 1972), pp. 222–23.

ism, class conflict, and the need for the state to wrest economic and political power from traditional landed and industrial groups, leaders in the Popular Unity coalition redefined the means to promote its objectives in the Chilean context.

By acknowledging the possibility of achieving radical change through a constitutional framework guaranteeing cultural pluralism and civil liberties, the Marxist coalition began its term in office with the area of normative conflict with official Catholicism significantly reduced. In fact, important normative agreement between Catholic and Marxist leaders on the desirability of democratic socialism and the contribution religion could make to it provided legitimation not only for relatively peaceful coexistence, but also for some cooperation between Church and state during Allende's presidency.

STRUCTURAL COMPATIBILITY BETWEEN CHURCH AND STATE

While there clearly was important agreement in official pronouncements by Church and state at the outset of the Allende government, we could accord more significance to these statements if we can also demonstrate that normative agreements were respected with a relatively high degree of consistency. In fact, we can go further. There is ample evidence that authoritative actions by Church leaders provided important legitimacy and support for governmental objectives during the first two and one-half years of Allende's term in office.

During the final part of the Popular Unity government, significant Church-state tensions developed as groups on both sides threatened the terms of mutual normative agreement. In this context, some significant public opposition to the government developed at lower echelons of the Church. Despite these developments, however, the hierarchy never moved to a position of open hostility to the regime, nor did the administration ever adopt measures limiting the Church's freedom.

Supportive Interaction of Religious and Marxist Leaders during the Transition Period (September–November 1970)

The bishops played an important constructive political role during the time between the popular balloting on 4 September and the inauguration on 3 November. During this eight-week period, when intense domestic and international efforts were underway to prevent Allende from taking office, the hierarchy refused to place the official weight of the Church behind the campaign to stop him.

The cardinal, in a private meeting with National Party leaders during

this period, refused to acquiesce to their request that the hierarchy denounce the UP.[32] Such an action by the official Church could have
paved the way for a Christian Democratic-National Party alliance in
Congress to choose Alessandri over Allende, or could have been read as a
tacit endorsement for a military coup that was under consideration.

As was revealed later, the U.S. government and several North American corporations were making concentrated efforts to provoke such a
coup between mid-September and mid-October. They also offered substantial bribes to Chilean congressmen to vote against Allende in the
upcoming plenary session of Congress. Furthermore, a Chilean right-
wing terrorist organization was encouraged by these signals to stage a
kidnapping attempt of the head of the army, mortally wounding General René Schneider just before the plenary session of Congress on 24
October.[33]

In this climate of intrigue, the bishops attempted to use their public
moral influence to preserve calm and allow traditional constitutional
processes to resolve the crisis. In late September the Episcopal Conference issued a declaration recognizing that "the Chilean people want to
continue in the same framework and style of liberty that they have defended for 160 years." The hierarchy urged citizens not to become paralyzed by fear of radical changes, nor to resort to violence as an alternative. They also stated that they wished "to continue to cooperate with
changes in the country, especially those which favor the poorest."[34]

The official position of the Church during the period immediately
following the popular balloting was not one of support for Allende's
confirmation as president. The hierarchy remained cautious and
publicly neutral concerning the final outcome. They refused, however,
to play an active role in legitimizing opposition to the UP, and this
was an important factor in avoiding a breakdown in democratic procedures.[35]

Within hours of the congressional vote of confirmation, however, a
delegation of bishops led by Cardinal Silva paid the traditional visit to
the new president in his home. In this conversation, the cardinal promised Allende active support for his new government, saying: "We are at

---

[32] Franz Vanderschueren and Jaime Rojas, "The Catholic Church of Chile: From
'Social Christianity' to 'Christians for Socialism,'" p. 30.

[33] U.S. Congress, Senate, Select Committee to Study Governmental Operations
with Respect to Intelligence Activities, *Alleged Assassination Plots Involving Foreign Leaders*, Report no. 94–465, 94th Cong., 1st sess., 1975, pp. 225–54.

[34] Secretariado General del Episcopado, "Declaración de los obispos chilenos sobre
la situación actual del país," pp. 29–30.

[35] Church neutrality and support for constitutional processes also contributed to
the atmosphere that encouraged PDC and UP leaders to work out an agreement for
a statute of democratic guarantees for the Constitution (Chapter VI, note 6). This
paved the way to PDC support in Congress for Allende's confirmation.

your disposal, Mr. President, to help you carry out your major programs to promote the common good."[36]

On 3 November Allende and his cabinet participated in a Te Deum, or Act of Thanksgiving, traditionally held in the cathedral of Santiago upon the inauguration of new presidents. At Allende's request leaders of the other religious denominations also participated. In his homily the cardinal stressed the importance for all Chileans to work together to promote further changes on behalf of the poor. He also prayed for the newly elected government officials, who "regardless of their personal ideologies or beliefs" deserve because of their "legitimate authority" the "respect and cooperation from all citizens in whatever promotes the common good."[37]

Hence, throughout the turbulent transition period, the actions of official spokespersons for the Church and the Left were highly consistent with their stated normative commitments. The hierarchy remained true to their promise to encourage respect for constitutional processes, and to accept whatever outcome might result. This not only promoted an atmosphere of calm and reasonable negotiation which led to Allende's confirmation, but also provided very important legitimacy for his administration as it took office. Their posture was diametrically opposed to subversive rightist forces within the country and to the activities of the U.S. corporations and government, and provided no encouragement to such efforts attempting to disrupt Chile's political traditions.

Conversely, the Left enhanced the credibility of its own stated objectives by respecting parliamentary processes, political freedoms, and religious traditions. Negotiations with the Christian Democrats, support for a statute of democratic guarantees in the Constitution, and participation in an ecumenical Te Deum were concrete proof of the Popular Unity's intentions of honoring its promise to inaugurate a democratic transition to socialism.

Throughout this transition period, therefore, strategies by official Catholic and Marxist leaders remained well within the boundaries of their mutual commitments. These decisions met with no formidable resistance at lower levels of leadership in either camp, and were given binding force by specific and clear actions by official spokesmen at the top of each organization. As in the case with the separation of Church and state in 1925 and the coexistence of the Church with a Popular Front government in 1938, strategies of religious and secular leaders

---

[36] "El saludo al Presidente Allende," *Iglesia de Santiago* 8 (October 1970): 11.

[37] Cardinal Silva, "Queremos ser constructores de un mundo más solidario," *Iglesia de Santiago* 8 (November 1970): 4.

were nonthreatening to one another and operationalized mutually overlapping interests effectively.

Institutional Compatibility during the Government's
Period of Popularity (November 1970–February 1972)

During the first fifteen months of the Popular Unity government,
action strategies by Church and Marxist leaders remained very consistent with mutual normative commitments tacitly agreed upon at the
outset of the regime. In fact, at critical moments the hierarchy gave important official support for some programs of the government. The administration in turn respected the institutional freedom and privileges of
the Church, encouraged Christian-Marxist cooperation, and made significant headway in promoting structural transformations within a constitutional framework.

The Popular Unity government moved quickly during its first year in
office to socialize the economy and effect a redistribution of income in
favor of wage earners. Congress unanimously approved total nationalization of the copper mines, and through stock purchases the state
gained control of two-thirds of the credit of the entire banking system.
By resort to laws dating back to the 1930s allowing state requisition of
enterprises, the government took over several key industries as well after
workers went on strike or seized them. By the end of 1971, over 150 industries had been put under state control. Agrarian reform was rapidly
accelerated, and by the end of 1971 the state had expropriated over 1,-
300 large farms—300 more than had been taken during the Frei Administration.

Through existing powers allowing the executive monetary initiatives,
Allende imposed price freezes on basic commodities, raised wages by
66.6 percent and the basic monthly salary by 35 percent, expanded
public works projects, and increased the money in circulation by 100
percent. The results of these redistributive strategies in 1971 were that
unemployment in Santiago fell from 7.1 percent to 3.7 percent, white
and blue collar share of income rose from 50 percent to 59 percent, and
inflation dropped from 34.9 percent to 22.1 percent. The gross domestic
product also increased dramatically during this period, rising 8.6 percent in response to additional consumer demand and the elasticity of the
manufacturing sector which had been operating at less than 70 percent
capacity when Allende took office.[38]

By operating within the existing legal framework, the new govern-

---

[38] Barbara Stallings, *Class Conflict*, pp. 131–32; Arturo Valenzuela, *Chile*, pp.
51–53.

ment made significant progress in beginning a transition to socialism and in providing expanded economic benefits for the poor. Traditional civil and political liberties were respected along with the right of legitimate dissent, and local mechanisms for worker participation in factories and on publicly-owned farms were begun. The popularity of these measures was reflected in the results of national municipal elections in April 1971 when Popular Unity candidates received 48.6 percent of the votes, a substantial increase over Allende's 1970 plurality of 36.2 percent.

On several occasions during the period of government popularity the cardinal demonstrated his sympathy for the goals of the government aimed at benefiting the working class, curbing the power of transnational corporations, and establishing more just relations between rich and poor countries. In early 1971, he participated in the annual May Day celebrations sponsored by the Central Confederation of Workers (CUT) which was given legal recognition for the first time by the Allende government. On this occasion he also urged the unity of all workers, even though the CUT traditionally had been dominated by the Communist and Socialist parties.[39]

A few months later he publicly endorsed the nationalization of copper, despite the fact that the government decided to give no compensation to the North American companies affected (Kennecott and Anaconda) on grounds of excess profits in past years. In a statement on national television in October 1971, the cardinal also appealed to the people of the United States to respect Chile's efforts to gain control over its own course of development stating that: "I think the process of nationalization of copper is constitutionally impeccable."[40]

Furthermore, when Kennecott Copper attempted to establish a legal embargo on the sale of Chilean copper in Western Europe on the grounds that it was stolen property, Cardinal Silva obtained a denunciation of these efforts by the Justice and Peace Commission of the French Catholic bishops. He was publicly thanked by Allende during a press conference. He also petitioned Cardinal Cooke of New York to ask President Nixon to intercede with the World Bank that it not cut off loans to Chile in 1971.[41]

Two months before the Third United Nations Conference on Trade and Development (UNCTAD III), to be held in Santiago in April 1972,

[39] Carta del Cardenal Raúl Silva Henríquez a la C.U.T., "Unidad de los trabajadores cumple la ley del Señor," *Iglesia de Santiago* 8 (May 1971): 28.

[40] "Estados Unidos debe contribuir a que Chile conquista su desarrollo," *Iglesia de Santiago* 9 (November 1971): 13.

[41] "Presidente de la República se refiere a actitud de la Iglesia," *Iglesia de Santiago* 10 (November 1972): 12–13. The information about Cardinal Silva's request to Cardinal Cooke of New York to intercede with President Nixon was given to me by Arturo Gaete, S.J., of *Mensaje*.

the cardinal wrote a strongly-worded Lenten message to European Christians urging them to take more seriously the just economic demands of third-world countries. The tone and orientation of this open letter closely paralleled the foreign policy of the Popular Unity regime on these issues. Allende again thanked the cardinal and said that such a letter proved that in Chile "men of good will characterized by different ideological persuasions" could still "arrive at a common position in face of serious problems confronting the poor."[42]

Attempts were also made at lower echelons of the Church to ease the transition to socialism. The Sacred Heart Fathers and the Jesuits announced in early 1971 that they planned to turn over some of their private high schools to the government so as to reorient them more toward service to the poor. The U.S.-based Congregation of the Holy Cross kept its one school (St. George's in Santiago) but raised the tuition for rich students so as to give more scholarships to those from working-class areas.[43]

While not endorsing the policy of turning over a large number of Catholic schools to the state, the hierarchy in 1971 publicly declared their intention of making diocesan schools "open to all Chileans without social or economic discrimination." To achieve this they petitioned Congress to authorize greater public subsidies for those Catholic schools still charging tuition (24 percent of the total) so that they could admit more poor students free of cost.[44]

This willingness on the part of sectors of the clergy and the hierarchy to cooperate with the new government in areas of education was a clear indication that at the outset of the new regime there was no deep-seated fear at official levels of the Church as to the intentions of the government regarding Catholic schools. Had there been a concern that Allende once in office planned to follow the example of Eastern European communist regimes and nationalize all private schools, such overtures would not have been forthcoming from the religious orders and hierarchy in regards to a closer alignment of Catholic education with socialist objectives.

[42] Cardinal Raúl Silva Henríquez, "Llamado a los cristianos de los países desarrollados, February 1972," Mensaje 21 (March–April 1972): 135–37; "President Allende se refiere a la carta abierta del Cardenal," Iglesia de Santiago 10 (March 1972): 8–9.
[43] "Congregación de los SS.CC. adopta posiciones ante futuro de sus colegios," Iglesia de Santiago 8 (August 1971): 22–24; "¿Democratización de colegios clasistas?," Mensaje 20 (November 1971): 554–58; "Análisis de un camino para la Integración Escolar," Iglesia de Santiago 10 (August 1972): 13–18.
[44] "Declaración del Comité Permanente del Episcopado sobre la entrega de colegios católicos al estado," Santiago, 24 August 1971, in Documentos del Episcopado, ed. Oviedo, pp. 110–11; "El Cardenal informó a Diputados sobre postular de la Iglesia en la Educación," Iglesia de Santiago 8 (August 1971): 21.

Throughout 1971 and early 1972 attempts were also made by several apostolic movements sponsored by the Church to instill greater social awareness among their members and to encourage their active participation in the transition to socialism. A national meeting in January 1971 of clerical, religious, and lay leaders affirmed a commitment to develop small base communities in tune with socialist goals. They urged Christians in these communities to display "a generous and constructive attitude," and not to remain as spectators in Chile's transition from "a capitalist to a socialist context."[45]

The Plan of Action of the Archdiocese of Santiago outlining pastoral goals for 1972 to 1974 also emphasized as priorities the promotion of small communities (especially in working-class neighborhoods) and the participation of their members in social and political organizations. The plan articulated as one of its objectives for the following three years "placing the goods of the Church at the disposal of the local civic community" for the promotion of human development.[46]

A national conference of Catholic youth organizations held in early 1972 included in its objectives closer coordination with the movement toward socialism in the country "along the lines of the Gospel as articulated at Medellín." To achieve this, the group committed its organizational networks to challenge the "individualistic and egotistical mentality" of many young Catholics and to alert them "at the same time to their responsibilities in the construction of a new Chile."[47]

Furthermore, in late July 1971, six Christian Democratic congressmen withdrew from their party on the grounds that it was moving away from its traditional commitment to "communitarian socialism." They stated that the leadership of the party had repeatedly rejected their suggestions for closer cooperation with the government to construct a type of socialism that was humanistic and democratic. They also feared that Christian Democracy was moving toward an alliance with the National Party to form a united electoral opposition to the Left, and claimed that this would be against the spirit of recent pronouncements and actions by the hierarchy which were now more progressive than the PDC in regards to the "construction of a socialist society in Chile."[48] This group, along with the leadership of the youth wing of the PDC and some members of MAPU, joined together to form the new Christian Left Party (MIC). It

[45] "Primer Seminario de Responsables de Pastoral en Chile," *Iglesia de Santiago* 8 (March 1971): 3–10.

[46] "Programa de Acción Pastoral, 1972–1974," *Iglesia de Santiago* 10 (March 1972): 13–17.

[47] "Pastoral Juvenil: Prioridades de la Acción Pastoral," *Iglesia de Santiago* 10 (April 1972): 3–5.

[48] "Renuncia Partido Demócrata Cristiano," *Política y Espíritu* 27 (August 1971): 77.

explicitly supported Popular Unity efforts to socialize the economy with guarantees for worker participation in decision-making.[49]

Throughout this period *Mensaje,* the most respected Catholic periodical in Chile, adopted a very positive stance toward the policies of the new government. In five of eleven monthly issues of the magazine between October 1970 and November 1971, there appeared editorials endorsing the general direction and objectives of the new government and encouraging positive support by Christians.[50] In addition, several articles published in *Mensaje* during these months stressed the compatibility of democratic socialism with Christian principles, and implicitly or explicitly emphasized the importance of a close working relationship between the PDC and the UP for making such a system a reality in Chile.[51]

The government on its part responded favorably to these initiatives at various levels of the Church to make its roles and structures more compatible with socialist objectives. Complete freedom of religion was respected and there was no attempt to limit the independence of Catholic schools or other pastoral programs. State subsidies to Catholic primary and secondary education continued at the same level as before Allende took office, and at the university level actually increased. In fact, throughout the entire three-year period, public subsidies to the Catholic university system grew steadily so that by 1973, 80 percent of the operating costs of the main branch in Santiago were provided by the state (as compared to 60 percent at the end of Frei's presidency). This enabled the university to accept a larger number of low-income students, and to continue many of the extension services and programs related to research on national development inaugurated after the 1967 reforms.[52]

The television station at the Catholic University of Santiago contin-

---

[49] "El pensamiento de la Izquierda Cristiana," *Punto Final* (Santiago), no. 137 (1971), pp. 2–4.

[50] "El triunfo de la Unidad Popular," *Mensaje* 19 (October 1970): 454–55; "Jugando con fuego," *Mensaje* 19 (November 1970): 509; "Los cristianos en la construcción de la nueva sociedad," *Mensaje* 19 (December 1970): 71–73; "Comienza un año," *Mensaje* 20 (January–February 1971): 9–11; "El cobre: un desafío para Chile," *Mensaje* 20 (November 1971): 519–22.

[51] John Biehl, "Salvador Allende ya no es candidato," *Mensaje* 19 (October 1970): 448–50; Otto Boye, "Comienzos de la administración Allende," *Mensaje* 19 (December 1970): 567–69; Sergio Molina and Hernán Larraín, S.J., "Socialismo democrático: alternativa al socialismo totalitario," pp. 75–83; Julio Silva Solar, "La construcción pluralista del socialismo," *Mensaje* 20 (June 1971): 210–17.

[52] This information was provided to me by José Zalaquett, deputy vice rector of academic affairs at the Catholic University of Santiago during 1973. For a statement by the rector affirming that the government of Allende had respected the Catholic University's freedom during its term in office, see Fernando Castillo Velasco, "Universidad: pluralismo y independencia política," *Mensaje* 22 (June 1973): 264–65.

ued to operate freely, although the director, Fr. Raúl Hasbún, was not favorable to socialist objectives. The government respected the right of the station to express dissent, but did refuse permission and additional subsidies to expand its transmissions through use of public transmittors throughout the provinces. This did not become, however, a major source of conflict between Church and state during this period of official cordial relations.

In addition to these overtures of good will by the Left, when the new Christian Left Party was formed in 1971 its leaders were immediately invited into the governing coalition and were given representation in several cabinets over the next two years. The administration hoped by this to precipitate more defections from Christian Democracy, and thus build a stronger bridge between progressive Catholicism and Marxism for its governing coalition. While the Christian Left remained a very small party and never attracted a large following of Catholics,[53] its continued support for the government's objectives and participation in the administration (along with MAPU) was an indication that strategic collaboration by Marxists and leftist Christians was realized at the highest levels of the Popular Unity government.

A final pattern of structural compatibility between Church and state which was established during Allende's first year in office (and which continued up to the military coup) was the freedom for the Church to receive substantial financial subsidies from abroad for its pastoral and social programs. Between 1970 and 1973 foreign Church agencies in Western Europe and North America continued to send very significant monetary and material support to projects sponsored by the Chilean Church (see Table 2.9).

Although the administration expanded public programs in areas where the Church previously was active (nutrition, housing, community organization), it made no efforts to restrict Church projects nor limit the entrance into the country of outside sources of finance supporting such programs. Ecclesiastical leaders, however, made no attempt to increase Church-sponsored programs, nor to link existing ones closely to those of the government. The Church basically attempted to maintain its presence in this area, and to conduct a holding operation of ongoing projects. There is no evidence that foreign Church money was used to mount a campaign of opposition to the regime while Allende was in office.[54]

[53] In the 1973 parliamentary elections, the Christian Left Party (MIC) polled 1.2 percent of the vote, electing one deputy and one senator to the Congress.
[54] The largest single foreign Church donor, Catholic Relief Services, continued to send large amounts of clothing and medicine as well as U.S. government food supplies (P.L. 480, Title II) to Chile during these years. There was some decline in the average yearly dollar value of material as compared to the Frei period, but no drastic reductions occurred. West German and (direct) U.S. government support to

Hence, throughout the first fifteen months of the Popular Unity regime, the government made a significant beginning toward a transition to socialism within the existing constitutional framework, respected traditional civil and political liberties, welcomed collaboration by commited Christians in its coalition, and respected the interests of the Church. In turn, the hierarchy and groups at lower levels of the Church used their moral and structural resources to promote autonomous national development and the distribution of goods and services favoring the poor. In some cases there was clear enthusiasm by Church elites for socialist objectives (e.g., the cardinal, *Mensaje,* some religious congregations and lay apostolic movements). In other cases there was acquiescence and at least a willingness to coexist peacefully with the state (the bishops, Cáritas-Chile, Catholic University T.V. station). There was no significant opposition to the government by official Church elites in this period, and authoritative decisions made at the top of the Church's organization to accept the basic direction of the government were transmitted down the layered administrative framework of the institution fairly consistently without any major conflict with the UP.[55]

Moderating Role of Church Leaders during Mounting Public
Opposition to the Government (February 1972–March 1973)

As resistance to the Popular Unity's nationalization policies developed in 1972, the public position of the Church continued to provide important legitimacy for the administration and its general objectives. Some lay groups closely associated with the Church (especially sectors of

---

Church-sponsored social projects in Chile ceased during the Allende years (see Table 2.9).

There is no indication that partisan political considerations influenced distribution of Church-administered materials within Chile. What is true, however, is that Cáritas-Chile (the local Church organization responsible for administering CRS materials) did not want to promote new social action projects within the country closely associated with the structures of the regime. While there was no direct conflict between Cáritas and the government, neither was there strong enthusiasm from Cáritas to identify itself closely with public programs. (Interview on 28 October 1977 in Washington, D.C. with Patrick Ahern, Program Assistant of Catholic Relief Services in Santiago from October 1971 to November 1973.)

[55] In an interview with a journalist in 1972, Luis Corvalán, secretary of the Communist Party, said he believed the Church had maintained "a friendly relationship with both the president and the government" during its first year in office. In commenting on the critical position toward the government expressed by Fr. Raúl Hasbún of Channel 13, the Catholic University television station in Santiago, Corvalán downplayed its significance in light of the officially supportive attitude expressed by the cardinal toward the administration:

There are opposing viewpoints and problems arising from contradictions within the Church itself. The point I would like to emphasize is the fact that the official policy of the Church as an institution is fundamentally positive and friendly toward the government, including the stance of the cardinal who is head of the Church.
[Labarca Goddard, *Corvalán, 27 Horas,* pp. 208–9]

the PDC) moved toward stronger opposition to the government and an alliance with the Right. Many clerical leaders, however (the cardinal, the Episcopal Conference, and *Mensaje*), maintained a publicly respectful stance toward the administration. In fact, at several key moments during this period they condemned illegal actions by extremist groups outside the government and urged compromise and cooperation between the UP and the PDC. By so doing, several Church elites attempted to play a moderating role amidst growing political polarization and thus prevent a breakdown of constitutional processes.

In February 1972, the opposition-controlled Congress approved a constitutional amendment requiring specific legislation for all past and future state takeovers of privately owned firms. Allende vetoed the amendment, arguing that existing laws dating back to the 1930s provided sufficient legal basis for his nationalization policies, and pushed ahead with his socialist program. Extremist groups on the Left (particularly the MIR) moved even faster than the administration, and staged illegal seizures of farms and factories not designated for nationalization.

In addition, black-market profiteering by merchants to avoid price regulations, disruptions in agricultural production due to accelerated land reform, and government distribution policies favoring working-class sectors, all combined to produce shortages of basic commodities in middle- and upper-income urban areas. Street demonstrations were orchestrated by opposition groups in which violent clashes between anti- and pro-government forces broke out.

During these emerging tensions and disruptions, the bishops issued a joint statement in mid-April 1972 supporting the basic orientations of the government and calling for mutual respect among opposing political factions. They praised such accomplishments of the administration to date as greater social participation, more equality, respect for freedom to dissent, and liberty of conscience. They also reminded citizens that the process of change taking place "corresponds to the will of the vast majority" and could not be realized without "sacrifice by those with privilege." Consequently, they invited all Chileans to work for the development of the country by supporting greater opportunity for the poor in health care, education, culture, employment, and housing. They recognized, however, that "only mutual respect and fraternal understanding could create a society of equal and united people" and warned against violence and narrow sectarianism.[56]

During the next several months, however, the economic situation worsened. This was accompanied by a hardening of political positions

---

[56] "Por un camino de esperanza y alegría," Punta de Tralca, 11 April 1972, *Mensaje* 21 (May 1972): 293–94.

on both sides. Domestic and foreign investment declined dramatically, loans and credits from the United States and international financial institutions heavily dependent on U.S. capital were drastically curtailed, and inflation climbed to over 30 percent for the first seven months of 1972. (By December it would reach 163 percent for the entire calendar year.) Conversations between the government and the PDC to settle differences on nationalization policies ended in stalemates in mid-July. Subsequently, Christian Democratic leaders announced an alliance with the conservative National Party for the 1973 parliamentary elections.

In August a series of strikes by shopkeepers in Santiago and in several of the provinces heightened political tensions. Roving bands of pro- and anti-government demonstrators clashed in major cities of the country. The administration declared a state of emergency and for brief periods suspended public meetings and constitutional guarantees, ordering the police to use more force to control disturbances. Finally, in early September Allende made a dramatic announcement that he had uncovered a right-wing plot abetted by foreign copper companies to overthrow the government.

At this point the official voice of the hierarchy intervened again, appealing for moderation and respect for law. On the same day as Allende's dramatic announcement of a possible coup, a message from Cardinal Silva was read over television. In it he warned that the "specter of fratricidal war" loomed on the horizon. "We must destroy hatred," he said, "before hatred destroys the soul of Chile." He condemned violence as a means to promote change and urged all citizens to "respect legality" and to modify laws "with the same processes by which they were made." He concluded by reaffirming his hope and his confidence in "our democratic institutions and in our public authorities, called to serve and guarantee national unity."[57]

While implicitly calling upon the government to establish with Congress a clearer legal framework for further nationalization and to remain within the law in curbing civil disturbances, the weight of his remarks was clearly directed against extremists outside the government and their use of violence. His affirmation of confidence in "democratic institutions" and "public authorities" was also an important sign of continued Church support for the existing government.

Furthermore, the position of *Mensaje* (unlike the late 1960s) closely paralleled that of the bishops throughout mounting tensions in early and mid-1972. Of the seven issues of the journal published between February and September, two carried editorials strongly denouncing ex-

[57] Cardinal Raúl Silva Henríquez, "Congoja y esperanza," Santiago, 2 September 1972, *Mensaje* 21 (October 1972): 618.

tremist slogans and violent tactics on the far Right and the far Left.[58] Two more editorials explicitly endorsed dialogue and cooperation between the UP and the PDC, arguing that a further distancing by Christian Democrats from the government, as well as accusations by sectors of the administration of fascist tendencies in the PDC, would seriously damage the prospects for democratic socialism.[59] Several articles appearing in *Mensaje* during this period stressed the necessity for more self-criticism within both the UP and the PDC, and emphasized the feasibility for mutual accommodation on the conditions for further nationalization of industry.[60]

In commenting on Cardinal Silva's T.V. message of early September, *Mensaje* also explicitly rejected the desirability of military intervention. A strongly worded editorial urged both government and opposition to take the cardinal's words to heart and admit their respective failures and ideological blindnesses. Otherwise, argued the editorial, extremist groups would precipitate a military coup leaving "thousands dead" and producing "economic paralysis."[61]

The crisis of August and early September passed, but a month later another series of strikes paralyzed the entire country for over three weeks. On 10 October, the Confederation of Truck Drivers (most of whom owned their own vehicles) began a nationwide strike demanding higher rates and protesting the establishment of a state trucking agency in one province in the south of Chile. They were joined by shopkeepers, taxi drivers, construction workers, independent farmers, physicians, and bank employees all protesting shortage of goods and again demanding more precise legal constraints on nationalization policies.

The government retaliated by jailing leaders of the trucking confederation and threatened requisition of all stores that shut down. Trucks of striking enterprises were requisitioned, and twenty-one of the twenty-five provinces were placed under military control to keep goods flowing into urban areas. The government also took over private radio stations to prevent possible distortion of information and incitement to riot, but relinquished them when the controller general declared such action illegal.

[58] "Enfrentamiento y madurez política," *Mensaje* 21 (May 1972): 236–39; "Lo Hermida: transformación de una tragedia," *Mensaje* 21 (September 1972): 508–11.
[59] "No a los extremismos," *Mensaje* 21 (January–February 1972): 11–16; "Nuevos ministros, conversaciones, C.U.T.," *Mensaje* 21 (July 1972): 376–80.
[60] Jaime Ruiz-Tagle, "De la reforma industrial al conflicto de poderes," *Mensaje* 21 (May 1972): 233–35; Ruiz-Tagle, "Tensión en la Unidad Popular," *Mensaje* 21 (July 1972): 369–72; Alejandro Foxley, "Convergencias y divergencias en los projectos socialistas para Chile," *Mensaje* 21 (August 1972): 443–48.
[61] "El mensaje del Cardenal: una lección de septiembre," *Mensaje* 21 (October 1972): 569.

All major opposition parties supported the strikes, and the PDC accused the government of flagrantly violating its promise to respect constitutional guarantees. Christian Democratic leaders also refused an invitation to confer with Allende in order to find a solution to the crisis. The hierarchy, however, accepted such a request by the president, and ten bishops met with Allende on 20 October, offering their assistance in resolving the conflict. The next day the Permanent Committee of the Episcopal Conference issued a public declaration reaffirming the official Church's belief that the great majority of Chileans favored "constitutional continuity, respect and obedience for legitimate authority, and the rule of law applied to all citizens." The bishops emphasized that most people favored the processes of change underway aimed at liberating the poor from injustice and misery and providing widespread participation at every level of decision-making. They also called upon Christians of all political persuasions to work together in finding a constructive solution to the crisis. Finally, they affirmed the belief that the vast majority of citizens wanted the upcoming congressional elections in March 1973 to take place in a "democratic atmosphere with the complete freedom of expression to which we are accustomed."[62]

The situation was resolved on 5 November when the president appointed the three commanders-in-chief of the armed forces to cabinet posts, and gave assurances that the government would not nationalize trucking firms. The administration returned all properties requisitioned during the strikes and abandoned legal actions and sanctions against striking unions or their leaders. This crisis passed, and both government and opposition forces turned their attention toward mobilizing their respective supporters for the March congressional elections.

Throughout these months of rising political tension in 1972, relations between the official leadership of Church and state remained cordial and constructive. While Christian Democratic leaders moved into a position of opposition to the regime and accused it of betraying its commitment to respect the Constitution, the hierarchy did not take such a public stance. They remained openly supportive of the basic social and economic goals of the government and levelled the brunt of their criticism at those who resorted to violence and disruption in opposing public policies. Furthermore, during the first serious attempt to unseat the administration in September and October when rumors of a coup were spreading, the cardinal, the Episcopal Conference, and *Mensaje* in no way abetted these efforts. In fact, they unanimously

---

[62] Comité Permanente del Episcopado de Chile, "Pedimos un espíritu constructivo y fraternal," Santiago, 21 October 1972, *Mensaje* 21 (November 1972): 682.

placed their respective moral prestige behind constitutional continuity and political accommodations to avoid further chaos or military intervention.

It was clear by the end of the year, however, that the bishops' appeals for dialogue and cooperation were not being heeded by key Catholic elites in the Christian Democratic Party. Nor was the government itself willing to compromise on its nationalization policies and seek an accommodation with Congress. It was also evident that many citizens in both middle- and upper-income sectors were losing confidence in normal political channels, and that the country had entered upon a phase of critical polarization and simmering violence.[63]

The social and political processes needed to guarantee reasonable accommodation of differences were experiencing very significant strain by late 1972. The Church's voice on behalf of civility in society was falling on deaf ears. This seriously limited its capacity to act as an effective legitimizing force for constitutional government.

Church-State Tensions during the Final Months of the Government (March–September 1973)

During the final months of Allende's presidency, Church-state relations were severely strained when the government proposed to overstep the boundaries of its earlier normative commitments in education. Conversely, the hierarchy began to articulate more critical attitudes toward the policies of the administration as disruptions grew more serious, and some groups closely affiliated with the Church clashed head-on with the government.

However, it is important to emphasize that the *official* posture of the Church never moved to a position of formal opposition. The bishops, notwithstanding private resentments and fears, to the very end made public efforts to promote reconciliation between the UP and its democratic opponents. Moderate forces within the government and the opposition welcomed such overtures and responded positively to them, unfortunately without success.

[63] A poll of 300 residents of Santiago in August 1972, commissioned by the weekly magazine, *Ercilla*, and carried out by the consulting firm, Ingenieros Consultores Asociados, indicated very serious polarization of opinion along class lines as to government performance. Seventy-five percent of those in low-income sectors indicated that it was easy for them to buy essential household products, whereas 99 percent of the upper class and 77 percent of the middle class said it was difficult. Conversely, 72 percent of the upper-income groups and 52 percent of the middle class expressed belief that government performance to date was poor, while 68 percent of the workers said it was good or adequate. An average of 83 percent of *all* respondents, however—including 98 percent of the rich, 92 percent from the middle-income brackets, and 75 percent of the poor—said that a climate of violence prevailed in the country. "¿Qué piensan los chilenos hoy?," *Ercilla*, 13–19 September 1972, pp. 10–11.

The elections of March 1973 did not break the stalemate between the executive and Congress. Votes for the Left totalled 43.9 percent—a substantial increase from the 36.2 percent Allende received in 1970, but below its 48.6 percent in the 1971 municipal elections. The combined opposition of Christian Democratic and National Party candidates gained a clear majority of 54.2 percent, but failed to win the two-thirds majority they had striven for in order to override presidential vetoes and possibly impeach Allende.

Each side interpreted the results differently. The united opposition argued their majority support was a clear mandate for a rollback in government policies. The administration, however, claimed a moral victory since, it said, in recent history it was unprecedented for a government to surpass its winning presidential vote in the next parliamentary elections.

The result was that the president (urged by left-wing forces in his own Socialist Party) decided to move ahead with nationalization policies, still refusing to negotiate an agreement with Congress as to the extent and quality of state controls.[64] Part of this thrust toward continued nationalization also involved private schools. Shortly after the election, the Ministry of Education announced an educational reform program to provide better opportunities for workers and establish a unifying educational ideology throughout the whole country.

This proposed National Unified School System (Escuela Nacional Unificada—ENU) included in its objectives the "harmonious development of the personality of youth formed in the values of socialist humanism." It also aimed to effect a "change in the consumer mentality associated with capitalist society" and to promote a "productive spirit of human solidarity" among all students. To achieve this, the state would establish greater coordination of all levels of education, include more technical and vocational training in curricula, set up comprehensive work-study programs, and offer greater extension services and adult education for workers.[65]

Under this reform plan, all private schools would be required to adopt the ideology and structures of ENU. Twenty-five percent of primary and secondary school enrollments were in private institutions, almost all controlled by the Church. Furthermore, the Ministry of Education was to begin the program in secondary schools within three months, and

---

[64] For a discussion of the various options open to Allende after the inconclusive results of the March elections and the pressures within sectors of the Socialist Party to move ahead more rapidly rather than seek accommodation with Congress, see A. Valenzuela, *Chile*, pp. 87–88.

[65] Ministerio de Educación Pública, "Informe sobre 'Escuela Nacional Unificada,'" *Cuadernos de la Realidad Nacional* (Santiago), no. 17 (July 1973), pp. 23–46.

would continue implementation until it had been established at all levels of education by 1976.[66]

At this point the Catholic bishops for the first time took a public position in clear opposition to a government policy. In their view, despite several positive aspects of the reform which they recognized, the government was overstepping the boundaries of its electoral platform commitments made in 1970 to respect diversity in education and to encourage widespread participation in proposed changes by groups affected by its reforms.

Consequently, on 27 March the Permanent Committee of the Episcopal Conference issued a public statement praising some elements of ENU, but strongly objected to the lack of pluralism and consultation. They supported some objectives, such as the integration of work and study, greater educational opportunities for every stage of life, and an end to discrimination on the basis of class. They claimed, however, that such a unified school system, as it was proposed, did not give sufficient consideration to the "religious values which are part of the spiritual patrimony of Chile." According to the bishops, the proposal was also based on an assumption that the majority of the country was in favor of the revolutionary ideology underlying ENU. They pointed out that a "considerable part of the country" was in disagreement, and further complained that the timetable set down for implementation was too rapid. They urged, therefore, that there be more discussion of the proposal by all sectors of the population affected by it, including parents, teachers, and students.[67]

---

[66] Although all sectors in the government coalition accepted the substance of this proposal (since it reflected the educational objectives outlined in the UP platform of 1970), differences existed within the administration as to the style of the rhetoric and timetable for its implementation. Jorge Tapia Valdés, the minister of education, with the backing of members of his Radical Party, sought to delay the plan until public discussion and wider consultation could occur as originally promised in the 1970 UP platform. Sectors of the Socialist and Communist parties in the ministry, however, pressed for the original draft, and it was this version which was released just after the March congressional elections. A. Valenzuela, *Chile*, p. 89.

[67] Comité Permanente del Episcopado de Chile, "Declaración del Comité Permanente del Episcopado de Chile sobre la Escuela Nacional Unificada," Santiago, 27 March 1973, in *Documentos del Episcopado*, ed. Oviedo, pp. 152–53. The military (whose leaders had withdrawn from the cabinet after the March elections) were also opposed to ENU, and commanding officers from the various branches of service made their objections clearly known to the minister of education. At a meeting with him, they claimed that ENU as proposed was an attempt to politicize in partisan fashion the country's youth, and that eventually this would have a deleterious impact within the ranks of the armed forces. ENU was, they said, a threat to national security and to the hierarchical chain of command in the military. *La Segunda* (Santiago), 12 April 1973; *La Prensa* (Santiago), 13 April 1973. Opposition parties in Congress, the conservative press, and associations of students and parents involved in private education also vigorously criticized ENU. For an assessment of the implications of the proposal and of the debate surrounding it, see Kathleen B. Fischer, "Political Ideology and Educational Reform in Chile, 1964–1976."

Reaction to ENU by other sectors of the official Church was stronger and more provocative. Fr. Raúl Hasbún, director of the Catholic University T.V. station in Santiago, escalated his criticisms of the government at this time, and stated publicly that he now believed a "confrontation between totalitarian Marxism and the Catholic Church is inevitable." He also attempted to expand the Catholic T.V.'s transmission beyond Santiago without government permission.[68]

When a local affiliate Catholic channel in Concepción was jammed by a corresponding public station, a mysterious bombing of the government transmitter occurred and an employee lost his life. Media publications of the Communist and Socialist parties launched a bitter personal attack on Hasbún, and charged that he conspired with agents of the reactionary and violent Fatherland and Freedom organization (Patria y Libertad) in the crime and was therefore guilty of the death of an innocent person.[69]

The bishops vigorously defended Hasbún and strongly criticized his detractors for making unsubstantiated accusations.[70] The charges were never proved to be true. During the same period clashes occurred in the streets of Santiago between Catholic school students, protesting ENU, and the police. These incidents further strained relations between the Church and the government.

Soon after official ecclesiastical criticism of ENU in late March (and with opposition mounting from other sectors), the minister of education sent a long, conciliatory letter to Cardinal Silva. He insisted that the reform plan did respect the values of Christian humanism, and observed that ideological pluralism in the program would be guaranteed by the fact that a diversity of political groups supported the government—Marxists, rationalists, Christians. The minister, however, did thank the bishops for their contribution to the debate, and announced a postponement of ENU until further discussion could occur.[71] The plan was shelved and not reintroduced while Allende was in office. Although a prolonged Church-state confrontation was thus avoided, the disagreement over ENU marked a cooling in the hierarchy's previously cordial relations with the government.[72]

---

[68] *La Tribuna* (Santiago), 26 March 1973.

[69] *El Siglo* (Santiago), 1 April 1973; Victor Vaccaro, "La caída del Comando de Cura Hasbún," *Chile Hoy* (Santiago), 2 June 1973, p. 7.

[70] Asamblea Plenaria del Episcopado, "Carta de adhesión al Pbro. Sr. Raúl Hasbún," Punta de Tralca, 11 April 1973, in *Documentos del Episcopado*, ed. Oviedo, pp. 158–59.

[71] The text of this letter is reproduced in ibid., pp. 156–58.

[72] In a more extensive document issued by the entire Episcopal Conference in June, the hierarchy claimed that ENU would turn schools into a battleground. Although the administration described the reform as "pluralistic," "democratic," and "humanist," the bishops argued that it was in fact dominated by a "Marxist-Lenin-

After the March elections the administration pushed on with its nationalization of industry in opposition to the newly elected Congress. This resulted in a hardening of ideological positions on both sides, and an increase of violence by extremist groups on the Right and Left. It became increasingly more difficult for the administration to maintain order, and, although the Church never formally withdrew its support, in the final months the hierarchy did manifest a more critical attitude of government performance than before the March elections.

After the election the new cabinet committed itself to nationalize forty firms that had been occupied by workers during the October truckers' strike. In April the Movement of the Revolutionary Left (MIR) engineered a series of new takeovers of factories and food distribution centers which resulted in a violent clash with the police. On the far Right, Fatherland and Freedom annnounced support in May for civil war as a last resort to overthrow Allende. At about the same time, a party convention of Christian Democrats passed by a narrow margin a resolution stating that Chile faced the prospect of a Marxist dictatorship and that the PDC's response had to be one of continued and increased opposition.[73]

Added to this escalating political polarization in May, was a series of strikes by copper miners charging that the government had cheated them of previously agreed upon wage increases. Violent clashes between police and miners followed, and when the administration refused the pay increases, the Congress impeached the minister of labor and the minister of mines. The Supreme Court also criticized the executive branch for an abuse of power when the secretary general of the government closed down a right-wing radio station for allegedly broadcasting false reports on disturbances in the mining strike.[74]

---

ist" ideology that did not respect the rights of parents to determine the style of education for their children. They also charged that it was unconstitutional, since the statute of democratic guarantees (added to the Constitution just before Allende's confirmation by Congress in 1970) stated that education be democratic, pluralist, and free from all politically partisan orientations. The bishops concluded by sketching an alternative Catholic view of educational reform allowing for more freedom of choice and decentralization of structures. "El momento actual de la educación en Chile: documento de trabajo," *Mundo '73* (Santiago), no. 61 (July 1973).

[73] By this point, conservative forces within the PDC (centering on the former president, Eduardo Frei) had gained predominance in the party's leadership. This group was adamantly opposed to major compromise with the government and was convinced that Allende and the Left were out to impose a Marxist dictatorship on the country. For an analysis of the strategies and counterstrategies of the PDC and the UP during the last six months of Allende's term in office, see A. Valenzuela, *Chile,* pp. 88–106.

[74] For a rather comprehensive factual summary of the week-by-week political and economic developments in Chile during these final months of Allende's term in office, see Lester A. Sobel, ed., *Chile and Allende,* pp. 109–40.

The literature on the events and causes that precipitated the downfall of the Pop-

In the context of this mounting crisis of authority and intensification of violence, nine bishops from the central provinces (including Cardinal Silva) issued a public letter in early June criticizing both the opposition and the government for what they considered to be illegitimate actions. They condemned black-market practices and the exodus of professionals from the country—strategies that characterized opposition groups exploiting economic scarcity for their own self-interest. For the first time since Allende took office, however, the hierarchy accused the administration of tendencies toward statism. In the wake of the PDC's May declaration of the danger of a Marxist dictatorship, the bishops warned Chileans of the same possibility:

> We are concerned about the tendency toward absolute statism without sufficient participation. . . . The Church has always denounced totalitarianism. Under this name we include all types of total and absolute systems, which, although founded on different and sometimes mutually contradictory ideologies, tolerate no opposition, no criticism, or countervailing forces.[75]

They also condemned other actions of which both pro- and anti-government groups were guilty—distortions in the media, incitement to hatred, violence in mining areas. Finally, they decried a hardening of positions across the political spectrum and once more appealed for mutual respect of persons despite ideological differences:

> We ask for people to look more at what unites them than at what divides them. We feel it is more necessary to serve real people with names and faces than to play with words and definitions. People count more than systems—persons are more important than ideologies. Ideologies divide people, but history, blood, common language, human love, and the common project which all Chileans share should help us form one family. Our words have no other objective or hope than to help all see each other as equals, as brothers. We as a people do

---

ular Unity government is vast, and much of it is heavily colored by the political and ideological commitments of the respective authors. A useful early critique of thirty-one books and articles on the subject has been done by Arturo and J. Samuel Valenzuela, "Visions of Chile," *Latin American Research Review* 10 (Fall 1975): 155–75. A good critique of twelve recent books has been done by Simon Collier, "Allende's Chile: Contemporary History and the Counterfactual," *Journal of Latin American Studies* (London) 12 (November 1980): 445–52. The best political analyses in English are A. Valenzuela, *Chile,* and Paul E. Sigmund, *Overthrow of Allende.* An excellent appraisal of the economic performance and failures has been done by Stefan de Vylder, *Allende's Chile: The Political Economy of the Rise and Fall of the Unidad Popular.* A very useful collection which includes appraisals by several ex-leaders of the UP administration is Federico G. Gil et al., eds. *Chile at the Turning Point: Lessons of the Socialist Years, 1970–1973.*

[75] Cardinal Silva Henríquez et al., "Solo con amor se es capaz de construir un país," Santiago, 1 June 1973, *Mensaje* 22, (July 1973): 336.

not deserve to live amidst anxiety, uncertainty, hatred, and vengeance.[76]

Although this letter included a strong criticism of the government, it also was another appeal for moderation by the opposition and for a willingness to communicate on both sides. That it was not read primarily as an attack on the government can be shown by press reaction to it. *El Mercurio,* the most prestigious daily paper in the country and a strong opponent of Allende, criticized the bishops for being too easy on the government. The tabloid of the far Left, *Clarín,* interpreted the letter as a clear denunciation of subversive tactics of the opposition.[77]

These calls for moderation by Church leaders, however, had little impact on the course of events over the next month. In mid-June more strikes by professionals and teachers were organized in five major provinces in support of miners demanding higher pay and in protest against the government's economic policies. Striking miners marched on Santiago and, despite a police blockade, many broke through and were welcomed at rallies on the campus of the Catholic University organized by anti-government student groups. Riots in Santiago and other major cities coincided with these incidents and troops were called out to quell shootings.

The leading opposition newspaper, *El Mercurio,* was closed for printing a National Party declaration saying that the government had repeatedly violated the Constitution and therefore was illegitimate. The courts overturned the closure order, and the president and the thirteen Supreme Court justices exchanged bitter accusations of each other's actions.

On 29 June, 100 rebel troops stormed the ministry of defense and presidential palace in Santiago with tanks. The attempted coup was put down by army forces loyal to the government, but Allende declared a week-long state of emergency throughout the country. Fatherland and Freedom claimed responsibility for the revolt, and in mid-July announced it would unleash a total armed offensive to overthrow the government.

It was revealed later that the CIA spent $6.5 million for covert activi-

---

[76] Ibid.

[77] *El Mercurio* (Santiago), 8 June 1973; *Clarín* (Santiago), 6 June 1973.
The editorial staff of *Mensaje,* like the bishops, also accused the government of committing some errors that were preparing the ground for statism. They still recognized, however, the possibility and desirability of constructing a form of socialism in Chile that would avoid the abuses of power perpetrated by existing Marxist regimes in other countries. They also condemned the exit of professionals from the country out of a desire to make more money. "Los que se alejan," *Mensaje* 22 (June 1973): 223–25.

ties (worth over $30 million when exchanged on the black market inside Chile) supporting opposition groups between 1970 and 1973. The money was furnished to media organizations, political parties, and private groups critical of the Allende regime.[78] While it is clear that domestic opposition to the administration had a capacity of its own to carry on resistance and even subversion, it is also undeniable that such massive financial assistance substantially reinforced the determination and effectiveness of these organizations, especially during Allende's last six months in office.

In the context of this final assault on the government and amidst growing rumors that both pro- and anti-government forces were stockpiling arms, the Episcopal Conference made another effort to promote dialogue. In mid-July the bishops issued an urgent warning that the scourge of "civil war" was imminent. They did not call upon the government to cease its efforts to promote socialism as a necessary means to avoid the catastrophe. In fact, they recognized that further structural changes were necessary in order to put "justice into practice" in a way that "guarantees the poorest and weakest a proportionate share of resources." The bishops also indicated that they believed there still was a "willingness to effect urgent and profound social changes" among the vast majority of citizens regardless of ideological differences. They affirmed that many "social and political groups within government and in the opposition" shared a common desire to construct "a new Chile, built on respect for every human being." They called upon such groups to create conditions of dialogue and mutual understanding so as to form a "national consensus" and thus allow "social transformations" to continue. "Each sector must put aside," they said, "the effort to make its interpretation of social reality the only valid one." Finally, they called for another serious attempt at negotiation between representatives of the government and the opposition parties in order to rebuild trust and reach a consensus.[79]

The bishops did not include in their pronouncements a clear rejection of military intervention. They seemed to be more preoccupied by the fear of civil war than of a coup. However, their statement in no way was an invitation to the armed forces to overthrow the government, and, in fact provided one more opportunity for civilian leaders to attempt a resolution of their differences.

[78] U.S. Congress, Senate, Staff Report of the Select Committee to Study Governmental Operations with Respect to Intelligence Activities, "Covert Action in Chile: 1963–1973," *Hearings Before the Select Committee to Study Governmental Operations with Respect to Intelligence Activities*, 94th Cong., 1st sess., 1975, vol. 7, Appendix A, p. 189.

[79] Comité Permanente del Episcopado de Chile, "La paz de Chile tiene un precio," Santiago, 16 July 1973, *Mensaje* 22 (August 1973): 396.

Mensaje was even more explicit than the bishops in opposing a military takeover. In an August editorial the journal bluntly stated that "a military coup at this moment would clearly entail a dictatorship of the Right." To avoid it, they urged military leaders not to "harbor in their ranks irresponsible groups bent on a coup," and encouraged the UP and the PDC "to find a minimum of consensus between them."[80]

Furthermore, the rectors of the six private universities in the country (including the three Church-related institutions—the Catholic University of Santiago, the Catholic University of Valparaíso, and the University of the North in Antofagasta) also issued a joint statement calling upon political leaders to "search for a certain level of loyal democratic consensus." They appealed to all citizens to respect "legally constituted authorities," and affirmed the necessity of continued loyalty by the military to democratic institutions. Finally, they urged the government to exercise leadership in engaging in dialogue with the opposition and in providing guidelines for a solution to the crisis.[81]

These appeals by religious and educational leaders for another effort at negotiation met with positive reactions among moderates in the government and the opposition. Two days after the bishops' call for a truce, the minister of defense invited the PDC to begin a dialogue. On the same day, spokespersons for the Communist Party warmly endorsed the hierarchy's call to negotiations and praised their statement as articulating the wishes of a majority of Chileans, not only those of religious believers. Two weeks later the PDC also responded favorably to the bishops, citing their 16 July statement as "opportune" and promising to begin talks with Allende out of a conviction of "moral and patriotic duty."[82]

Extremist groups on the far Right and Left, however, opposed the suggestions of the bishops. National Party spokespersons reminded the hierarchy that more than peace was at stake in Chile. The Church, they said, should be more vigilant in protecting all the other values of Christian culture threatened by communism, and should explicitly denounce "violent sectors" associated with the government. The Right also referred to possible dialogues between government and opposition leaders as "a waste of time." Fatherland and Liberty rejected such conversations, as did the MIR. Leftist sectors of Allende's own Socialist Party

[80] "Hacia una democracia," *Mensaje* 22 (August 1973): 346–48.
[81] "Declaración de los rectores de las universidades no estatales," *Mensaje* 22 (August 1973): 383–84.
[82] "Carta del Senador Luis Corvalán, Secretario General del Partido Comunista, al Cardenal Raúl Silva Henríquez," *El Siglo,* 18 July 1973, p. 1; "La necesidad del diálogo en Chile," *El Siglo,* 18 July 1973, p. 4; "Carta del Senador Patricio Aylwin, Presidente de la Democracia Cristiana, al Cardenal Raúl Silva Henríquez," *El Mercurio,* 30 July 1973, p. 26.

also categorically ruled out "all dialogue with parties and organizations who openly or secretly promote or participate in the counterrevolution."[83]

Notwithstanding extremist opposition to further attempts at political negotiations (and some serious doubts among Christian Democrats), Patrico Aylwin, president of the PDC, conferred with Allende for two days at the end of July. Oral agreement was reached by the two leaders regarding the necessity for a constitutional reform bill clearly delineating areas of the economy that would be under state control. The Christian Democrats, however, made several other demands as well: (1) the disarming of paramilitary groups on the Right and Left; (2) the restoration of factories and farm properties seized by workers after the aborted June 29th coup; and (3) a role for the military at lower levels of government, not merely in cabinet posts. Allende indicated he needed time to win support for these demands among his coalition, especially within his own Socialist Party.[84]

Over the course of the next two weeks, however, no action was taken by the government while Allende was negotiating within his own coalition on the PDC's demands. During this time truck owners launched another nationwide strike, joined by many professionals and shopkeepers, and this was openly endorsed by the PDC. Sabotage by extremist groups resulted in the assassination of Allende's naval aide-de-camp and the bombing of power stations and railroad lines. Fatherland and Liberty claimed responsibility for most of these actions, and announced in late August that their aim was to accelerate chaos and precipitate a military takeover. Further violent street clashes occurred between pro- and anti-government forces in urban areas, and the military killed several workers in attempting to search factories for caches of arms.[85]

The cardinal, at Allende's request, made a final effort at reconciliation in mid-August. He invited both the president and Aylwin to lunch in his home on 17 August, at which time Allende again promised to implement several demands of the PDC in the near future. Opposition within the UP coalition to compromise continued, however, and no immediate action was taken by the administration after this second meeting between Allende and Aylwin.[86]

On the Christian Democratic side, groups sympathetic to some sort of

[83] "Declaraciones del Diputado Nacional Mario Arnello sobre el llamado del Cardenal y la favorable respuesta del Partido Comunista," La Tribuna, 25 July 1973; "En torno a declaraciones del Cardenal," La Tribuna, 25 July 1973; La Nación, 24 July 1973, p. 29; Ruiz-Tagle, "Los obispos, el diálogo y la 'Via Chilena,'" Mensaje 22 (September 1973): 401–2.

[84] Sobel, ed., Chile and Allende, p. 133.

[85] Ibid.

[86] "Hechos del diálogo," SELADOC (Santiago) 1 (June 1974): 24.

military solution were becoming more outspoken while others escalated their attacks on the UP. The party leadership sponsored a bill in Congress accusing the government of violating the law and calling on the military "to guarantee the constitutional order." The PDC newspaper, *La Prensa,* printed an article on 25 August claiming that Chile was being taken over by a "Jewish Communist cell" occupying key posts in government and industry.[87] Aylwin himself, while publicly denying that his party favored anything but a democratic solution to the crisis, reportedly was saying in private that if he had to choose between "a Marxist dictatorship and a dictatorship of our military, I would choose the second."[88]

On 9 September, the Christian Democrats called upon Allende and all elected officials to resign and allow new elections to resolve the strike crisis. Before any further attempts at political settlement were made, the military intervened on 11 September and overthrew the government.

Thus, during the final six months of the Popular Unity period groups associated with the government and with the Church strained the parameters of previous agreements. The precipitous launching of ENU by the administration, the bitter attacks on Raúl Hasbún by sectors of the Left, the executive's failure to negotiate effective legal agreements with Congress on nationalization policies, and the increasing resort to repressive force all damaged the credibility of the government's commitment to democratic procedures in the eye of many Catholic leaders. Conversely, illegal transmissions and escalated attacks on the regime by the T.V. station of the Catholic University, anti-government demonstrations orchestrated by Catholic schools, the tactical alliance of the official leadership of the PDC with reactionary forces on the Right, their support for public chaos and their public silence in face of the impending coup, all tarnished Chilean Catholicism's image of unqualified support for democracy.

Nevertheless, the *official* leadership on both sides remained committed to their respective normative commitments to the very end. Allende was not, nor did he ever attempt to become, a dictator. When the courts declared the actions of his administration illegal, he always complied with

---

[87] Marvine Howe, "Allende's Ouster Not Aim, Foe Says," *New York Times,* 27 August 1973. This article in the *Times* also pointed out that the PDC was playing a dual role in the current crisis, since it was calling for a democratic solution but at the same time was supporting the wave of strikes and demonstrations aimed at bringing down the government.

[88] Marlise Simons, "Allende Accuses Opposition of Seeking to Spur Armed Coup," *Washington Post,* 26 August 1973. Simons also observed that it was common knowledge in Santiago that an important sector of the PDC had hammered out a mutual agreement with the military during the last two weeks of August. The cool treatment of leaders of the PDC by the military officers in the coup after September 11th, however, casts some doubt on the validity of this opinion.

their judgment. He never abrogated the right to legitimate peaceful dissent, respected the full gamut of human rights—including complete religious freedom—and withdrew ENU once the hierarchy expressed their strong objections. Conversely, the official voice of the Church as articulated by the Episcopal Conference and the cardinal never endorsed treason. To the very end of the Allende period, despite some fears and reservations about the government's ability to manage the crisis, significant public efforts were made by the cardinal and bishops to preserve constitutional processes and facilitate a political settlement by civilian leaders. Furthermore, even amidst growing tensions between Church and state, the public position of the hierarchy remained committed to continual social and economic transformation.[89]

Important as was this contribution of the Church's leadership to promoting a moral framework for a transition to democratic socialism, it is also clear that the hierarchy could effectively exercise supportive legitimation only so long as there remained a fundamental agreement by all major political groups as to the rules of the game. Once this consensus broke down, and subversive elements increased their attacks with substantial assistance from abroad, the Church's moral influence on behalf of civility and law was minimized. Even within Church ranks, appeals from the bishops for respect for constitutional processes and continued efforts to reach a democratic solution were not heeded by all. Some clerics (such as Hasbún) and important Catholic lay leaders in the PDC lost confidence in a constitutional outcome, and once this happened official Church leaders no longer could keep their members loyal to democracy.

POST FACTUM JUDGMENTS OF ECCLESIASTICAL LEADERS
REGARDING THE CHURCH'S FREEDOM UNDER ALLENDE
AND THE NECESSITY OF MILITARY INTERVENTION

Up to this point in my analysis of Christian-Marxist coexistence in Chile I have relied primarily on documentary evidence from the period itself. Given the importance of the normative and structural compatibilities as well as the emergence of some contradictions toward the

---

[89] Three weeks before the coup, *Chile Hoy,* a prominent weekly journal closely associated with Allende's branch of the Socialist Party, printed a positive assessment of the official Church's contribution to the construction of Chilean socialism. The article (written by a congressman of the Christian Left) praised the hierarchy for their "open and understanding attitude in face of a process of radical transformation" since 1970. It also hailed the cardinal's forthright position in condemning terrorism, and recognized the important efforts of the Episcopal Conference to avoid civil war by its public intervention in mid-July. It ended with a favorable judgment regarding the neutral political position of the official Church, claiming that it "has abandoned the narrow path of party identification." Luis Maira, "Opciones políticas para la iglesia," p. 6.

end of the period, it would be useful to know the judgments of those who had been involved directly in these events after the experience was over and opinions crystallized.

I was unable to conduct systematic interviews with Marxist leaders in Chile during 1975 due to the political climate at the time and their unavailability. I did, however, ask almost all the Church leaders whom I interviewed how they evaluated the impact of the policies of Allende's government on the freedom of the Church to perform its mission. Table 7.1 indicates that over 80 percent of the bishops, and more than 70 percent of the priests interviewed, felt there were no official attempts by the government to limit the Church's activity beyond the case of ENU which never fully materialized. Only two bishops felt the Church's freedom was actually threatened at the local level, and three felt it might have occurred in the future but did not materialize during Allende's years in office.

A considerable percentage of the nuns (39.4 percent) declined to answer, apparently because they considered the question too political. A significant minority (24.2 percent) were inclined to interpret the Left's efforts at ideological and political mobilization as a threat to the Church's pastoral programs. (I shall indicate some of the reasons for this interpretation in the next chapter which focuses on the internal life of the Church during the Allende years.) The great majority of lay leaders who answered the question (62.7 percent), agreed with the bishops and priests that, aside from ENU, there was no official attempt by the government to restrict the Church's freedom of activity.

In elaborating his response to this question, the cardinal made a spontaneous comparison between the Church's freedom under Allende and its position under the subsequent military junta:

> Aside from project ENU, there was nothing else harmful. The Church had more freedom under Allende than it does now. . . . The government of the UP was not a Marxist regime but a stage in the preparation of one. Marxists respected the power of the Church, much more than did the old liberals. . . . The government of Allende, despite all its problems, was a government with which poor people identified, but in no way do they identify with this government.[90]

I shall return to a comparison of the range of the Church's institutional freedom under Allende and under the military junta in Chapter 9. This remark by the cardinal in the context of the responses of other bishops in Table 7.1 supports the conclusion, based on the documentary

[90] Interview with Cardinal Raúl Silva Henríquez, Punta de Tralca, 25 October 1975.

evidence presented earlier, that official actions of top echelons of the government were very consistent with their original promises to respect the Church's freedom.

Despite contradictions and tensions that occurred during the last six months of Allende's presidency, Church leaders two years later in looking back on the overall experience of rapprochement with Marxism at the external policy level felt the Church's liberty survived relatively unimpaired. This judgment gives added credibility to the possibility that Leftists in France and Nicaragua whose religiopolitical contexts are somewhat similar to that of Chile between 1970 and 1973 will also honor their promise to respect religious freedoms.

I also included in my survey a question to probe the *private* opinions of Church elites regarding the coup. I wanted to see whether or not these corresponded to the *public* positions articulated by the bishops and many local Church leaders in 1973 favoring constitutional government. I discovered that over 70 percent of all respondents said that military intervention was necessary at the time. Table 7.2 shows that nearly 90 percent of the bishops, 76 percent of the priests, over half of the nuns, and almost two-thirds of the laity whom I interviewed all indicated that they believed there was no other viable alternative at that time.

A significant number of respondents (15.8 percent of the total) refused to answer the question—especially women religious leaders—on the grounds that it was too sensitive. The repressive political context of 1975 during which the interview was conducted also may have accounted for a response favorable to the military among some others. The question, however, was included at the end of the interview (which averaged between one and two hours), and by that time the vast majority of the respondents felt rather comfortable with my survey. They also were speaking their opinions quite frankly on a whole range of religious and political issues. In addition, I deliberately used the term "military intervention," a more neutral description of the event than "military coup" (leftist terminology) or "military pronouncement" (rightist terminology), so as not to betray my own interpretation of the action.[91]

The results, while somewhat tentative, suggest the prevalence at every level of the layered administration of the Church of a very serious loss of confidence in the possibility of a civilian solution to the crisis of late 1973. This does not detract from the importance of the *public* legitimating role of ecclesiastical leaders in support of constitutional government right up to 11 September. It does indicate, however, the presence of an underlying feeling among clerical, religious, and lay elites that the con-

[91] The exact wording of my question in Spanish was as follows: "¿Piensa que la intervención militar fue necesaria in septiembre de 1973?"

Table 7.1

"Do You Feel That During the Government of Allende There Was Any Attempt to Limit the Freedom of Church Activity?" (1975)

	Bishops (N = 29)	Priests (N = 70)	Nuns (N = 33)	Laity (N = 51)	Totals (N = 183)
1. No, not that I recall; not officially or directly	51.7% (15)	38.6% (27)	24.2% (8)	43.1% (22)	39.3% (72)
2. Yes, but only in one or two inconclusive instances, e.g., ENU	82.7 { 31.0 (9)	72.9 { 34.3 (24)	12.2 (4)	62.7 { 19.6 (10)	65.0 { 25.7 (47)
3. Not directly; had the government lasted longer, there would have been more limits put on the Church	10.4 (3)	7.1 (5)	—	7.9 (4)	6.6 (12)
4. Yes, there were limits on the Church's pastoral ministries in several areas (growing politicization and hatred; Marxist propaganda; pressures on people not to attend Church; ENU)	6.9 (2)	11.4 (8)	24.2 (8)	17.6 (9)	14.8 (27)
5. Don't know, no answer	—	8.6 (6)	39.4 (13)	11.8 (6)	13.6 (25)

NOTE: Not asked = 3

Table 7.2

"Do You Think the Military Intervention Was Necessary in September 1973?" (1975)

	Bishops (N = 27)	Priests (N = 72)	Nuns (N = 33)	Laity (N = 51)	Totals (N = 183)
1. Yes, there was no other alternative	88.9% (24)	76.4%* (55)	51.5% (17)	64.7% (33)	70.5% (129)
2. No, there were other alternatives still possible	3.7 (1)	12.5 (9)	9.1 (3)	23.5 (12)	13.7 (25)
3. Don't know, no answer	7.4 (2)	11.1 (8)	39.4 (13)	11.8 (6)	15.8 (29)

NOTE: Not asked = 3

tinuing inability of political leaders to control chaos would lead to a military coup.

The forty-year absence of military intervention, their moderating influence in Allende's cabinet in late 1972, and their defense of civilian government during the aborted June 1973 coup, all led many Chileans to believe the armed forces might save the country from civil war in September and restore order without prolonged damage to constitutional processes. Some political leaders believed the armed forces would engineer a "white coup" with little or no bloodshed, restore peace, and almost immediately hand back the government to a different group of civilians (led by the PDC). Those harboring such hopes were naive. They badly underestimated the tragic consequences of what would follow once the military were in power.

The results of the responses to my question, therefore, do not necessarily imply that those holding positions of responsibility at various levels of the Church supported an authoritarian regime. (As we shall see in Chapter 9, there is severe dissatisfaction with, and significant opposition to, the present regime in the Church—especially at lower echelon levels.) Many of the respondents in my 1975 survey explicitly made a distinction between accepting some military action at the time and disapproving what actually later transpired.

One bishop who agreed that the intervention was necessary pointed to the devastating impact the military regime has had on structures of social participation:

> The social network of participation was destroyed. This network saved us from Marxism, but now there is no more defense against the power of the state. This is very dangerous.[92]

Another member of the episcopacy approved the legitimacy of the intervention to restore order, but rejected the prolongation of military rule:

> The government of Allende had become illegitimate because of its arbitrary actions (*atropellos*). Intervention by the military was legitimate. But continuation of military government for thirty years—No![93]

Several lower-level leaders also expressed a double feeling—original hope in the military and later disillusionment with the style and impact of the intervention. A priest in a lower middle-class urban parish in Osorno said:

[92] Interview no. 012, 24 June 1975.
[93] Interview no. 007, 29 April 1975.

Table 7.3

"Do You Think the Military Intervention Was Necessary in September 1973?"
(Priests, Nuns and Lay Leaders in Urban and Rural Working-Class Areas in 1975)

	Priests (N = 31)	Nuns (N = 24)	Laity (N = 17)	Totals (N = 72)
1. Yes	61.3% (19)	58.3% (14)	47.0% (8)	56.9% (41)
2. No	25.8 (8)	12.5 (3)	41.2 (7)	25.0 (18)
3. Don't know, no answer	12.9 (4)	29.2 (7)	11.8 (2)	18.1 (13)

> I do not like communism and fear it. I was happy to see the military intervention. The Chilean military, however, have acted like Nazis. This was not necessary. We could have had another alternative from them.[94]

A white-collar employee in Santiago also frankly admitted his mixed feelings about the event and its aftermath:

> I can't say yes or no emphatically. When I remember what Chile was like on September 10, 1973, I must admit with profound pain, yes. When I look at Chile in July 1975, two years later, I have to say, no.[95]

A public school teacher in Chillán expressed similar ambiguous feelings:

> The intervention was necessary, yes. It saved more blood than would have been spilled in a civil war. . . . In any case, for *that* moment military action was necessary, but *not* for the present.[96]

In disaggregating according to social class of the parish, and focusing exclusively on urban or rural working-class areas, it is clear that the percentage of those who favored the intervention was still very high— nearly 60 percent. Only among the lay leaders in working-class communities was there a sizable number who said they opposed the intervention (41.2 percent), but even among them a plurality (47 percent) indicated it was necessary. These responses suggest far more acquiescence to the coup even among clerical, religious, and lay leaders in poor areas than previously thought.

Again, many of these respondents in working-class areas manifested the same ambiguity as others in my survey from middle-class parishes. A priest in a shantytown in Santiago said that the poor were suffering from the economic chaos that existed and many had hopes that the military could prevent a civil war:

[94] Interview no. 064, 23 April 1975.
[95] Interview no. 120, 7 July 1975.
[96] Interview no. 135, 1 July 1975.

I believe the country had arrived at a point where democratic dialogue was impossible. It was not merely a question of economic collapse in which the ones who suffered the most were the poor. It was also unknown just how far we could go before a civil war would occur. I think the military had the support of the majority of Chileans and many placed their hope in them.[97]

A nun in a working-class neighborhood in Concepción expressed a similar judgment:

The intervention was a lesser of two evils. I would never in principle want a military government. At that moment, however, the people couldn't bear up under the conditions any longer.[98]

A sister working in the countryside outside Temuco said: "Given the failure of the dialogues to reach a mutual understanding among civilian leaders, the intervention was necessary to stop the hatred."[99] Another sister in a poor neighborhood in the capital indicated, however, that she never expected the tragic consequences that the intervention brought:

I don't think we could continue to suffer the chaos in which we were living much longer. . . , although I never suspected what really was going to happen after the intervention. We needed a change badly, but what occurred was very severe and brought much suffering to our people. The cost in terms of lives lost and tortures perpetrated I just cannot accept.[100]

Finally, a lay leader in another low-income neighborhood in Santiago also expressed dismay at what for him accompanied a desired return to order:

It was unnecessary to go so far as to murder people, but it was necessary to control the license of all the political parties and the masses in general.[101]

All of these personal responses from Church leaders in low-income areas reveal neither authoritarian attitudes nor a betrayal by the Church of constitutional government. The public words and actions of the Church's leadership right to the end of Allende's administration do not substantiate such a conclusion. The responses do indicate, however, that many with responsible positions at various levels of the Church *privately* felt the country was in a cul-de-sac in September 1973. They strongly believed that the military could save the country from worse suffering, and so were relieved when the armed forces intervened. While

[97] Interview no. 095, 9 December 1975.
[98] Interview no. 168, 7 July 1975.
[99] Interview no. 169, 4 July 1975.
[100] Interview no. 183, 20 September 1975.
[101] Interview no. 152, 4 November 1975.

this judgment did not alter the public actions of the vast majority of bishops, priests, nuns, and lay leaders before the coup, nor lead to subversive or treasonous activities by them, it did affect how the highest level of Church leadership related to the junta as soon as it came to power. I shall examine this in Chapter 9.

BEHAVIORAL COMPATIBILITY IN ELECTORAL POLITICS

It would be important to know if there were shifts to the Left in Catholic political preferences during the Allende years. Such information is crucial for evaluating the overall impact of the Church on the political system, since, as we have seen in previous chapters, its public influence depends largely upon the attitudes and choices of its lay membership. This is particularly significant for ascertaining whether religious practice can become less of an obstacle to the Left in its attempt to expand its base of support during a transition to socialism.

In examining surveys from the Centro de Opinión Pública for shifts in correlations between party preference and religious practice in Santiago during the Allende Administration, it is clear that the Left made significant gains among all types of Catholics during its nearly three years in power. The UP doubled its support among practicing Catholics between 1970 and 1973, and increased its base by over 60 percent among both occasionally practicing and nonpracticing Catholics. The Christian Democrats, however, experienced a resurgence of Catholic support, although their gains after 1970 were not proportionately as large as those of the Left—a 50 percent increase among the regulars, a 70 percent gain among occasionals, and a slight loss among the nonpracticing. The Right remained about the same in each category, hovering around the 10 percent mark.

What is also interesting to note about Table 7.4 is that the Left's largest gains proportionately among Catholics were made between 1970 and 1972 during its period of greater public popularity. While it continued to gain in 1973 among the practicing Catholics over its 1972 percentage, its support fell off that year (still remaining ahead of its 1970 level) among both the occasionally practicing and nonpracticing. Moreover, the Christian Democrats in 1973 gained among these groups of Catholics about the same amount that the Left lost. This indicates that, while religion was not seriously hurting the Left (particularly among the most devout), other political and economic factors were. By 1973 the Christian Democrats (not the Right as in 1970) were perceived by those critical of the government as the leading opposition party.

In contrasting Catholic political preferences in Chile in 1973 to those in France, Italy, and Spain at about the same time, it is clear that regularly practicing Chilean Catholics were considerably further to the Left by the end of the Allende years—twice as much so than those in France and Italy, and one-third more so than those in Spain. Conversely, the overwhelming proportion of regularly practicing in France still backed the Right (in the absence of a viable DC or other centrist party), and about the same percentage in Italy supported the Christian Democrats. In Spain, a plurality of practicing Catholics were behind the governing centrist party (the UCD) in about the same proportion as Chilean practicing Catholics favored the PDC.

In all *three* of these Western European nations the Left's effective support base among Catholics was predominantly concentrated among the nonpracticing, with two-thirds to three-fourths of those who were not churchgoers favoring socialist-oriented parties. Such, however, was clearly not the case in Chile in the last free elections in 1973. Nonpracticing Catholics were far more diversified (and even undecided) in their political choices than their European counterparts. Anticlericalism simply was not the significant attractive force for the Left among nominal Catholics in Chile as it has continued to be in much of Western Europe.

When we examine public attitudes in Santiago in 1973 regarding the desirability of socialism, we find that intensity of religious practice among Catholics was associated with negative responses. Nearly three-fifths (57.5 percent) of those who practiced regularly were against Chile becoming a socialist country, whereas only one-third of them favored such a prospect. However, less than one-half of the nonpracticing Catholics and those of other faiths were supporters of socialism. Only among the minority of nonbelievers who expressed no religious identification (a small proportion of the population) did socialism gain overwhelming support. The vast majority of the sample (71.5 percent) representing occasionally practicing and nonpracticing Catholics and those of other religions were almost *equally* divided in their opinions.

Nor can we account for this split by class differences. When we disaggregate the sample by occupational categories and examine the working class (the industrial and the nonindustrial laborers) and the middle class (white collar employees and small businesspersons) we find some surprising results. Among the industrial workers (the hard core of urban support for the Left) less than one-half (49.3 percent) expressed a sympathy for socialism in February 1973 in Santiago, and two-fifths (40.7 percent) said they opposed this alternative. Among the nonindustrial workers (who constituted one-third of the poor in the capital city in 1970 and whose numbers and political importance were growing) the lack of enthusiasm for socialism was even more dramatic—53.7 percent were against it, and only 34 percent favored it. Among those groups in the middle class that the UP had placed some hopes in 1970 as potential

Table 7.4
Party Preference and Religious Practice of Chilean Catholics, 1970–1973, Greater Santiago

Party Preference	Regularly Practicing			Occasionally Practicing			Nonpracticing		
	August 1970 (N = 171)	April 1972 (N = 129)	February 1973 (N = 120)	August 1970 (N = 246)	April 1972 (N = 394)	February 1973 (N = 329)	August 1970 (N = 119)	April 1972 (N = 194)	February 1973 (N = 143)
UP (Left)	17.0%	27.9%	34.2%	21.1%	45.2%	35.6%	27.7%	54.6%	43.3%
PDC (Center)	29.2	34.1	43.3	22.8	28.7	37.1	27.7	17.5	26.6
PN (Right)	12.9	14.0	10.0	11.4	7.1	11.8	7.6	7.7	7.7
Undecided	40.9	24.0	12.5	44.7	19.0	15.5	37.0	20.2	22.4

SOURCE: Centro de Opinión Pública, Santiago, Chile.

Table 7.5
Comparative Catholic Party Preference: Chile (1973), France (1973), Italy (1968), and Spain (1978)

Party Preference	Regularly Practicing				Occasionally Practicing				Nonpracticing			
	Chile (N = 120)	France (n.a.)	Italy (N = 937)	Spain (N = 2,117)	Chile (N = 329)	France (n.a.)	Italy (N = 667)	Spain (N = 1,251)	Chile (N = 143)	France (n.a.)	Italy (N = 288)	Spain (N = 1,091)
Left												
Marxist	34.2%	13.0%	3.5%	1.8%	35.6%	38.0%	16.8%	6.6%	43.3%	67.0%	46.5%	15.5%
Nonmarxist	—	—	12.5	19.0	—	—	33.3	34.8	—	—	27.8	48.2
Center												
Christian Democrat	43.3	—	77.2	—	37.1	—	40.9	—	26.6	—	18.1	—
Other	—	16.0	1.2	41.4	—	13.0	1.5	33.8	—	11.0	2.8	16.9
Right	10.0	70.0	5.6	16.1	11.8	47.0	7.5	4.6	7.7	20.0	4.8	2.4
Undecided	12.5	1.0	—	21.7	15.5	2.0	—	20.2	22.4	2.0	—	17.0

SOURCES: Data for the survey of French Catholics is taken from an IFOP poll of 927 adults conducted in February 1973. See "Les elections legislatives des 4 et 11 Mars 1973," *Sondages* 35 (1973): 26. See also Guy Michelat and Michel Simon, "Religion, Class and Politics," pp. 159–86. The Italian data is a subsample of a poll of 2,500 adults conducted in 1968 by CISER and reported in Samuel H. Barnes, "Italy: Religion and Class in Electoral Behavior," p. 195. Data on Spain is from a subsample of a national survey of 5,898 persons conducted by Juan Linz and associates in September 1978. I am grateful to Professor Linz for showing me his data and giving me permission to cite it. More of his findings are reported in Juan J. Linz, "Religion and Politics in Spain." Data for Chile is from the February 1973 survey of Santiago taken by the Centro de Opinión Pública.

Table 7.6
*Support for Chile's Becoming a Socialist Country According to Religion
Greater Santiago, February 1973*

	Catholics			Protestants, Jews, Others (N = 67)	No Religion (N = 99)	Totals (N = 754)
	Regularly Practicing (N = 120)	Occasionally Practicing (N = 329)	Nonpracticing (N = 143)			
Yes	33.3%	43.5%	47.6%	49.3%	72.6%	46.8%
No	57.5	47.1	42.0	40.3	23.2	44.2
Don't know, no answer	9.2	9.4	10.4	10.4	4.2	9.0
Percentage, Total	15.9	43.6	19.0	8.9	12.6	100.0

SOURCE: Centro de Opinión Pública, Santiago, Chile.

Table 7.7
Support for Chile Becoming a Socialist Country According to Occupation and Religion
Greater Santiago, February 1973

A. Industrial Workers (Skilled and Unskilled) — Working Class

	Catholics			Protestants, Jews, Others	No Religion	Totals
	Regularly Practicing	Occasionally Practicing	Nonpracticing			
Yes	36.2	45.3	54.8	43.6	76.7	49.3
No	48.3	44.6	37.0	46.2	18.6	40.7
Don't know, no answer	15.5	10.1	8.2	10.2	4.7	10.0
	N = 58 (16.1%)	N = 148 (41.0%)	N = 73 (20.2%)	N = 39 (10.8%)	N = 43 (11.9%)	N = 361 (100%)

B. Nonindustrial Workers (Artisans, Independents, Domestic Services) — Working Class

	Catholics			Protestants, Jews, Others	No Religion	Totals
	Regularly Practicing	Occasionally Practicing	Nonpracticing			
Yes	31.0	30.2	35.5	41.2	57.1	34.0
No	65.5	60.3	51.6	29.4	14.3	53.7
Don't know, no answer	3.5	9.5	12.9	29.4	28.6	12.3
	N = 29 (19.7%)	N = 63 (42.9%)	N = 31 (21.1%)	N = 17 (11.6%)	N = 7 (4.7%)	N = 147 (100%)

C. White Collar Employees and Small Businesspersons — Middle Class

	Catholics			Protestants, Jews, Others	No Religion	Totals
	Regularly Practicing	Occasionally Practicing	Nonpracticing			
Yes	28.0	45.2	44.8	85.7	71.9	48.9
No	68.0	44.1	41.4	14.3	28.1	43.0
Don't know, no answer	4.0	10.7	13.8	—	—	8.1
	N = 25 (13.4%)	N = 93 (50.0%)	N = 29 (15.6%)	N = 7 (3.8%)	N = 32 (17.2%)	N = 186 (100%)

SOURCE: Centro de Opinión Pública, Santiago, Chile.

supporters of socialism—shopkeepers, civil servants, clerks, salespersons, officeworkers—there was almost an even split on the question—48.9 percent for, and 43 percent against.

Lack of any religious faith was correlated with strong positive responses among each group, but these nonbelievers were not numerous. The dissatisfaction with socialism in Santiago in 1973 among so many of its supposed sympathizers could not be blamed on Churches.

When we examine correlations between party preference and religion in the same survey we find similar results. Religious identification was a cleavage factor, but not a powerful one, and stated support for the UP among both low and moderate income groups in Santiago just before the last election was not overwhelming.

Among blue-collar workers, just over one-half (52 percent) expressed identification with the Left. Only among the nonbelievers was the percentage of leftist support overwhelming, and thus similar to the European industrial working-class pattern. This group, however, constituted only about one-tenth of the blue-collar population. Moreover, among the nonindustrial workers in Santiago the UP received just over one-fifth support and their combined backing for the PDC and the Right was over one-half (53.1 percent). Among this critical group of poor, religion played no consistent role in party choice. Finally, in the middle-class occupations leftist support was well under two-fifths, but the backing for the combined opposition was nearly one-half (46.2 percent). Among these groups, it was only the minority of nonbelievers who expressed strong identification with the government parties.

Despite increased mobilization efforts by the Left after 1970, the unionization of some previously unorganized workers, significant economic gains for wage and salary earners in 1971, and the enfranchisement of illiterates during the same year, serious cleavages still remained in the UP's stated support base in Santiago in 1973.[102] Galloping inflation, shortages from hoarding and black-market profiteering, recurrent strikes, cyclic civil disorders, mounting violence, and U.S. economic pressures and political subversion all combined by 1973 to produce serious damage to the Chilean social fabric and political economy. It was not the rich who suffered so much, since their investments and savings left the country early on and they could afford to pay black-market

[102] On the basis of aggregate electoral and ecological data, Arturo Valenzuela believes that there was no dramatic shift in the base of support for the Left nationwide between the 1969 and the 1973 congressional elections. In each election, the Popular Unity coalition received 43.9 percent of the vote. He concludes that there seems to have been some gains for the Left in areas with small concentrations of blue-collar workers in the early 1970s, but also some erosion of middle-sector support between 1969 and 1973. The Hamuy survey data for Santiago would support this conclusion. A. Valenzuela, *Chile,* pp. 85–87.

Table 7.8
Party Preference According to Occupation and Religion
Greater Santiago, February 1973

A. Industrial Workers (Skilled and Unskilled)

Working Class

Party Preference	Catholics			Protestants, Jews, Others	No Religion	Totals
	Regularly Practicing	Occasionally Practicing	Nonpracticing			
UP	43.1	47.9	58.9	46.2	72.1	52.0
PDC	43.1	37.2	24.7	30.8	11.6	31.9
PN	1.7	2.7	2.7	7.6	—	2.8
Undecided	12.1	12.2	13.7	15.4	16.3	13.3
	N = 58 (16.1%)	N = 148 (41.0%)	N = 73 (20.2%)	N = 39 (10.8%)	N = 43 (11.9%)	N = 361 (100%)

B. Nonindustrial Workers (Artisans, Independents, Domestic Services)

Party Preference	Catholics			Protestants, Jews, Others	No Religion	Totals
	Regularly Practicing	Occasionally Practicing	Nonpracticing			
UP	20.7	20.6	19.4	35.3	28.6	22.4
PDC	48.3	39.7	35.4	23.5	14.3	37.4
PN	17.2	19.1	12.9	5.9	14.3	15.7
Undecided	13.8	20.6	32.3	35.3	42.8	24.5
	N = 29 (19.7%)	N = 63 (42.9%)	N = 31 (21.1%)	N = 17 (11.6%)	N = 7 (4.7%)	N = 147 (100%)

C. White Collar Employees and Small Businesspersons

Middle Class

Party Preference	Catholics			Protestants, Jews, Others	No Religion	Totals
	Regularly Practicing	Occasionally Practicing	Nonpracticing			
UP	36.0	28.0	34.5	28.6	65.6	36.6
PDC	32.0	37.6	27.6	42.8	6.3	30.1
PN	25.0	17.2	17.2	—	12.5	16.1
Undecided	7.0	17.2	20.7	28.6	15.6	17.2
	N = 25 (13.4%)	N = 93 (50.0%)	N = 29 (15.6%)	N = 7 (3.8%)	N = 32 (17.2%)	N = 186 (100%)

SOURCE: Centro de Opinión Pública, Santiago, Chile.

prices for anything they wanted. It was middle-class groups and many in the working class who bore the brunt of these disruptions in the last year and a half of Allende's term in office, and this was reflected in their luke-warm support for the Left by 1973.

The assumption of some scholars (Petras, Zeitlin, D. Johnson, Stall-ings) that the Chilean Left enjoyed very substantial support among workers during the Allende years is not verified by careful analysis of survey data in Santiago. Even among the group of industrial workers (who constituted two-thirds of the poor in Santiago in the early 1970s) support for the Left, although up from the 40 percent level of 1970, was not overwhelming (52 percent). Moreover, among the workers who were employed in nonindustrial occupations and who are frequently classi-fied as part of the bourgeoisie by Marxist scholars but who constituted at least one-third of low-income groups in Santiago in 1973, the Left's sup-port was only 22 percent. Finally, critical sectors of the Santiago mid-dle-class whom the UP had hoped to attract on the basis of a solid eco-nomic performance were also severely divided in electoral behavior in 1973.

There is no extant survey data of national public opinion on political preferences in Chile during the Allende years. There is good reason to believe, however, that the serious cleavages in working-class and mid-dle-class political behavior in Santiago were representative of patterns elsewhere in the country. The Christian Democratic Party made inroads into leftist support in the unions during the early 1970s, nearly captur-ing the presidency of the Central Confederation of Workers (CUT) in July 1972. The PDC also benefited from the dissatisfaction among strik-ing miners demanding higher salaries throughout 1972 and 1973, and also maintained a strong competitive base vis-á-vis the Left in the con-tryside due to previous social and political organizational work among peasants and small farmers. Had the Popular Unity parties enjoyed an overwhelming (two-thirds) majority among industrial and nonindustrial workers, peasants, miners, small farmers, employees, and small mer-chants (who constitute a combined total of over 80 percent of the eco-nomically active population), they would have won a clear majority in the 1973 parliamentary elections, rather than halting at the 44 percent level.[103]

The fact that the government was unable to continue its social and economic successes of 1971 badly damaged its chances to attain the

[103]   For an excellent analysis—based on ecological data—of the cleavages in vot-ing behavior among the urban subproletariat, small and medium farmers, and small and medium shopkeepers in Chile up to 1971, see Urs Müller-Plantenberg, "La voz de las cifras: un análisis de las elecciones en Chile entre 1957 y 1971," *Cuadernos de la Realidad Nacional,* no. 14 (October 1972): 152–74.

Table 7.9
Supporters of Socialism and of the Left in the Working and Middle Classes According to Religion
Greater Santiago, February 1973

	Supporters of Socialism			Supporters of the Left		
	Working Class				Working Class	
Religion	Industrials (N = 178)	Nonindustrials (N = 58)	Middle Class (N = 91)	Industrials (N = 188)	Nonindustrials (N = 33)	Middle Class (N = 68)
Catholics						
Regulars	49.4%	56%	53.8%	51.1%	57.6%	51.5%
Occasionals						
Nonpracticing						
Other Religions	50.6	44	46.2	48.9	42.4	48.5
Nonbelievers						

SOURCE: Centro de Opinión Pública, Santiago, Chile.

overwhelming electoral support of these low and moderate income groups in the 1973 congressional elections. Without such strength, the chances for it to gain an electoral majority, and subsequently make the necessary legal changes to continue a transition to socialism within a constitutional framework, were badly damaged.

When we analyze the support for socialism and for the Left in Santiago in 1973 among working and middle classes according to religious identification, the political wisdom of Allende's respect for the Church becomes apparent. Almost one-half (49.9 percent) of socialism's supporters among blue-collar workers were regularly or occasionally practicing Catholics. Well over one-half of its sympathizers among nonindustrial workers and in middle-class occupations were also persons with regular or occasional contacts with the Catholic Church.

The same pattern holds true for leftist supporters in both classes. One-half or more of the UP's sympathizers in working-class occupations (51.5 percent of industrials and 57.6 percent of nonindustrials) and in the middle-class were Catholics who went to Mass on a regular or occasional basis.

Religion, therefore was much less of an obstacle to the Left in 1973 than it had been in 1964 and 1970.[104] In fact, the mutually correct relations between the Catholic Church and the UP government between 1970 and 1973 made eminent political sense for the Left. The UP's electoral base in the capital among critical occupational groups would have been smaller than it actually was had there been serious Church-state tensions throughout Allende's term in office.

CONCLUSIONS

The Chilean case between 1970 and 1973 offers some very significant learning experiences for other Christians and Marxists attempting a rapprochement at the external policy level. While all of these may not

---

[104] The conclusion of Langton and Rapoport that the "plurality coalition of Salvador Allende was seriously constrained in its efforts to mobilize support for its government" because of significant numbers of "political Catholics hostile to the left" throughout the early 1970s is wrong. They make this judgment on the basis of the dramatic findings in Hamuy's 1964 preelection survey (which I also reported in Chapter 5), and on *conjecture* that the negative impact of religion against the expansion of the Left's vote *probably* did not diminish in the early 1970s since religiosity remained at the same level among the Chilean people. Although they claim to have had access to Hamuy's surveys of 1970 and 1972 (and cite some statistics on religiosity from these polls), they did not analyze any correlations between religious practice and political choices for these years. Such type of conjecturing, without careful empirical analysis of possible changes in relations between religious practice and party preferences over time (when you have the data available to do so), is methodologically poor and substantively misleading. Kenneth P. Langton and Ronald Rapoport, "Religion and Leftist Mobilization in Chile," pp. 277–308.

be duplicated in the other situations, they illustrate that peaceful coexistence is possible under certain conditions. They also point to critical areas where tension is likely to occur, and where the boundary limits for strategic cooperation are located.

(1) *Classical normative conflicts between Catholicism and Marxism can be reduced significantly, thereby removing some ideological obstacles for a transition to democratic socialism.* Traditional Catholic concerns about social participation and the official Church's new openness to some forms of socialism resonate with recent developments in sectors of Marxism espousing radical economic change within a constitutional framework. When leaders in both camps emphasize these areas of compatibility, they can, despite other normative disagreements, establish a framework in which the potential for public conflict can be minimized in electoral politics.

In Chile, an ideological framework for coexistence was made possible by permissive signals from the Vatican regarding socialism, a new articulation of Catholic social norms by the local hierarchy, and by a reinterpretation of classical Marxism by the Chilean Left to fit the country's democratic traditions. Overlapping normative interests publicly articulated by both Marxists and Catholics reduced moral impediments to the Left's coming to power and also allowed the official Church to give added legitimacy for the inauguration of a transition to socialism. These factors prevented Church-state conflict at the start of Allende's term in office and enhanced the possibilities for a peaceful transfer of power.

On the basis of these mutual ideological advances at the beginning of the Popular Unity government, there is reason to believe that Catholics and Marxists in Italy, Spain, and Portugal at some point in the future could reach some agreements at the ideological level. In these countries it would be more difficult due to much longer entrenched antipathies and suspicions on both sides. The Chilean case at least shows that reaching normative accommodations between the Church and the Left during the latter's rise to power is more than a theoretical possibility or an illusory premise employed by Marxists to fool Catholics.

(2) *Institutional conflicts between the Church and a democratically elected Marxist government can be minimized, since each side is capable of maintaining previous normative agreements.* The first two and a half years of the Popular Unity government are proof that official policies of Church and state under a Marxist coalition administration can maintain previous agreements fairly closely over an extended period of time. This not only eliminates the possibility of significant Church-state conflict during the initial stages of a transition to socialism, but also enables the Church to play an important public moral role as the project proceeds.

The action strategies of both religious and Marxist elites in the immediate period following the 1970 election in Chile and throughout the first year of the UP administration were an indication that initial normative overtures on both sides were sincere. Church leaders did not endorse efforts to prevent Allende's confirmation as president, and their neutrality was a positive support for constitutional procedures during the delicate period of political negotiations. They also acquiesced to, and in some cases positively endorsed, the economic policies of the new government.

In addition, the roles and structures at lower levels of the Church reflected the position of the hierarchy. Several Church apostolates adapted their programs to fit socialist objectives, while others (including those heavily dependent on international Church finances) maintained a publicly neutral position vis-à-vis government policies.

The layered institutional network of the Church, therefore, translated official normative commitments into specific actions that not only minimized religiopolitical conflicts but also provided additional moral legitimacy for the government. Structural linkages with other national Churches (in terms of personnel and money) did not, as in the early 1960s, make the Chilean Church a staunch opponent of Marxism nor an alternate channel for Christian Democratic interests.

Conversely, the initial action strategies of leftist leaders and the policies they followed were a proof of their commitment to constitutional processes and democratic freedoms, including religious liberty. They made a significant start toward a transition to socialism within a legal framework, respected human rights, allowed the Church to function without restriction, continued public subsidies to private elementary and secondary schools, and increased state support for Catholic higher education.

Even during the period of mounting opposition to the government during Allende's second year in office, there were no major conflicts between Church and state. The bishops continued to provide public moral support for the process of change that was taking place, and they frequently condemned violent and illegal efforts to create political instability. In fact, the hierarchy played a more positive role in favor of government objectives than did the Christian Democratic Party during 1972. The government, in turn, continued to respect the institutional interests of the Church and worked within constitutional limits to resolve public crises.

This evidence from Chile bodes well for Church-state relations in other countries should the Left gain power and begin a transition to socialism. In fact, official Church leaders could play an important moderating role if societal tension develops, and may be counted on to back the legitimacy of public authorities so long as they exercise power within constitutional limits, and respect the Church's freedom.

(3) *The establishment of areas of normative and structural compatibility between Catholicism and Marxism does enable the Left to expand its electoral support among rank-and-file Catholics.* Antipathies of regularly and occasionally practicing Catholics for Marxist parties can be reduced concomitant to an official rapprochement between Catholicism and Marxism on external policy issues. In a nonthreatening context, the hierarchy need not forbid Catholics to vote for Communist and Socialist parties and can remain neutral in electoral politics. Catholics, in turn, can be free to make political choices on other than religious grounds, and this reduces one of the classic obstacles to leftist support in nominally Catholic countries.

The Chilean case shows that in a relatively short time span of three years some significant changes in Catholic political preferences can occur, particularly among those groups that are potentially the Left's greatest source of support—various workers and sectors of the middle class. In fact, given political and economic obstacles to mobilizing greater support for the Left in Chile, regularly and occasionally practicing Catholics constituted a significant part of the Popular Unity electoral base among these groups in 1973. It made eminent political sense, therefore, for Allende and other leftist leaders to treat the Church as respectfully as they did—not merely to avoid needless conflict with the hierarchy, but also to maintain and even expand important backing for their coalition among lower and medium-income Catholics with regular or occasional rates of Mass attendance.

This learning experience is perhaps not as crucial for Marxist parties in Western Europe whose base of strength is predominantly among those with little or no contact with the Catholic Church. Nevertheless, the Chilean case does show that religion's negative impact on voting for the Left under certain conditions can be reduced in a nominally Catholic society. In closely contested elections in France, Italy, Spain, or Portugal, small changes could possibly tip the balance in favor of victory for a Marxist coalition in the future. Chile at least shows that such incremental gains need not be short-circuited primarily because of religious practice.

(4) *Amidst severe societal polarization and a breakdown of normal democratic mechanisms to resolve conflict, cordial relations between the Church and an elected Marxist government are harder to maintain.* So long as traditional mechanisms to resolve conflict in a democratic society function effectively, the possibility that many Church groups and those on the Left can maintain nonconflictual relations is relatively good. The Chilean experience shows, however, that the dynamics of Church-state relations can change significantly once severe societal polarization and political stalemate set in. In such a context, groups on both sides are more likely to break the parameters of mutual agreement and thus strain Church-state relations.

During the last six months of Allende's administration, some elements in the government and in the Church clashed openly with one another. The hasty proposal of ENU by sectors in the Ministry of Education, the mobilization of groups of Catholic schoolchildren against the government, the refusal of the president to establish legal limits on nationalization policies with Congress, the mounting criticisms of the government by the Catholic T.V. station, and the hard-line policy of the PDC leadership all strained Catholic-Marxist relations. Elements on both sides were responsible for overstepping the boundary lines of previous agreements.

Whether such mutually threatening actions between Catholics and Marxists are inevitable in a democratic society where the Left is in power is still an open question. Had other pressures not been so severe—international economic strangulation, foreign subsidization of domestic opposition, internal sabotage, mounting violence, black-market profiteering, a hardening of ideological positions—provocative actions by sectors within the Church and in the government toward one another might have been avoided. In a different set of circumstances where these other pressures do not reach such a peak of intensity, a pattern of cordial Church-state relations (that characterized most of Allende's term in office) might possibly be maintained for a much longer period.

What the Chilean case does show regarding Church-state tensions, however, is that despite a *private* loss of confidence in the government's ability to resolve crises among leaders at every level of the Church by September 1973, the official *public* position of the institution remained committed to a democratic solution by civilians. In fact, when all other normal means of negotiation failed, it was the hierarchy, and especially the cardinal, who continued efforts to bring government and opposition leaders together. The highest leadership of the Church never withdrew public support for constitutionalism, and to the end proved to be a positive force for Allende. Conversely, despite some antagonistic actions from the Marxist side, the freedom of the Church to perform its religious mission and also exercise a critical, but constructive, public function was never seriously hampered by official government policies.

This sustained public rapprochement between the highest echelons of leadership on both sides is a very important lesson for Catholics and Marxists in other situations. While neither side can expect the other to be a totally credible ally amidst growing social polarization, all-out public confrontation at the external policy level between Church and state is not inevitable. The Chilean case has shown this dramatically, and both the Left and the bishops in other nominally Catholic countries should take this into account in assessing the possibility for mutual coexistence in their respective situations.

(5) *The official Church's ability to protect the moral basis of societal consensus is limited, and cannot prevent a breakdown of democratic processes.* While the Church may function as an important moral force favoring constitutionalism during a transition to socialism, it cannot prevent the undermining of democratic government. Once the regular secular channels for negotiating differences and mobilizing sufficient popular support for public policies no longer function adequately, the moderating role of official Church spokespersons cannot be effective. Their efforts are one contributory factor that can help maintain public civility in a nominally Catholic country, but not the only nor most important one.

Chile's Popular Unity government never achieved a clear majority at the polls due to significant cleavages in political choice among its potential base of support. This serious weakness, coupled with severe international pressures, predictable resistance by landed and industrial interests, sabotage, and deep antagonism between leftist and centrist party leaders, precipitated escalating societal tension and political stalemate. While official Church leaders were not a major source of any of these problems for the Left, neither could they resolve them nor save constitutional government.

The dead end reached by the Popular Unity government was not brought about by the impending danger of a Marxist-imposed dictatorship, as suggested by both Christian Democratic leaders and the military junta. It resulted from the opposite problem—widespread anarchy. The administration and the president himself had lost their ability to control the country. Many domestic and international forces accounted for this, including divisions and ineptness within the Marxist coalition, disloyal opposition by Christian Democrats, and subversion by the U.S. government and private enterprise.

The Chilean experience between 1970 and 1973, however, does not rule out either the possibility of a democratic transition to socialism nor of effective public moral support by the Church for basic societal consensus during such a process. In other situations where a Marxist coalition might achieve a clear majority of the electorate on its own (55 percent of the national vote or more), or establish a majority electoral coalition with centrist parties,[105] and where international financial

---

[105] The downfall of Allende precipitated a series of criticisms of the Chilean Left by the Italian Communist Party (PCI) in the fall of 1973—the UP's concentration on winning a 51 percent majority of the vote on its own, its refusal to deal with the Christian Democrats, and its insistence on a government of leftists only. Renato Sandri, "Cile: analisi di un' esperienza e di una sconfitta," *Critica marxista* (Rome) 11 (September–October 1973): 15–40. Enrico Berlinguer, Secretary General of the PCI, in a series of articles in *Renascita* in the same period under the title, "Reflections on Italy after the Events of Chile," first broached the idea of the *compromesso storico* for Italy, calling for an alliance of reform-minded Christian Democrats, socialist parties,

strangulation and foreign subversion does not occur to such a critical extent, then a transition to socialism within a democratic framework might be possible. The Left under such conditions could effectively handle both legal dissent and domestic social and economic sabotage since it would have preponderant political power based on popular support. Provided it also continued to respect constitutional processes and guarantees, it could expect a rapprochement with the Church. Moreover, the public moral influence of the hierarchy in such circumstances might very well be a significant reinforcing element to help keep the social fabric of society intact.

What the Chilean case does highlight, however, is that fear of civil war from prolonged chaos is a far more powerful force than moral persuasion or rationality when people feel that life, limb, and pocketbook are all threatened at once. These fears cannot but play into the hands of reactionary elements who are always ready to exploit popular anxiety for their own ends. Religious believers and Marxists alike in other nations who want to collaborate in promoting radical economic change within a democratic framework must ponder this learning experience from Chile very seriously. Once the social fabric of a society is stretched to the breaking point (regardless of who is to blame), the demand for order outweighs the desire for justice among most people. This reversal of priorities plays directly into the hands of the minority seeking an authoritarian solution. In such circumstances, religion and morality—even in their most noble expression—cannot trump economic self-interest nor control human passion.

---

and the PCI. Joan Barth Urban, "Moscow and the PCI: Kto Kovo?," *Studies in Comparative Communism* 13 (Summer–Autumn 1980): 110.

A different strategy was followed by parties of the French Left in the 1970s. After a period of electoral coalition between Communists and Socialists from 1975 to 1978, the French Communist Party decided to go it alone since the gains made by a united Left were predominantly won by the Socialist Party. After 1978 the Socialists continued their expansion of public support culminating in the presidential victory of François Mitterrand in March 1981 and the subsequent majority won by the Socialists alone in the April 1981 parliamentary elections. Mitterrand did include, however, four Communists in his cabinet. Given the bitter historical controversies between the Church and all sectors of the Left surrounding education in France, and the fact that at least one-third of the present French legislators are former public school teachers or professors, may make the full nationalization of schools (a Socialist platform promise) more problematic for Church-state relations in Mitterrand's France than it was in Allende's Chile. Suzanne Berger, ed., "Introduction," *Religion and Politics in Western Europe*; Frank J. Prial, "What Will Mitterrand Do to the French School System?," *New York Times*, 8 September 1981, pp. C1, C4.

8 Christian-Marxist Synthesis: Internal Church Dynamics during the Allende Years

The other challenge of rapprochement is a synthesis between the values and strategies proper to each system. For Marxists this is not a critical question since they do not accept the transcendental claims of religious faith. They believe religion will pass away when the classless society is established and the reasons that give rise to religion have disappeared. Christians, however, whose religious faith motivates them to combine a belief in a life after death with a desire to make life on earth more humane, have shown considerable interest in this issue. In fact, some have made efforts to use aspects of Marxism to criticize and transform oppressive economic and social structures.

Over the past decade groups of Christians in Latin America and Western Europe have adopted Marxist analysis and some Marxist-oriented strategies of action to effect radical political and economic change. Many liberation theologians, radical priest movements, and Christians for Socialism organizations since the late 1960s have explicitly endorsed the use of Marxist insights. While disavowing some of the philosophical tenets of Marxism (atheism, materialism and economic determinism), they find others compatible with their faith—a belief in the economic and ideological conditioning of cultural values and symbols, the inevitability of socialism, the necessity of conflict in promoting change, and the impossibility of political neutrality amidst class struggle. They emphasize that these insights and methods are essential to make Christianity vital and to restore to it many of the original emphases in the Bible itself.

Liberation theologians in Latin America, for example, stress that the Church for too long has focused on spiritual and individual faith and downplayed the biblical notion that religious salvation involves liberation from oppressive economic and political structures as well.[1] They argue that traditional religious symbols such as charity, reconciliation, and salvation of souls have come to serve the interests of the powerful since they have been frequently invoked by Church leaders to avoid the

---

[1] Gustavo Gutiérrez, *A Theology of Liberation*, pp. 148–87; Ignacio Ellacuría, S.J., *Freedom Made Flesh: The Mission of Christ and His Church*, pp. 3–19, 87–126, 160–61; Hugo Assmann, *Theology for a Nomad Church*.

conflict that is necessary to achieve radical economic change.[2] Further-more, the official Church's insistence on neutrality in partisan politics, they claim, is in reality a tacit political choice since it actually legiti-mizes the status quo.[3] Finally, these theologians emphasize that unity among Christians is only a myth so long as there are oppressed and op-pressors within their ranks. They thus call upon the official Church to make a radical commitment to the poor and take an active stance on their behalf amidst class struggle so as to liberate both oppressed and oppressors. Only in this way, they argue, can genuine unity and reconcil-iation ultimately be achieved.[4]

In addition to such attempts made at the theoretical level to assimi-late Marxist values into Christian theology, there have been serious ef-forts made by clerical and lay groups in several Western countries to apply these insights in practice. Radical priest movements such as Gol-conda in Colombia, Movement of Priests for the Third World in Argen-tina, and ONIS in Peru emerged in the late 1960s using Marxist analysis to critique forms of capitalism in their respective societies. They also acted as pressure groups inside the churches in these countries, en-couraging the bishops to take a more prophetic stance against exploita-tion of the poor. Some members of these movements also engaged in radical political organizations to concretize their commitment to the working class and give religious legitimacy to the objectives of these sec-ular groups.[5]

In the early 1970s a number of Christians for Socialism movements arose in Chile, Spain, Italy, Portugal, Holland, Canada, and the United States explicitly endorsing socialism as the only valid economic and po-litical option for Christians in the contemporary world. These groups include clergy and lay groups from various Christian denominations actively engaged in the struggles of the working class in their respective countries. While not definitely endorsing violence, they have adopted an explicit class-conflict model to effect change. Rather than fearing a strategic alliance with Marxists, they argue that their faith demands it and that an understanding of genuine Christianity can only be experi-enced from within a revolutionary commitment joined with a scientific Marxist perspective. International meetings have been held by repre-sentatives of national Christians for Socialism organizations (Santiago, 1972; Avila, 1973; Bologna, 1973; Quebec, 1975) to promote solidarity

[2] Juan Luis Segundo, S.J., *The Liberation of Theology*, pp. 40–47.
[3] Gutiérrez, *Theology of Liberation* , p. 266; Segundo, *Liberation of Theology*, pp. 71–75.
[4] Gutiérrez, *Theology of Liberation*, pp. 272–79; Segundo, *Liberation of Theology*, pp. 208–40; Ellacuría, *Freedom Made Flesh*, p. 146; Assmann, *Theology for a Nomad Church*, pp. 138–39.
[5] See Chapter 2, note 23 and Chapter 7, note 10 for sources on these movements.

among themselves and forge more effective cooperation at the global level.[6]

There have been considerable efforts made in recent years both at the theoretical and practical levels to forge a synthesis between Marxism and Christianity. These attempts have been made exclusively on the Christian side, and by groups who claim it is not necessary to abandon their faith in order to make such an assimilation. In fact, their goals have included both a sharpening of their revolutionary commitment through Christian symbols and motives, and a transformation of the Church into a more effective agent for radical structural change of society.

It is too early to predict the future impact of these various new currents of thinking and organization on the post-Vatican II Church. They still represent only a minority of Christians, and in Latin America where much of the original impetus for these movements arose the predominant authoritarian context since the mid-1970s has not permitted their overt growth. The quality of scholarship and leadership, however, as well as the dedication of members of these movements have all been excellent. Their ideas and strategies have taken hold in parts of North America, Western Europe, and in several third-world countries. Young clergy and student groups in several areas of the world have found some of their ideas and methods useful for integrating religious faith with a critical social analysis and action strategy for radical change. Hence, while at present they are only a minority, and in many places are unable to function overtly or attract many adherents, such movements may be significant in the future for key sectors of the Church, especially those ministering to the poor.

Perhaps more than in any other national Church to date, Chilean Christians made the most sustained and serious effort to forge a synthesis between their faith and Marxist methods and strategies. Between 1971 and 1973 a well-organized movement of Christians for Socialism (*Cristianos por el Socialismo*—CpS) functioned with an active membership of several hundred priests, religious, laity, and Protestant pastors, many of whom lived and worked with the rural and urban poor.[7] The group drew heavily upon the writings and the advice of liberation theologians (such as Gustavo Gutiérrez of Peru, Juan Luis Segundo of Uruguay, and

---

[6] Bartoloméo Sorge, "El movimiento de los 'Cristianos por el Socialismo,' " pp. 488–97; Arthur F. McGovern, S.J., *Marxism: An American Christian Perspective* (Maryknoll, N.Y.: Orbis Books, 1980), pp. 236–38.

[7] Estimates of clerical involvement in the Chilean Christians for Socialism movement (either as active members or as publicly known sympathizers) reached as high as 300—or approximately 12 percent of the total number of 2,500 priests in the country in the early 1970s. Franz Vanderschueren and Jaime Rojas, "The Catholic Church of Chile," p. 58.

Hugo Assmann of Brazil). They established local chapters in almost every province of the country, and published monthly bulletins, articles, and pamphlets (with a circulation of over 500 copies) commenting on aspects of the Chilean transition to socialism and giving theological justification for an integral role for Christians both as individuals and communities in it. In their pastoral work they also made efforts to raise the social awareness of their parishioners in small base communities and so enhance the mobilization of workers and peasants for the Left.

Christians for Socialism in Chile during these years also established close communication with radical priest movements in other parts of Latin America, such as ONIS in Peru and Movement of Priests for the Third World in Argentina. They sponsored the first international conference of Christians for Socialism in Santiago in April 1972, which was attended by 400 Catholic and Protestant representatives from twenty-six countries.

The movement acted as a catalyst among priests within Chile, and some members of CpS formed a parallel organization (the group of "200") whose goal was to promote a new style of priestly ministry closer to the concerns of the laity, especially the poor. This organization also served an important legitimating function for those Catholic lay men and women who were attempting to forge a personal synthesis of Christian and Marxist perspectives during the Allende years, although its primary focus was on religious issues.

The Chilean Christians for Socialism movement offers important learning experiences to groups in other countries who wish to confront the assimilation-synthesis aspect of Christian-Marxist rapprochement. While the organization functioned for less than two years in Chile, the quality of its theological reflections and impact both within the Chilean Church and on the universal Church was considerable. Its members made some very significant breakthroughs, especially at the theological level, in showing the contribution of Marxist analysis to Christian thought and in promoting serious reflection on the various dimensions of the political role of the Church as an institution.

Serious tensions between Christians for Socialism and the Chilean bishops arose, however, on the extent to which such an assimilation of Marxist categories and tactics can be made within the Church without damaging its essential religious mission. Although the hierarchy did not condemn the movement during the Allende years, five months before the coup they began to prepare a document critical of CpS's theological and practical aspects which was finished just after the government was overthrown. The attempts made by CpS, "the 200," and many young laity to make a synthesis with Marxism within the Church, in fact, precipitated a far more harsh reaction by the bishops than did the attempts made by other Catholics to work out coexistence and limited cooperation with the government at the external policy level.

This chapter analyzes both the advances in and the obstacles to the assimilation-synthesis aspects of Christian-Marxist rapprochement in Chile. I shall focus on those aspects of the challenge that liberation theologians, radical priest movements, and Christians for Socialism in other parts of the world have emphasized as priorities—the rooting of religious salvation in a socialist revolutionary praxis, the responsibility of the official Church to employ its full political weight to promote radical change in society on behalf of the poor, the legitimacy of class conflict in achieving ultimate Christian unity, and the engagement of international Church linkages in advancing all of these objectives.

NORMATIVE CHALLENGES OF CHRISTIANS FOR SOCIALISM

As the bishops were attempting to establish grounds for Church-state coexistence and limited cooperation during the early months of the government, others within the Church began to forge very close links between Catholic and Marxist values. In April 1971, before the Episcopal Conference issued its pastoral letter, "Gospel, Politics and Various Types of Socialism," eighty priests, primarily from working-class areas in Santiago, met to discuss their responsibilities as pastors amidst the transition to socialism. Several had been meeting regularly for over a year to reflect on the implications of the Medellín documents for their own ministry among the poor. The election of Allende had given further impetus to their discussions, and they intensified their efforts to form a more cohesive force among priests who were sympathetic to socialism. Eight of them met for several days in mid-April 1971, and afterwards issued a public statement calling for explicit ecclesiastical support for the tasks being undertaken by the Allende Administration.

While paralleling the cardinal's November 1970 remarks about the compatibility of Christianity with many socialist values, these priests went much further. They endorsed several specific UP programs, such as the "nationalization of mineral resources, the socialization of banks and monopoly industries, the acceleration of agrarian reform." They also stated that "criticism should be formulated from within the revolutionary process, not from outside it," and said they as priests "must do what we can to make our own modest contribution" to socialist objectives.[8]

---

[8] "Declaration of the 80," Santiago, 16 April 1971, in *Christians and Socialism*, ed. John Eagleson, pp. 3–6.

Within a week, the hierarchy reacted publicly to this pronouncement of "the 80." While recognizing the admirable commitment of these priests to the poor, they criticized them on several counts for challenging some crucial official Church teachings. They reminded the priests that the Church is not tied to any political system, nor is it competent to make pronouncements on contingent solutions to complex social and economic problems. They also warned priests against "taking partisan political positions in public" since this resurrected "an outdated clericalism," hampered the "liberty of Christians" to make their own political choices, and threatened the "unity of the Christian people with their pastors."[9]

A month later, their pastoral letter, "Gospel, Politics and Various Types of Socialism," outlined in detail episcopal reservations about official Church identification with specific economic or political strategies and about public involvement in partisan politics by representatives of the institution (cited in Chapter 7). They also vigorously supported the potential contribution to unity and dialogue a politically neutral Church can make in any social system.[10]

The warning by the bishops, however, did not end the debate. In July and again in October 1971 "the 80" published two major theological reflections in reaction to "Gospel, Politics and Various Types of Socialism." One criticized the bishops' pastoral letter for its lack of sufficient structural analysis of capitalism, its oversimplistic view of Marxism, and the abstractness of its perspective. It also stated that the "liberal ideology of capitalism" underlay the social analysis of the hierarchy's document, and that the thrust of "Gospel, Politics and Various Types of Socialism" was therefore an "option for reformism"—and "we know very well which group in Chilean politics proposes a reform in the capitalist system."[11]

The second critique of the pastoral letter published under the auspices of "the 80" (and written by the Uruguayan liberation theologian Juan Luis Segundo, S.J.), sharply challenged any possibility of a politically neutral Church and criticized the basically conservative implication of espousing Church unity. The critique bluntly stated that the Chilean bishops in their May letter were opting to maintain the political status quo, since they were implicitly saying that no form of socialism was acceptable as an alternative to capitalism. The critique also argued that no bond of spiritual unity can exist among Christians when some are exploiters and others are exploited. Finally, it concluded that the Chilean

---

[9] "Declaration of the Bishops of Chile," Temuco, 22 April 1971, in ibid., p. 14.
[10] La Conferencia Episcopal de Chile, "Evangelio, política y socialismos," nos. 69–70, in *Documentos del Episcopado*, ed. Oviedo, p. 92.
[11] Secretariado sacerdotal de los "80," *El compromiso político de los cristianos*, p. 14.

Church could not foment change in society and also identify with all the Chilean people at the same time, since a "Church open to all is not really capable of serving the masses: it is intrinsically conservative."[12]

These two reflections published in mid and late 1971 by "the 80" were in fundamental disagreement with public positions staked out by the hierarchy earlier in the year. The feasibility of official Church neutrality in politics was denied as well as the possibility of any type of Church unity in a society badly divided along class and political lines. At the deeper theoretical level, "the 80" were presenting direct challenges to two of the perennial and central characteristics of the Roman Church—a general (not specific) articulation of social norms in relation to political and economic issues, and universal membership patterns cutting across social classes—both of which pertain to the performance of its religious mission as traditionally conceived.

Aside from publicly disagreeing with the bishops, the two critiques by "the 80" misrepresented positions of the hierarchy. They claimed that the bishops in their letter ruled out all forms of socialism, which, as seen in the previous chapter, was not true. "Gospel, Politics and Various Types of Socialism," while cautious, was clearly an advance from earlier episcopal adamancy against Marxism and left the door open to various forms of democratic socialism.

They also accused the hierarchy of tacitly endorsing Christian Democracy. While their *personal* sympathies undoubtedly were closer to Christian Democracy than to Marxism, the *public* normative position of the bishops during the 1970 election and its aftermath provided, as seen in Chapter 7, important moral legitimacy for both a peaceful transition of power to the Left and for Christian participation in the construction of socialism. The fact that the bishops did not enthusiastically endorse socialism, and were also concerned about protecting the religious unity of the Church against sectarianism, could not be interpreted as a public endorsement of reformism nor of Christian Democracy. Allende and the Communist Party certainly did not interpret the public stance of the bishops in such a way, and they were delighted with the declared neutrality of the episcopacy during the crucial first year of the new administration.

A month after the publication of their second critique of "Gospel, Politics and Various Types of Socialism," in November 1971 "the 80" priests formed the first Christians for Socialism (CpS) movement in Latin America. The core administrative arm of the organization was made up of the secretariat of "the 80." The new organization also

[12] Segundo, *La iglesia chilena ante el socialismo* pp. 9, 10, 12, 23.

included religious, lay, and Protestant leaders from Chile and other Latin American countries, including Peru, Argentina, Bolivia, and Brazil.

In April 1972, they hosted a major conference in Santiago for over 400 priests and lay leaders, primarily from Latin America but including observers from Europe and the United States. Two hundred were priests and nuns, 40 were Protestant leaders and 160 were Catholic lay men and women, mostly Chileans. At the end of the week-long exchange, the participants issued a consensus document which spelled out in more detail the basic position prefigured by "the 80" a year before: the necessity of socialism as the only legitimate Christian option, the religious obligation to involve oneself in a revolutionary process and to identify with working-class parties, the impossibility of eventual unity in the Church without first endorsing class struggle, and the requirement that priests form political movements.

They stated that there is no "middle-ground position between capitalism and socialism" as proposed by the Christian Democratic Party. The "Cuban revolution and the Chilean transition toward socialism" are the best and most hopeful models available to achieve socialism, they said, since these "propose a return to the wellsprings of Marxism and a criticism of traditional Marxist dogmatism."[13]

The group proposed that the specific Christian contribution to establishing socialism could not be experienced outside of, or prior to, engagement in the process itself. A Christian "discovers the liberative power of God's love, or Christ's death and resurrection" from within the revolutionary praxis, they said. Within this struggle, at the theoretical level a Christian's specific obligation is to unmask the "ideological justifications" that traditionally have manipulated Christian faith, theology, and social doctrine to serve the interests of the ruling classes. They concluded that at the practical level Christians must join only the "parties and organizations that are authentic instruments of the struggle of the working class."[14]

In the past, the meeting asserted, Christians have not understood the rationale proper to class struggle, since they have tried "to deduce their political approach from a certain kind of humanistic conception, e.g. the 'dignity of the human person,' 'liberty,' and so forth," all of which only has produced "political naiveté, activism, and voluntarism." Instead, they argued, religious believers must adopt class conflict as the only ef-

[13] "Final Document of the Convention," 30 April 1972, in *Christians and Socialism*, ed. Eagleson, pp. 165–66.
[14] Ibid., pp. 170, 173.

fective strategy to effect ultimate Christian unity, since the "revolutionary struggle, which reveals the superficial unity of the Church today, is fashioning the authentic unity of the Church tomorrow."[15]

Lastly, the group stated that "priests and ministers are making a growing commitment to the poor" and that their "personal commitment induces them to take on a political responsibility." This obligation can involve prophetic denunciation of injustice, but also can include the formation of "specific organizations of their own" which "represent a positive contribution to the Latin America process of liberation."[16]

All of these major points emphasized in the final document of the convention placed this new movement of Christians for Socialism (CpS) in direct public opposition to the Chilean hierarchy, similar to the situation of their predecessors, "the 80." While the bishops had come to a cautious acceptance of some types of socialism and Marxism at the general theoretical level, CpS went considerably further by identifying specific forms of Marxist socialism (in Cuba and Chile) as authoritative. Like "the 80" they ruled out the possibility of a neutral political position for the Church, and further specified the parties of the Left as the only legitimate Christian option—positions clearly in contradiction to the hierarchy's publicly stated views.

Finally, like "the 80," CpS denied the existence of a deeper bond of unity in the Church that perdures despite severe social and ideological differences. In their view, only present exacerbation of class conflict—as intense in the Church as in the social system—could lead to ultimate unity of Christians by finally eliminating social and economic divisions among groups. This position also was in direct opposition to traditional Catholic belief, reaffirmed by the Chilean hierarchy in their 1971 pastoral letter, that the Church is open to all classes and types of people and that the Gospel can provide a common bond among Christians "more powerful than the differences that separate them on other levels."[17]

It is clear, therefore, that Christians for Socialism were interested not only in forming a closer ideological alliance between Catholicism and Marxist socialism, but in the process in laying the theological foundations for a very different type of Church. Members of the CpS in Chile articulated this goal more explicitly several months after the April 1972 convention. At a November meeting of their national organization (where 350 delegates participated, of which 200 were priests and nuns), Gonzalo Arroyo, S.J., the executive secretary, stated that one of the

---

[15] Ibid., pp. 170, 174.
[16] Ibid., p. 168.
[17] La Conferencia Episcopal de Chile, "Evangelio, política y socialismos," no. 70, in *Documentos del Episcopado*, ed. Oviedo, p. 92.

major goals of the group was to create "a new Church." It would be, he said, "less institutionalized, more centered at the base community," although not necessarily independent of the hierarchy.[18]

Diego Irarrázaval, another member of the secretariat of CpS and an ordained deacon, in a December lecture at the parish for university students in Santiago outlined in more detail the nature of this new and less institutionalized Church. He described the celebration of the sacraments as being closely linked with participation in revolutionary struggle, and espoused small, homogeneous, and politically committed base communities modelled along the lines of a sect:

> We will celebrate the Eucharist amidst the struggle of the working class and in gratitude for insertion into it. We will give thanks because the people are advancing towards the revolutionary goal of the kingdom of God. . . . This celebration will be possible insofar as each member of the community has a revolutionary commitment and insofar as the community is homogeneous. . . .
> This new type of community also will have a public political dimension. It will participate as a group in destroying exploitation and creating forms of power exercised by the people.[19]

Some of the members of the Christians for Socialism secretariat who were specifically interested in the transformation of the Church formed a separate organization for priests called "the 200." Under the direction of Sergio Torres, a diocesan priest from Talca, this movement held annual meetings in 1971, 1972, and 1973 to discuss a new style of priestly ministry, one more identified with the life of the laity and with the process of socialism. The principal characteristics of the new form of priestly ministry in a socialist society proposed by "the 200" included: (1) engagement in secular work as the means for self-support, rather than dependence on stipends or contributions from the faithful; (2) optional celibacy and the integration of ex-priests who have married back into the

---

[18] Gonzalo Arroyo, S.J., "Historia y significado de CpS." Excerpts of this speech are translated and reprinted in Vanderschueren and Rojas, "The Catholic Church of Chile," pp. 44–45.

[19] Diego Irarrázaval C., "Cristianos, compromiso revolucionario, comunidad de creyentes," pp. 6–7. Other statements by Christians for Socialism in their bulletins and pamphlets also articulated a new model for the Church—smaller, decentralized, more homogeneous and exclusive in membership commitments, and more structurally involved in the active promotion of socialism. Juan Menard, "¿La iglesia de hoy es para el mundo de ayer?," *Pastoral Popular* (Santiago) 22 (March–April 1972): 51–64; "Informe CpS—Regional Concepción," *Boletín de CpS*, 7 December 1972; Secretariado Nacional de los Cristianos por el Socialismo, *El pueblo camina . . . ¿y los cristianos?* (Santiago: Prensa Latinoamericana, 1972); Irarrázaval, "¿Qué hacer?: cristianos en el proceso socialista," translated and reprinted by CRIPS (Church Research and Information Projects), New York, 1975.

active ministry; and (3) a political involvement by priests compatible with the process of liberation of the poor underway in Chile.[20]

Hence, during the years of the Popular Unity government when both ecclesiastical and political leaders were discovering several areas where normative agreement was possible, there were emerging major internal Church disagreements between the bishops and some clerics on the extent to which Marxist and Christian values could be synthesized. What was at stake was more than diverse political analyses or preferences, as some have claimed. Fundamental theological and pastoral differences over the nature of the Church and its mission divided the bishops and the priests.

As seen in Chapter 2, different opinions on the specificity of Church social teaching (Tables 2.1 and 2.2), the nature of episcopal authority (Table 2.4), and the extent and quality of Church membership (Table 2.5) characterized the hierarchy and local church leaders in 1975. These already were beginning to surface publicly during the Allende years. With greater decentralization of responsibilities, inauguration of small base communities, and more serious involvement in the concerns of the working class (all of which began or were accelerated in Chile after 1968), some clerics by the early 1970s were publicly opting for explicitly sectarian and political models of the Church. This was further accelerated by the growing politicization of secular society after 1970. Such options, however understandable, were precipitating serious open normative conflicts with the hierarchy by 1972.

Christians for Socialism made Marxist assumptions and methods central to their pastoral commitments by arguing for the close association of revolutionary action and religious salvation, the religious obligation to support socialism, the explicit politicization of ecclesiastical roles and structures, and the promotion of class conflict inside the institution. In so doing, they challenged the legitimacy of some of the traditional Catholic normative concerns and went beyond the parameters of permissible shared consensus with Marxism as laid down by the bishops in their May 1971 statement.

BREAKDOWN OF AUTHORITY FLOWS ACROSS THE
HIERARCHICAL STRUCTURES OF CHURCH LEADERSHIP

What were the structural consequences for the Church of the important normative disagreements between Christians for Socialism and the Chilean bishops? Merely articulating and espousing new theological

---

[20] "Conclusiones de la Jornada de delegados de los 200," mimeographed (Padre Hurtado, 29–30 January 1972); Jose M. Camarero, "Los 200, ¿Qué son?," pp. 31–33.

and political opinions does not necessarily precipitate serious structural conflicts or authority crises. In fact, as seen in Chapter 2, throughout the history of Catholicism reforms have often arisen among religious or lay groups which appeared to threaten the Church when they began but later became legitimized by the hierarchy. In Chile itself, the emergence of Christian Democracy was nearly short-circuited in 1947 when the Falange Nacional clashed with the bishops, as described in Chapter 4. Later, however, it became the preferred political option for Catholics (including the bishops) in the mid-1960s.

When we examine the action strategies chosen by many leaders of Christians for Socialism in Chile between 1971 and 1973, however, we find that serious and prolonged disruptions of authority flows developed in the institution. On several occasions members of this movement went beyond the guidelines set down by the bishops for priests and this precipitated some strong reactions by the hierarchy who did not share their vision of the Church. In fact, during the last year of the Allende regime the movement functioned almost as a parallel magisterium (teaching office) in the Church. It publicly contradicted the bishops at several crucial moments when the Episcopal Conference was attempting to function as a moderating force amidst growing societal polarization.

Breaches of Discipline among the Clergy during the
Initial Stages of Societal Polarization

One of the crucial areas of normative disagreement between Christians for Socialism and the bishops was the question of clerical involvement in politics. The hierarchy defined the issue in rather strict terms, whereas spokespersons for CpS did not consider that open support for socialism necessarily entailed identification with specific parties. In early 1972 when opposition to the government was mounting and societal polarization worsening, members of Christians for Socialism publicly clashed with the bishops over political issues, causing a strain in relations across the hierarchical chain of command in the Church.

The first conflict occurred during the preparation for the international conference of Christians for Socialism held in Santiago in late April 1972. A series of public letters were exchanged between the secretariat of CpS and Cardinal Silva over the nature and purpose of the convention. In turning down an invitation to attend the meeting, the cardinal accused the group of planning a "political meeting" whose aim was to "commit the Church and Christians to the struggle on behalf of Marxism and Marxist revolution in Latin America." They responded by denying that they were opting for a specific party or seeking power, but agreeing that they were political in the sense defined by Medellín— actively engaged in the struggle for liberation of the poor. While neither the cardinal nor the Episcopal Conference forbade the priests to hold the convention, their dissatisfaction with the meeting was rather clear, and despite invitations to all the hierarchy no Chilean bishop participated in the conference.[21]

A second and more serious public confrontation between the movement and the bishops occurred just prior to the April convention itself. In early March a group of twelve clerical leaders of Christians for Socialism (ten priests and two seminarians) went to Cuba at the invitation of Fidel Castro. They issued a public message to Latin American Christians from Havana at the end of their visit denouncing all reformist solutions to the problem of underdevelopment on the continent, criticizing the Church for its past failures, and calling for more radical strategies for change, including the use of violence.

They concluded that "socialism is the only way . . . to break effectively and realistically the chains of capitalistic and imperialistic oppression." They asked public pardon for the Catholic Church's "great historical sin" of an alliance with a "small minority who have dominated and exploited working people." Finally, they affirmed that Latin American Christians must identify with the struggle of those being exploited, and said that if "reactionary violence opposes our efforts to construct a just and egalitarian society, we must respond with revolutionary violence."[22]

The statement of the twelve received significant media coverage in Chile, Cuba, and other parts of Latin America. A further complicating factor was the timing of this statement. After February 1972 the Popular Unity government began to experience considerable congressional opposition to its policies. For the first time, serious economic disruptions emerged across the country accompanied by violent clashes between pro- and anti-government forces. In such a context, the bishops wanted to play a moderating role amidst growing societal conflict. The statement by the twelve clerics seemed to commit the official Church to one side, and also appeared to legitimize violence as a valid means to promote change.

Hence, in mid-April when the Chilean bishops issued their statement (cited in Chapter 7) praising the accomplishments to date of the Allende Administration but calling for mutual respect among opposing political factions,[23] simultaneously they released a reprimand of the declaration

---

[21] "Initial Response of Cardinal Silva to Gonzalo Arroyo," Santiago, 3 March 1972, in *Christians and Socialism*, ed. Eagleson, p. 41; "Response of the Coordinating Committee to Cardinal Silva," Santiago, 20 March 1972, ibid., p. 60.

[22] "Mensaje de 12 sacerdotes católicos sobre Cuba," *Política y Espíritu* 26 (April 1972): 96. The original text first appeared in *Granma* (Havana), 6 March 1972.

[23] Los obispos de Chile, "Por un camino de esperanza y alegría," Punta de Tralca, 11 April 1972, *Mensaje* 21 (May 1972): 293–94.

from Havana made by the twelve members of CpS. In the document, the hierarchy recognized the validity of priests' sharing the life style of the poor, but criticized the twelve for taking what the bishops considered a political stance dangerous for the Church:

> We do not approve the partisan political attitude which the group has publicly expressed in their manifesto. It openly goes against the guidelines of the Church, reiterated by the Synod of Bishops in Rome last year and by ourselves on recent occasions forbidding a priest from exercising undue influence in the temporal and political realm.
>
> We believe this situation of ambiguity does harm to the life of the Church. . . .
>
> As a consequence, we ask those priests and aspirants to the priesthood . . . to limit their actions to ministerial tasks.[24]

The bishops were clearly more annoyed than in April 1971 when they publicly responded to "the 80." On this occasion they asked the seminarians involved in the action to reconsider their "priestly vocation," and for each priest, after "dialogue with his bishop and religious superior," to "ask to be relieved from his priestly ministry for a period of time," if he "believes his vocation is to be political."[25]

Thus, in the early months of 1972, as serious societal disruptions were beginning, very different normative commitments of the hierarchy and Christians for Socialism led to quite different action strategies on the

---

[24] Asamblea Plenaria del Episcopado, "Carta a los sacerdotes que firmaron el 'Mensaje a los cristianos de América Latina' en La Habana 3 March 1972," Punta de Tralca, 11 April 1972, in *Documentos del Episcopado,* ed. Oviedo, p. 132. The same international Synod of Bishops in Rome of October 1971 which issued the strong exhortation of Church commitment to justice (cited in Chapter 1) also published a separate document on priestly ministry. In it the bishops urged that priests today "must keep a certain distance from any political office or involvement," and they forbade "active militancy on behalf of any party" by priests without consent of the hierarchy. Synod of Bishops, "The Ministerial Priesthood," pt. II, no. 2, *Catholic Mind* 70 (March 1972): 44–45.

[25] Asamblea Plenaria del Episcopado, "Carta a los sacerdotes," in *Documentos del Episcopado,* ed. Oviedo, p. 133.

It is important to note the difference in the styles of statements made by the bishops regarding public social and political issues and those pertaining to internal Church affairs. As seen in Chapter 7, the bishops' documents on the former for the most part remained general in analysis and prescription throughout the Allende years. On matters of ecclesiastical doctrine or discipline, however, the hierarchy spoke much more specifically and left much less room for interpretation once they considered the essential aspects of the Church to be at stake in these latter points. This reflects a perennial pattern in the Roman Church, described earlier in Chapter 2. In Chile in the early 1970s this meant that while lay persons continued to enjoy a wide degree of freedom in making political choices, clerics did not. They shared in ecclesiastical authority and their public actions represented, and touched more closely, the core of the institution. It also meant that behavior of priests could be canonically sanctioned more easily than that of lay persons by threats of dismissal from their official positions in the institution.

part of each group. The leaders of CpS viewed the emerging political opposition to Allende as a signal for more active commitment by themselves and other Christians to bolster the legitimacy of the transition to socialism. They saw this as being consistent with their moral commitment to the poor and to a new vision of the Church which was more decentralized and partisan. The bishops, however, considered the proper role of official Church spokespersons to be one of advocacy for public moderation and mutual understanding among contending factions in society. This flowed from their understanding of the Church which was politically neutral, open to all parties, and guided by hierarchical decision-making. They criticized the public actions of the CpS secretariat in planning the April 1972 convention and the statement of the twelve made in Cuba both as breaches of clerical discipline and also as undermining the possibility for the official Church to act as a force for dialogue in a polarized society.[26]

Challenges to Episcopal Authority during
Allende's Last Year in Office

In late 1972 and early 1973 when social and political polarization reached a critical stage, public differences between CpS and the bishops became severe. During the month-long truckers' strike that paralyzed the nation in October 1972, the day before the Permanent Committee of the Episcopal Conference made its public appeal for cooperation among all contending factors to resolve the strike and to respect constitutional processes (cited in Chapter 7), the secretariat of CpS issued a press release placing blame for the incident squarely on "powerful egotistical interests" who were provoking chaos and blocking the just aspirations of the poor. The statement praised the efforts of workers and leftist organizations to break the strike and called upon all Christians to join them in their struggle for emancipation.[27] While the analysis of CpS may have been correct, the timing and tone of their statement (which the media publicized) at such a critical moment was very much at odds with that of the Episcopal Conference and seemed to challenge (and even preempt) the bishops' public moral authority.

---

[26] A further confirmation of the open divisions emerging among clerics on political issues in early 1972 in Chile was the publication of a letter signed by over 250 priests who opposed the strategies of CpS. The statement appeared just before the April international convention of Christians for Socialism and criticized the leaders of the movement for "trying to revive, despite their good intentions, positions of clericalism and paternalism" which "contradict the explicit thinking of our bishops and of the worldwide episcopate." "Sacerdotes chilenos a su pueblo," Santiago, April 1972, *Iglesia de Santiago* (May–June 1972): 29–30.

[27] "Comunicado del Secretariado Nacional 'Cristianos por el Socialismo,'" Santiago, 20 October 1972, *Boletín de CpS,* 1 November 1972.

In the months between the October strike and the March congressional elections, while the hierarchy were attempting to maintain a neutral position for the official Church in the campaign, Christians for Socialism more definitely identified themselves with the government cause. The CpS secretariat invited representatives of parties of the Left (Communist, Socialist, Christian Left, MAPU, and MIR) to their national meeting in late November. All of these organizations sent spokespersons, and frank discussions occurred on strategic and tactical differences that divided them. While not explicitly identifying with any one party or faction, the leaders of Christians for Socialism considered a major function of their organization to be the promotion of unity among *all* leftists as a necessary precondition for political victory in the March elections and the continuance of a transition to socialism amidst mounting opposition.[28]

During the electoral campaign the CpS organizational network actively promoted the slate of candidates supporting the government and publicly criticized that of the united opposition (consisting primarily of National and Christian Democratic party representatives). A flier circulated widely in January 1973 by the national secretariat of Christians for Socialism presented the choice in quite simple terms, and came close to identifying a vote for the Left with a commitment to Christ:

> In the elections of March the rich are running against the poor, the exploiters against the exploited. When we vote, we are not voting for one or other persons. Basically, either we vote for the capitalist class and its National and Christian Democratic parties or we vote for the working class and the political parties of the Left.
> ... Can a real Christian vote for the oppressors against his people?
> ... We win when we have more of a revolutionary consciousness. We win when we gain more power. And in this whole struggle Christ accompanies us and we encounter God.[29]

In addition to explicitly identifying with parties of the Left during the election, in the last six months of Allende's administration members of CpS on two separate occasions publicly contradicted the hierarchy on issues which the bishops considered of vital importance both to Church and society. After the hierarchy had taken a clear and unequivocal position in opposition to the ENU proposal in March 1973 which would inaugurate a unifying ideology in all private and public schools, Chris-

---

[28] F.Z., "Cristianismo revolucionario," *Chile Hoy* 1 (1–7 December 1972): 7; Françoise Esquerré, " 'Cristianos por el Socialismo,' política y fe cristiana," pp. 47–53.

[29] Secretariado Nacional de los Cristianos por el Socialismo, "Cómo cristianos: ¿por qué nos importan las elecciones de marzo?," mimeographed (Santiago, January 1973).

tians for Socialism issued a document strongly endorsing ENU as an effective means to promote socialist values and liberation of society from capitalist ideology.[30] In June, when the bishops of the central provinces warned the government against tendencies toward statism, but also appealed for mutual respect on all sides, Fr. Pablo Richard, a founder of CpS, publicly rejected such positions as reflecting only the values of the bourgeoisie.

In an article in late June in the periodical *Punto Final*, published by the extreme left MIR, Richard accused the bishops of expressing the "feelings of the rich, not the feelings of the poor and exploited" and of using the notion of unity as an ideological instrument to obfuscate the reality of class struggle. He concluded by demanding that the hierarchy take a stand on the side of the exploited since there was no room for reconciliation of differences among classes:

> We demand that [the episcopate] pronounce itself clearly—about whether it is on the side of exploitation or on the side of liberation. The Chilean process does not admit spectators or arbitrators. It does not admit ambiguous situations. Christ very clearly divided his audience: one group followed Him, the other group murdered Him. And it was not the poor, nor the sick, nor the oppressed who crucified Christ. It was the powerful . . .
> . . . We are concerned about the bishops' statement. It points in a very dangerous direction—to a path against history, against revolutionary changes, against the poor and exploited.[31]

Hence, during the last year of the UP administration when Church-state relations became somewhat strained, but while the bishops were making efforts to promote public moderation, representatives of Christians for Socialism were acting almost as a separate teaching office in the Church. While their intention was to offset what they considered to be implicit and unquestioned reformist political tendencies on the part of the bishops, they came to appear as a quasi-official religious voice directly paralleling, and vying with, that of the episcopacy inside the Church itself.

Several of the serious normative differences between Christians for Socialism and the hierarchy outlined in our previous section in fact led to quite divergent action strategies by both amidst the growing polarization of secular society. While some of these flowed from different political sympathies and frameworks of social analyses, they also reflected

---

[30] Secretariado Nacional de los Cristianos por el Socialismo, *La ENU: ¿control de las conciencias o educación liberadora?*

[31] J. Pablo Richard G., "Los obispos y la prédica de la pequeña burguesía," pp. 26–27. Translated and reprinted in *Christians for Socialism: Highlights from Chile's Religious Revolution*, pp. 29–31.

contradictory visions of the Church itself. Once an explicit endorsement of socialism, an activist political role for clergy, and the promotion of class conflict among Christians all were put into practice by members of CpS it was clear that a very different type of Church was emerging that was hard to reconcile with the one officially espoused by the hierarchy.

THE IMPACT OF TRANSNATIONAL ECCLESIASTICAL LINKAGES FOR THE ASSIMILATION OF MARXISM IN THE CHILEAN CHURCH

One of the critical factors that enhanced the efforts of Christians for Socialism in Chile between 1971 and 1973 was their effective use of the transnational linkages of the Church. Those engaged in CpS received important support from like-minded church groups in other countries, and in turn contributed significantly to the development of movements similar to their own in other parts of the world.

Nevertheless, paralleling the tensions that emerged within the Chilean Church over CpS, there developed significant criticisms of liberation theology and Christians for Socialism both in Rome and in the Latin American Episcopal Conference (CELAM) in 1972 and 1973. Those opposed to efforts to assimilate Marxist theories and strategies within the Church also mobilized key resources of international Catholicism to block such a synthesis, and the Chilean case was one that attracted much of their attention, and even venom.

Reinforcing Interactions between CpS in Chile and the International Church

As seen in previous chapters, an important variable for understanding the development of change-oriented forces in Chilean Catholicism throughout most of the 1960s was the large influx of foreign priests and religious into the country during this period. They brought with them new ideas and material and financial resources and were assigned by the bishops primarily to urban and rural working-class areas.

Although the rate of influx of foreigners slowed after 1968 due to a decline in vocations throughout the Church after Vatican II, many of those who already were in Chile at the time of Allende'e election were favorably disposed to the objectives of his administration. They had grown impatient with what they considered too slow a pace of change during the Frei government and shared intimately in the frustrations of their parishioners. Foreigners therefore provided a substantial part of the clerical group attempting to make an assimilation of Marxism within the Church during the Allende years. In fact, about one-half of the group of eighty priests who publicly endorsed the Chilean transition to socialism in April 1971 were foreign-born. Many of the participants in the Christians for Socialism movement also were foreigners, since this organization drew heavily upon clerics and religious in working-class areas of Chile.

The Chilean bishops recognized this phenomenon, and resented what they considered to be imprudent intervention in Chile's domestic affairs by foreigners who, in their judgment, did not fully understand the Chilean context. In September 1970, after the election but before the congressional confirmation of Allende as president, they publicly asked "priests from other countries . . . not to express opinions on party politics" since they had not "shared profound and prolonged experience over many years with our people."[32] In April 1972, when they reprimanded members of Christians for Socialism for their statement in Havana, the bishops asked the foreigners in the group who were "in a country . . . not their own" to be "more prudent in making statements that are political in nature" and "even more than the Chileans to remain on the margins of political affairs."[33]

In the 1960s most foreign clergy shared a common vision with the bishops and undertook many of the reforms in the Church which made it more visible and effective among the poor. By the early 1970s many of these same priests, however, had become radicalized by what they had seen and experienced in working-class areas. They moved decidedly to the Left in both their theological opinions and their social analysis, and in so doing came to outflank the hierarchy both on religious issues and political strategy. The same transnational linkages that provided the Church with a consistent force for reformist change a decade earlier, by the 1970s had come to be a support for more radical positions. This shifting phenomenon exacerbated further the tensions between the higher and lower leadership of the Church.[34]

Throughout the Allende years groups in Chile attempting an assimilation of Marxist and Christian values and tactics also drew upon the intellectual capital of liberation theologians and leftist clerics in other parts of Latin America. Gustavo Gutiérrez of Peru, Juan Luis Segundo

[32] Los obispos de Chile, "Carta de los obispos de Chile a los consejos de presbiterio y a los superiores de congregaciones religiosas," Punta de Tralca, 24 September 1970, in *Documentos del Episcopado*, ed. Oviedo, p. 32.

[33] Asamblea Plenaria del Episcopado, "Carta a los sacerdotes" ibid., p. 133.

[34] The uneasiness of a significant number of bishops with the behavior of some foreign clerics during the early 1970s helps account for the divided opinion of the hierarchy in responding to my question on the performance of foreign clerics as a whole in my 1975 interviews. A clear majority of bishops (55.2 percent) were completely positive in their evaluations, saying that priests from abroad had provided a very effective support for the Chilean Church over time. A significant minority (44.8 percent), however, felt that many foreigners wasted their energies on the wrong concerns or did not adapt well to Chile (see Table 2.8).

of Uruguay, and Hugo Assmann of Brazil all visited Chile several times to provide theological expertise for "the 80," for Christians for Socialism, and for "the 200." Such theologians gave workshops and made substantial contributions to the preparation of key documents published by CpS in Chile, such as the final declaration of the First International Convention of Christians for Socialism held in Santiago in April 1972. Leaders of radical priest movements in other Latin American countries (ONIS in Peru, Golconda in Colombia, Movement of Priests for the Third World in Argentina) assisted those in Chile who inaugurated Christians for Socialism and provided them with much of their inspiration and organizational insight.[35]

While "the 80" and Christians for Socialism benefited substantially from contacts with like-minded groups and individuals in other countries, they also made a contribution to the development of Christian-Marxist rapprochement at the international level. The first international meeting of Christians for Socialism was organized by the Chilean group, but about one-half of all the participants in the week-long meeting were foreigners. The documents and conclusions from this conference were translated into several languages and circulated throughout Latin America, Western Europe, and North America. The success and media interest in this meeting encouraged Christians in other countries to start additional national organizations of Christians for Socialism. The April 1972 Santiago meeting also was an important precedent and inspiration for later international gatherings of Christian Marxists, such as the one held in Avila, Spain, in January 1973, in Bologna, Italy, in September 1973, and in Quebec, Canada, in April 1975.[36] Thus, by 1973 the Chilean experience began to be duplicated by Christians in other parts of the world, and the movement was taking on global dimensions and receiving significant international attention.

Negative Feedback from the International Church

The stronger the Christians for Socialism movement became and the more international acclaim its ideas and strategies received in the media, the more there arose criticisms both from the Vatican and from groups closely identified with the Latin American Bishops' Conference (CELAM) headquartered in Bogotá. Those who were concerned about CpS's implications for the universal Church (and who held very different theological and political positions) also began to use the network of the Church to discredit it and mobilize resources to stop it.

Roger Vekemans, the Belgian Jesuit who had organized many of the

---

[35] Eagleson, ed., *Christians and Socialism,* pp. 19, 141–42; Vanderschueren and Rojas, "The Catholic Church of Chile," pp. 41–42.

[36] Sorge, "El movimiento de los 'Cristianos por el Socialismo,' " p. 489.

Chilean Church's social action programs in the early 1960s with substantial amounts of foreign money, left Chile within days of Allende's
popular election. From Bogotá in 1971 he launched a campaign against
both liberation theology and radical priest movements in Latin
America. He was concerned by what he considered dangerous movements to the Left throughout the Latin American Church in the late
1960s and early 1970s, and in December 1971 sent a letter to Misereor
(the German bishops' fund that supports social and humanitarian projects in the third world) requesting a grant to monitor closely liberation
theology.

In the letter he accused liberation theology of promoting a "revolution of the Church, challenging the Church's hierarchical authority"
and brushing aside official Church pronouncements "as obsolete if not
counterrevolutionary." He charged that it was a "theology of violence"
guilty of "indiscriminate collaboration and often almost a fusion" with
Marxism. He concluded with a bitter indictment of the threat to the
Church that liberation theologians and Christians for Socialism were
purportedly mounting:

> The really weird aspect of this process is that it is not something shape-
> less or marginal, but it has now solidified into a movement and has
> succeeded in penetrating some of the institutional Church's nerve cen-
> ters. Not only theologians highly regarded for their specialities, but
> many priests and Christian militants are, like real agitators, making
> full use of ecclesiastical structures, with the naive acquiescence of weak
> authorities and sometimes with logistical, intellectual, and financial
> support from abroad.
>
> The saddest part is that to combat this brutal and unscrupulous at-
> tack we see only scattered and intermittent reactions that seem to ac-
> knowledge beforehand their inevitable defeat.[37]

As seen in Chapter 6 regarding the case of ILADES in 1968, the German bishops were sympathetic to those who feared Marxist penetration
of the Chilean Church, and they reacted positively to Vekemans's request for aid. In 1972 with German Catholic funds, Vekemans began a

---

[37] An English translation of this letter was published in Lima in *Latinamerica Press,*
21 April 1972. It also appears in *The Theology of Liberation,* pp. 56–57. Adveniat, the
West German bishops' fund for the support of religious programs in Latin America,
later set aside money for a series of meetings on liberation theology held in Germany,
Italy, and Colombia between 1973 and 1976. Only clerics and theologians opposed
to this current of thought, however, were invited to these discussions. A number of
German theologians (Catholic and Protestant) favorable to liberation theology
strongly criticized the use of Church funds for such partisan actions in a public letter
in November 1977. See, "We Must Protest," *Cross Currents* 28 (Spring 1978): 66–70.
For a rebuttal to these criticisms by Vekemans, see, "Ubicación, valor y significación
de las fuentes aducidas por los memorandos acerca de Adveniat," *Tierra Nueva* 28,
(January 1979): 83–94.

major research project to critique the theology of liberation and to warn against radical movements such as Christians for Socialism which drew some of their inspiration from it.

Vekemans amassed considerable documentation on "the 80" and the new Christians for Socialism movement in Chile, and as early as July 1972 began to publish these materials in a new quarterly journal, *Tierra Nueva*, launched that year to offset the influence of what he considered extremely radical tendencies in the Latin American Church. The texts of liberation theology and the Chilean CpS he published, however, while accurate and representative, only appeared in excerpted form and were also interspersed with a rather critical and negative commentary by the editor.[38] As a result, a critical voice (and that of a powerful international Church figure) began to be heard throughout Latin America by mid-1972 regarding liberation theology and Christians for Socialism, and the Chilean case was singled out as his primary target to be discredited and destroyed.

Vekemans, however, was not the only formidable opponent on the continent to Latin American liberation theology and Christians for Socialism in the early 1970s. In June 1972 the Episcopal Commission of the Department of Social Action in CELAM issued a strong criticism of the growing "political instrumentalization of the Church in Latin America." Although the document mentioned both capitalism and Marxism as being guilty of this fault throughout the continent, only one brief paragraph focused on the former. The greater part of the document concentrated on Marxism as the real threat to Latin American Catholicism. It accused Marxists of trying to manipulate base communities at the local level of the Church, weakening their ties to the hierarchy and seeking to promote "new forms of revolution within the Church."[39]

The statement specifically criticized the documents from the April 1972 international convention of Christians for Socialism in Chile for purportedly justifying Marxist ideological and tactical infiltration of the Church. It concluded by suggesting that all the episcopal conferences throughout Latin America promote investigations of where and how such methods were being employed in their own countries to "destroy or weaken the institutional Church" or to manipulate "small base communities, popular religiosity, and Church organizations."[40]

---

[38] "La iglesia chilena, microcosmos latinoamericano: crónica," *Tierra Nueva* (Bogotá), no. 2 (July 1972), pp. 24–41, and no. 3 (October 1972), pp. 80–91.
[39] Comisión Episcopal del Departamento de Acción Social del CELAM, "La instrumentalización política de la iglesia en América Latina," *Política y Espíritu* 28 (April 1973): 76–77.
[40] Ibid., pp. 77–78.

In late 1972, there was also a general change at the top level of CELAM itself, away from the more progressive orientation of the late 1960s. Conservative bishops were elected to the two key posts of president and secretary general of the organization—Eduardo R. Pironio of Mar del Plata, Argentina, and Alfonso López Trujillo of Bogotá, Colombia, a close collaborator of Roger Vekemans. In the eyes of some, this change in the leadership of CELAM signalled a pullback on the part of many Latin American bishops from their Medellín commitments. Local grass-roots Church groups in several Latin American countries had begun to move faster and more radically than anticipated by the bishops in implementing the guidelines of Medellín, and by 1972 several episcopal conferences wanted to slow down the pace of change and also avoid too much Church involvement in political issues. This was interpreted by the progressive clerical and lay sectors of the Latin American Church, however, as thwarting the spirit and original thrust of Medellín.[41]

López Trujillo, soon after his election as secretary general of CELAM, published an extensive article in *Tierra Nueva* showing what he considered to be major incompatibilities between Marxist analysis and Christian faith. In his essay he also included a long section on what he believed to be a naive and dangerous assimilation of Marxism in the final document of the April 1972 Christians for Socialism convention in Santiago.[42]

Concern about liberation theology and Christians for Socialism also began to preoccupy the Vatican at about the same time. A document from the Holy See was sent to bishops and papal nuncios in 1972 warning against the implications of liberation theology.[43] In December 1972 the Sacred Congregation for Catholic Education in Rome also sent a letter to the Latin American hierarchy criticizing the "increased politicization of Catholic education" and the tendencies in CELAM-sponsored projects of "being oriented consciously or unconsciously in many cases towards questioning, criticism, and flirting with negative ideologies."[44] In early 1973, an apostolic visitor was sent from Rome to investigate criticisms against Bishop Leonidas Proaño of Riobamba, Ecuador, for purportedly moving too far in establishing socially commited base communities in his diocese.[45]

[41] Agoŝtino Bono, "Five Years After Medellín: Social Action Fades in Latin America," pp. 1, 6, 11; Phillip Berryman, "Latin American Liberation Theology," pp. 393–95.

[42] Bishop Alfonso López Trujillo, "Análisis marxista y liberación cristiana," pp. 5–43.

[43] Berryman, "Latin American Liberation Theology," p. 395.

[44] Bono, "Five Years After Medellín," p. 1.

[45] Gary MacEoin, "Church Renewal on Trial in Ecuador," *America,* 4 August 1973, pp. 61–63.

Thus, the reinforcing international currents for a synthesis between Marxism and Christianity running to and from Chile by early 1973 were encountering powerful opposing forces also operating through the transnational network of the Church. Money from West Germany, theological expertise from other parts of Latin America, and disciplinary warnings from Rome against leftist tendencies in the Church all combined to mount a major campaign against liberation theology and Christians for Socialism by the last year of Allende's presidency. Such an international Church context reinforced the growing antipathy of the Chilean bishops for these trends, and paved the way for their own strong condemnation of Christians for Socialism written during Allende's last months in office.

CONDEMNATION OF CHRISTIANS FOR SOCIALISM BY THE CHILEAN HIERARCHY

A definitive break between Christians for Socialism and the Chilean hierarchy finally occurred in 1973. The bishops later claimed they held off for quite some time in publicly condemning this movement out of a desire to keep open the lines of communication with its members and sympathizers for as long as possible.[46] They were also concerned about the possible repercussions for Church-state relations that an open break between themselves and CpS might precipitate, given the strong support for government objectives manifested by the group. Attempts were made at dialogue by some bishops and leaders of the movement during 1972, but they failed to reconcile differences. As the hierarchy began to distance themselves from the policies of the government after March 1973, they also decided to forbid further participation by clerics and religious in Christians for Socialism.[47]

[46] In a report to an international Synod of Bishops held in Rome in October 1974, the Chilean hierarchy stated that the reason for their delay in publicly condemning Christians for Socialism was "their overriding desire not to break with the socialist priests and not to cause important sectors of workers, peasants, and university students from cutting off their ties to the faith." La Conferencia Episcopal de Chile, "Sínodo de obispos, 1974," p. 13.

[47] Allende himself was pleased to have a group within the institutional Church publicly endorsing the specific goals of his regime and a Christian-Marxist synthesis. Domestically and internationally it was a clear indication that religiously devout Chileans were open to his goals and that there was also ample freedom for a positive contribution to socialism by Church members, even priests. From time to time, therefore, in private conversations with the cardinal and bishops he would praise Christians for Socialism as a sign of how much the Church was changing. He also would advise the hierarchy to avoid a public condemnation of the movement which, in his view, would be a major setback for progressive Catholicism and Christian-Marxist cooperation. In early 1973, however, when Allende learned that the bishops were finally planning a public denunciation of Christians for Socialism, he urged the

They reached this decision at their semiannual meeting in early April, but decided to delay promulgation of the disciplinary decree until a document could be prepared giving all the reasons for the condemnation.[48] Approval of the final text of the statement by the Permanent Committee of the Epsicopal Conference did not occur until 13 September, two days after the military coup. The committee decided to shelve the document due to the dramatic change in the country and the suppression of all political movements. The secretary of the Episcopal Conference, Bishop Carolos Oviedo Cavada, however, released the statement on his own in mid-October, and sent copies to other national episcopal conferences in Latin America.[49]

In this statement, entitled "Christian Faith and Political Activity," the bishops acknowledged some positive elements they saw in Christians for Socialism: a "critical examination" of Church structures so that it might divest itself of "special interests," a sensitivity to "socioeconomic factors that condition the moral and spiritual life," and a "vitalization of theology by bringing it into open contact with the historic problems of the day."[50] The major thrust of the document, however, was negative and harsh. It focused both on areas of incompatibility of Christian faith and Marxism, and on what the bishops considered to be an attack against the Church's mission, unity, and hierarchical authority made by Christians for Socialism.

The document claimed that by closely identifying genuine religious experience with revolutionary activity, CpS robbed the Gospel of its transcendence since "Christian liberation stems from Christ's resurrection, and not from social processes or struggle."[51] The bishops also accused Christians for Socialism of having "taken over wholesale the main features of Marxist methodology," many of which, they argued, are incompatible with central values in the Gospel: charity, reconciliation,

---

leaders of CpS to talk with the hierarchy and then to submit to episcopal demands. He could not afford a schism in the Church precipitated by a dissident Catholic movement in close sympathy with the government. This would leave the Popular Unity regime supporting a sect and would precipitate official Church opposition to the regime. (This information and analysis was provided to me by Arturo Gaete, S.J., of Centro Bellarmino, who closely followed these conversations and developments as an advisor to the hierarchy on Christian-Marxist dialogue during this period.)

[48] *Documentos del Episcopado,* ed. Oviedo, p. 176.

[49] Oviedo, a known critic of CpS and also a sympathizer to the military in the months following the coup, was replaced by the assembly of bishops as secretary of the Episcopal Conference in December 1973, two months after he publicly circulated this document on his own authority. Bishop Carlos Camus, a man of more moderate political views, succeeded him in this position.

[50] "Christian Faith and Political Activity," no. 17, 16 October 1973, in *Christians and Socialism,* ed. Eagleson, pp. 188–89.

[51] Ibid., no. 46, p. 201.

peace, human freedom, and the autonomy of moral and spiritual virtues. They denied that such values are merely "bourgeois ideologiza-
tions," nor that class conflict can serve to realize them in any authentic
way. "We do not believe," they said, "that man can arrive at the 'reign
of liberty' by exacerbating conflict to the utmost." They stated that
"class struggle is not the specific means which Christ gave his Church to
contribute to the ultimate triumph of justice in the world."[52]

The bishops thus categorically rejected the position espoused by
Christians for Socialism: that class differences and struggles made belief
in the present unity of the Church impossible and illusory. The promotion of unity belongs to the "innermost nature of the Church," claimed
the bishops, offering an invaluable service to society *especially* when the
very foundations of its social fabric are coming apart. Through a fundamental unity of faith and charity that goes beyond all political and class
differences, they said, the Church can help "to make the moral climate
of the country more humane and serene."[53]

As in "Gospel, Politics and Various Types of Socialism," the hierarchy
again stressed that the only way the Church could continue to perform
such a public service was by preserving an officially neutral position in
the political arena. They admitted that the Church does try to influence
political policies through its social teachings, through education, and
through the interior renewal of human beings so that they might dedi-
cate themselves to the struggle for justice. The bishops denied, however,
that the official position of the institution was partisan. The reasons
given were that "it does not offer any political model," that is "properly
its own," and that it "does not try to be effective by exercising power."[54]

Christians for Socialism, said the bishops, while claiming to be nonpartisan, in reality were using tactics aimed at unifying parties of the
Left and mobilizing Christian support for them. Such behavior "is totally out of line with the apolitical character of the Church and her
priests," they said, and seeks to introduce a new form of clericalism into
areas that are primarily secular.[55]

Finally, the bishops stated that both the analysis and the strategies of
Christians for Socialism were causing serious pastoral problems within
the internal life of the Church itself. CpS's assumption that Marxism
and Christianity "are compatible, and even convergent," at the doctrinal level, said the bishops, is contrary to official Catholic teaching and
causing confusion among the faithful. The reconciliation of a "supernatural and divine meaning of existence with dialectical and historical ma-

[52] Ibid., nos. 19, 23, 58, 68, pp. 190, 192, 207, 211.
[53] Ibid., nos. 14, 79, pp. 187, 216.
[54] Ibid., nos. 35, 40, 47, pp. 196–97, 199, 202.
[55] Ibid., nos. 36, 37, pp. 197–98.

terialism" is an impossible task and goes against warnings by the hierarchy.[56]

Christians for Socialism, therefore, come "dangerously close" to becoming a sect, they said, and thus "detract from the nature of the Church and her essential institutionality." The movement openly contradicts the "disciplinary directives" of the hierarchy "in full view of the faithful," and its secretariat "exercises a kind of teaching function parallel to that of the bishops":

> Thus the group inevitably ends up by somehow "sacralizing" its own cause and making it a Church within a Church—or rather the "true Church," a new sect, only marginally associated with the hierarchical ties of the ecclesial community.[57]

While admitting that other movements within the Church "exhibit distortion of the Church's temporal role," the bishops justified their treatment of this movement in greater detail on the grounds of its organizational network and well-publicized positions throughout the country over the past two years. They also claimed that "utilization of the faith in the opposite direction," while just as regrettable, "does not call for such extensive examination for obvious reasons":

> It is not crystallized in organized groups, it does not have the same impact on public opinion, it does not invoke the label "Christian" so explicitly, it does not entail militancy on the part of priests and religious, it is not formulated in written documents, it does not propound a distinct doctrine or vision of the Church, it does not call the fundaments of the faith into question in the same way, and it does not oppose the ecclesiastical hierarchy in the same measure.[58]

The bishops, therefore, concluded their harsh rebuttal to CpS with a disciplinary pronouncement forbidding "priests and religious from be-

---

[56] Ibid., no. 73, p. 214.

[57] Ibid., nos. 74–75, pp. 214–15.

[58] Ibid., no. 81, p. 217. During most of the three-year period of the Popular Unity government, many of those active in the right-wing Catholic movement, Tradition, Family and Property (TFP), were in self-imposed exile in Brazil and Argentina. They reappeared in Chile in early 1973, and issued advertisements in various newspapers charging that the clergy and hierarchy in Chile were bringing about the "self-destruction" of the Church and "exercising a deadly influence . . . in the dramatic process of communizing the country." Sociedad Chilena de Defensa de la Tradición, Familia y Propiedad, "La autodemolición de la iglesia, factor de la demolición de Chile," *La Tribuna*, 27 February 1973. See also, "La Iglesia '73," ¿*Qué Pasa?* (Santiago), no. 105 (19 April 1973), pp. 7–9. The fact that TFP did not conduct a prolonged and sustained attack on the bishops throughout the Allende period, and that their leadership was not clerical, diminished their threat to Church unity and hierarchical authority in the minds of the bishops. As we shall see in the next chapter, however, the TFP was to become a much more serious threat to episcopal authority once the political context changed after 1973 and the military were in power.

longing to that organization" or from engaging in any "activity we have denounced in this document."[59]

The immediate practical effect of this condemnation was not significant, since it did not actually appear until after the military coup when formal public activities and pronouncements of Christians for Socialism had ceased. It was in preparation, however, for several months before the downfall of Allende and its content (but not the timing of its release) did receive final approval of the executive committee of the Episcopal Conference. Its import, therefore, lies in the issues it raises for wider questions of Christian-Marxist rapprochement more than in the immediate impact it had on religiopolitical developments in Chile in October 1973.

It is an indication that, while there can be great room for maneuverability in the external relations of the Church with a Marxist regime that respects its freedom, the hierarchy is likely to set much stricter limits on the adaptation of Marxist categories and strategies in the internal life of the institution itself. The legitimation of socialism as the only viable Christian political option, the espousal and active promotion of political strategies by clerics, the sustained public challenge to episcopal authority, and the use of class conflict as a pastoral strategy all presented much more of a threat to the integrity of the Church than did coexistence and limited cooperation with a Marxist regime in Chile between 1970 and 1973.

All of these points challenged three key issues that the hierarchy traditionally have considered to be central to the religious mission of the Church—general articulation of social norms so as to prevent official identification with partisan movements, hierarchical authority flows under the control of the bishops, and universal membership scope for all social classes. Once these fundamental characteristics of Catholicism appeared to be under attack, the hierarchy reacted strongly to defend core interests of the institution as they perceived them. The fact that threats to these core interests were also perceived by others (including the Vatican) at the international level of the Church (the fourth critical dynamic in Catholicism) made it easier for the Chilean bishops to take disciplinary action against Christians for Socialism.

Clerical movements in other contemporary Latin American countries which have employed Marxist analysis and have at times attempted to act as forces for moving the Church closer to socialism have encountered similar problems with the hierarchy once they publicly have challenged

[59] "Christian Faith and Political Activity," no. 80, in *Christians and Socialism*, ed. Eagleson, p. 217.

episcopal authority and have become engaged in partisan politics. In Colombia, the Golconda movement of the late 1960s encountered strong public opposition from the bishops when some of them endorsed the revolutionary position of Fr. Camilo Torres and also became active in the presidential campaign of Rojas Pinilla in 1970.[60]

On the other hand, the experiences of ONIS in Peru and the Movement of Priests for the Third World in Argentina have shown that clerical organizations sympathetic to Marxism and committed to promoting change within the Church in the direction of socialism can function without encountering episcopal condemnation. In both these situations, leaders of the respective movements made a conscious effort to maintain good personal relations with the hierarchy, and avoided active participation in parties. In the late 1960s and early 1970s these movements concentrated their efforts on denouncing forms of injustice in secular society and in sensitizing their respective hierarchies (both traditionally conservative) to the need for structural change.[61]

In the Chilean situation, however, Christians for Socialism, despite some efforts to maintain communication with the hierarchy, as time went on took more independent positions in public. Authority flows across the hierarchical command system of the Church broke down, and the bishops felt obliged to take a more critical stance toward a Christian-Marxist synthesis within the Church than they had done regarding rapprochement in the secular arena.

BEHAVIORAL STRAINS AMONG LAITY
DURING THE ENCOUNTER WITH MARXISM

Thus far we have concentrated on the major normative and structural dimensions of the assimilation-synthesis aspect of a rapprochement between Catholicism and Marxism attempted by clerics and religious in Chile. As in previous chapters, it would also be important to know what impact the encounter with Marxism had on rank-

---

[60] Daniel H. Levine and Alexander W. Wilde, "The Catholic Church, 'Politics' and Violence: The Colombian Case," 231–34; *Social-Activist Priests: Colombia, Argentina,* pp. 19–41. In November 1976 (after the fourth international meeting of Christians for Socialism held in Quebec in 1975), the sixty-five bishops of Colombia issued a condemnation of Christians for Socialism, rejecting claims that Marxist analysis is scientifically valid and capable of separation from its atheistic ideology. In September 1976 the Ecuadorian hierarchy published a similar rejection of CpS on the basis of statements signed by the Quebec meeting. McGovern, *Marxism,* p. 237. See also, *Latinamerica Press,* 13 January 1977, pp. 5–6 and 27 January 1977, p. 4.

[61] For information on both of these movements, see Chapter 2, note 23. For a comparative analysis of the ideology and strategies of the Movement of Priests for the Third World in Argentina and Christians for Socialism in Chile, see Michael Dodson, "The Christian Left in Latin American Politics."

and-file Catholic attitudes and behavior—particularly on their religious faith and allegiance to the Church. This would be particularly significant for lay Catholics today in other parts of the world who are proposing that it is possible to combine a vibrant religious belief with Marxist economic and political analysis and strategy.

Although there has not been sufficient empirical research to date on this aspect of rapprochement in Chile during the Popular Unity government, the evidence that does exist raises some serious questions about how successfully such a synthesis can be made by lay persons while still remaining committed Christians. Furthermore, the Chilean experience indicates that amidst the societal polarization that can accompany a transition to socialism it is very difficult for the Church to develop new evangelization programs and to keep the ones it has from being seriously politicized.

A Weakening of Church Allegiances among Young Leftist Catholics

As desribed in Chapter 6, during the final years of the Frei Administration many young Catholics became disillusioned with Christian Democracy. A small group moved to the Right, but the majority of the disenchanted moved Left. A considerable number joined MAPU, the Christian Left, or the Socialist Party. Others who experienced a strong attraction to classical Marxism and a purer revolutionary commitment went even further to the MIR, the extreme left organization which proposed violence as the only effective method to achieve radical structural transformations.[62]

Those who have studied the religious trajectory of these young Catholics in Chile as they adopted Marxist ideas and commitments have concluded that there was a considerable decline in their allegiance to the institutional Church. Moreover, in many cases a loss or weakening of religious faith also occurred. Pablo Fontaine, a Chilean priest who has followed this phenomenon closely, has argued that a steady evolution developed among these young Christians from religious commitment, to social awareness and involvement, to a search for more global solutions to economic and political problems, to an encounter with Marxism as an all-encompassing system. In this final stage of growth, some simply abandoned their faith. Others bracketed it and relegated it only to those

---

[62] This trajectory by the Catholic Action members from Christian Democracy, to MAPU or the Christian Left or the Socialist Party, and then to the MIR was described to me by several Chilean priests who had been active as university chaplains or teachers in the late 1960s and early 1970s. (Interviews with Humberto Guzmán, Arturo Gaete, S.J., Sergio Zañartu, S.J., and Patricio Cariola, S.J., Punta de Tralca, 20 September 1975.)

issues pertaining to ultimate destiny, making revolutionary ideology and commitment their urgent concern.[63]

Some few did find religious faith a source of inspiration and motivation in their struggle. By and large, however, according to Fontaine, there was a strong tendency among young leftist Catholics to reduce everything to politics, and to reduce politics to class struggle. In such a context, if personal faith itself was not substantially weakened, allegiances to the institutional Church certainly declined.[64]

Hervi Lara, a Chilean sociologist who studied this same question, has concluded that many young Catholics in Chile also were affected by the growing process of secularization that was developing in Latin America during the late 1960s and early 1970s. At this time, the Church and its institutions appeared to some as unnecessary. Lara concludes that to Christians who made a commitment to Marxism and the Left in this cultural context, organizational structures of the Church seemed to hamper revolutionary commitment since its official position was not 100 percent behind radical change:

> In the perspective of Christians on the Left, the Church should have used its power, authority, and prestige to fight the capitalist system and actively promote socialism. The Church, however, refused to do so—partly because it was in some ways identified with the present system, and also because those of its leaders more aware of the implications wanted to avoid the errors of the past and maintain the liberty of the institution.[65]

According to Lara, a combination of secularization, the encounter with Marxism, and the refusal of the official Church to throw its weight fully behind the transition to socialism in Chile all led to a weakening of faith on the part of many leftist Catholics during the Allende years.[66]

Other studies on religious attitudes of Catholics during the same period confirmed the fact that the chronically weak allegiances to the institutional Church (described in previous chapters) actually worsened during the Allende years. Mass attendance declined from the 1960

---

[63] Pablo Fontaine, SS. CC., "Algunos aspectos de la iglesia chilena de hoy," pp. 246–51 (esp. pp. 249–50).

[64] Ibid., p. 250.

[65] Hervi Lara B., 'Cristianos por el Socialismo': manifestación de crisis de fe, pp. 86, 95.

[66] While he was conducting his research in 1975, Lara showed me summaries of several extensive interviews he conducted with young lay Catholics who had attempted to make a synthesis between Marxism and religious faith in their personal lives. Although these conversations do not appear in his published work, the evidence he showed me all supported the same conclusions reached by Fontaine —namely that Marxist ideology and/or leftist political commitment gradually replaced their religious faith, or put it, as it were, in a state of suspended animation, and that alienation from the institutional Church was part of this process.

levels, especially among women, youth, and children. Those studying this phenomenon within the Church (OSORE, Centro Bellarmino) concluded that, in addition to the impact of societal secularization, rapid changes within the Church resulted in a disillusionment with the institution by some adults and a deterioration of religious training for youth.[67]

While Marxism by itself did not cause the weakening of ties with the institutional Church, the fact that both associational participation and personal religious development were declining made it very difficult for those Christians who did attempt to integrate Marxism into their personal lives to hold on to their faith in the process. Marxism was so pervasive and attractive among many young idealists in Chile during these years that it replaced tenuous and declining religious allegiances in their lives instead of melding with them into a new synthesis.

Short-Circuiting of New Evangelization Programs and Internal Politicization of Base Communities

There never was sufficient time nor opportunity to develop new religious socialization mechanisms during the Allende years to offset the attractive power of Marxism among younger Catholics. Although the bishops inaugurated new religious programs after 1968 (small base communities, lay leadership groups, catechist and deacon training programs), these structures did not significantly grow during the rapid social and political changes of the late 1960s and early 1970s.

There was no overt attack on the institutional network of the Church by the Allende Administration. There was, however, an intensification of mobilization efforts by all political parties between 1968 and 1973 and an accelerated politicization of society after 1971. In such a context, it became difficult for the Church to compete with other social organizations for associational participation since politics took on an all-pervading importance.

While the Marxist parties did not discourage people from going to Church, they (like other parties) often used Sundays—the only non-working day in the week for most Chileans—or evenings to hold mass rallies and conduct neighborhood meetings. These were the precise

---

[67] Oficina de Sociología Religiosa de la Conferencia Episcopal (OSORE), "Secularización," mimeographed (Santiago, December 1971); Carmen Galilea y Josefina Puga, *Religiosidad y secularización en Chile*. The study by Galilea and Puga was based on secondary analysis of a random sample of 886 adults in Santiago conducted in April 1972 in cooperation with the Centro de Opinión Pública of Eduardo Hamuy. Galilea and Puga found that among the Catholics (N=721) in the sample, those between eighteen and twenty-seven years of age were the most alienated from the Church in terms of religious practice, obedience to episcopal teachings, and personal piety (pp. 39–40, 58, 66).

times new Church programs were holding their sessions and this made it more difficult for those with political interests or commitments to participate in such Church activities. Hence, cross-pressures were operating which made it hard for the Church to conduct effective evangelization programs during these years.

In my interviews with Chilean religious elites in 1975 (especially with priests, nuns, and lay leaders), on several occasions I was told that Marxist parties scheduled activities in working-class neighborhoods precisely at those times when the new base communities would be meeting for worship, prayer, or study. This helps explain why a significant percentage of these local leaders (between 11 and 24 percent) indicated to me that they believed that there was an attempt to limit the freedom of Church activity during the government of Allende (see Table 7.1). There certainly was no concerted effort to hinder such Church activities at the *top* level of government, but the negative effect on Church participation at the *local* level by intense leftist mobilization efforts was resented by many priests, nuns, and lay leaders. (The Left, of course, was not the only party guilty of drawing people away from Church activities since the PDC was also very active in trying to expand its working-class cadres during the Allende years.)

Many of the new small communities that did function during the Popular Unity administration were quickly drawn into the vortex of politics. In some cases, priests sympathetic to the transition to socialism made explicit efforts to raise the political awareness of their new communities, and demanded of the membership an active commitment to the leftist cause and to the transition to socialism.[68] In other cases, the participants themselves often injected political issues into the small group discussions of these communities, and in religious meetings openly clashed with other members who had different political convictions.[69]

Hence, although unintended, the impact of Marxism on the internal dynamics of the Church during the Allende years was to diminish its capacity to develop new mechanisms for viable religious socialization. Given the already weak structural underpinnings and membership allegiances of the Church when it entered the Allende era, it was addition-

[68] For example, the declaration of principles for a Christian base community inaugurated in Valparaíso in October 1971, and guided by one of the priests active in Christians for Socialism, required that all members be both Christian *and* revolutionary and that no one could participate without previous acceptance by the membership. Ignacio Pujadas, "Comunidades de cristianos revolucionarios: declaración de principios," pp. 48–50.

[69] This problem of internal politicization of religious meetings was fairly widespread, especially during the latter part of the Allende Administration, according to many of the local Church religious and lay leaders I interviewed in 1975 throughout Chile.

ally harder to promote solid doctrinal and spiritual training among young people desirous of making an assimilation of Marxism.

POST FACTUM JUDGMENTS BY CHILEAN CHURCH LEADERS OF THE IMPACT OF MARXISM WITHIN THE CHURCH

In my interviews with Chilean Church leaders in 1975 I included several questions about how elites at various levels of the institution evaluated the overall consequences of the encounter with Marxism two years after the Allende period, as compared with what the bishops had written at the height of the turmoil in 1973. I asked the bishops, priests, nuns, and lay leaders in my sample what they felt were the most positive and negative experiences for the Church itself during those years. I also asked them their opinions concerning the extent and the consequences of clerical involvement in politics to see if there were any significant differences of judgment across leadership levels of the Church.

Regarding the positive experiences for the Church during the Allende period, only 8.6 percent stated that they believed there was anything fruitful for the life of the Church, and an equal number felt that *nothing* positive at all for the Church resulted from this close encounter. A little over one-quarter (28.5 percent) indicated that Marxism forced the Church to take the problems of the secular world more seriously, especially the concerns of the poor. The plurality (31.7 percent) of respondents, however, expressed their answers in very defensive categories related to the survival of the institution. They stressed the fact that the Church had to define its doctrine more clearly, or that it had gotten through these years (albeit with much suffering) with its unity and independence intact.

These responses are in contrast to the rather good external policy relations maintained between Church and state during the Allende years and the significant contributions to democratic procedures made by the official Church in that period. It highlights again what was illustrated earlier (Table 7.2)—namely, the hierarchy *privately* harbored reservations about Marxism despite correct and positive public relations with the Allende government. This is also manifested in some of the responses to my other question, the negative experiences for the Church during the Allende period.

Over two-fifths of Church leaders (41.4 percent) felt that the most negative experience for the Church was the divisiveness and confusion that arose inside Christian communities, the penetration of Marxist doctrine into the Church, or the decline of participation in the life of the Church by Catholics. Another one-quarter (25.8 percent) considered politicization of the clergy as being the most damaging effect, and many

Table 8.1

"What Do You Feel Was the Most Important Positive Experience for the Church During the Period of Allende?" (1975)

	Bishops (N = 30)	Priests (N = 72)	Nuns (N = 33)	Laity (N = 51)	Totals (N = 186)
1. Positive encounter with Marxism itself (we learned how to coexist and dialogue with Marxists; we found we could cooperate with them on certain projects)	13.3%	11.1%	—	7.8%	8.6%
2. Positive encounter between Church and world (especially the world of the poor; greater social awareness)	23.3	30.6	39.4%	21.6	28.5
3. Survival of the Church (it maintained its unity or independence; it was forced to define itself more; suffering purified us; general defensive position)	36.7	33.3	12.1	39.2	31.7
4. Combination of the above	16.7	2.8	3.0	2.0	4.8
5. Nothing positive at all	10.0	11.1	3.0	7.8	8.6
6. No answer	—	11.1	42.5	21.6	17.8

singled out Christians for Socialism or "the 80" as prime examples. Very few (5.9 percent) indicated that Marxist groups *outside* the Church threatened its interest by trying to manipulate it for political gain.

These two tables taken together indicate that what predominated in the consciousness of Chilean religious elites at every level of the Church in 1975 was that an assimilation of Marxist theory and practice *into* the Church was responsible for much damage to its integrity during the Popular Unity years. This negative impression was so overwhelming two years after the coup that, above all else, these leaders could recall the most positive experience to have been one of sheer survival of the institution from a serious internal threat.[70]

Many of the negative assessments focused on the political actions of the clergy during these years and their consequences, particularly those who attempted to identify the Church closely with the Left. Over 80 percent of all the respondents in my interviews said that priests over the past decade had become too much involved in political activities, and most said that partisan activities had occurred on both sides of the political spectrum. When asked to specify what types of activities they felt were harmful in this area, just under two-fifths (37.6 percent) mentioned identification with parties in general. One-quarter (24.9 percent) indicated divisive actions, such as political sermons, clerical participation in public demonstrations, and the use of religious symbols by priests for political purposes—predominantly activities of clerics with socialist sympathies during the early 1970s. Almost one-fifth (19.1 percent) included in their responses involvement with parties of the Left or the actions of Christians for Socialism and "the 80" (with bishops and priests mentioning this the most). Very rew respondents (1.3 percent) singled out the public identification of priests with the PDC, and only one person named involvement with parties on the Right as having been a problem among priests since 1965.

A moderate appraisal of clerical involvement in parties was made by only one bishop who did not seem disturbed by the phenomenon. While not condoning it, he found it understandable due to the pressures on clerics from the groups whom they serve:

> One should not consider politics as something terrible, dangerous, or immoral. Did not Pius XII say that politics is the most noble expres-

---

[70] One bishop told me that in his judgment the most damaging impact of an assimilation of Marxism occurred among the laity who were not prepared for it:

The most harmful experience for the Church was the absence of a solid formation among Christians. They were weak in the face of Marxism. They lacked a depth of comprehension of the Church. There was a lot of sentimentality among them which was not able to resist in the ideological combat with Marxism.
[Interview no. 022, 23 September 1975]

Table 8.2
"What Do You Feel Was the Most Harmful Experience for the Church during the Same Period?"
(1975)

	Bishops (N = 30)	Priests (N = 72)	Nuns (N = 33)	Laity (N = 51)	Totals (N = 186)
1. Hatred, divisiveness, confusion inside Christian communities; penetration of Marxist doctrine into the Church; decline in Church participation	50.0%	40.3%	45.4%	35.3%	41.4%
2. Politicization of members of the clergy; divisive action by priests or lay leaders; actions of Christians for Socialism or "the 80"	36.7	31.9	6.1	23.5	25.8
3. Utilization of religion or of the Church by government or its followers for their own material or political interests	3.3	6.9	—	9.8	5.9
4. Combination of the above	10.0	2.8	3.0	2.0	3.8
5. Other (indecisiveness of bishops; inability of Church to contribute more to development of the country)	—	5.6	6.1	3.9	4.3
6. No harmful experience	—	4.2	—	7.9	3.8
7. No answer	—	8.3	39.4	17.6	15.0

Table 8.3
"What Types of Political Activities by Priests Do You Think Were Harmful for the Church over the Past Decade?" (1975)

	Bishops (N = 29)	Priests (N = 70)	Nuns (N = 24)	Laity (N = 34)	Totals (N = 157)
1. Enrollment or involvement in political parties in general	37.9	35.7	20.8	53.0	37.6
2. Divisive actions (political sermons; participation in marches, strikes, land seizures; too much social action; use of religious symbols for political purposes)	17.3	22.9	33.3	29.4	24.9
3. Involvement or enrollment in parties of the *Left* (among other actions mentioned above)	6.9 ⎫ 31.0	12.8 ⎫ 22.8	4.2	2.9	8.3 ⎫ 19.1
4. The actions of Christians for Socialism or "the 80" (among other actions mentioned above)	24.1 ⎭	10.0 ⎭	8.4	2.9	10.8 ⎭
5. Involvement or enrollment in Christian Democracy	—	2.9	—	—	1.3
6. Involvement or enrollment in parties of the *Right*	—	—	—	2.9	.6
7. Combination of #1 and #2	10.4	5.7	20.8	—	7.6
8. Combination of #4 and #5	3.4	1.4	—	—	1.3
9. No answer	—	8.6	12.5	8.9	7.6

NOTE: Twenty-nine respondents (15.6 percent) did not feel priests had become too much involved in political activities over the past decade.)

sion of charity? A priest who lives the life of his times cannot avoid politics . . . and to live in a party is sometimes a necessity. A priest serving in the workers' world cannot ignore the Communist Party, nor can a military chaplain ignore the military mentality. Very few priests joined parties in Chile in the last few years. A priest should not join a party, but it is not really a serious error if he does. I think a priest should be critical, serious, and not become politically involved in a party, but I do not consider it a moral sin if he does not measure up to these ideals.[71]

The vast majority of the bishops, however, were quite critical. One made a distinction between Church involvement in politics in general and identification with specific parties. While admitting that "the Church is always involved in politics," he argued that as clerics "we should not utilize the Gospel to legitimate a party."[72]

Another prelate also emphasized the negative effect on the pastoral mission of the Church:

There is an efficacy based on the Paschal Mystery—the power of the Gospel—and an efficacy based on politics. In recent years some priests living and working with the poor who became impatient to improve their lot began to place greater emphasis in their ministry on political effectiveness. This was understandable, given their situation and their desire to rectify the problems immediately. Furthermore, many years ago Chilean Catholic Action began to emphasize temporal problems and afterwards politics. This was the dynamic in the Chilean Church for some time. But the Gospel has an efficacy of its own and priests have to give this first priority in their ministry. It seems to me that some used the Gospel to support a contingent political position and this was bad.[73]

Some bishops made a distinction between the close sympathies between the Church and Christian Democracy and the preference for socialism publicly manifested by leftist clerics. They argued that there were important differences between these two cases that had to be kept in mind when analyzing the Church's involvement in politics over the past decade. Two of them emphasized that the link made by some between the Church and a partisan position was much more direct and explicit in the case of socialism than in regards Christian Democracy. One said:

. . . The identification with the PDC was made despite a very prudent stand taken by the Church. There were some who made this identifi-

---

[71] Interview no. 010, 18 June 1975.
[72] Interview no. 014, 2 July 1975.
[73] Interview no. 028, 29 October 1975.

cation but this was not the official position of the Church. In any case, it is historically understandable because the leaders of the Christian Democratic Party were activists in Catholic Action. They wanted to implement the principles of the social doctrine of the Church. . . .

In contrast, I believe those who wanted to take the Church on the road to socialism made moves which were wrong. They presented politics as absolute and implied that a commitment to the Gospel invariably led one to socialism. This was a betrayal—it was a total identification with a political option. This was not only a practical, but a theoretical mistake.[74]

Another also affirmed this distinction:

. . . A mixture of religion and politics is somewhat inevitable. But to use religion in the service of a party—yes, this is dangerous. In regard to the PDC, one thing is a pastoral strategy, the other is contact, friendship, et cetera. The bishops and the leaders of the PDC were all boyhood friends. This is legitimate. This is not utilizing religion. Their cultural and moral values are good. . . . In regard to socialism, Medellín was pointing in this direction. I do not see a danger in that. There may be danger when some wish to make a direct link—by logic—between the Gospel preference for the poor and socialism. This was the error of Christians for Socialism.[75]

The vast majority of priests whom I interviewed also shared these views regarding the dangers of clerical identification with parties, and believed the most egregious examples of this in the last decade in Chile were on the Left. One priest in the far North caustically (and too simplistically given the activities of Fr. Raúl Hasbún described in Chapter 7) remarked: "If such activities existed among priests on the other side [the Right] of the political spectrum, they passed unnoticed!"[76] Another priest in Concepción made the same point about the close, but unofficial, links between the Church and Christian Democracy, saying that "sympathetic relations" not "official support of the Church for this party" accounted for the phenomenon.[77]

More than just friendship, and historical factors tied the official Church closely to the PDC in the early 1960s. The remarks of these priests and of the bishops cited above are too simplistic in their assessments of the degree and reasons for such an association. As described in Chapter 5, the Chilean hierarchy clearly used their public moral influence to help the Christian Democrats in the early 1960s, differing only in degree and style from the efforts of Christians for Socialism in the early

[74] Interview no. 022, 23 September 1975.
[75] Interview no. 023, 4 October 1975.
[76] Interview no. 033, 27 August 1975.
[77] Interview no. 052, 26 June 1975.

1970s to do the same for the Left. The PDC in the period just prior to the 1964 election, however, was not a threat to any of the traditional religious concerns and dynamics of the Church, but rather was a reinforcement for them and a carrier of its official positions into secular politics. A decade later, CpS not only used religion for political purposes (as did the bishops in the early 1960s), but did little in return to shore up the traditional aspects and goals of the institutional Church. They were a direct threat to several of its core interests and wanted to change these drastically. The bishops, committed canonically to defending these characteristics, found CpS, therefore, far more dangerous for the institution than clerics (including the bishops themselves) publicly identified with the PDC ten years earlier.[78]

Not all local Church leaders, however, were critical of Christians for Socialism. Some pointed to what they considered a positive impact made by the commitment of these clerics on the poor. One priest in Arica pointed to the subtle, less visible, but damaging effect of more traditional Church leaders who identified with the Right as compared to those working for a new Church among the poor:

> . . . The activities of traditional clerics and laity close to the establishment are often less conspicuous but they cause damage just the same. They are upset by activity of a more committed type. The masses, on the contrary, have discovered through priests dedicated to the interests of the poor, the "new" face of the Church. Conversely, the attitudes of a more traditional type committed to the "established order" make the masses feel divorced from a Church which appears identified with those considered the exploiters of the poor.[79]

A young female student from a working-class family in Santiago also denied the partisan aspects of the commitment of these priests. She said their activities could in no way be considered harmful since they were dedicated to the poor in their ministry:

> I do not think these priests were making a partisan political commitment when they made a commitment to the masses. Perhaps it appears harmful because their form of commitment may not have been understood. (I am referring to the ones who were or who are with the people on the Left.)[80]

Several of the Chilean leaders of CpS whom I was able to interview in exile here in the United States in 1974 also expressed positive judgments about the overall impact of their movement, and some were critical of

---

[78] I am indebted to Professor Juan Linz of Yale for this incisive comparative judgment.

[79] Interview no. 032, 30 September 1975.

[80] Interview no. 115, 12 October 1975.

the bishops for failing to comprehend the significance of their efforts. Fr. Sergio Torres, a former member of the executive secretariat of CpS and national coordinator for "the 200," told me that in his judgment the Chilean Christians for Socialism movement was the first real attempt in a socialist society by a group of committed believers to place the official Church definitely on the side of the poor, and that this was a hopeful encouragement to groups in other parts of the world to forge closer ties with the Left. The bishops in Chile, he said, did not understand the movement primarily because they did not live closely with the poor nor share in their daily concerns and struggles. As a result, their theological way of thinking remained very traditional and removed from a new view of the faith emerging among those living among workers and peasants—a belief that is primarily expressed in works of justice and which leads to a reinterpretation of the Gospel from the perspective of the poor.[81]

Fr. Martin Gárate, another Chilean priest who also was a member of the executive secretariat of CpS, told me that he believed the problems between bishops and Christians for Socialism were based mainly on political rather than theological differences. CpS in his opinion was a major breakthrough in demonstrating the possibility of radical political commitment by Christians. He said that the Chilean hierarchy reacted negatively since they were wedded to a reformist political ideology and strategy closely associated with the PDC. Their apparent openness to Allende, especially in 1970 and 1971, was based upon fear and uncertainty as to where the country was going. He believed, however, the bishops were always against both Marxism and socialism, and, once they were convinced Allende could not succeed (in 1973), they felt it safe to criticize the government openly and also condemn Christians for Socialism.[82]

Diego Irarrázaval, an ordained deacon and also a member of the executive secretariat of the movement, gave me a somewhat more nuanced post factum assessment of Christians for Socialism in Chile. He was more self-critical than Torres and Gárate, and did not place all the blame on the bishops for their final break with CpS.

Irarrázaval indicated that he felt there were at least three very important accomplishments by Christians for Socialism both for Chile and for the rest of the Church:

(1) The movement was a clear proof that it is possible to be on the Left politically while remaining a committed Christian.

[81] Interview with Fr. Sergio Torres, Maryknoll Seminary, Maryknoll, N.Y., 4 December 1974.
[82] Interview with Fr. Martin Gárate, C.S.C., Notre Dame University, Notre Dame, Indiana, 20 November 1974.

(2) Christians for Socialism offered a very practical approach to Christian-Marxist cooperation.

(3) The group helped to develop a new expression of Christianity different from the reformist model associated with Christian Democracy—one that was more concrete, compatible with socialist values and more resonant with the experience of the working class.

Irarrázaval, however, also recognized some serious failures of the movement which he attributed both to tactical errors and to a lack of time for the movement to mature. Among these errors he included the following:

(1) It never reached out sufficiently to include lay men and women of the working classes, and for most of its two-year history remained elitist and heavily clerical in its membership and leadership.

(2) At the beginning it identified too closely with government objectives, and at the end was too much oriented in its official position with strategies of the extreme Left (especially the MIR).

(3) The leadership of CpS as a whole never gave sufficient attention to the possibilities of linking its values and symbols to expressions of popular religiosity.

(4) The movement did not give adequate thought to the implications of promoting divisions inside the Church as intense as the polarizations of secular society. As a result it collided head-on with the bishops whose priority was to avoid serious public splits within the institution.[83]

Clearly it was this last mistake of CpS that precipitated the final break with the hierarchy. Notwithstanding the contributions of the movement as articulated by these three former leaders, the overriding impression that Christians for Socialism created was that they were committed to an explicitly partisan political option and were willing to risk ultimate schism within the Church in pursuing this objective. Once this became the dominant image of CpS, despite all their other valid contributions and justified criticisms of the Church, the reaction by the bishops was predictable.

The judgment of a considerable number of other Church leaders (clerical, religious, and lay) two years after the fact also coincided with the conclusion reached by the bishops. Christians for Socialism, therefore, had not only become alienated from the top level of leadership in the Church but also had failed to convince most of their peers and the laity that their tactics and goals were fruitful for the life of the Chilean Catholic community at the time.

---

[83] Interview with Diego Irarrázaval C., Chicago, Illinois, 18 November 1974.

CONCLUSIONS

The attempts made by Christians for Socialism to forge a synthesis of Marxist and Christian perspectives, and the fallout effect a close encounter with Marxism in general had within the Chilean Church, provide some critical insights for similar efforts elsewhere. The Chilean case was characterized by several unique experiences that do not yet exist in other contexts, some of which need not, nor cannot, be duplicated. The results of the Chilean situation, however, do highlight what positive contributions an attempt at assimilation can offer to churches elsewhere. The Chilean experience also indicates what will likely be ruled out by the top Church leadership in any situation, and what are still open questions regarding this challenge.

(1) *Marxist analysis can provide an important method to critique the ideological uses of religious symbols, and to stimulate a more comprehensive assessment of the political impact of the Church in societies undergoing radical change.* Christian emphases on societal peace, reconciliation among contending factions, and the unity of all believers can become too closely identified with existing social and economic structures, or at least can be used to legitimate only reformist methods to change them. The critique provided by Christians for Socialism in Chile helped to unmask some of these ideological aspects of Christian belief, and pointed to other combinations of Christian and secular values that are possible in a society undergoing a transition to socialism.[84]

They showed how Marxist emphases on radical equality and justice for the poor are compatible with the original biblical values of full human liberation. People of genuine religious faith must work to change the structures of chronic economic exploitation even if this involves the use of conflict. Such efforts had a purifying impact on the symbolic level of Catholicism (recognized even by the bishops themselves), and made some believers more clearly aware of the temporal consequences and responsibilities of their faith. The writings of CpS made some Christians more conscious of exploitative aspects of economic and political structures which reformist ideology overlooked or downplayed.

Furthermore, the Marxist method employed by Christians for Socialism in Chile forced a healthy rethinking of the political nature of the Church itself. An institution with the resources of the Roman Catholic Church must face more honestly the unavoidable political consequences

[84] In official Catholic social doctrine (traditional and recent), the role of conflict in promoting justice is minimized. Peace, harmony, and reconciliation among contending classes and factions are all given priority, and assumed to be possible, in the pursuit of equitable social and economic change benefiting the poor. David Hollenbach, S.J., *Claims in Conflict: Retrieving and Renewing the Catholic Human Rights Tradition*, pp. 118, 142, 161–66.

of its actions, including its intended and unintended impact on competition in a multiparty system. While the Chilean bishops in their pastoral letter, "Christian Faith and Political Action," finally acknowledged a political role for the Church, they defined this in very spiritual and personalistic terms—moral education and guidance for individual lay Christians to act on their own in the political arena. The analysis of Christians for Socialism was more sophisticated and complete, and focused on the wider impact the Church has as a major ideological and structural force in a traditionally Catholic culture. They also correctly pointed to the political uses of religion by official Church representatives (including the bishops) to assist the PDC in its rise to power, a factor that the hierarchy has refused to acknowledge adequately.

(2) *Too facile an assimilation of Marxism can undermine fundamental doctrines central to Catholicism, and thereby precipitate specific normative condemnations by the hierarchy.* There are several conflicts at the level of principle between Marxism and Christianity that make a synthesis of the two systems very difficult, if not impossible. Tension results from contrasting beliefs: economic determinism versus spiritual transcendence and individual freedom; unlimited perfectability of humankind versus sinful human nature; violence as a legitimate means for social change versus commitment to nonviolence; severe class conflict versus deeper unity among believers regardless of economic differences.

Christians for Socialism, despite their personal beliefs and intentions, frequently gave the impression in public statements that they were not taking such normative contradictions between the two systems seriously, and by so doing were ignoring or diminishing some essential Christian beliefs—the gift of God's grace to all persons regardless of class differences, the sinfulness in the individual human heart as well as in social relationships and structures, the distinction between the kingdom of God and human achievement. The critique of the ideological aspects and uses of these and other religious symbols also *appeared* to be a denial of any deeper objective meaning contained in them, even when CpS did not actually intend this.

Furthermore, Christians for Socialism seriously challenged some central objectives of the Church traditionally associated with preserving these doctrines and making them effective in various types of societies—no identification of Catholic official social teachings with any political party or movement, the openness of the institution to all persons and groups, its public responsibility to promote moral values that affect all citizens. While the official Church does not always live up to these stated objectives, or realize them consistently in many historical contexts, the rejection of their feasibility or desirability *in principle* is an attack on the core symbolic system of Catholicism itself. Once such a direct and sustained normative attack is made, the leadership of the institution will react vigorously to preserve what it considers central to the performance of the Church's religious mission.

The Chilean case also shows that prolonged challenges to official teaching by a vocal group within the Church moving to the Left precipitates the articulation of greater doctrinal caution by the bishops against new combinations of religious and radical values. It was not only the tactics of some associated with Allende's government that frightened the bishops into pulling back from some of their initial openness to Marxism, but also the strategies of the groups within the Church itself who clearly overstepped the official parameters of the original normative openness to the Left. The articulation of social norms by the hierarchy remained general and diffuse regarding relations with a leftist government at the *external* level for most of the Popular Unity administration. When a threat to the doctrinal integrity of the Church occurred from *within* the institution, however, by those sympathetic to the UP, their normative statements became much more specific and binding, and therefore more restrictive, against further rapprochement with Marxism by Catholics.

(3) *Public action strategies of clerics that involve explicitly partisan political commitments tend to undermine the Church's moral influence in society, and also threaten its own internal discipline.* It is correct for radical priests to point out and criticize the close ideological and strategic ties between Catholicism and Christian Democracy that were forged in the past. This is a phenomenon that has characterized not only Chile but several nominally Catholic countries in Western Europe (and continues to do so in some). It has also damaged the Church's claims to nonpartisanship authorized by Vatican II. It is equally damaging for the Church, however, for such priests to continue to inject clericalism into party politics by using their public prestige on behalf of leftist movements or organizations, even when they appear more committed to the poor than reformist movements.

The fact that priests share in canonical authority in the Church and act as official spokesmen for the institution often creates the impression when they endorse parties of any type that theirs in the only legitimate option for all Catholics. While some lay persons obviously will not reach this conclusion when they see priests involved in partisan politics, others do and this seriously impairs the credibility of the Church to serve as a conscience for the values of the whole of society instead of just for one sector. Christians for Socialism certainly made it clear by their words, and more importantly by their actions, that to be a good Catholic during the Allende period one *had* to support the Popular Unity in electoral politics and that no other position was religiously or morally defensible.

As societal polarization became more intense during these years in Chile, the bishops' voice for moderation and minimal respect among contending factions was hampered by the strategies of CpS who attempted to throw the official weight of the Church exclusively behind the Left. The hierarchy could not have saved the country from a coup by themselves, given the breakdown of many of the secular requirements of democracy by mid-1973. The clerics in Christians for Socialism who publicly endorsed and campaigned for the Popular Unity coalition, however, did not help the hierarchy's chances for promoting dialogue and compromise, and made the official Church appear inconsistent in the pursuit of this goal. (In all honesty, so did the actions of Fr. Raúl Hasbún, although he was never sanctioned by the bishops nor did he disobey any orders since they never were given. He was only one cleric, as compared to the 300 involved with CpS).

When a *group* of priests within the Church publicly and continuously goes against positions articulated by the hierarchy, however (as CpS seemed to be doing), such an authority crisis always has led to severe disciplinary reprisals by the bishops against the offenders, regardless of how such a reaction will be interpreted politically in society at large. When a parallel teaching office in the institution seems to be emerging threatening that of the bishops, such a felt threat will bring about episcopal condemnations of the movement, thus short-circuiting some of its other more positive contributions toward new ideological or practical options for Catholics.

(4) *Resource transactions with the international Church can provide important stimuli for new thought and action, but when these get out ahead of officially approved guidelines, and are dramatically publicized, reverse feedback can also occur through the transnational network of the Church.* When a group of radical Christians gets well out in front of official positions of Catholicism (especially when they do not have the strong backing of their local bishops), other jurisdictional centers in the international Church are likely to become concerned about the potential carryover effect of such movements. Given the transnational linkages in the Roman Church, what happens in one local Church does affect developments in others, and Rome, regional bishops' conferences, and national hierarchies all have the responsibility to think about the wider impact of any new development in one Church, especially if it seems to be setting a very new and different direction for Catholicism.

Since the Chilean Christians for Socialism were not only attempting an assimilation of Marxism in their own specific context but were also using the international network of Catholicism to propagate a new model for the Church at large, seemingly opposed to the traditional one, both Rome and the Latin American Episcopal Conference (CELAM) felt obliged to intervene. Furthermore, conservative, and even reactionary, sectors in international Catholicism totally opposed to any type of rapprochement with Marxism are, under such conditions, able to wield considerable influence and gain an effective hearing for their position in several authoritative decision-making centers of the Church.

What this experience highlights is not that new ideas and strategies in the Church are impossible per se (including closer ties to Marxism in the future), but that their development and eventual acceptance depends at least in part upon the tactics used by their proponents and the degree to which Rome is drawn into the process before these gain general acceptance both in the local Church and at the international level. Those attempting an assimilation of Marxism inside the Chilean Church in the early 1970s did not use prudence and restraint. They precipitated a crisis of authority inside their own domestic church, simultaneously bringing down upon themselves the wrath of key sectors of the international Church, including those still adamantly opposed to any rapprochement with Marxism. While the Chilean Christians for Socialism initially gained from their utilization of international Church resources, the overall impact of this key component of Catholicism went against them and was an added factor in the final break with their own bishops.

(5) *The challenges presented by the Chilean Christians for Socialism movement need not reach such a critical level of conflict with national and international Church leaders.* Some of the factors aggravating the Chilean bishops, CELAM, and Rome in the statements and actions of CpS need not be duplicated elsewhere. The tone and style of their statements did not give sufficient attention to some of the difficult normative contradictions between Marxism and Christianity. The group was exclusively clerical in its leadership, and predominantly so in its membership (over one-half of whom also were foreigners). Its action strategies constantly confronted episcopal authority head-on, seemed to undermine official Church objectives for societal reconciliation, and threatened formal unity of the Church both in theory and practice.

Other movements in the Church sympathetic to socialism need not emulate such tactics, nor are the social contexts in which they operate the same as those of Chile in the early 1970s. Neither the ONIS movement in Peru nor the Movement of Priests for the Third World in Argentina publicly challenged the authority of their respective hierarchies with the same intensity, nor identified so explicitly with specific party options. Their efforts in the late 1960s and early 1970s were focused instead on articulating a socialist critique of the economic structures of capitalism in their countries, and convincing (successfully) sectors of the hierarchy that they, too, should adopt such a prophetic stance in face of the chronic problems of dependent development. Such strategies for clerics are far less threatening to internal Church discipline, and in the long run, by maintaining good communication with the top level of the Church, these radical priests can have far more positive impact on its official policies.

Furthermore, in Western Europe and North America where Christians for Socialism movements (albeit smaller) continue to function, the leaderships and memberships are not so heavily clerical or foreign, and the social context is less polarized. They are predominantly lay organizations, national and frequently ecumenical in character, and are attempting a synthesis with Marxist viewpoints without representing the official Church to the extent that priest-led movements do. They, therefore, do not present the same challenge to episcopal authority. Nor are they a threat to formal Church unity to the same degree, since the social fabric of the societies in which they operate is at the moment stronger. Under such circumstances, these groups can and do play an important prophetic role in offering a critique of capitalism not usually heard in Churches in such countries, and in making Christians consider a variety of possible alternatives to the status quo.

Hence, the possibility for assimilating some Marxist insights and strategies into the Church by elite groups is still open. All such efforts need not encounter episcopal condemnations. Several national movements of Christians for Socialism continue to offer important critiques from the Left within the Church, and have chosen a more prudent strategy than that of direct confrontation with the hierarchy.

(6) *A necessary precondition for any prolonged positive encounter with Marxism within a national Church is the development of deep faith commitments by lay members and effective structures for evangelization.* Without strong lay allegiances and well-developed socialization mechanisms to maintain them, a Church is likely to suffer considerable losses among its constituency when they attempt to come to serious terms with Marxism. A structurally weak Church with tenuous influence over most sectors of its baptized laity cannot sustain such an encounter without experiencing considerable damage to the performance of its pastoral mission.

Those lay members who attempt to make a synthesis with Marxism in their personal lives and still remain Christians in more than name only need deep internal resources and very mature faith. Otherwise, the attraction, power, and demand for total loyalty that Marxism makes will likely sweep away what weak religious allegiances that do exist in such persons. There will not be a true synthesis of two different value systems but a substitution of one set of commitments by another.

This phenomenon of drainage or value substitution will be felt especially among middle-class elites (intellectuals, clerics, students, professionals). Due to education, background, exposure, and level of political awareness, they will be the ones most likely to attempt such a synthesis in their own personal lives. If they have not yet developed deep religious convictions, they will become estranged from the Church. This will in turn diminish the potential ranks of new top-level leaders for its various religious and social projects.

Lay Catholics in the working class, while providing more numerically significant support for the Left in electoral politics than the middle class, will be less interested in making such a synthesis in their value systems with Marxism, and therefore will not be as susceptible to losing their faith. More deeply ingrained patterns of popular religiosity will militate against such an assimilation. However, while these are the groups that will be most favorably impressed by Church efforts to come to terms with Marxism, they are not likely to participate more frequently in the Church's public religious life during a transition to socialism. In fact intense efforts at political mobilization by leftist and centrist parties among the poor will diminish their already weak patterns of ritual participation. This cross-pressure will also limit the effectiveness of new Church efforts to change traditional styles of personalistic piety among the poor into more communal forms closely associated with the spirit of Vatican II, Medellín, and Puebla.

From the perspective of the institutional Church, therefore, it is evident that chronically underdeveloped structures are a clear liability in attempting to conduct effective evangelization in a highly polarized society. The Chilean case shows that a Church which has a very low rate of lay participation in its religious programs, which has never adequately educated vast sectors of its members as to the implications of their faith, and where nominal members have very weak commitments to its official goals, the consequences of entering into a serious encounter with Marxism in a democratic context can be very damaging.

Such a Church will experience severe divisions and also losses, since it has no way of moderating or blunting inside its own ranks the conflict that is taking place in wider society. Without adequately developed structures that can withstand some of these external pressures, it is almost impossible for a Church under such circumstances to maintain significant allegiances, to carry out effective religious training, or to deepen commitments among its nominal members. It rapidly becomes as severely politicized and fragmented as the society at large, and is in danger of splintering into a number of sects or losing contact with its congregation in several social strata.

National Churches in other parts of the Western world which are, or in the future may be, facing a close encounter with Marxism in a democratic context (France, Italy, Spain, Portugal, Nicaragua) also suffer similar attitudinal and behavioral weaknesses among their members as did the Chilean Church in the Allende period. These are nominally Catholic cultures in which personal allegiance and degrees of association with the institutional Church are very tenuous among large numbers of baptized Catholics, especially among students, intellectuals, and workers who are most susceptible to the attraction of Marxism. While such Churches may very well be able to maintain correct relations with Marxist coalition governments at the *external* policy level in these societies, this does not bode well for an effective synthesis *within* the Church of religious and radical political perspectives among many Catholics, or for effective pastoral work by the Church during such periods. This is not necessarily the fault of the Marxists, but a reflection of traditionally weak Churches.[85]

Unless such national Churches develop new forms of religious socialization *before* a serious encounter with Marxism, then they, too, are likely to experience similar contradictions, tensions, and losses among laity as did the Chilean Church. Despite all the efforts to inaugurate new forms of evangelization and ministry *during* a transition to socialism in a democratic context, the Chilean case shows that this is very difficult to achieve, especially if the wider society becomes severely polarized in the process.

The European situation, however, could be different. If the Left were to gain a strong majority of the electorate on its own or in a coalition with Center parties and also can avoid some of the other major domestic and international obstacles encountered by Allende in Chile, severe polarization and economic disruptions could possibly be avoided in Europe. If the Catholic Church also has the imagination and time to prepare itself creatively for such an encounter in these countries by strengthening its own internal cadres and rank and file allegiance commitments, it, too, might escape severe drainage and internal politicization during such a democratic transition to socialism in France, Italy, Spain, or Portugal. Only time will tell.

---

[85] Since the Nicaraguan revolution in 1979 the Catholic bishops, while open to democratic socialism, are becoming increasingly concerned with a declining interest in the Church by laity, and with the government's attracting away from Church-sponsored programs some of its best catechists (Delegates of the Word). Dodson and Montgomery, "Churches in the Nicaraguan Revolution."

PART IV

The Prophetic Role of the Church under Authoritarianism

9 The Church and the Chilean Military Regime, 1973–1980

The final major religiopolitical challenge facing Catholicism that needs to be analyzed in order to complete the assessment of the range of the Church's adaptive capacities in a modern context is its recently announced commitment to oppose abuses of public power by repressive governments. This perhaps is the most difficult and complex of the problems confronting the post-Vatican II Church, given the ambiguous historical relationships the institution has traditionally maintained with authoritarian and totalitarian states.

Throughout the eighteenth and nineteenth centuries, the Catholic Church forged alliances with several authoritarian governments in Europe, and identified with many of their values and objectives, such as order, social harmony, suppression of anarchical groups and radical political movements. In the twentieth century, Catholicism's record in the face of the rise of corporatism, fascism, and nazism was indeed mixed. In Italy, Portugal, Spain, Austria, Brazil, and Argentina, Catholic bishops provided no resistance to the emergence of corporatist and fascist regimes in the 1920s and 1930s. In Germany only a few prelates openly opposed National Socialism and warned against the dangers of nazism as Hitler's strength mounted in the early 1930s.[1]

While the hierarchy did not actively encourage such authoritarian rulers as they came to power, neither did they as a group prophetically denounce systematic violations of human rights nor other atrocities perpetrated by these dictators while in power. Nor have Catholic bishops in the Soviet Union and eastern Europe provided sustained public criticism of repressive policies of communist regimes once they were firmly in power. In Cuba the bishops were openly opposed to some of the Castro government's practices during its first two years, but public opposition

---

[1] D. A. Binchy, *Church and State in Fascist Italy*, pp. 100–166; Thomas C. Bruneau, "Church and State in Portugal," pp. 468–75; Norman B. Cooper, *Catholicism and the Franco Regime*, pp. 6–13; Alfred Diamont, *Austrian Catholics and the First Republic*, pp. 256–90; Margaret Todaro Williams, "Church and State in Vargas's Brazil," pp. 446–48; *Iglesia Argentina: ¿fidelidad al evangelio o conquista del poder?* (Lima: CELADEC, 1975), pp. 5–6; Guenter Lewy, *The Catholic Church and Nazi Germany*, pp. 8–56.

by the Church diminished considerably with the consolidation of the revolution after 1961.[2]

The Vatican also normally has taken a flexible position once totalitarian and authoritarian governments are well established, and has attempted to open or maintain lines of communication with them through papal nuncios or delegates. The strategy of ecclesiastical leaders at both the national and international levels in face of strong rulers, on the Right and the Left, has been to use private negotiations to win government acquiescence for continued religious ministries by the local Church.

Moreover, there are theological and sociological reasons why leaders of a church-type religious organization such as Roman Catholicism normally are not prophets in the classical sense of the word—namely, speaking and acting critically in the face of abuses of religious or secular power. In the Judeo-Christian tradition (and in other major religions) prophecy is a charisma given to specific persons by God, and it is not ex officio bestowed on those who exercise jurisdictional authority. This role is usually played by heroic individuals or sectarian groups within larger religious communities. It is rarely identified with the priestly caste who have the responsibility of carrying on ritual traditions and maintaining the survival of the ecclesiastical structures as a means to accomplish this.[3]

Bishops of the Roman Catholic Church in more recent years, however, have appropriated to themselves the prophetic function of critiquing abuses of public power. The Fathers of the Second Vatican Council stressed the responsibility of leaders of the Church to "pass moral judgments, even on matters of the political order whenever basic personal rights . . . make such judgment necessary."[4] The Medellín documents of the Latin American bishops in 1968 also committed pastors of the Church "to denounce everthing which, opposing justice, destroys peace" and "to defend the rights of the poor and oppressed."[5] Eleven years later at Puebla these bishops reiterated their prophetic commitment, and in so doing denounced authoritarian governments in the Americas that perpetrate or permit "assassinations, disappearances, arbitrary imprisonment, acts of terrorism, kidnappings, and acts of torture."[6]

[2] Gerhard Simon, "Catholic Church and the Communist State"; Leslie Dewart, *Christianity and Revolution,* pp. 116–73; Margaret E. Crahan, "Religious Freedom in Cuba," pp. 22–27.

[3] Max Weber, *Sociology of Religion,* pp. 46–59.

[4] "Pastoral Constitution on the Church in the Modern World," no. 76, in *Documents of Vatican II,* ed. Walter M. Abbott, S.J., p. 289.

[5] CELAM, "Peace," nos. 20, 22, in *The Church in the Present-Day Transformation of Latin America,* 2:81.

[6] CELAM, "Evangelization in Latin America's Present and Future," no. 1262, in *Puebla and Beyond,* ed. John Eagleson and Philip Scharper, p. 279.

In many third-world countries where the state has systematically violated human rights in recent years, many Church leaders have begun to exercise this prophetic function of religion. In the Philippines, South Korea, Uganda, Rhodesia, South Africa, Brazil, Paraguay, Argentina, Bolivia, El Salvador, Guatemala, and Nicaragua there have been clashes in recent years between Church and state over issues of repression. Catholic bishops and Protestant pastors in these countries have spoken out against murder, torture, disappearance of persons, lack of democratic freedoms and free unions, and denial of basic human needs stemming from severe economic measures that place the burden of development on the poor.[7] Bishops have been persecuted and harassed, religious and clergy have been murdered, jailed, or expelled, Church schools have been restricted or contravened, and Church publications and access to the secular media curtailed or denied.

The structures of Catholic and Protestant Churches, despite persecutions, in many of these countries have been expanded to include actions on behalf of human rights. Churches are often the only places persons in trouble can go to seek assistance when authoritarian governments have smashed or brought under control all other social structures mediating between the individual and the state. Throughout the southern tier of Latin America, for example, a whole series of ecumenical human rights organizations sponsored by Catholics and Protestants are operating at the local level to provide legal aid, assistance to prisoners, economic assistance to families of the disappeared, and self-help cooperatives for the unemployed. They also collect and disseminate abroad accurate data on the extent of human rights violations in these various countries.[8]

Thus far, however, there has been no systematic analysis of what the range of possibilities are for Churches to check the power of a repressive state or how this new critical role is affecting the internal life and religious mission of Churches themselves. Again, the Chilean case since late 1973 offers a context in which to explore these issues. The Church hierarchy over the past several years has gained the reputation of being defenders of human rights and opponents of the military government. Catholic, Protestant, and Jewish communities soon after the military coup established a short-term ecumenical committee to assist foreign political refugees and another one of longer duration to provide a whole

[7] Robert Youngblood, "Church Opposition to Martial Law in the Philippines"; Elaine Windrich, "Church-State Confrontation in Rhodesia," pp. 67–73; *Journal of Current Social Issues* 15 (Summer 1978); José Marins, Teolide M. Trevisan and Carolee Chanona, eds., *Praxis de los Padres de América Latina*, pp. 681–84, 690–730, 833–45, 860–79, 967–76, 979–83, 989–1008. Adrian Hastings, *A History of African Christianity, 1950–1975.*

[8] Brian H. Smith, "Churches and Human Rights in Latin America."

panoply of legal and social services of Chilean citizens being deprived of their rights. This second organization (the Committee of Cooperation for Peace) received substantial acclaim and support from international Church agencies, and quickly became a model for other new ecumenical efforts to defend human rights in the southern tier of the continent.

Furthermore, in the wake of the coup, the Catholic Church became a critical focal point for the articulation of the needs of the poor, and acted as a surrogate form of social participation for them in a period when all their other normal channels of influence (labor unions, political parties, neighborhood organizations) came under heavy government surveillance or were outlawed or dissolved. The local structures of the Church took on a new vitality and meaning, new forms of ministry emerged (including more responsibilities for women), and the class orientation of the Church became more focused on the interests of workers and peasants than at any time in its history.

All of these developments have precipitated some serious clashes with the state, and some Church programs have suffered restrictions on their freedom. These activities and new directions have also disturbed some traditional Catholics who want a predominantly spiritual emphasis in the Church, and have strongly alienated others who support the repressive policies of the military regime for political or economic reasons. For all of these reasons, the Chilean Church since 1973 offers a considerable amount of data to explore some of the benefits and costs of a critical role by Catholicism under recent authoritarian regimes.

In this chapter I shall assess to what extent the bishops have denounced abuses of power committed by the Pinochet government. I shall also trace the origins of new roles and mechanisms across the layered network of the Church, their effectiveness in promoting human rights, and the impact on the institutional freedom of the Church which its opposition to the state has produced. An analysis of the attitudinal and behavioral changes at the local level of the Church will also be made, resulting from a clearer identification of ecclesiastical structures with the poor and from new responsibilities for laity and women religious. Finally, the role of linkages with international Church agencies will be examined to determine whether they foster the capacity of a local Church to blunt the repressive power of a government. By drawing upon multiple experiences at different levels of the Chilean Church over the past several years, some general conclusions will be offered regarding the effectiveness of this new prophetic role for the Church which could be useful for religious institutions in other contemporary authoritarian contexts.

AMBIGUOUS PROPHETIC ROLE OF THE HIERARCHY

Despite the prophetic image of the Chilean bishops abroad as forthright opponents of the current military regime, closer analysis of their public statements during the first seven years of the regime indicates a more ambiguous, and sometimes inconsistent, record. As a group they voiced some reservations at the outset, but also provided important moral legitimacy for the regime in its first months of office, with some individual bishops explicitly endorsing its principles and programs. During 1974 and 1975 the Episcopal Conference publicly criticized some violations of human rights and attempted to present an alternate moral perspective to that being offered by the regime. During this period of consolidation of the new government's power and institutionalization of its methods of repression, however, the hierarchy articulated their criticisms at first specifically and later more vaguely, and on each occasion included praise for what they considered to be good intentions and some sound accomplishments of the junta. It was not until the repression of the regime touched the bishops personally and lay elites close to them after mid-1976 that they began to issue unambiguous condemnations of the systemic aspects of the repression and to ask for a return to democracy.

*Moral Legitimacy for the Regime by the Hierarchy during
the First Six Months (September 1973–March 1974)*

Despite a consistent *public* policy of correct relations and some cooperation with the Allende government, the majority of leaders at all levels of the Church *privately* believed in September 1973 that a military coup was necessary to put an end to chaos and prevent civil war (Table 7.2). They hoped, as did many Chileans, that the long-standing respect for constitutionalism manifested by the armed forces would make the intervention relatively bloodless and short-termed. Hence, the hierarchy did not in the immediate period before or after the coup issue warnings that a military takeover could lead to a reign of terror or suppression of civil liberties, as they did in late 1969 when rumors of such an occurrence were prevalent during the relatively stable Frei government.

The initial promise of the four-man military junta, in fact, reinforced the mistaken expectations of Church leaders. On the day of the coup they stated that their purpose was to restore "order and constitutional rule" and that they would remain in power only so long as this was necessary. They also promised workers that the "economic and social benefits they have achieved up to the present will not suffer fundamental changes."[9] Despite these stated objectives the actions of the armed forces from the outset raised serious questions about their real intentions. The junta closed the Congress, outlawed Marxist parties, placed others in recess, and began to round up leaders of Allende's government. They also conducted raids on factories (despite minimal popular resistance to the coup), and carried out massive arrests of working-class and student leaders.

Although spokespersons for the new regime admitted to few casualties during the week following the coup (claiming less than 100 dead), domestic and foreign observers placed the mortality figures well into the thousands. Furthermore, during October and November the fact-finding teams sent to Chile by the International Commission of Jurists and by Amnesty International reported that executions without trial, use of torture, and massive preventive detentions all were common occurrences.[10]

On 13 September, Cardinal Silva and the Permanent Committee of the Episcopal Conference issued a public declaration decrying the spilling of "blood which has reddened our streets . . . the blood of civilians and of soldiers." The statement also asked for "respect for persons fallen in battle" and first of all for "him who was until Tuesday, September 11, the president of the Republic." It asked for "moderation toward the vanquished and that there be no needless reprisals," and that "progress achieved by former governments for the workers and peasant class not be ignored." Finally, these leaders of the Episcopal Conference affirmed their trust in the "patriotism and selflessness" of the military junta, and asked all citizens to cooperate with them so as to "return soon to institutional normality."[11]

Hence, the first official reaction of the Church was somewhat critical, and did not offer explicit legitimacy for the coup. Neither did it condemn the overthrow of the previous government, however, but tacitly

---

[9] "Bando No. 5 de la Honorable Junta de Gobierno de Chile, el 11 de septiembre de 1973," in Chile, *Libro Blanco del cambio de gobierno en Chile,* pp. 248–49; Lester A. Sobel, ed., *Chile and Allende,* p. 141.

[10] Even the C.I.A. reported several months later that 11,000 persons were killed between the time of the coup and the end of November 1973. The U.S. State Department said it was prepared to accept estimates up to 20,000 dead. Sobel, ed., *Chile and Allende,* pp. 148, 151, 168.

[11] "Declaración del Señor Cardenal y del Comité Permanente del Episcopado Chileno," Santiago, 13 September 1973, *Mensaje* 22 (October 1973): 509. The PDC and the National Party both expressed support for the new government on the same day this first statement of the bishops was released. Ex-president Eduardo Frei in an overseas phone call to a son the next day said his party was given guarantees by the military for new elections within twelve months. Sobel, ed., *Chile and Allende,* p. 145.

accepted what had transpired and seized upon the promise of the military to restore constitutional rule as a hopeful sign.

Five days later, prayer services were conducted throughout the country commemorating national independence, but no celebration of an Act of Thanksgiving for the new government. In Santiago representatives of the four major religious faiths (Catholic, Protestant, Greek Orthodox, and Jewish) gathered for the ceremony. They met, however, not in the customary place of the Catholic cathedral but in a less prestigious edifice, the Church of National Gratitude. Cardinal Silva presided, but he addressed the four members of the junta as chiefs of the armed forces and not as heads of state. Afterwards, on the steps of the cathedral, he also did not exchange with them the handshake normally given to a president on such occasons.[12]

The cardinal's choice of words in his homily during the service, however, was less cautious than the original episcopal declaration of 13 September. He did pray for "those who have fallen," and that "there not be among us either conquerors or conquered." He also said, however, that the Church offered its "impartial collaboration to those who at a difficult time have taken upon their shoulders the very heavy responsibility of guiding our destiny."[13]

Ten days later on 28 September, after the military regime had been recognized by several major Western governments, including the United States, the Permanent Committee of the Episcopal Conference met with the four members of the junta. At the end of the conversation, the committee issued another brief statement wherein they thanked the junta "for the deference that the new authorities have extended to the bishops in every part of the country" and expressed a desire that the Church continue its "authentic preaching of the Gospel message." It reiterated the bishops' offer of "collaboration in the work of reconstruction," especially in "developing the social gains of the workers."[14]

While all other major social organizations in the country had been outlawed or placed under heavy surveillance or in recess, the Church was the one remaining institution allowed to function openly. In fact, as we shall see later in the chapter in discussing the institutional role of its layered network, the Church quickly became a focal point for the needs of vast numbers of foreigners and Chileans suffering the brunt of the regime's repression. Efforts to assist them began to develop at lower levels

[12] Carlos Condamines, "Chili: l'Eglise et la Junte," p. 507.

[13] "Homilia del Señor Cardenal en el acto ecuménico de oración por la patria," 18 September 1973, *Mensaje* 22 (October 1973): 510–11.

[14] "Episcopado ofrece colaborar en la reconstrucción," *El Mercurio,* 29 September 1973.

of the Church immediately after the coup, and by late September and early October the Catholic, Protestant, and Jewish communities had formed organizations to assist the persecuted—a National Committee to Aid Refugees, and the Committee of Cooperation for Peace.

These September declarations of the cardinal and Permanent Committee of the episcopate reflected the desire of the official ecclesiastical leadership to preserve the Church's institutional freedom to carry out both religious and social programs during what they considered an emergency situation. In exchange for this guarantee, the Episcopal Conference rejected the strategy of clear and specific denunciations of abuses of power. Hence, objectives at the structural level placed restrictions on the prophetic capacities of the Church at the normative level.

An early October meeting between the four members of the junta and Cardinal Silva finalized this understanding between Church and state. For its part, the government would not curb the institutional freedom of the Church to conduct both pastoral and humanitarian activities. The Church, in turn, would accept the legitimacy of the government and would attempt to play a constructive role during the reconstruction period. These mutual agreements were revealed by the cardinal in a press conference immediately following a session on 9 October in his office with the leaders of the new military regime. He said:

> The Church has always maintained cordial relations with governments of this country. We desire to be of service. The Church is not called upon to install governments or to take power away from them, nor to give or withold recognition of governments. We accept the governments which the people want and we serve them. There is, moreover, a cordial understanding between Church and state in this task: the task of reconstructing Chile and of removing the great difficulties in which the country now finds itself.[15]

The cardinal also indicated the junta would facilitate the role which the Church desired to play in this task—that of a "good Samaritan" healing wounds and diminishing pain, referring to the humanitarian efforts already underway at lower levels of the Church.

This statement by the cardinal revealed a pragmatic decision to accept a de facto situation and make the best of it. It was the strategy he and the other Chilean bishops had followed during the initial months of the Allende government, and then it had paid off. The cardinal was counting on the same good faith of the military regime both to carry out its promises to the country and also to respect the Church as Allende

[15] "La iglesia tiene absoluta fe en el futuro de Chile," *La Tercera* (Santiago), 10 October 1973.

had done. He actually expected more. In an interview with ABC television in late October he told the U.S. commentator that the Church had promised the junta the same cooperation it gave the Allende government. He said the military could even "expect more from us" since they were "Christian" and so "we can understand each other in many fields."[16]

Despite these public expressions of confidence in the government on the part of the cardinal and the Permanent Committee of the Episcopal Conference, repression in the first month after the coup did not subside. Rather it increased in severity, and expanded to include economic sanctions against the urban and rural poor. By mid-October workers who were union leaders or sympathizers of the former government were being summarily dismissed from their jobs. Delivery of food, medicine, and other social services to shantytowns was drastically cut back. Wage readjustments were kept much lower than approved rises in prices in order to stimulate confidence on the part of investors. In December land reform programs were suspended, and cooperatives and socialized farms instituted by Frei and Allende respectively were broken up, and small plots parcelled out to individual poor families who had neither the tools nor the credit to work the land productively.[17]

Throughout these months, however, the cardinal and the Episcopal Conference refrained from further public criticisms of the regime. They naively considered such actions as short-term and necessary in a period of emergency to restore order and economic stability. They were also counting on their own personal access to military leaders to blunt some of the effects of repression.[18]

The initial responses to the regime by other prelates were far less complex and nuanced. Some bishops did not realize the severity of the repression at first since in many of the provinces the military were not as brutal as in major urban areas.[19] Others, however, were anxious to express gratitude and relief upon the end of the chaos that characterized the final months of Allende's presidency, and simply were blind to the

[16] *Religious News Service* (Washington, D.C.), 29 October 1973, p. 10.

[17] Sobel, ed., *Chile and Allende,* pp. 153, 162.

[18] Many of the thirty bishops whom I interviewed in 1975 told me that in the months following the coup they personally intervened with local military commanders in their provinces on behalf of those in prison. They claimed that they had been successful in achieving better treatment for many of these individuals, and that they believed private conversations with the authorities at that time were very effective in alleviating suffering.

[19] This was the judgment of several bishops in rural areas whom I interviewed, and was another reason why a strong and consistent policy on denouncing human rights violations was not forthcoming from the Episcopal Conference as a whole during the initial period following the coup.

bloodshed occurring around them. The statement of several bishops following the coup were far more specific and clear in providing legitimacy for the new government than those of Cardinal Silva and the leaders of the Episcopal Conference.

On the day of Allende's death, Bishop Francisco Valdés of Osorno composed a public prayer thanking God for having freed Chile from "the worst clutches of lies and evil that have ever plagued poor humanity."[20] Archbishop Juan Francisco Fresno of La Serena in early October publicly gave a similar justification for the coup. He stated that "the soul of the populace was in the process of being destroyed," and affirmed that the military did not perpetrate a fascist or brutal coup but rather liberated the country.[21] Alfredo Cifuentes, the retired archbishop of La Serena and a staunch opponent of Marxism since the 1930s, publicly presented his episcopal ring to the junta saying it was a "modest contribution to the work of reconstruction of Chile."[22]

A month later, Archbishop Emilio Tagle of Valparaíso, the second largest city in the country and an area where the repression and killing after the coup was very severe, read a prepared statement over television in which he thanked the military for having prevented the country "from falling irrevocably under the power of Marxism." While admitting that "the country has lost some blood," he said this was outweighed by saving "Chile as a free and sovereign nation."[23] Bishop Eladio Vicuña of Chillán stated publicly in December that it was "very beneficial that the honorable junta has imposed a long period of political silence."[24] He subsequently wrote an article for foreign consumption, published in Spain and excerpted in Argentina, in which he denounced the Allende regime, accused it of preparing a plan to murder the heads of the armed forces (the mysterious and illusory "Plan Z" which never has been proven) and called the coup an "act of patriotic heroism."[25]

In a press interview in early March 1974, Bishop Augusto Salinas of Linares (who had clashed with the Falange Nacional nearly thirty years before over the issue of communism) described the coup as a just rebellion against an illegitimate government. He also praised the armed forces and police for carrying out their task with "swiftness" and "precision." He frankly admitted that the Church provided legitimacy to the

[20] Bishop Francisco Valdés S., "La oración de Chile neuvo," 11 September 1973, *DOCLA* (Santiago) 1 (September 1973): 20.

[21] *El Mercurio*, 10 October 1973.

[22] *El Mercurio*, 4 October 1973.

[23] *El Mercurio*, 14 November 1973.

[24] *El Mercurio*, 24 December 1973.

[25] Bishop Eladio Vicuña, "La verdad sobre Chile," *Boletín CIO* (Madrid), no. 160 (16 February 1974). This article was also reprinted in *Cruzado Español* (Barcelona) 17 (15 May 1974), and excerpted in *Roma* (Buenos Aires) 8 (November 1974), pp. 2–3.

new regime, and placed September 11th on the same level of importance as national independence from Spain in 1810.[26]

Such public declarations by several bishops revealed not only deep-seated fears and resentments of Marxism formerly kept private while Allende was still in office, but also manifested gross insensitivity and blindness to the systematic repression and terror being perpetrated by the junta and its followers. Moreover, these statements were clearly political in their content and impact. They were given widespread coverage in the government-controlled media to provide moral legitimacy for the regime during its first months in office. Some of the same bishops who had condemned Christians for Socialism for going against episcopal guidelines regarding clerical involvement in politics and identifying their priestly office with partisan political movements, now were guilty of even worse actions themselves, condoning bloodshed and lies. No public criticisms, however, were voiced against them collectively or individually by other bishops.[27]

While not mentioning these six bishops who openly and completely supported the junta, two others expressed some personal reservations publicly. Fernando Ariztía, auxiliary bishop in the western zone of Santiago and cochairman of the ecumenical Committee for Peace which aided the persecuted, issued a moderately critical statement in December. While saying that it was a "very positive" gain "that the streets are quite orderly," he said that one must hope for more—namely, "freedom of the press and of assembly . . . liberty for unions and political freedom."[28] Bishop Jorge Hourton of Puerto Montt issued a mimeographed letter at Christmas to pastoral leaders in his diocese wherein he recognized "certain beneficial effects" of the military intervention—liberation from the threat of Marxist dictatorship, an end to hyperpoliticization of the country and exacerbated class conflict, and a return to discipline at work and public administration. He also criticized, however, several very specific abuses of the regime which he considered unnecessary—preventive detentions, tortures, repression, political and economic discrimination, disproportionate penalties by courts, and limitations on freedom of expression and association (especially for manual workers).[29]

Hence, during the first several months after the coup the official pub-

---

[26] *El Mercurio*, 3 March 1974.

[27] The jurisdiction of individual bishops is supreme in their own dioceses, subject only to that of the pope. Episcopal conferences exercise only an advisory function regarding the words and actions of individual prelates.

[28] Bishop Fernando Ariztía, "Signos e instrumentos de reconciliación," *Mensaje* 22 (November-December 1973): 578–79.

[29] Bishop Jorge Hourton P., "Mensaje de Navidad de 1973," mimeographed (Puerto Montt, 17 December 1973).

lic position of Church leaders as a group was not prophetic. The expression of social norms of the hierarchy was general and contradictory. Despite a wide gap between the principles and the practices of the new regime, the bishops, with two exceptions, did not criticize the widespread violations of human rights. This resulted from a desire to protect the institutional interests of the Church and from a judgment that the Church could do little except to alleviate some of the effects of repression. It also flowed from a naive trust in the promises of the junta and an unwillingness to believe how bad and systematic the brutality actually was, particularly in large industrial areas. Finally, a vocal minority of six projunta bishops made it impossible for the Episcopal Conference as a body to articulate a consistent public critique of the violence and bloodshed during the first six months.

Cautious Criticism of the Regime during the Consolidation of Power (April 1974–April 1976)

By early 1974 the extent of the repression was more widespread and harder to deny, despite a *Declaration of Principles* by the junta in March that recognized the importance of human rights and organizations of social participation (*gremios*) other than parties.[30] Disappearances, arrests without charges, the use of torture, and arbitrary executions were all spreading to small cities and some areas of the countryside. Unemployment was steadily growing due to summary dismissals of politically undesirable workers and the policy of the government to cut back on public investments. Parishes throughout the country became focal points for complaints and requests for legal and material aid, and both the local and national offices of the ecumenically sponsored Committee of Cooperation for Peace were by now providing the bishops with undeniable evidence of continued violation of human rights and denial of basic needs by the government.

In face of continuing repression in society and mounting pressures on the hierarchy from groups at lower levels of the Church, in late April 1974 the bishops as a group issued their first major criticism of the government, entitled "Reconciliation in Chile." While praising the junta's recent *Declaration of Principles* for "its explicitly Christian inspiration," and for offering "a basis to orient civic and social action during this situation of emergency," the bishops also recognized "certain insufficiencies in the formulation of the Christian ideal for social and political life." They did not present a detailed analysis of the government's declaration, but did suggest that such principles be incorporated into a new constitution only after a "free acceptance by our people" and a "discus-

[30] Chile, *Declaración de principios del gobierno de Chile,* pp. 7, 13, 16–19, 21, 29–31.

sion in which all citizens can actively and conscientiously participate."[31]

For the first time since the coup, the bishops also criticized abuses of the regime. The hierarchy softened their denunciations by admitting that they had no doubts about the "good intentions nor the good will of our governmental authorities," but then stated that they saw practical obstacles to the achievement of genuine reconciliation among Chileans. They included among these concerns the "climate of insecurity and fear . . . and lack of participation and information." They also expressed anxiety about "arbitrary dismissals for ideological reasons" and the fact that workers "bear too much of the quota of sacrifice" during the recovery period. For the first time as a body they acknowledged mistreatment of prisoners, and obliquely referred to torture:

> . . . We are concerned that in some cases there are no effective juridical safeguards to insure personal safety against arbitrary or prolonged detentions which result in neither those affected nor their families knowing the specific charges against them. We are also troubled by interrogations which include physical or moral constraints, by limitations on the possibilities of legal defense, by unequal sentences given for the same charges in different parts of the country, and by the restriction of the normal right of appeal in the court system.[32]

The bishops concluded their list of concerns by recognizing the legitimacy of "short-term suspension" of the exercise of some rights in "particular circumstances." They reminded the government, however, that there are certain rights which "pertain to the very dignity of the human person, and those are absolute and inviolable."[33]

A delegation of bishops met with members of the junta before issuing this document and informed them of its content. In presenting the statement subsequently to the press, Cardinal Silva indicated that the bishops had "no pretensions that our judgment is the only correct one" and that they respected "those who disagree with us." He explained to the representatives of the foreign and domestic press that the fact that the government, once informed of the content of the document, respected the Church's freedom to promulgate it "constitutes the greatest proof of the existence of a right to dissent in Chile and of the prevalence of law in the nation."[34]

Despite such qualifications and obsequious exaggerations, the document had no impact on changing government policy. It also drew strong

---

[31] Los obispos de Chile, "La reconciliación en Chile," *Mensaje* 23 (May 1974): 197.
[32] Ibid.
[33] Ibid., pp. 197–98.
[34] "Presentación de la declaración del Episcopado sobe la reconciliación en Chile, hecha por Eminencia, el Cardenal Arzobispo de Santiago, Presidente de la Conferencia Episcopal de Chile," *SELADOC* 1 (December 1974): 5.

criticisms by those closely associated with the administration. One of the four members of the junta, General Gustavo Leigh of the Air Force, said he had "great respect for the Church, but like many men, without realizing it, they are vehicles for Marxism."[35] Letters appeared in the press (which was controlled by those favorable to the regime) attacking the cardinal for his criticisms of the present government, and complaining that he had been too easy on the former administration which had been responsible for the present climate of insecurity in the country.[36]

Furthermore, within the Episcopal Conference serious public differences again emerged, and this time over the proper interpretation of the meaning and thrust of the bishops' own declaration. Four voted against some sections of the statement in private deliberations, and two (Archbishops Fresno and Tagle) expressed their dissent in public once it was released. Both these senior prelates again praised the actions of the junta for purportedly saving the country, and pointed to the order and respect in schools, factories, and streets as proof of the benefits of the coup. Tagle also specifically justified "severe restrictions" for reasons of national security since, he said, traces of Marxist "aggression" were still present in Chile.[37]

Such statements detracted from the critical thrust of the bishops' joint declaration, made it more easy for the military to disregard its contents, and opened the door for differing responses to the document among the laity. The most widely read pro-government newspaper in the country, *El Mercurio,* praised both Archbishop Fresno and Archbishop Tagle for having "clarified" the meaning of the Episcopal Conference's declaration. The paper thanked them for emphasizing "loyalty" and respect for the government's policies as the best way to achieve national reconciliation, and for not "crossing the line into political positions."[38]

For the next year and a half, the hierarchy as a group issued no more joint statements pertaining to policies of the government. Private conversations between individual bishops and military authorities occurred from time to time, and, particularly in provincial areas, these led to some lenience or release from prison on a case-by-case basis. It was also at this time (late 1974 and early 1975) that the Church was expanding its human rights activities to include a whole range of social and economic services to the poor (especially in large urban areas). The cardinal

---

[35] Sobel, ed., *Chile and Allende,* p. 171.

[36] Jaime Ruiz-Tagle, "La iglesia frente a la prensa," p. 267.

[37] Archbishop Juan Francisco Fresno, "Es necesario superar la situación de vencedores y vencidos," *El Día,* (La Serena) 19 May 1974; Archbishop Emilio Tagle, "Acerca de la reconciliación," *La Revista Católica* 73 (January-April 1974). Both are reprinted in *SELADOC* 1 (December 1974): 14–18.

[38] "Reconciliación nacional," *El Mercurio,* 19 May 1974.

and other liberal bishops wanted the Church to be left free to engage in this work, and preferred not to risk a major public confrontation which might jeopardize such programs.

By mid-1975, however, the institutionalization of political and economic repression was reaching extremely serious proportions. A secret police organization (DINA) begun in November 1973 (and legally established in June 1974) was by 1975 operating several centers in the vicinity of Santiago where torture was used on a regular basis. The "shock treatment" plan of economic recovery begun in early 1975 was inflicting almost unbearable pain on low-income Chileans by mid-year. Unemployment rose from 10.3 percent in June 1974 to 16 percent in June 1975, and 40,000 public employees were let go in the first six months of 1975. The purchasing power of wage earners since the coup had fallen over 60 percent by September. Former President Frei in May 1975 for the first time openly criticized the government for the severe social cost of its economic measures, and indicated that alternative policies were possible that entailed less sacrifice for the working class.[39]

Graphic accounts of torture, disappearances, hunger, and despair among workers were coming to bishops from local Church leaders, especially in major urban areas. Many were requesting that the bishops speak out once more against the repression which by now was taking on very definite systemic proportions.

In early September, just before the second anniversary of the coup, the Episcopal Conference issued its third major statement since late 1973, entitled "Gospel and Peace." The document identified some of the most basic human rights that must be respected as a precondition for peace in any society, such as the right to life and bodily integrity, and the right to participate.[40] The hierarchy, however, did not say that torture was actually occurring in Chile, nor that the authoritarian model being imposed by the regime was suppressing genuine participation.

While questioning some of the extremist attitudes and reactions of anti-Marxists associated with the regime, the bishops went out of their way to thank the military for "freeing" the country "from a Marxist dictatorship which appeared inevitable and would have been irreversible"[41] (a judgment for which there was no solid evidence).

The bishops criticized the gains being made by some at the expense of the poor, and expressed concern over the decline in public services which

[39] José Aldunate L., S.J., "Remuneraciones y costos de vida," pp. 634–36; Aldunate, "Salarios y precios: ¿cómo sigue la situación?," pp. 186–88; Emilio Filippi, "Frei analiza la situación económica," *Ercilla,* no. 2078 (28 May-3 June 1975), pp. 8–12.

[40] Comité Permanente del Episcopado de Chile, "Evangelio y paz," Santiago, 5 September 1975, pp. 465–66.

[41] Ibid., p. 466.

was hurting the poor. However, they also renewed their confidence in the "spirit of justice of our armed forces," praised some of the palliatives for the poor (such as the minimum employment program) and lauded the personal efforts made by wives of the military to aid children and the aged.[42]

Despite the oblique references to some abuses of power, the most striking aspect of the document was its extremely deferential attitude toward the military. After two years of sustained violation of civil, political, social, and economic rights of its citizens, the military received the public thanks of the bishops as a whole for having saved the country from Marxism. The atrocities committed by those associated with the regime were unheard of during Allende's term in office. Yet, in September 1975 the hierarchy chose not to condemn these specifically, nor to raise fundamental questions about the structure of the political economy which clearly violated social teachings of the Church.

One major reason for this deference was that some bishops still believed it possible to influence government leaders through private negotiations. A good number continued to maintain good personal relations with representatives of the government in their provinces, and were treated respectfully and cordially by local military commanders. Hence, many bishops still did not take a systemic view of the deeper structural contradictions that were causing both economic exploitation and political repression, and believed that quiet diplomacy was the best strategy for them to employ in order to alleviate the abuses that did exist.

One bishop in a rural area remarked to me in an interview in June 1975 that he believed his own private conversations with military leaders in his diocese had been successful in stopping abuse of prisoners:

> There are specific cases calling for public denunciation but this is not common. There were cases of torture here in my diocese during the first days of this government. I went to the authorities and was successful in my complaints. The form of the protest is important. We must avoid politics. At the level of principle we have to speak the truth.[43]

---

[42] Ibid., p. 471. A minimum employment program (*plan de empleo mínimo*) was begun by the government in early 1975, offering jobs on a day-to-day basis in public works projects. The plan was very inadequate since it paid less than the minimum wage (offering about $1.00 a day) and assisted only 15 percent of those out of work due to severe cutbacks in public service jobs. Ruiz-Tagle, "Cesantía y solidaridad nacional: el programa de empleo mínimo," *Mensaje* 24 (September 1975): 341–344. Furthermore, the military regime provided less, not more, assistance to the crippled, to children, and to the elderly than the former two administrations. They emphasized these projects in the media (with the assistance of their wives) as an attempt to convince the public of their good will despite cutbacks and controls in essential services.

[43] Interview no. 011, 21 June 1975.

Another bishop in the provinces told me in the same month that not only were private conversations with the government more effective than public condemnations, but that confrontation would precipitate greater harm for those at lower levels of the Church:

> Dinners, private letters, or conversations are more effective than public denunciations.
>
> This clearly is not prophetic, but it is also certain that we have to live in this country. We can't leave, and we bishops won't pay the consequences, but the clergy and the laity will. . . . Torture isn't everything. . . . The person tortured affects 50 to 100 persons. But there are many other social and economic problems that affect more Chileans. For many the situation is now better—no strikes, no chaos, order has returned, threats and abusive language have ceased, children can go to school in peace and are able to pursue their studies. The situation is far more complex than a foreign journalist can understand.
>
> The clergy and the religious and the laity are split. A prophetic challenge is not useful—not because the structures of the Church must be maintained . . . but rather to preserve the presence of the Church. Prudence is needed. I am content with the present Chilean Church—it has the independence and freedom to criticize. More than this is not useful or prudent.[44]

An added reason for the very cautious and deferential tone that characterized several parts of "Gospel and Peace" was the hierarchy's concern for unity, especially in the Episcopal Conference itself. Many wanted to avoid open disavowal by some of their brother bishops of the general thrust of the document after it was released, as happened subsequent to their April 1974 statement. A few conservative bishops insisted that the new joint declaration contain special words of praise for the military, and, although some of the most laudatory paragraphs were not present in the original draft, they were added in the final stages of its preparation to satisfy those who strongly supported the government.[45] While this strategy minimized the possibility of later public utilization of episcopal disunity by government sympathizers for political purposes, it also produced a document that was riddled with contradictions, full of generalities, and openly supportive of the military.

In early July, two months before "Gospel and Peace" appeared, one

[44] Interview no. 010, 18 June 1975.

[45] My own conversations with the hierarchy in 1975 confirmed this fact. The original draft of "Gospel and Peace" did not have as many references to the accomplishments of the regime, or praise for the contributions of the wives of the military to the poor. These were put in at the end of the deliberations upon the urging of just a few bishops, especially Archbishop Tagle of Valparaíso. This is comparable to what happened to the Chilean bishops' pastoral letter of 1962 (as described in Chapter 5) when, at the behest of a few conservative prelates, very strong condemnations of communism were written into the final version of the document.

bishop told me frankly that he was uneasy with official Church concern for unity, both in Rome and at the national episcopal level. He believed this would result in public positions by the bishops that provided the government with more legitimacy:

> There are divisions among us. There is a game going on between collegiality and unity (badly understood) and uniformity. The pope wants unity in the Church. . . . However, unity can result in a position of supporting the government.[46]

A concern with such political consequences, however, did not characterize the majority of bishops in mid-1975.

Despite the extremely respectful attitude toward the government expressed in the pastoral letter, even the mild criticism and suggestions it contained had no impact on public policy. In a major speech delivered a week later on the second anniversay of the coup, Pinochet announced no changes in his political and economic policies. The press made no editorial comment on the bishops' statement, and *El Mercurio* printed it serially over several days, burying it in the back pages of its Santiago edition.

No dissenting views were expressed by bishops after the publication of "Gospel and Peace," but a week later, on the second anniversary of the coup, some bishops ignored a public recommendation by the Permanent Committee of the Episcopal Conference that there be no special religious ceremonies on September 11th commemorating the coup. In several dioceses prelates presided at public Masses of thanksgiving in which military officials participated.

At the military academy in Santiago, Bishop Francisco Gillmore, the head of military chaplains and himself a general in the army, celebrated a Mass with twenty-four other chaplains. The members of the junta were present, along with representative delegations from the four branches of the armed services and the civilian public, including delegations of children from several high schools. The Mass was broadcast nationwide on the government television station, and general absolution for sins (without vocal admission of guilt) was extended to all present at the beginning of the ceremony—a privilege allowed to soldiers only before entering battle when there is no opportunity for private confession. In his homily the bishop-general also thanked God that the "torch of freedom reappeared in the hands of the armed forces" and that "the hope of order, respect, dignity, and work returned" to the country after so much anxiety and hatred of the recent past.[47]

---

[46] Interview no. 014, 2 July 1975.

[47] "Misa de Acción de Gracias en la Escuela Militar," *El Mercurio*, 12 September 1975, pp. 21, 30. In 1975 there were thirty-three full-time priest-chaplains in the Chilean military, and sixty-two others serving in a part-time capacity (4.5 percent of

Despite efforts within the Episcopal Conference to work for consensus statements rather than risk further public dissension among themselves, some prelates found ways to express unequivocal support for the military. This not only played into the hands of the government, but also further undermined the public credibility of even mild criticisms of the regime by the hierarchy as a whole.

Two incidents in late 1975 did precipitate some tension between the hierarchy and those close to the government. Both involved affronts to episcopal dignity and authority—one involving Bishop Carlos Camus, the secretary of the Episcopal Conference, and the other directed against the cardinal.

An off-the-record news briefing to foreign correspondents by Bishop Camus in late September was taped by a Bolivian journalist and sold to the Chilean pro-government tabloid, *La Segunda*. The editors of this paper printed excerpts of the tape over a several-day period, taking some of the bishop's remarks out of context. Included in the excerpts were some frank criticisms of government economic policies, and an admission by the bishop that he believed that some Chileans with Marxist sympathies were working in the Committee of Cooperation for Peace. The media sensationalized the incident, demanding Camus's immediate removal as secretary of the Conference for unjustly criticizing the government to foreigners. Six bishops (three of whom openly supported the government) criticized Camus publicly for what they considered serious indiscretion.[48]

When Camus subsequently circulated a full transcript of the interview (made from his own personal tape), showing that some of his words were taken out of context or simply misquoted, the hierarchy closed ranks. The Permanent Committee clarified the errors of interpretation and criticized the media for its unfairness. Later, the bishops confirmed him in his position as secretary of the Conference at their December

---

the total of 2,111 priests in the country). *Guía de la Iglesia en Chile*, 1976, pp. 437–39, 506.

Military chaplains are a special breed of clergy, not only in Chile but in other Western countries as well. They normally hold officer rank, and very closely identify with the values and goals of the armed services of which they are an integral part. In Nazi Germany, the most nationalistic and pro-Hitler member of the Catholic hierarchy was the head of the military chaplains, Army Bishop Franz Josef Rarkowski. Lewy, *Catholic Church and Nazi Germany*, pp. 236–42. During the Vietnam conflict, U.S. chaplains by and large supported the war efforts of this country whole-heartedly, and never publicly criticized any of the tactics of our military.

[48] "Infiltración Marxista," *El Mercurio*, 12 October 1975, p. 3; Pablo Rodríguez Grez, "El obispo y sus nuevos feligreses," *La Tercera*, 13 October 1975, p. 3; Ernesto Murúa F., "Análisis de un periodismo de campañas," *Mensaje* 24 (December 1975): 579–83. *El Mercurio*, 10 October 1975 pp. 1, 12; *El Mercurio*, 15 October, p. 18; *El Mercurio*, 20 October, p. 17.

Table 9.1

Opinions on the Prophetic Role of the Church under Authoritarian Regimes (1975)

"Throughout history the Church has had to coexist with authoritarian regimes whose ideologies or practices are in conflict with Catholic doctrine (e.g., Nazi Germany, various communist governments in Eastern Europe and Asia). Leaders of the Church frequently have adapted to the situation in such societies rather than publicly confront governments, because they wish to maintain the structures of the Church and the possibility of administering the sacraments."

"Are you in agreement with this position and strategy, or do you think that the institutional Church should be more prophetic under these conditions?"

	Bishops (N = 30)	Priests (N = 72)	Nuns (N = 33)	Laity (N = 51)	Totals (N = 186)
1. First Position (Prudence is needed; depends on the situation; Church really does not have that much power; Church must clarify doctrinal issues; private conversations better than public denunciations; satisfied with present stance of Chilean Church)	90% (27)	40.3% (29)	12.1% (4)	29.4% (15)	40.3% (75)
2. Second Position (Church should speak and act more decisively, including Chilean Church)	10 (3)	47.2 (34)	57.6 (19)	56.9 (29)	45.7 (85)
3. Combination of both strategies—dialogue and cooperation when possible combined with strong public defense of human dignity and rights	—	8.3 (6)	—	—	3.2 (6)
4. Don't know, no answer	—	4.2 (3)	30.3 (10)	13.7 (7)	10.8 (20)

meeting. This episcopal support for a brother bishop, remarked one prelate at the time, shows "that yellow journalism does not rule the Church."[49]

The second incident involved an affront to Cardinal Silva by a Catholic lawyer close to the junta. In November 1975 several Chilean priests were arrested (and three foreign nuns expelled) for having assisted some of the remaining leaders of the MIR (one of whom was badly wounded) to obtain medical assistance after a police shoot-out and subsequently to gain political asylum in foreign embassies. The cardinal at the time publicly forbade priestly involvement in terrorism, but approved on the grounds of Christian mercy the legitimacy of preserving life regardless of the political consequences. Jaime Guzmán, chief legal adviser to the junta and leader in the Catholic Integralist movement, twice on national television criticized the cardinal's interpretation of mercy as a "serious error," and called upon people to turn over to the proper authorities all those wanted by the police even if they seek ecclesiastical help.[50]

The cardinal's reaction was immediate and crystal clear. He defended mercy and humanitarian aid for any wounded person, and threatened Guzmán with excommunication for attempting to "undermine the power of ecclesiastical authorities."[51] Guzmán publicly retracted, and the government released the priests from jail before Christmas. In December the bishops replaced the cardinal as president of the Episcopal Conference, choosing as his successor Archbishop Francisco Fresno, a public supporter of the junta. They also issued no more public statements on political or social issues for the next several months.

Hence, during these two years of consolidation of power the bishops' public statements moved away from the moderately denunciatory position of early 1974. Open divisions within their ranks, a desire to protect the institutional Church, and the continuing belief by many in the efficacy of private conversations with military leaders all led to a more deferential episcopal stance vis-à-vis the government.

Dissenting Views Within the Church in 1975 over the Desirability of a More Prophetic Stance from the Top

Some bishops chose a cautious style of language in "Gospel and Peace" purportedly to protect their local leaders engaged in humanitarian work from a frontal attack by the government. These same local leaders, however, wanted a much clearer denunciation of the regime in 1975.

I asked all those in my survey, carried out between April and Novem-

[49] El Comité Permanente del Episcopado, "Declaración del Episcopado," Santiago, 27 October 1975, *El Mercurio*, 5 November 1975, p. 21; Guillermo Blanco, "Hora de decisión en la iglesia," pp. 3–5.

ber 1975, whether or not they agreed with the position frequently taken historically by the official Church under authoritarian regimes to adapt to the situation as a way of protecting the institution and guaranteeing the possibility of continuing its specifically sacramental mission. While 90 percent of the bishops said they agreed with this strategy, almost one-half of the priests and nearly three-fifths of the nuns and laity said they preferred Church leaders to be more prophetic under such conditions.

Many of those at the local level also took this question as an opportunity to speak about current Church-state relations in Chile. Despite the realization that they themselves might very well suffer more directly the costs of a prophetic position by the bishops, they still voiced a preference for a clearer denunciatory role on the part of the hierarchy.

A priest in a lower-middle-class parish in Santiago, for example, stated frankly that the official Church "must be prophetic and courageously denounce injustice without weighing strategies or various alternatives." Church leaders "should be faithful to the Gospel. . . . Evil from whatever source must be challenged."[52]

A layman in a working-class neighborhood in the capital voiced a similar opinion. He also contrasted what he considered the clear public position of the bishops against "Project ENU" under Allende to the "evasive" one "now when many people have been assassinated or tortured." For the poor, he said, "this implies that the Church has taken a position in favor of the government."[53]

A nun doing pastoral work in a shantytown in Santiago recognized the complexity of the issue and the legitimate concern of the hierarchy for Church unity. Nevertheless, she too expressed a desire that the Chilean bishops be more prophetic and "that they unmask falsehood and indicate what is erroneous, even though this implies conflict and a direct persecution of the Church."[54]

Many religious, clerical, and lay leaders in the Church saw the effects of political and economic repression more directly than the bishops due to the close daily contact with people and involvement in new programs designed to alleviate their suffering. Many of these leaders by mid-1975

[50] "Declaración pública del Arzobispado de Santiago," Santiago, 5 November 1975, *Mensaje* 24 (December 1975): 596; "Comentario de Jaime Guzmán Errázuriz transmitido por Televisión Nacional el 6 de noviembre y repetido el 8," *Mensaje* 24 (December 1975): 596–97.

[51] Departamento de Opinión Pública del Arzobispado de Santiago, "Evangelio y misericordia: réplica a un comentarista de TV Nacional," Santiago, 10 November 1975, *Mensaje* 24 (December 1975): 599.

[52] Interview no. 094, 8 December 1975.

[53] Interview no. 107, 20 October 1975.

[54] Interview no. 183, 12 September 1975.

believed that the time for prudence, dialogue, and private negotiation between the Church and government was over, and that clear and specific public denunciations were the only tactic that was then honorable. Several told me they believed that even if a formal persecution of the Church did result from a more prophetic stance by the bishops, they themselves and their parishioners would not suffer any more pain than they were already.

Throughout 1975, however, the hierarchy as a whole continued to judge otherwise. No form of repression aimed at the Chilean people was sufficient to resolve the internal divisions in the Episcopal Conference, nor to make them risk limitations by the government on the freedom of the Church to perform its religious and humanitarian functions. It was such preoccupation with defending the institution, however, that eventually sensitized the bishops to the deep systemic character of the repression and moved them to alter substantially their public stance after mid-1976.

Episcopal Prophecy amidst Mounting Attacks on the Church (May 1976–December 1980)

After mid-1976 the articulation of social norms by the bishops became more specific and consistent. This resulted from a series of direct frontal attacks on several of themselves, laity closely associated with the Church or the PDC, and Church structures and programs. Public divisions among the hierarchy ceased. They began to criticize not merely individual aberrances of power, which formerly they considered transitory and correctable, but the systemic character of the regime as the cause of political and economic repression.

Throughout 1974 and 1975 criticisms of the government were made by spokespersons for the PDC, particularly regarding the junta's economic policies and its refusal to allow meaningful social participation. In turn, the government systematically removed PDC leaders or sympathizers from positions of influence in education and labor, and forced it to close its major journal of critical thought, *Política y Espíritu*.[55]

In 1976 both sides escalated the conflict. During the Sixth Assembly of the Organization of American States held in Santiago in June, six prominent Chilean lawyers closely associated with the PDC presented a letter to all the foreign ministers in attendance protesting the continuing state of siege in Chile, as well as arbitrary detentions, abuses by the secret police, and the abdication of responsibility by civilian courts in face of human rights violations. Two of the six, Eugenio Velasco (former dean of the Law Faculty at the University of Chile and ex-justice on

[55] Paul E. Sigmund, *Overthrow of Allende,* p. 255.

the Supreme Court), and Jaime Castillo (minister of justice under Frei), were subsequently expelled from the country for purportedly threatening Chile's national security.

In mid-August a frontal attack was made by persons associated with the government against members of the hierarchy themselves. On 12 August seventeen bishops from various Latin American countries (including three Chileans) were arrested at a meeting in Riobamba, Ecuador, which focused on new pastoral developments. The military government of Ecuador charged that the prelates were discussing "subversive themes of a Marxist orientation," and after detaining the bishops expelled them from the country. Several Chilean newspapers and the national television station published criticisms of the three Chileans (Enrique Alvear, Fernando Ariztía, and Carlos González) who attended the Riobamba session, calling them "leftist bishops" and denouncing what was considered more clerical involvement in politics. The bishops upon returning home were met at the airport in Santiago by a group of pro-government demonstrators, including members of the DINA, who shouted insults, threw stones, and physically mistreated those accompanying the prelates. The police did nothing to restrain the demonstrators, and instead arrested some relatives and friends of the bishops.[56]

The Permanent Committee of the Episcopal Conference reacted decisively to both these events, and issued two strong statements on the same day—one critizing the treatment of the prominent Christian Democrats, and the other threatening excommunication for those involved in the attack on the bishops. These were the first unequivocal statements by the hierarchy as a group in almost three years of military rule.

In the first, they denounced the arbitrary expulsion of Castillo and Velasco "without a decision about their culpability by a free and impartial judge." They concluded by asking that if this could happen to "two prestigious professional people . . . what could happen to simple and ignorant citizens?"[57] No acknowledgment was made, however, of the fact that thousands of "simple and ignorant citizens" had already been expelled or forced to leave the country since 1973 without due process.

In the second statement they defended the Riobamba meeting as strictly pastoral in orientation and convoked with ecclesiastical approbation. They affirmed that only the Roman Pontiff has the "authority to

[56] R.A.H., "Sentido del episodio Riobamba-Pudahuel," *Mensaje* 25 (October 1976): 455–60. For a summary and analysis of the coverage of these events in the Chilean press, see Guillermo Blanco, *Los incidentes de Riobamba y Pudahuel en tres diarios chilenos.*

[57] El Comité Permanente del Episcopado Chileno, "Declaración," 17 August 1976, *Mensaje* 25 (September 1976): 446.

define the ambience of our pastoral competence," and that the arrest of the bishops in Ecuador "represented a clear act of hostility against the Catholic Church." The bishops also protested against the "violence and verbal aggression" against the Church by the communications media, including *La Segunda, El Cronista* (the official paper of the government), and the national television station. They also denounced "with indignation" the insulting demonstrations at Pudahuel airport, named specific members of the DINA who had taken part in the incident, and reminded them that canon law automatically imposes excommunication on those Catholics who "perpetrate violence against an archbishop or bishop."[58]

On this occasion the Episcopal Conference also moved beyond the specific threats to themselves and raised serious criticisms about the fundamental characteristics of the system being imposed throughout Latin America by military governments:

> The actions which we denounce and condemn are not isolated incidents. They are part of an overall process or system that is very clearly delineated in its characteristics and which threatens to impose itself relentlessly throughout Latin America. By a constant appeal to national security, a model of society is being consolidated that takes away basic liberties, runs roughshod over the most fundamental rights and subjugates citizens to a dreaded and omnipotent police state. . . .
>
> The Church cannot remain passive or neutral in face of such a situation. The legacy which it has received from Christ demands that it speak out in favor of human dignity and for the effective protection of the liberty and rights of the person.[59]

The hierarchy as a group was coming to realize that abuses of power by the Chilean security forces were not isolated, transitory, or unavoidable mistakes. They were part of a whole system of repressive state power present in Chile and several other Latin American countries in the mid-1970s. It took, however, a direct attack on themselves and prominent laity in the PDC to open their eyes to this fact.

In late 1976 and 1977, after Pinochet had announced that the military

---

[58] "Declaración del Comité Permanente del Episcopado," Santiago, August 1976, pp. 436–37.

[59] Ibid. By mid-1976 the bishops were becoming more conscious of the dangers of an exaggerated emphasis on national security that characterized the words and actions of the government. They began to discuss this problem among themselves and commissioned studies on national security doctrine by lay persons closely associated with the Church. In a sermon on the anniversary of national independence, Bishop Santos, a philosopher and one of the prelates most concerned about this ideology, presented a comprehensive analysis of where the doctrine diverged from traditional Christian values and from the *Declaration of Principles* of the junta itself published in March 1974. José Manuel Santos, "La seguridad nacional, condición del bien común," Valdivia, 18 September 1976, *Mensaje* 25 (November 1976): 597–99.

would remain in control of the state indefinitely to protect national security, the Christian Democratic Party again stepped up its activities against the government. Its members became more involved in legal defense of prisoners and the disappeared, and the PDC radio station (Radio Balmaceda) increased its broadcasts on repressive aspects of the government's political and economic policies. The party leadership, encouraged by Jimmy Carter's election as president of the United States, inaugurated internal discussions on feasible scenarios that would bring an end to military rule and also establish a tactical alliance between the PDC and moderate sectors of the Left.

The junta responded decisively. At the end of January 1977 it closed down permanently Radio Balmaceda. On 12 March Pinochet also announced the dissolution of all political parties, and justified this by claiming that the Christian Democrats had broken the political recess imposed in September 1973 on all non-Marxist parties.

In the wake of these latest reprisals against the PDC, the bishops issued another clear denunciation of the regime. The pastoral letter, entitled "Our Life as a Nation," included an analysis of the structural weaknesses of the system as a whole, and placed the Church clearly behind those urging an early return to constitutional and representative government.

The first point of disagreement with the government which the bishops raised was the problem of disappeared persons and the lack of information as to their whereabouts. They explicitly asked that the president of the Republic "make sure that the government give its total cooperation to the courts in order to clarify once and for all the fate of each of those who had disappeared" since September 1973. Without such cooperation, they argued, the families of these persons will have no rest, nor will there be genuine peace inside the country and Chile's image abroad will remain tarnished.[60]

The statement did not mention the suppression of the PDC as such, but addressed itself to what the bishops considered a basic flaw in the regime which the dissolution of the party reflected. In accordance with traditional Catholic social teaching about subsidiarity, the bishops argued that intermediate organizations between the state and the individual must not be suppressed. Such institutions, they said, guarantee both social and political participation and a healthy pluralism of ideas which are essential ingredients in the pursuit of the common good. They also affirmed that social, labor, and professional organizations had manifested "a maturity as well as a realistic and patriotic understanding,

---

[60] Comité Permanente de la Conferencia Episcopal de Chile, "Nuestra convivencia nacional," Santiago, 25 March 1977, p. 167. (Reprinted in *Latin American Bishops Discuss Human Rights,* LADOC "Keyhole Series" no. 15, pp. 41–54.)

even when they have dissented from government viewpoints." Such groups, they argued, deserved not more restrictions but "greater possibilities to express themselves and thus collaborate in generating an authentic consensus."[61]

Using the same line of argument, the hierarchy criticized the economic plan of recovery for not being subject to wider societal debate or allowing for more popular input into its formulation. They asked that economic decision-making "not be reserved to only one scientific school of thought or to some of the most privileged economic sectors." They stated that "more wisdom is bound to result from the open discussion of various opinions, rather than from only one judgment that is handed down dogmatically . . ."[62]

Finally, the bishops called for an end to government by decree, and urged popular ratification of any future constitution or set of laws:

> We believe that there will not exist full guarantees for the respect of human rights so long as the country does not have a constitution, old or new, ratified by popular vote. Such guarantees will also be lacking so long as laws are not written by legitimate representatives of the citizenry, or while all the structures of the state, from the highest to the lowest, are not subject to the constitution and to a set of laws . . .[63]

This was the first time in three and a half years that the hierarchy implied that the military were not the legitimate representatives of the people. It was also the first time that they acknowledged that inadequate protections for personal, political, and economic rights were due to the absence of accountable government rather than to failures by some individuals within the administration. It was also clear that the factor that precipitated the bishops' criticism of the lack of the regime's legitimacy and their most comprehensive analysis to date of its structural weaknesses was the suppression of the Christian Democratic Party.

The reaction of the government and its supporters was swift and acerbic. *El Mercurio* accused the bishops of having for the first time adopted a "political position in face of the military regime," thus overstepping their "pastoral authority." The minister of justice publicly called the bishops "useful fools, ambitious, bad-intentioned, and resentful" who have "abandoned the care of souls" and have "launched a hypocritical political attack on the government."[64]

Although the minister was removed from his position, no positive action was taken by the government in response to the hierarchy's request

[61] Ibid., pp. 167–68.
[62] Ibid., p. 169.
[63] Ibid., p. 168.
[64] "Posición política de los obispos," *El Mercurio*, 27 March 1977; Gregorio Meneses V., "Acontecimientos de marzo," *Mensaje* 26 (May 1977): 174.

for more freedom and genuine participation and for a return to representative government. In fact, in July 1977 Pinochet announced that a return to civilian rule would not occur until 1985, nor would the new institutional order allow for political parties or a popularly ratified constitution.[65]

Over the course of the next three years the Episcopal Conference continued to issue critical statements of the regime, and, for the most part, each declaration focused on a specific aberration of public power. At Christmas 1977, they issued an appeal for amnesty to those in forced or voluntary exile. At about the same time they sent a public letter to the junta asking for a postponement of a precipitously announced referendum rigged to guarantee a favorable outcome for the government.[66]

Throughout 1978 the members of the Episcopal Conference addressed themselves to three more problems—restrictions on salaries and rights of workers, the lack of information on the disappeared, and the harassment of the clergy. The Permanent Committee of the Conference issued six separate public statements criticizing specific government actions or programs that aggravated these situations.[67]

In 1979 the bishops denounced government policies that undermined the cultural identity and right to land by the Mapuche Indians. They also issued a long critical analysis of the junta's agrarian program, claiming that it denied small farmers access to credit, technical assistance, and adequate power to protect themselves against large landholders. The conference also publicly requested the government to surrender for Christian burial the bodies of those murdered and concealed in large common graves after the coup.[68]

In April 1980 the Episcopal Conference called for "a return to institutional normality" and asked that public approval of a new constitution be done amidst "ample freedom of information, effective respect for the privacy of conscience, and true seriousness and honesty" throughout the approbation process. In August, when the government suddenly announced a plebiscite for early September, the bishops reiterated their appeal for equal access to the media for all viewpoints and for guarantees that the voting procedures would be fair. Their voice went un-

[65] *El Mercurio,* 10 July 1977.

[66] Episcopado Chileno, "El sufrimiento del exilio," Santiago, 25 December 1977, p. 84.

El Comité Permanente del Episcopado, "Carta del Comité Permanente del Episcopado a cada uno de los Srs. Miembros de la Honorable Junta de Gobierno," Santiago, 30 December 1977, *Mensaje* 27 (January-February 1978): 101.

[67] These statements all were published in *Mensaje* in the respective issues of June, July, and December 1978, and January-February 1979.

[68] These statements were published in 1979 in the July, September, and October issues of *Mensaje* respectively.

heeded by the government, and the Church was severely criticized (and even calumniated) in the media. Finally, in December 1980, the bishops of Linares (Carlos Camus), Talca (Carlos González and Alejandro Jiménez), Temuco (Sergio Contreras), and Ancud (José Luis Ysern) declared as automatically excommunicated those in their respective dioceses who torture, those who order it, and those who fail to stop it.[69]

None of these clear and pointed statements by the hierarchy between 1976 and 1980 had any significant impact on the government's political policies. Nor did the junta make any substantial change in its economic measures, and continued to impose a heavy burden on the basic needs and rights of workers.

This whole series of public declarations by the bishops after mid-1976 signalled, however, a definite distancing of the official Church from many of the principles and tactics of the regime. Once the bishops themselves and the party they considered closest to the Church's position were subjected to direct and sustained attack, most came to share the judgments of the majority of local Church leaders and those in society suffering the brunt of political and economic repression.

As during the Allende years, there was a "cooking time" in which private dissatisfaction among the bishops regarding the government was growing for quite some time before a public change. In the Allende period this abrupt change did not occur until after the coup, but the private fears of the bishops regarding Marxism helped to explain their apparently surprising tolerance for the junta when it came to power. Under the military government the continual imposition of unbearable economic costs on the poor during recovery, the sniping attacks on episcopal authority by government supporters, the development of national security doctrine in opposition to traditional Catholic social teachings, and persecution of prominent Christian Democrats all were preparing the way for a greater critical consensus within the hierarchy regarding government policies and principles. Something more, however, was needed to galvanize this emerging dissatisfaction into a consistent prophetic stance, and this was provided by the direct attack on three bishops at Pudahuel airport in mid-1976 and the suppression of the PDC in early 1977.

Closer examination of the public stance of several other national hierarchies in Latin America living under military rule in the 1970s

[69] "Declaración del Comité Permanente de la Conferencia Episcopal de Chile," Santiago, 12 April 1980, *Mensaje* 29 (May 1980): 228; "Declaración sobre el plebiscito," Santiago, 23 August 1980; Bishops Carlos González C., Alejandro Jiménez L., and Carlos Camus, "Excomunión a torturadores," *Mensaje* 30 (January-February 1981): 68.

shows the same pattern. The bishops in Brazil, Guatemala, Argentina, Bolivia, Paraguay, and El Salvador have only slowly come to take a prophetic position in face of government repression. In these countries, as in Chile, "cooking time" has elapsed between the institutionalization of human rights violations by such regimes and a clear denunciation of these practices by the respective hierarchies.[70] In all of these cases, the bishops initially have accepted military rule and have done their best to maintain good relations with the regime. Only when they considered core interests of the Church to be under attack (usually the lives or safety of clergy) have they spoken out clearly and critically against the wider structures of oppression affecting the whole of society.

THE CHURCH AS INSTITUTIONAL COUNTERWEIGHT
TO REPRESSION

Despite the cautious and often inconsistent public statements of the bishops regarding human rights during the early period of the military regime in Chile, the organizational resources of the Church were a significant factor right from the start in alleviating some of the effects of brutality. With the collapse or entrenchment of other major social institutions after the coup, the Church provided a protective umbrella under which a whole range of humanitarian programs could be maintained, as well as accurate information on human rights violations disseminated. Chronic structural weaknesses in the Church, however, coupled with intense government pressure on its newly emerging programs, placed restrictions on the capacities of the institution to mount a campaign of strong opposition to the regime.

Decisive Action on Behalf of Human Rights
at Lower Church Levels

Due to the acquiescence of the Catholic bishops to their intervention, the military were willing to allow Churches to set up programs to assist the persecuted. All denominations were besieged with requests for assistance, and within a month after the coup a united ecumenical effort was undertaken by several religious communities (Catholic, Protestant, Greek Orthodox, Jewish) to coordinate emergency services to the persecuted.[71]

---

[70] Smith, "Churches and Human Rights in Latin America."

[71] The leaders of other Christian denominations (Lutheran, Greek Orthodox, Anglican, Methodist, Baptist) all followed fairly closely the position of the Catholic bishops—namely, initial acceptance of the coup, some cautious public criticisms, growing private dissatisfaction, and continual cooperation at the local level to help persecuted persons and those suffering the costs of economic recovery. Most funda-

A National Committee to Aid Refugees (CONAR) was set up by the Churches before the end of September, and by February 1974 had helped approximately 5,000 foreigners to leave the country safely. In early October leaders from these various denominations inaugurated the Committee of Cooperation for Peace (COPACHI) in Santiago under the copresidency of Lutheran bishop Helmut Frenz, and the Catholic auxiliary bishop of Santiago, Fernando Ariztía. The organization's purpose was to provide legal assistance to prisoners and workers arbitrarily dismissed from their jobs as well as economic aid to families of both of these groups of Chileans. Over the next several months, local offices or representatives were established in twenty-two of the twenty-five provinces throughout the country to provide the same type of services as in the capital.[72]

From October 1973 to December 1975 the Committee of Cooperation for Peace initiated legal actions on behalf of more than 7,000 persons in Santiago alone who were arrested, condemned, or who had disappeared. Its members also defended more than 6,000 workers dismissed from their positions for political reasons. It was successful in obtaining reduced sentences for many who were brought to trial (a small minority of those arrested or disappeared), as well as compensation for countless numbers of those who had been peremptorily fired.[73]

During 1974 and 1975 the committee expanded its services to include a whole range of projects aimed at alleviating the suffering inflicted on the poor by the economic model of recovery. It provided technical and financial assistance for 126 self-help enterprises initiated and managed by workers themselves. In the countryside, it helped set up ten cooperatives for small farmers, and in Santiago supported health clinics in working-class neighborhoods where more than 75,000 patients were treated during the first two years of military rule. Moreover, by the end of 1975, approximately 400 soup kitchens for preschool children suffering from severe malnutrition were in operation throughout the coun-

---

mentalist evangelical churches (which account for the vast majority of the 1 million Protestants in Chile), however, were openly supportive of the junta from its first days in office and most did not participate in ecumenical human rights activities. Soon after the coup, the new government gave significant subsidies to the evangelicals for the completion of a large temple in downtown Santiago. In December 1974 Pinochet attended the dedication ceremonies of the edifice (where he was warmly received by a capacity crowd of several thousand Pentecostals), and he affirmed his support for freedom of conscience and religious practice for all Churches in Chile. Pedro Puentes Oliva, *Posición Evangélica.*

[72] P.N., "¿Qué hacen las iglesias por la paz?," *Mensaje* 22 (November-December 1973): 561–63.

[73] El Comité de Cooperación para la Paz en Chile, "Crónica de sus dos años de labor solidaria."

try (the majority in Santiago) providing a hot lunch to more than 30,000 youngsters daily.[74]

None of these projects effected any significant changes in government policies, nor did they reach anywhere near the actual number of people in need. In addition to reducing the sufferings of many, however, the Committee of Cooperation for Peace established a network of communication. Its nation-wide staff of over 300 full-time lawyers, social workers, and medical personnel provided detailed information for almost every area of the country on arrests, disappearances, torture, unemployment, sickness, and malnutrition. As a result of this network of communication, rather thorough regular reports were prepared every few months by the Santiago office of the committee on the basis of these facts and sent to the bishops as well as international Church organizations supporting COPACHI's work. This contribution not only provided the outside world with some of the most accurate first-hand testimonies of human rights violations in Chile, but also was an important factor in sensitizing some bishops in the country early on to the systemic nature of the repression.

Furthermore, the work of the Committee for Peace acted as a catalyst to encourage many other types of community projects at the local Church level. Drawing upon the experience and the advice of the skilled staff of the committee, small groups of working-class people at the parish and neighborhood level established self-help employment projects, daycare centers, and independent soup kitchens. While all these were only palliatives and could not affect the deeper causes of political and economic repression, such projects were another network of communication and of participation. They nourished a sense of solidarity among the persecuted and their families, and enabled many to survive who otherwise might have lost all hope.

These new social projects had a profound impact on the mentality of many local clergy and religious as well. By working on a daily basis with those suffering the consequences of the repression, priests and nuns in low-income areas were exposed more directly to the consequences of the repression than were the hierarchy. Though not in a position to exercise the same type of public influence as the bishops, they acted as a constant

---

[74] Ibid. For more information on the operations of the Committee of Cooperation for Peace, see Juan Zerón Domínguez, "Una experiencia de trabajo ecuménico: Comité para la Paz," pp. 54–56; U.S. Congress, House, Subcommittee on International Organizations of the Committee on International Relations, "Prepared Statement of José Zalaquett Daher, Chief Legal Counsel, Committee of Cooperation for Peace in Chile," *Chile: The Status of Human Rights and Its Relationship to U.S. Economic Assistance Programs,* 94th Cong., 2nd sess., 1976, pp. 57–65.

source of pressure on the prelates to speak and act more critically against the government.

While such suggestions were not always heeded by the bishops, the flow of information and criticisms continued to move up the vertical chain of command in the Church throughout the period of consolidation of the regime's power. It did have a gradual impact on the attitudes of individual bishops long before the hierarchy as a group developed a consistent prophetic position against the government after mid-1976. From my own experience as assistant pastor in Santiago in 1975, for example, it was evident that priests' senate meetings, pastoral planning sessions, and periodic interchanges between bishops and clerics and women religious frequently were occasions in which local church leaders respectfully, but forcefully, pressured those at the top to define a more clearly critical position for the Church as a whole. The cardinal and three auxiliary bishops in Santiago did, in fact, come to share such opinions long before bishops in other parts of the country.[75]

Rectories and convents also became places of refuge for those seeking to escape arrest and subsequent torture or execution, especially those formerly active in leftist parties or unions. With the assistance of those closely associated with the Committee of Peace, priests, nuns, ministers, and lay men and women enabled many of these persons to exercise their right to political asylum in foreign embassies and leave the country unharmed. The story is yet to be told of the countless numbers of lives these courageous men and women saved, risking their own lives to do so.[76]

In addition to these actions on behalf of human rights, the Jesuit-sponsored monthly magazine, *Mensaje,* provided a balanced but critical viewpoint on public events right from the outset. During the initial period after the coup, like the bishops the journal expressed cautious acceptance of the regime as the only alternative to civil war. Its editorials early on, however, specifically condemned the widespread use of violence and torture, stressed the need for the reestablishment of traditional freedoms and an early withdrawal of the military from power, and sup-

[75] Under an authoritarian government progressive clerical, religious, and lay leaders were less prone to disagree as openly with the hierarchy as when there was more freedom in the political system under Frei and Allende. In a repressive context they felt the need for the bishops' protection of their local structures and programs, and also saw the public prestige of the hierarchy as useful for potentially withdrawing legitimacy from the regime. Hence, such local leaders, even when they disagreed with the tactics of the bishops, were more interested in winning them over than in subverting their authority.

[76] For an account of some of the heroic efforts of these Christians, see Sheila Cassidy, *Audacity to Believe.*

ported the continued desirability of some form of socialism in Chile.[77]

During this period of consolidation of government power in 1974 and 1975, *Mensaje* voiced a concern over the lack of adequate social and political participation. During these two years the magazine also published articles describing the devastating impact of the government's economic policies on the purchasing power and quality of life of workers and other low-income sectors of the population.[78]

In 1976 *Mensaje* also stepped up its criticisms of the government as the bishops came to express more open disagreements with the junta. It expanded its coverage of sensitive issues such as the continued inaction of the courts in face of violations of constitutional rights, government censorship of the media, the lack of information on the whereabouts of disappeared persons, and the chronic suppression of workers' rights and the denial of adequate salaries.[79] Like the bishops, the magazine in 1977 and 1978 pressured editorially for a speedy return to democratic government. As intermediate steps towards this goal it also urged a termination of the state of emergency, the reconstruction of voting lists, the election of a constitutional assembly, and freedom for nongovernmental organizations (unions, universities, the press) to function without severe government controls.[80]

The articles appearing in *Mensaje* after 1976 also continued to provide some of the best analyses of the effect of repression on various aspects of public life—labor, health, agriculture, the legal system, and practices of the DINA (which was replaced in 1978 by the Center for National Information—CNI). As a result of this expanded critical stance assumed

---

[77] "Pronunciamiento militar," *Mensaje* 22 (October 1973): 468–70; "Un grito de alerta," *Mensaje* 22 (October 1973): 470–71; "Hacia un nuevo año," *Mensaje* 23 (January-February 1974): 9–10; "¿Rectificando una línea?," *Mensaje* 23 (March-April 1974): 78–80.

[78] Aldunate, "Remuneraciones y costos de vida," pp. 634–36; "Salarios y precios: ¿cómo sigue la situación?," pp. 186–88; Ruiz-Tagle, "El estatuto social de la empresa," *Mensaje* 24 (May 1975): 145–47; Alejandro González Poblete, "El anteproyecto del Código del Trabajo," *Mensaje* 24 (August 1975): 371–75; Sergio Molina, "La encrucijado actual de la política económica," *Mensaje* 24 (October 1975): 439–44.

[79] "¿Resquicios legales al revés?," *Mensaje* 25 (July 1976): 269–71; "Medios de comunicación social: libertad y bien común," *Mensaje* 26 (June 1977): 249–52; "Los detenidos desaparecidos: tragedia nacional," *Mensaje* 27 (July 1978): 357–61; "1° de mayo, día del trabajo," *Mensaje* 25 (May 1976): 141–45; "Demandas sindicales," *Mensaje* 27 (May 1978): 195–98.

[80] "¿Nueva institucionalidad?," *Mensaje* 26 (July 1977): 315–18; "Un plazo razonable," *Mensaje* 26 (September 1977): 471–74; "Pax interior y seguridad externa," *Mensaje* 26 (November 1977): 626–29; "El impasse de 1977 en el retorno a la democracia," *Mensaje* 27 (January-February 1978): 3–9; "La consulta: ¿un paso hacia la democracia?," *Mensaje* 27 (March-April 1978): 105–09; "Unica salida: la democracia," *Mensaje* 27 (May 1978): 191–94.

by the journal in recent years, the circulation jumped from 5,000 in 1974 to 11,4000 in 1976 to over 12,000 in 1979.[81]

Reprisals against Church-sponsored Programs

The government and the communication media soon came to recognize the political implications of these critical activities in Church-sponsored institutions and took steps to discredit their work and frighten their leaders. By mid-1974 strong attacks on the Committee of Peace appeared in *La Segunda* and in *El Mercurio* criticizing the ecumenical organization for sending damaging information abroad about internal domestic affairs and for disturbing the prevailing peace and order in the country.[82] By late 1974 periodic arrests of members of COPACHI in Santiago became regular occurrences. Those working in local social action projects of the Church, such as soup kitchens and self-help employment projects, were also raided at irregular intervals by the police and participants detained for short periods of time. In addition to this type of direct harassment, the government offered money to unemployed workers to attend neighborhood Church meetings and to report back on what was said and who was present.[83]

In November 1975, after a group of priests and nuns, some of whom were members of COPACHI, assisted four members of the MIR to gain asylum in foreign embassies, severe pressure was brought to bear on Church leaders to dissolve the ecumenical organization. Over a two-week period in November, eighteen clerical, religious, and lay participants in COPACHI were arrested. During this time Pinochet also sent a letter to the cardinal urging him to close down the organization since, he

---

[81] Eugenio Bergloid, "La situación sindical después de cuatro años," *Mensaje* 26 (December 1977): 697–700; Jorge Jiménez de la Jara, "Salud: orientaciones y realidades en los últimos tres años," *Mensaje* 25 (November 1976): 573–77; José Franco Mesa, "Agricultura 78: fuerte caída de la producción," *Mensaje* 27 (July 1978): 399–405; Felipe Adelmar R., "Variaciones de la neuva legalidad chilena," *Mensaje* 25 (September 1976): 409–14; Alejandro Quezada, "La lección de la DINA," *Mensaje* 27 (July 1978): 362–72.

[82] "¡Calumniadores contra Chile!," *La Segunda*, 16 May 1974, p. 1; *El Mercurio*, 6 July 1974; Ruiz-Tagle, "La iglesia frente a la prensa: los ataques al Comité para la Paz," pp. 265–67.

[83] In Santiago the phenomenon of "paid spies" attending Church activities was a well-known occurrence in 1975. The parishioners themselves were understanding of hungry neighbors who engaged in such activities in order to be able to put food on the table for their children. This did, however, make them cautious and fearful whenever repression arose as a topic for discussion in Church meetings or programs. I was asked by members in my community not to preach critical sermons on social issues, for fear of it being reported back to the police that they had attended a political rally.

said, it was "a means whereby Marxist-Leninists were creating problems threatening the civil order."[84]

The Greek Orthodox and Baptist Churches had withdrawn from the ecumenical committee out of concern that its activities were becoming too political, and Archbishop Tagle and Bishop Salinas openly criticized the priests and religious who had assisted members of the MIR in obtaining political asylum[85] Amidst such mounting criticisms and pressures on COPACHI, Cardinal Silva acquiesced to Pinochet's request that the organization be disbanded. In granting this concession, however, the cardinal denied that the committee had been "simply an instrument used by Marxist-Leninists to disturb the peace," praised the organization for the humanitarian work it carried out "under very difficult circumstances," and committed the Church to continue such activities on behalf of the poor "within our own respective ecclesiastical structures."[86]

The ecumenical committee, therefore, was formally closed by the Church at the end of December 1975. The next month, however, the cardinal immediately set up a new organization, called the Vicariate of Solidarity. While there were some changes in personnel, the new organization continued the same services of COPACHI and was made an integral part of the juridical structures of the Archdiocese of Santiago. While the Church had lost a tactical skirmish with the government, the strategy of the cardinal was shrewd and foresighted. The new Vicariate of Solidarity was more closely tied to the official Church than its predecessor, making it both easier for the bishops to control and harder for the government to smash without directly attacking the core of the Church itself.

The Vicariate quickly established regional offices in twenty of the twenty-five provinces associated closely with chanceries, and over the course of the next four years provided legal, health, nutritional, and occupational services to more than 700,000 persons throughout the coun-

---

[84] *Chile-América 3* (November-December 1975): 41. The fact that Bishop Carlos Camus in late September had acknowledged in his off-the-record press interview that there were those with Marxist sympathies working in the Committee of Cooperation for Peace added fuel to the fire of government opposition to the organization.

[85] "Iglesia Ortodoxa se retiró del Comité por paz," *El Mercurio*, 10 November 1975, pp. 1, 8; "Obispos reprueban ayuda a los Miristas," *El Mercurio*, 9 November 1975, pp. 1, 8.

The Lutheran Church had undergone a formal schism due to strong opposition to COPACHI's work by its pro-junta German-speaking members. A majority of its congregations (mainly in the South) split off and formed a second Lutheran Church in June 1975, leaving only a minority headed by Bishop Helmut Frenz (copresident of COPACHI) as participants in the ecumenical human rights organization. Fernando Salas, S.J., "Crisis en la Iglesia Luterana Chilena," *Mensaje* 24 (July 1975): 312–15.

[86] *Chile-América 3* (November-December 1975): 42.

try. In 1979 alone, over 5 million hot meals were served to hungry children, and a whole series of training, credit, and technical assistance programs were expanded in the countryside.[87]

The Vicariate also inaugurated the publication of a biweekly bulletin (*Solidaridad*) that circulates in parishes throughout the country. It publishes accounts of the various projects the Vicariate has undertaken, as well as articles on problems affecting workers, peasants, and students. *Solidaridad* has reached a circulation of over 30,000 copies which are distributed gratis throughout the network of parishes, small base communities, and social action projects of the Vicariate. In addition, the Vicariate has undertaken the printing and dissemination of pamphlets or supplements in its bulletin on special topics of poular concern, such as the status of investigations regarding disappeared persons, the opinions of labor leaders on the rights of unions, and recent papal and international episcopal statements on social justice and human rights.[88] In such a way, an effective source of communication and information among Church personnel and others at the local level has been maintained that can counter the distortions presented in the secular media.

Although public attacks and harassment of the Vicariate was unleashed by the media and the government in late 1976 (similar to those that had been launched against the Committee of Cooperation for Peace before), the bishops stood firmly behind it. Unlike its predecessor, the Vicariate is not an ecumenical organization and is considered an integral part of the Catholic Church. Furthermore, by the time government leaders and sympathizers began to discredit the Vicariate, the Catholic bishops had already closed ranks and decided upon a more consistent policy of public opposition to the regime, especially in cases where they judged the core interests of the institutional Church to be at stake. The Vicariate, therefore, has continued to function with strong episcopal support, and besides basic humanitarian services provides a surrogate form of social participation and a network of accurate information in the absence of viable secular means to accomplish these ends.

In late 1975 the junta also made some initial attempts to silence *Mensaje*. The government sent a letter to the bishops individually expressing concern over what it considered a continuing policy of irresponsibility by *Mensaje* and asking how strongly each prelate supported the journal. This occurred just at the time the media was mounting another campaign to discredit Church leaders (Bishop Carlos Camus, the secretary for the Episcopal Conference, and the cardinal himself), as described

---

[87] *Vicaría de la Solidaridad: segundo año de labor*, p. 171; *Vicaría de la Solidaridad: cuarto año de labor*, pp. 60-69, 83, 104.

[88] *Vicaría de la Solidaridad: un año de labor*, pp. 123-32; *Vicaría de la Solidaridad: segundo año de labor*, p. 171; *Vicaría de la Solidaridad: tercer año de labor*, p. 81.

previously. In this context, the Permanent Committee of the Episcopal Conference, responding to a request from the editors of *Mensaje,* issued a strong public endorsement of the magazine. In their statement, the bishops said that in recent years *Mensaje* had become "more closely linked to the mission of the Church," and expressed a "fervent desire" that it continue its "positive effort of clarification" of crucial issues affecting the country.[89] The government ceased in its efforts to have the bishops disassociate themselves from *Mensaje* as a preliminary step to suppressing it, but only after having won from them what the administration considered to be a more important concession—the dissolution of the Committee of Cooperation for Peace in December 1975.

An important structural resource of the Church for public influence that was successfully curtailed by the government is its educational institutions. The Catholic University network accounts for over 16 percent of all enrollments in higher education, and the Church's primary and secondary system educates approximately 18 percent of all schoolchildren in the country. By 1973, however, 90 percent of the operating budget of the Catholic university system and approximately 50 percent of the finances for Catholic primary and secondary schools came from public subsidies. Unlike Allende, the junta exploited this dependency of Catholic education on the state. It moved quickly to consolidate control over all levels of education, both public and private, so as to eliminate what it considered Marxist influences in schools and universities.

The junta appointed military rectors in all universities in October 1973, including those in the Catholic university system in Santiago, Valparaíso, and Antofagasta. They exercised the same hiring and firing privileges as their counterparts in the state universities, and used these powers to dismiss countless faculty and students formerly sympathetic to the Popular Unity or Christian Democracy. Furthermore, courses in social sciences, journalism, and fine arts in the Catholic University of Santiago were severely curtailed, and greater emphasis was placed on science and technology along with required courses on aspects of national security. The television and radio networks associated with these universities were also given over to government sympathizers. Moreover, scholarship assistance was cut back considerably and students from low-income families constitute a much lower percentage of the student body

[89] "Carta de los obispos a *Mensaje,*" Santiago, 30 December 1975, *Mensaje* 25 (January-February 1976): 1. In this letter the bishops were sending a message to both the junta and to the editors of *Mensaje.* To the former, they were saying implicitly that if you attack the magazine you are attacking the Church. To the latter, they were gently but clearly chiding the Jesuits for distancing themselves from the hierarchy in 1968 (described in Chapter 6), and reminding them to stay close to the bishops if they wanted continued protection against the state.

than in the Frei and Allende years. Between 1973 and 1978 state subsidies were curtailed 10 percent each year, and the number of first-year students at the Catholic University in Santiago declined by over 11 percent.[90]

The military also placed restrictions on Catholic primary schools, subjecting them to the same controls imposed on public schools. Books which local military commanders believed an attempt "to indoctrinate students with strange ideologies" were banned, parents' councils were limited in their scope of activities, public subsidies were reduced, and health and nutritional services administered through schools cut back. By 1977 enrollments in private grammar and high schools (the majority of which are Catholic) had fallen by more than 13 percent since the coup, and the ones most affected were students from families of modest income.[91]

The opposition of the hierarchy to such controls on Catholic education has been less vigorous and successful than their strong criticism of the restrictions only contemplated by Allende. Unlike the ENU plan of Allende, however, the junta never announced a comprehensive plan or ideology for education that openly challenged the Church's freedom and objectives. They continued to espouse educational principles in public that are close to those of the Church—the primacy of spiritual values, the importance of community participation in the learning process, the crucial significance of the private sector in education. The controls they imposed on private schools were originally justified as emergency short-term measures necessary to eradicate Marxist influence on education. Given the cautious and optimistic public positions of the bishops regarding the regime during its first three years in power, the bishops as a group chose not to confront the government on a problem many believed to be short-term in nature and not based upon fundamental differences of principle between themselves and the military.[92]

[90] Paul P. Meyers, "La intervención militar de las universidades chilenas," *Mensaje* 24 (August 1975): 379–84; Centro de Investigaciones Socioeconómicos (CISEC), "Estudios sectorales de la estructura social chilena 1978: sector universidad," mimeographed (Santiago, May 1978), p. 23; Ernesto Livacic G., "Nuevos caminos para la universidad," *Mensaje* 29 (September 1979): 573–75. The best comprehensive treatment in English of the changes in universities effected by the military has been done by Daniel Levy, "Chilean University Policy under the Junta."

[91] *El Mercurio*, 10 October 1973, p. 21; Carlos Hurtado E., S.J. "Las subvenciones de la educación particular gratuita," *Mensaje* 24 (October 1975): 447–50; "¿Qué pasará con los colegios subvencionados?," *Mensaje* 26 (August 1977): 432–38; Dr. Luis Bravo, "Cuatro aspectos de la crisis del sistema educacional escolar," *Mensaje* 27 (August 1978): 484–90.

[92] *Declaración de principios de gobierno de Chile*, p. 36; Raimundo Barros, S.J., "¿Crisis educacional superada? ideales y realidades," *Mensaje* 27 (July 1978): 413–17. The cardinal, however, did resign his post as chancellor of the Catholic University in Santiago in October 1974 in protest over the firing practices of the military rector.

Moreover, the hierarchy has much less possibility of effecting changes in government policies in education now than they did under Allende. Even in 1976 when they finally came to recognize the threat to the Church's interest posed by the government both in principle and in practice, the bishops had little opportunity for exercising effective influence. They could successfully fight Allende on this issue since they joined with other cogent allies (the military, some of the press, opposition party leaders) who were also against ENU. Allende by early 1973 was also in a vulnerable position politically, and wanted the continued legitimating support of the Church to hold together a consensus for constitutional government. None of these factors characterized the political context under the military junta who enjoy absolute power, who allow no party or congressional opposition to their policies, and who have consistently ignored the Church's message even after 1976 when it has been clear and specific.

The most significant factor of all that accounted for the hierarchy's relative silence and ineffectual opposition to greater public control over Catholic education, however, has been the financial dependency of Church-sponsored universities and schools on the state. Under such conditions, the potentially important structural resource of the Church to inculcate critical attitudes among youth in opposition to the ideology of the regime has been severely handicapped. Other organizational apostolates sponsored by the Church since the coup, such as human rights committees, nutritional and health services, neighborhood self-help programs, and *Mensaje,* are all financially independent from the Chilean government, and hence far less vulnerable to its control. Catholic schools have not enjoyed such autonomy over the past generation which has been a result of the incomplete extrication of the Church from the state in 1925 (described in Chapter 3) and the lack of adequate lay support for the Church's educational apostolate. While this was not a major problem during the Frei and Allende administrations which were both willing to support private education as it became more attuned to issues of social change and the needs of the poor, such lack of financial autonomy has become a serious drawback for the Church under a government that is afraid of academic freedom and insensitive to the poor.

This strategy had no impact on the junta's educational controls or policies.

In 1975 the cardinal, with financial aid from the West German bishops and subsequently from the U.S. Inter-American Foundation, established the Academy of Christian Humanism to provide research support for professors and scholars of various ideological persuasions who lost their university jobs for political reasons. The academy supports about a dozen full-time research associates and close to 100 part-time affiliate scholars. They conduct research on various social, economic, and political issues affecting Chile, publishing the results in a journal called *Análisis.* Francisco Lopez F., *La crítica de la iglesia chilena,* pp. 61–62.

SUPPORTIVE INTERNATIONAL RESOURCES FOR CHILEAN
CHURCH COMMITMENTS TO HUMAN RIGHTS

The most significant factor in sustaining the Chilean Church's words and actions on behalf of human rights is its resource transactions with the international Church. Since 1973 papal, Vatican, and international episcopal statements all provided strong legitimation for involvement in the promotion of human rights by national Churches around the globe. In some cases moral and political support has been given by these international Church groups to the Chilean Church's particular efforts in this area. Furthermore, at the regional level of Latin America itself the Latin American Episcopal Conference (CELAM) has focused attention on the dangers of the national security state and has emphasized the Church's responsibility to oppose it. What has been even more important has been the significant increase of financial assistance to the Chilean Church since the coup from international ecclesiastical and secular sources in support of its various programs for the defense of human rights. Without such massive outside help none of these new commitments would have been possible.

*Moral and Political Support from the International Church
for Commitments to the Defense of Human Rights*

International Church leaders since 1973 have provided strong encouragement for local Churches to concern themselves with the defense of human rights. Documents issued by Pope Paul VI and Pope John Paul II,[93] by the Vatican,[94] by international bishops' meetings,[95] and national episcopal conferences[96] in recent years have all stressed the necessity for the Church to make part of its work the protection of the basic rights of all persecuted persons throughout the world.

Pope Paul VI also expressed concern over human rights violations in Chile specifically at several key moments during the first months after the coup, thus encouraging the local hierarchy to take a public position. On 16 September 1973, three days after the first critical statement by the Permanent Committee of the Episcopal Conference, Pope Paul

---

[93] Pope Paul VI, "Message on XXV Anniversary of Human Rights Declaration," *L'Osservatore Romano* (English Edition), 20 December 1973, p. 3; "Evangelization in the Contemporary World," *L'Osservatore Romano* (English Edition), 25 December 1975, pp. 1-6, 11-13; Pope John Paul II, *The Redeemer of Man*, no. 17, pp. 35-39.

[94] Pontifical Commission for Justice and Peace, "The Church and Human Rights" (1975), pp. 344-93.

[95] Synod of Bishops, Fourth General Assembly, "Evangelización y derechos humanos," pp. 591-92; El Episcopado de la Región Andina, "La iglesia y la Integración Andina," Lima, 4 May 1976, *Mensaje* 25 (June 1976): 255-57.

[96] U.S. Catholic Conference, Administrative Board, "Human Rights Violations in Chile," Washington, D.C., 13 February 1974, p. 19.

publicly expressed deep regret over the "tragic drama" occurring in Chile. On 7 October in a Sunday allocution he remarked that the "violent oppressions" in Chile were causing him "profound concern."[97] In April 1974, just prior to the meeting of the Chilean bishops that produced their first acknowledgement of human rights violations in the country, the pope sent them a cable urging a renewal of their commitment "to help those most in need, especially the poorest sectors" of the population.[98] The pope also gave strong support to Cardinal Silva on each of his annual visits to Rome after the coup, encouraging him and the other members of the Chilean hierarchy to continue their various programs on behalf of human rights.

Moreover, the United States Catholic Conference (USCC), in conjunction with several Protestant Church agencies in the United States, in 1974 mounted public education and lobbying efforts to effect changes in U.S. aid policies to authoritarian governments in Latin America, and particularly to Chile. The Office of International Justice and Peace of the USCC, the Human Rights Office of the National Council of Churches, and the Washington Office on Latin America (sponsored by twenty-two different Protestant and Catholic Church groups) all have acted as effective channels of communication to the North American public on human rights violations in Chile since the coup, and have testified before congressional subcommittees considering limitation on U.S. aid to the Chilean military government.[99]

While these efforts by themselves were not the only determining factors in changing U.S. government policy toward Chile between 1977 and 1980, they were important contributory elements encouraging the Congress and the Carter Administration in their own new initiatives in this area. They were also signs of a growing international ecclesiastical concern that supports the promotion of human rights by local Churches in authoritarian regimes.

Hence, unlike Christians for Socialism movements in the early 1970s which encountered significant opposition from several key sectors of the international Church, the promotion of human rights by local Church groups under authoritarian regimes has received strong encouragement at all major levels of the international Church. This provided the Chilean Church with significant moral and political reinforcement to sustain its own efforts in this area in face of government opposition.

---

[97] L'Osservatore Romano, 17–18 September 1973, p. 1; L'Osservatore Romano, 8–9 October 1973, p. 1.

[98] Excerpts of the cable are reprinted in Franz Vanderschueren and Jaime Rojas, "La iglesia católica y la junta militar: I Parte," Chile-América 4 (January-February 1976): 50.

[99] Philip L. Ray and J. Sherrod Taylor, "The Role of Nongovernmental Organizations in Implementing Human Rights in Latin America," pp. 484–89; Lewis H. Diuguid, "Lobbying for Human Rights," Worldview 21 (September 1978): 9–12.

Financial Support from International Sources for the
Chilean Church's Programs to Promote Human Rights

Even more important than the moral and political support provided by various international religious organizations for the Chilean
Church's commitment to human rights has been the massive amount of
financial and material aid from Church and government sources in
Western Europe and North America. None of the new projects begun
under the auspices of the Chilean Church since 1973 could have been
inaugurated or sustained over time without very considerable outside
support.

The first part of Table 9.2 graphically portrays how important foreign
aid has been to the Chilean Catholic Church since the coup as compared
to internally generated sources of support. Catholic organizations in
Western Europe and North America have donated more than $67 mil-
lion in money and materials (food, clothing, medicines) to Chile between 1974 and 1979. The Inter-American Foundation funded by the
U.S. Congress and Zentralstelle of the West German government have
together provided an additional $20 million in grants to Church-spon-
sored projects, all of which have as their goal the promotion of economic
development or human rights. Despite steady increases in contributions
by Chilean lay Catholics to their Church over the same period, the total
amount collected from annual tithing campaigns (CALI) has been only
$4 million.[100]

The second part of Table 9.2, however, illustrates how small this foreign assistance to the Church has been in comparison to the support
given to the Chilean government by public and private agencies in
Western Europe and the United States during the same time span. Despite citizen pressures on governments in these regions not to help the
Chilean junta (reflected in declining public aid to the regime since
1976), private banks in the United States and Western Europe have
more than made up for losses in public assistance. Part three of the table
shows that since 1976 foreign private banks substantially increased loans
to Chilean private businesses, which greatly profits from a stable regime
that represses labor and reduces public enterprise.[101]

---

[100] Various Protestant agencies in Western Europe and North America have also
sent considerable financial assistance to Church-sponsored human rights projects
since 1973, much of which has been channeled through the World Council of
Churches in Geneva. Although exact figures are not for public distribution (and
therefore are not included in Table 9.2), it is estimated that for this six-year period
the total amount of assistance to both Catholic and Protestant projects coming
through just the World Council of Churches was in the vicinity of $10 million.

[101] The severe repression of labor organizations, the selling of state enterprises back
to private groups, and a reduction of tariff barriers to an average of 10 percent on
imported goods (except automobiles) by the late 1970s was attracting much new
private foreign capital into Chile. Aside from some new investments, almost all in
the mining sector (amounting to less than $500 million net), the vast bulk of the new

Table 9.2
Foreign Aid to Chile, 1974–1979
(In U.S. Dollars)

A. Contributions to Chilean Church-sponsored Programs

Year	West European Catholic Church Organizations		North American Catholic Church Organizations		West German Government	U.S. Government	Chilean Catholics
	W. Germany	Other Countries	U.S.A.	Canada	(Zentralstelle)	(IAF)	(CALI)
1974	$ 2,462,556	$ 407,214	$ 4,439,982	$ 226,268	$ 168,699	$ 975,787	$ 155,106
1975	2,536,525	570,432	5,184,454	309,784		2,791,545	201,241
1976	3,146,290	1,749,228	5,333,296	312,300	1,425,000	2,370,240	361,636
1977	4,194,374	1,098,051	8,568,166	240,900		3,143,180	707,479
1978	6,104,151	1,323,373	4,448,800	211,200	2,126,042	1,817,824	1,160,873
1979	6,362,305	2,177,450	6,019,858	175,900	3,911,136	2,231,994	
Totals	$24,806,201	$7,325,748	$33,994,556	$1,476,352	$7,630,877	$13,330,570	$4,015,889

B. New Public and Private Loan Commitments to Chilean Government (in millions of U.S. Dollars)

Year	Western Governments	International Public Organizations (IMF, IBD, IBRD)	Private Banks in U.S. and Western Europe	Total Loans
1974	$307.9	$137.9	$ 304.7	$ 750.5
1975	119.1	65.5	216.6	401.2
1976	140.3	97.3	245.0	482.6
1977	23.4	64.9	871.9	960.2
1978	55.1	26.7	1,676.9	1,758.7
1979	2.5	34.2	768.7	805.4
Totals	$648.3	$426.5	$4,084.8	$5,158.6

C. New Loan Commitments to Chilean Private Enterprise (in millions of U.S. Dollars)

Year	Private Banks in U.S. and Western Europe
1974	$ 48
1975	228
1976	131
1977	208
1978	589
1979	992
Totals	$2,196

Foreign Grants to Church	$ 88.5 (1.2%)
Foreign Loans to Government	5,158.6 (69.3%)
Foreign Loans to Private Enterprise	2,196.0 (29.5%)
Total Foreign Grants or Loans to Chile	$7,443.1 (100%)

SOURCES: Data in Part A of Table 9.2 includes contributions from all the same Catholic organizations in Western Europe and North America mentioned in Table 2.9. In addition, this table includes contributions from Trocaire in Ireland, Briderlech Delen in Luxemburg, and CEBEMO in the Netherlands. CEBEMO, like Catholic Relief Services in the United States and Misereor in West Germany, channels significant amounts of government aid to development projects sponsored by Catholic Churches in third-world countries. Between 1976 and 1978, CEBEMO provided approximately one-third of all non-German European assistance to the Chilean Church, which included significant amounts from the Dutch government. Data for Part A of the table was provided to me by CIDSE in Brussels, the coordinating federation to which most of them belong.
Data in Part B of Table 9.2 is from International Bank for Reconstruction and Development (IBRD), World Debt Tables, EC–167/80 (Washington, D.C.: IBRD, 1980), 1:46, 48, 50.
Data in Part C of Table 9.2 is from Banco Central de Chile, Boletín Mensual, no. 628 (June 1980), p. 1053.

Heavy reliance of the Chilean Church on outside funding, documented earlier, substantially increased after the coup. The number of Chilean families contributing 1 percent of their annual income to the Church (CALI) did grow significantly from 70,566 in 1973 to 160,682 in 1979, and this increased autonomous financing for the Church. This was still totally inadequate, however, to sustain its new programs on behalf of human rights. Without the massive resource transfers from religious and governmental agencies abroad, the expansion of the infrastructure of the Chilean Church to perform humanitarian tasks would not have been possible.

Vulnerability of the Chilean Churches
from Dependency on Foreign Support
   While internal Church tensions regarding foreign Church aid subsided after the coup, a different set of problems emerged affecting Church-state relations. Neither the government of Frei nor of Allende placed any restrictions on foreign assistance to Chilean Catholic organizations. The present military government, however, has made several efforts to discredit and reduce foreign sources of Church support despite how small these have been relative to the total foreign aid flowing into Chile.

---

capital flowing into Chile since the 1973 coup has been in the form of loans from foreign private banks. Very little of these loans to the government and to Chilean businesses, however, have been used to expand the country's industrial capacity, or its production of basic goods for the domestic market. The bulk has gone to repay former foreign debts, to support expanded imports of manufactured goods and basic food commodities, or to bankroll speculators charging extremely high interest rates (50 percent or more annually) for short-term loans to Chilean businesses. The result has been very harmful for the social and economic needs of the workers, peasants, and much of the middle class. Not only have government-subsidized social services been severely curtailed, but trends in the private sector have reduced employment opportunities for blue collar and white collar workers. Other than financial speculation and export-oriented mining (copper) and agriculture (fruit and wood products) the Chilean economy since 1973 has been seriously depressed. Both the government and private enterprise have become dependent on ever-increasing loans from foreign banks—not revenues from an increased tax base or earnings from expanded production—to pay their debts. Juan Guillermo Espinosa, "El endeudamiento externo entre 1973 y 1979: una comparación internacional," in *Chile: liberalismo económico y dictadura política,* ed. Sergio Bitar, pp. 68–93; Karen Remmer, "Public Policy and Regime Consolidation: The First Five Years of the Chilean Junta"; Patricio Meller, René Cortázar, and Jorge Marshall, "Employment Stagnation in Chile, 1974–1978," *Latin American Research Review* 16 (1981): 144–58; Tomás Moulián and Pilar Vergara, "Estado, ideología y políticas económicas en Chile: 1973–1978," *Colección Estudios CIEPLAN* (Santiago), no. 3 (June 1980):65–120; Ricardo Ffrench-Davis, "Liberalización de las importaciones: la experiencia Chilena, 1973–1979," *Colección Estudios CIEPLAN,* no. 4 (November 1980):39–78; Pilar Vergara, "Apertura externa y desarrollo industrial en Chile: 1973–1978, *Colección Estudios CIEPLAN,* no. 4 (November 1980):79–117.

In early 1975, the military issued a decree requiring organizations with a private law juridical personality to report all their currency transactions with groups outside Chile. The main target of the edict was the Committee of Cooperation for Peace. The purpose was to gain full and detailed disclosure of all COPACHI's financing.

COPACHI ignored this requirement since, from its founding in late 1973, it was covered by the legal personality of the Archdiocese of Santiago. Under the terms of the separation of the Church and state in 1925, described in Chapter 3, the Catholic Church was recognized as having public law juridical personality (*personalidad jurídica de Derecho Público*). While the nature of the committee was ecumenical in sponsorship and administration, it was also legally affiliated to the Roman Catholic Church and therefore enjoyed the privileges of the Church under the law. Since 1975, however, all Protestant denominations, none of which have a public law juridical personality, have had to make disclosures to the Chilean government regarding the assistance they receive from abroad.

In late 1977 the government renewed its campaign against foreign contributions to Chilean Catholic and Protestant Churches. In November, Pinochet publicly accused the Vicariate of Solidarity of helping communists, and criticized one of its primary benefactors—the World Council of Churches—for financing subversion in Africa and for sending over $2 million annually to Chile to underwrite similar subversive activities. A statement of the Archdiocese of Santiago defended both the Vicariate and the World Council of Churches. It praised those working in both organizations for their "selfless work of evangelical service." The Vicariate publicly termed such accusations falsehoods. It also emphasized that the Roman Catholic Church and the World Council of Churches in recent years have established closer cooperative relationships in different parts of the world, strongly suggesting that a vilifying campaign against the council was also an attack on the Catholic Church.[102]

The government ceased its public criticisms of foreign Church organizations, but soon thereafter attempted to stop the assistance coming to Chilean Churches from the Inter-American Foundation, an agency of the United States government. In January 1978 security forces in a search operation captured documents related to IAF's grants to Chilean groups critical of the government. Shortly afterwards, *El Mercurio* printed a full-page disclosure of the programs supported by the IAF in Chile after the coup, almost all of which were under the aegis of the

[102] Salas, "Crisis en la Iglesia Luterana Chilena," p. 313; "Declaración del Arzobispado," Santiago, 29 November 1977; "Respuesta del Boletín 'Solidaridad,' " Santiago, 29 November 1977, *Mensaje* 27 (January-February 1978): 80–82.

Catholic Church, thus attempting to create the impression of large-scale foreign support to dissident groups in Chile.[103] Subsequently the Chilean Central Bank in one instance froze funds coming into Chile from the IAF through the Inter-American Development Bank (IDB) which dispenses some of the funds at the IAF's disposal.

The United States ambassador, members of the U.S. Congress, and representatives of the IDB all protested strongly against such tactics, and the Chilean Central Bank subsequently released the funds. The Chilean government could not afford to alienate both the U.S. Congress and international lending institutions simultaneously, since it had to renegotiate the scheduling of its large debt payments to the United States and international public financial institutions. Such interferences with the free flow of currency could have also undermined its attempts to maintain and attract more foreign private loans and credits and establish a favorable climate in Chile for international business. Given these serious economic constraints, the Chilean government ceased such harassments, and IAF support continued to provide very considerable assistance to Chilean Church-sponsored projects in the area of social development in the late 1970s.[104]

While the Chilean Church was able to avoid effective restrictions on its foreign finances it has not been as successful in defending its foreign personnel. About one-half of all the priests in Chile between 1960 and 1973 were foreigners (see Table 2.7). While this created no serious Church-state problems before 1973, after the coup the junta forced

---

[103] "La Inter-American Foundation y sus programas en Chile," *El Mercurio*, 25 January 1978, p. 24. The piece printed the requests presented to IAF, and also the matching funds sought from other sources, by twenty-one different projects in Chile between late 1973 and 1977—almost all of which were Church-affiliated. The total sum purportedly given by IAF listed at the end of the article came to just over $37 million for the four-year period. This was a definite distortion of the facts. Based on data provided by the IAF itself, Table 9.2 shows that its total assistance to programs affiliated with the Chilean Church between 1974 and 1977 was less than one-fourth ($9 million) of what *El Mercurio* insinuated.

[104] Beginning in 1980 the Chilean government began to repay its outstanding debt to the United States directly to the U.S. government in dollars instead of pesos. This would have as one of its primary effects limiting the money available to the IAF to spend in Chile. Since the 1960s Chile, like many Latin American countries, had been repaying its U.S. debt in its own national currency. Such currency was not given to the U.S. Treasury but was deposited each year in the Social Progress Trust Fund administered by the Inter-American Development Bank for recycling back into social and economic programs in each of the respective countries. The IAF is the only U.S. government agency allowed to draw upon the fund, and between 1977 and 1979 it used the equivalent of US $6.2 million in Chilean pesos deposited in the fund by the Chilean government to support projects in Chile. After 1980, however, the IAF will have to rely only on direct U.S. congressional appropriations (which have tended to be much less each year than what was available in the fund) for its Chilean activities since Chilean pesos are no longer available. (Telephone interview with James O'Brien, Inter-American Foundation, 28 January 1981).

many of the priests to leave the country. Table 9.3 indicates that during the first two years after the coup the Church suffered a loss of 380 clerics, the overwhelming majority of whom were foreigners (314 of 380). While the number of Chilean priests increased significantly after 1975, the number of foreigners continued to decline so that after six years of military rule the Church had suffered a net loss of 265 priests (11 percent of the 1973 total).

Many of these foreigners had been sympathetic to the Christians for Socialism movement, or had publicly identified with the goals of the Allende Administration. After the coup a few were murdered, several were arrested and expelled, and others had their permanent residency permits revoked by the government. Some simply left the country soon after the coup knowing full well that they were marked persons, and could not continue to function in Chile without serious danger to themselves and their parishioners.

The mainline Protestant Churches also experienced some losses of their foreign-born pastors who were expelled or left under duress after the coup. Many of these had also been sympathetic to Allende's goals and some were active members of Christians for Socialism.

The most critical loss among the liberal Protestants was Bishop Helmut Frenz, the German-born head of the Lutheran Church and co-president of the Committee of Cooperation for Peace. Frenz was responsible for much of the original funding of COPACHI, which came from Protestant sources in Western Europe upon its founding in 1973. Thereafter, he made frequent trips to Western Europe to collect additional funds and disseminate information about COPACHI. In June 1975, the secular media mounted a major vilification campaign to discredit Frenz for allegedly spreading lies about Chile abroad and for openly defending the Allende government in Europe.[105] As he was leaving the country in September 1975 on a trip to visit friends and family in Germany, his residency permit was revoked.

In my interviews with Catholic Church leaders in 1975 I asked them about the expulsion of priests and how they evaluated the impact on the Church. Two-thirds of the bishops (nineteen out of thirty) told me that their dioceses had lost some priests since the coup, indicating that the loss affected many dioceses throughout the country. Table 9.4 indicates that, in those areas that lost priests, the great majority of the bishops (68.4 percent) felt that it was better that such men left since the hierarchy considered them controversial personalities. Local Church leaders in these dioceses, however, were far more divided in their opinions. A significant percentage of the priests, nuns, and lay leaders did not express a

---

[105] "Las iglesias de Chile," *El Mercurio*, 24 June 1975, p. 2.

judgment on the issue due to a lack of personal knowledge of the men who left or due to the sensitivity of the question, but only one-third or less in each group agreed with the bishops' conclusion that it was better for the Chilean Church that they departed. Many of these local leaders (including one-quarter of the priests, one-fifth of the nuns, and nearly one-third of the laity) considered the loss to be crucial.

Although there was widespread consensus at all levels of the Church that many priests had become too much involved in politics during the past decade, as described in Chapter 8, only the bishops expressed a positive opinion about the expulsion of such men by the military. So deep was their concern over what they considered a challenge to hierarchical authority and to the formal unity of the Church presented by such clerics that the bishops considered the exodus of these priests as a positive benefit to the good order of the institution. Leaders at the lower echelons less responsible for such organizational concerns, however, felt the loss of these foreigners more deeply since it left the Church much weaker pastorally than before.

Had the hierarchy vigorously protested and defended these men during the first months after the coup when the junta sought legitimacy from the Church, it would have been more difficult for the government to expel them. Nevertheless, the revocation of residency permits to foreigners was much easier for the junta to execute than blocking foreign private and public money from coming into the country. This is a prerogative of political sovereignty and could be done without fears of political or economic sanctions from abroad. The absence of such external pressures on behalf of these priests, coupled with the acquiescence of the hierarchy, sealed the fate of the clerics and paved the way to their quick exodus.

Regardless of how leaders at different levels of the Church judged the explusion of these foreign clerics, the effect of their withdrawal was to reduce significantly the number of priests available for sacramental ministry in the country. The Church suffered a net loss of 11 percent of its priests in six years with the result that each priest in Chile in 1979 had to minister to 1,500 more baptized than in 1973. Although this provided an additional stimulus for new lay ministry, it also meant that the celebration of the Eucharist and the granting of absolution (functions that only priests can perform) were less available to Catholics in Chile than before the coup, especially in poor areas where most of these foreign priests served.

The expulsion of foreign clerics has also occurred in recent years in Africa (South Africa, Rhodesia, Uganda) and Asia (South Korea, the Philippines). In other Latin American countries besides Chile between 1968 and 1978, several hundred (mostly foreigners) were expelled by

Table 9.3
Nationality of Clergy in Chile, 1973–1979

Year	Chilean Priests	Foreign Priests	Total	Catholics per Priest
1973	1,289 (51.7%)	1,202 (48.3%)	2,491	3,251
1975	1,223 (57.9%)	888 (42.1%)	2,111	4,336
1979	1,402 (63%)	824 (37%)	2,226	4,760
Net Change Since Coup:	+113	−378	−265 (−11%)	+1,509

SOURCE: Office of Religious Sociology (OSORE), Episcopal Conference of Chile; Raimundo Barros, S.J., "Vitalidad de la iglesia chilena," *Mensaje* 29 (January–February 1980): 27–28.

Table 9.4
Opinions Concerning the Loss of Foreign Priests in Dioceses Where Some Were Forced to Leave (1975)
"Do you think the loss of foreign priests since the end of 1973 is a very crucial one, or do you think it is better that they have left because they were controversial?"

	Bishops (N = 19)	Priests (N = 31)	Nuns (N = 24)	Laity (N = 35)	Totals (N = 129)
1. It is better that they left	68.4% (13)	33.3% (17)	29.2% (7)	22.9% (8)	34.9% (45)
2. It is a very crucial loss	10.5 (2)	25.5 (13)	20.8 (5)	31.4 (11)	24.0 (31)
3. In some cases it was better that they left, but in other cases it is a loss since they were doing good pastoral work	21.1 (4)	7.9 (4)	16.7 (4)	8.6 (3)	11.6 (15)
4. Don't know, no answer	—	33.3 (17)	33.3 (8)	37.1 (13)	29.5 (38)

military governments for purportedly meddling in politics. Such losses are a definite impairment of the religious mission of Churches. They are also proof that dependency on foreign personnel makes religious institutions very vulnerable to governments who consider such foreigners threats to national security.[106]

SHIFTING CLASS ALLEGIANCES AND LATENT TENSIONS OVER NEW MINISTRIES BY NONCLERICS

One of the most significant factors that has helped to offset the loss of a considerable number of priests in Chile since 1973 has been an increase of lay initiatives, especially among those previously alienated from the Church or those with no close association with it—middle-class Catholics with leftist sympathies, and working-class people. While Mass attendance has not increased dramatically, lay men and women from these groups have come forward to staff the new structures emerging in the Church at the diocesan and parish levels to promote human rights.In addition, small base communities, Bible and catechetical circles, and lay leadership programs all have taken on a new vitality since the coup.

These new developments have not occurred without some serious problems, both overt and latent. Wealthy Catholics, those with more conservative religious orientations, and reactionary groups have all expressed varying degrees of public opposition to the post-1973 Church that is more closely identified with the poor and respected by the Left. In addition, there are indications that serious differences of opinion, and even frustrations, are developing across levels of the Church's leadership regarding the degree to which the laity and women religious should be incorporated into ministerial positions.

---

[106] Since 1968, over 850 religious and clergy were arrested, tortured, expelled, or murdered in Latin America (many of whom were foreigners). "Amérique Latine: Dix ans de répression contre l'Église, *DIAL* (Paris), no. 497 (11 January 1979). In August 1980 Brazil further institutionalized the process by promulgating the "Lei dos Estrangeiros," whereby the Ministry of Interior could determine which foreigners could enter and stay on the basis of national security reasons and the economic priorities of the country's development plan. The law also gave the Ministry of Interior the right to move foreigners at will to different parts of the country, including priests (similar to the anticlerical Mexican Constitution of 1917). Although purportedly meant to protect Brazilian jobs against immigrant labor, a major purpose of the law was to exercise greater control of the Church, especially in the Amazon region where Church-state tensions over the murder of Indians are critical. Forty percent of priests in Brazil are foreign-born, and despite personal appeals by Pope John Paul II, by December 1980 the law was being used to expel some of those the government found troublesome. Roberto Suzedelo, "Church versus State," *Isto É* (São Paulo), 11 December 1980, p. 22.

New Adherents among Middle and Low-Income
Sectors Sympathetic to the Left

In the period following the coup among those who first volunteered their services to staff new Church-sponsored organizations to assist the persecuted were Catholics with leftist sympathies. The Committee of Cooperation for Peace, and later the Vicariate of Solidarity, attracted the support and participation of those who formerly had been active in MAPU and the Christian Left Party (MIC). Many of these young Catholics had criticized the Church in the late 1960s for its lack of evangelical simplicity and its slow-moving institutional apparatus. Now, in a different context, they saw ecclesiastical structures as assets since its organizational network offered a unique opportunity to work for human rights.

Of the more than 300 professional and staff personnel (lawyers, social workers, physicians, clerical help) who initiated projects of the Committee of Cooperation for Peace throughout the country, the majority were leftist Catholics previously alienated from the institution, and a few were non-Catholics formerly active in the Communist or Socialist parties.[107] They were later joined by increasing numbers of Christian Democrats as the PDC became more disillusioned with the goals and practices of the junta, but, along with several priests and nuns, the backbone of the original core team—both in Santiago and in the provinces—were Catholics formerly associated with leftist parties. Their participation in ecumenically-sponsored Church programs after the coup did not necessarily entail a return to participation in its sacramental life, but it did signal a renewal of respect for the Church, and in many instances a rekindling of religious faith.[108]

A similar pattern of closer identification with the Church by those with leftist views occurred among groups in the working class as well. The majority of those helped by the various social projects undertaken under the auspices of of the Committee of Cooperation for Peace, the Vicariate of Solidarity, and small base communities at the neighborhood level have been those who formerly supported Allende. Legal aid programs, assistance to prisoners and their families, self-help employment projects, day-care centers, and soup kitchens for children of those out of work have benefited the poor in general, but especially those persecuted or penalized by the regime for their political affiliations. Some of those administering such programs (at the neighborhood level) are lay people who in previous years had very little formal contact with the

---

[107] This judgment is based upon my own personal observations and conversations with several persons active in the Committee of Cooperation for Peace in 1975.

[108] Pablo Fontaine, "Algunos aspectos de la iglesia chilena," pp. 249–50.

Church due to their sympathies for, or involvement in, organizations closely linked with the Communist or Socialist parties.

While not engaging in overt partisan political activities, these programs do offer such persons the opportunity to preserve a sense of human solidarity and service to their neighborhoods. These projects have also included those sympathetic to Christian Democracy. Hence, practical cooperation in humanitarian activities is paving the way to greater mutual understanding and respect across progressive party lines that was sadly lacking in the last months of the Allende regime.[109]

Such new forms of tactical cooperation between the political Left and Center in poor areas under the auspices of the Church is a major concern of the military, and explains the continual harassment of human rights projects sponsored by the Committee of Cooperation for Peace and the Vicariate of Solidarity as well as surveillance of even strictly religious events. The attitudes of party leaders of the Left, however, have become even more positive toward the Church than they were during the early 1970s.

Luis Corvalán, secretary general of the Chilean Communist Party, said in exile in 1977 that he believed "religion is losing its character as 'opium of the people' " and the Church is becoming "more an inspirational force in the struggle for peace, liberty and justice." He specifically praised the Church in Chile for having "raised its voice in defense of human rights" and for demanding a return to constitutional order subject to the will of the people.[110]

Carlos Altamirano, secretary general of the Socialist Party, also gave a fairly positive assessment of the role of the Chilean Church. In a book analyzing the causes for the downfall of Allende published in 1977, he criticized those bishops who publicly have supported the military but expressed warm praise for what he believes to be a "sustained campaign" of resistance carried on by many clerics, especially those who "risked their freedom and their lives to hide those persecuted by the police."[111]

Hence, both the impact of the programs undertaken by the Church on behalf of human rights and the fact that those with leftist sympathies are participating significantly in their implementation have opened up whole new possibilities for Christian-Marxist rapprochement, especially

---

[109] This judgment is based upon personal observations and experiences in the parish I served in Santiago, and on conversations with priests, religious, and lay leaders in other working-class parishes throughout the country in 1975.

[110] Corvalán gave this interview to *Excelsior* in Mexico City in June, but parts of it subsequently were reprinted in Chile. "La iglesia chilena vista por Corvalán," p. 7.

[111] Carlos Altamirano, *Dialéctica de una derrota,* pp. 264-65.

at the neighborhood level in poor areas. While it is too early to say whether lasting changes are occurring in attitudes, there is no doubt that bridges of communication and cooperation are being constructed between Catholics and Marxists at the popular base that go far beyond the contact among elites that occurred during the Allende years—top echelon political leaders, intellectuals, and clerics. This cannot but have a significant effect on the future relationships between the Church and leftist parties, as well as the possibilities of a Center-Left civilian cooperation once the military have withdrawn from power.

Alienation of Upper-Income Catholics

Allegiances to the Church among upper-income sectors have deteriorated since 1973. Many find the new emphases in the Church on lay initiative and social awareness distasteful, and Integralism is still an attractive ideology among a small, but influential, group of Catholic intellectuals who support the military government. Some reactionary Catholics have openly denounced the hierarchy as heretics for not being more critical of Marxism and for not giving total support to the present government.

Several of the bishops and priests whom I interviewed in different parts of the country in 1975 remarked that they were concerned about the quality of faith and commitment to the new Church among wealthier Catholics. While Mass attendance was still higher in these areas in 1975 than in poorer sections, lay men and women were reluctant to volunteer their services for new forms of ministry—deacons, catechists, Bible study leaders, et cetera. These ministries and nonsacramental activities are done in small groups and require a sense of solidarity and willingness to share one's faith in public, but upper-income Catholics still prefer more private forms of piety. Furthermore, there is also reluctance by many of them to consider concern for social and economic problems as part of their religious commitment, and some find such new emphases in the Chilean Church as directly threatening to their security.[112]

One young university student from an upper-income neighborhood in Santiago rather caustically described to me what he believed to be the predominant style and priorities of his parish in 1975:

---

[112] Vatican II reinstituted the permanent lay deaconate in the Catholic Church, thereby permitting married laymen (especially in areas where there are not sufficient numbers of priests) to preach, baptize, distribute the Eucharist, and officiate at weddings and burial services. "Dogmatic Constitution on the Church," no. 29, in *Documents of Vatican II,* ed. Abbott, pp. 55–56. By 1975 there were over 100 married men functioning as deacons in the Chilean Catholic Church, but very few from upper-income groups.

... It is easy to sense a lack of interest on the part of the faithful, and a lack of attention to the sermon. In a word, Sunday Mass seems like one more obligation to fulfill.

The spirit of the residents who participate is one of self-justification and a means of tranquilizing their own consciences. I do not think there is any faith, much less a sense of Christian vocation present there.

Neither is there any denuciation by the priests as to the disappearance of people from our neighborhood. On the contrary, after the events of 11 September 1973 many people took advantage of the situation to denounce their own neighbors who had lived in the area for years, and who had expressed sympathies or identification with the Left. Others toasted the fall of the former government with champagne.

All this among those who ceremoniously rush to Mass every Sunday.[113]

Such an analysis may very well be overdrawn, and is certainly too simplistic in its conclusion as to a complete absence of faith among the rich. There are clearly many committed Christians in the comfortable neighborhoods of Santiago, some of whom I met personally and who assisted me in my working-class parish with contributions of money and time to alleviate some of the sufferings of the poor. Nevertheless, the general vitality of parish life in upper-income areas and willingness on the part of the laity there to take more responsibility in the formation of a new Church are much weaker than in middle and low-income sectors. Thus far very little progress has been made in developing their allegiances to a post-Medellín Church, and in some instances these people have distanced themselves from the institution.[114]

In addition to this problem of apathy to the Church among the more comfortable, there still is a small but influential group of intellectuals in

[113] Interview no. 124, 26 May 1975.

[114] During one of my interviews in 1975, a bishop from a major urban area (other than Santiago) confirmed this problem of reluctance among the rich to be part of the newly emerging Church. He told me that in his diocese:

Those above the middle class are totally lacking in a positive feeling towards the Church.... They are on the margin of the life of the Church. They send their children to Catholic schools. Many go to Mass and also receive Communion once a year, but the Church is not an important element in their lives. [Interview no. 013, 27 June 1975.]

See also Renato Poblete, S.J., "Los católicos de derecha," pp. 251-52. In a more recent (1980) study of religious attitudes in Santiago conducted by Centro Bellarmino, the same patterns were found. Wealthier Catholics as a group went to Mass more often and had a better knowledge of doctrine than did the poor, but they were more critical of the clergy, felt more alienated from the Church, and were less willing to accept a commitment to justice and to human development as integral parts of Christian life. Renato Poblete B., S.J., Carmen Galilea W., and Patricia van Dorp P., *Imagen de la iglesia de hoy y religiosidad de los chilenos,* pp. 156-58.

Chile who continue to propose Integralism as the only legitimate social ideology for Catholics. During the Allende years many of the proponents of Integralism became active in political organizations such as the National Party or the militant Fatherland and Freedom movement. Since the coup, however, the Integralists have reappeared as an independent force. Several hold key positions in the government, especially in the National Secretariats of Youth and of Women respectively. They also have been active in the communications media, providing much of the propaganda and intellectual capital for the junta's ideology.[115]

Furthermore, since the purging of many with Christian Democratic associations at the Catholic University of Santiago, those sympathetic to Integralism have once more become influential in the faculties of history and law, and members of Opus Dei hold important positions in the administration. At the Catholic University of Valparaíso there is a small but vocal group of Catholic Integralists who in their monthly journal, *Tizona*, have published articles justifying the principles of the junta as being most compatible with traditional Catholicism and insinuating that the Latin American Church (and particularly the Chilean Church) has been infiltrated by Marxists.[116]

All of these groups from upper and upper-middle-class sectors constitute a small percentage of the total Catholic population in the country, and have little support among the hierarchy and lower clergy. The positions of influence which adherents to this brand of Catholicism have occupied in the years following the coup in Chile, however, gives them access to private and public power far beyond what one could assume merely from their numbers. Given the current political context and the desire on the part of the government to find justifications for its principles and policies, Catholic Integralism has once again surfaced and acts as a formidable ideological force in government, in education, and in the media.[117]

A very militant expression of Integralism after the coup was articulated by the Society for the Defense of Tradition, Family and Property (TFP). The organization maintained a relatively low profile during Al-

---

[115] Thomas G. Sanders and Brian H. Smith, "The Chilean Catholic Church During the Allende and Pinochet Regimes," p. 16. See also the discussion of Catholic Integralists in Chile in Chapter 3 and Chapter 6.

[116] "El significado de la derrota marxista en Chile," *Tizona* (Valparaíso) (September-October 1973); "El marxismo invade la iglesia," *Tizona* (November 1973). These articles have been reprinted in Miguel Poradowski, ed., *El marxismo invade la iglesia.*

[117] In 1980 a renewal of strong criticism, and even libel, against the present leader)hip of the Chilean Church occurred in the secular media by some groups sympathetic to Catholic Integralism. Ruiz-Tagle, "Iglesia, gobierno y pueblo," *Mensaje* 29 (July 1980): 308-11.

lende's presidency, with some of its members joining right-wing movements and others going into self-imposed exile in Brazil or Argentina. The movement reappeared once the military were in power, and in 1976 launched a major public campaign to discredit the bishops. In a 450-page book published in February 1976, entitled *The Church of Silence in Chile,* the TFP claimed to represent the views of all those conservative Catholics in Chile who purportedly had been betrayed by their clergy and no longer had any voice in the Church. They argued that since 1960 almost all bishops and a decisive part of the priests in the country had been undermining traditional Catholic orthodox positions on social issues, especially in regard to private property and Marxism. They claimed, therefore, that the leadership of the Chilean Church was in heresy, and that Catholics had the right and the duty to resist such bishops and clergy. Opposition, they said, should take the form of condemning these ecclesiastical leaders publicly, preventing them from using their prestige to further damage the Church and Christian civilization in Chile, and severing all spiritual relations with them even to the point of refusing the sacraments from their hands.[118]

The reaction of the bishops to such a frontal attack on their own authority and upon the unity of the Church was as decisive as was their rejection of Christians for Socialism in October 1973. In early March 1976 the Permanent Committee of the Episcopal Conference issued a short but pointed public declaration, even more severe than the condemnation of CpS three years earlier. The bishops described the TFP as another example of a "parallel teaching office" that has plagued the Chilean Church in recent years. They reminded Catholics that the Church "is founded on Jesus Christ in communion with the Holy Father and the bishops" who are appointed with sole governing responsibilities, and that those "who do not accept this doctrine do not belong to the Catholic Church." They clearly stated that members of TFP who had "collaborated in these writings and in the campaign . . . have by their actions placed themselves outside the Catholic Church." The bishops also remarked that they found it "strange" that a government which proclaims Christian principles would allow such a publication to be circulated by persons who offend "Holy Mother the Church and call for disobedience to her legitimate pastors."[119]

---

[118] Sociedad Chilena de Defensa de la Tradición, Familia y Propiedad, *La iglesia del silencio en Chile,* pp. 377–400.

[119] "Declaración del Comité Permanente," Santiago, 9 March 1976, *Mensaje* 25 (July 1976): 316. In their reaction to the slander against the Church in the secular press in early 1980 the hierarchy made a similar link between the propagators and the government itself: "It seems strange to us that in the context of restrictions on the

Hence, the attitudes of many upper-income Catholics in Chile since the coup have presented a challenge both to the internal unity and discipline of the Church as well as to its efforts to effect a religious renewal among the laity according to the guidelines of Vatican II, Medellín, and Puebla. Some find the new emphases in the Church not in accord with their religious tastes, while others hold onto an outdated form of Catholic social philosophy that they find more compatible with their political and economic interests. While the bishops do employ sanctions when there is a clear challenge to their own authority (as they also did formerly in the case of Christians for Socialism), they have difficulty gaining the voluntary compliance of such wealthy Catholics to new pastoral directions that are not strictly matters of doctrine or discipline. Even ecclesiastical sanctions are insufficient to stop serious public attacks on Church leaders when such campaigns coincide with government interests and are given free rein in the controlled media.

New Styles of Evangelization and
New Attitudes about Ministry

One of the major problems that confronted the Church during the Allende period was its inability to attract significant numbers of the laity into its newly emerging religious programs at the local level—small base communities, lay deaconate, Bible study, catechetical projects. Since the coup, important headway has been made at the neighborhood level in the area of religious evangelization.

By 1975 it was estimated that there were at least 20,000 actively committed lay members of small base communities. These included about 10,000 catechists who have received a two-year intensive training program in doctrine and Bible study and in turn have helped prepare over 100,000 adults to teach religion in their own homes. There were also over 100 married men functioning as deacons throughout the country (which reached 167 by 1979) who have also undergone intense theological and pastoral training and who can celebrate many of the sacraments (not Confession and the Eucharist). Substantial numbers of young people are also participating in social and religious formation activities of the small communities, and by 1978 there were over 10,000 involved in such programs.[120]

---

press in Chile it is possible to print calumnies against the Catholic Church with such facility." Comité Permanente del Episcopado de Chile, "Yo soy Jesús, a quien tú persigues," Santiago, 29 May 1980, *Mensaje* 29 (July 1980): 364.

[120] Enrique García Ahumada, F.S.C., "Neustra catequesis actual," *Mensaje* 26 (November 1977): 657–61; Carlos Sánchez, "El difícil despertar de la juventud chilena," *Mensaje* 27 (January-February 1978): 17–20.

Moreover, the catechetical, deacon, and youth programs are attracting low-income people who never had had much contact with the Church. For the first time in its history, the Chilean Catholic Church is beginning to evangelize the poor effectively and small, but well-trained, cadres of leaders are emerging in working-class urban neighborhoods.

Furthermore, many of the small base communities do include in their concerns some form of engagement in the social and economic problems of their civic communities. Incorporated into their structures are fraternal aid committees responsible for looking after the economic needs of citizens in their areas (*comités de ayuda fraterna*). These are led by those who also are involved in cathechetical training, Bible study, or prayer groups. Hence, participants in religious activities are often the ones who also initiate social action projects in their neighborhoods, such as soup kitchens, day-care centers, self-help employment projects, thus fulfilling the goals articulated at Medellín and Puebla.[121]

The greatest responsibility for preparing laity for these new tasks in the Church has been in the hands of women religious. Almost one-half of the 5,500 nuns in Chile are now engaged in direct pastoral work at the local level, particularly in poor areas. Due to the scarcity of priests, these sisters have also been given administrative responsibilities over entire parishes where no clergy are available. By 1976, 80 of the 750 parishes throughout the country (10.7 percent of the total) were under the exclusive control of such women, and, although not ordained, they perform many priestly functions except the granting of absolution for sins or saying Mass.[122]

As a result of these new forms of evangelization and leadership, there is evidence that some critical differences of opinion are emerging across levels of the Church. In my surveys with Church leaders in 1975, I asked all the respondents their opinions concerning the usefulness of liberation theology as a pastoral strategy, the possibility of married priests and of incorporating women into official ministerial positions. On all three of these issues I found criticial differences between bishops and local Church leaders.

Although nearly nine out of ten bishops (86.9 percent) felt there was no place for liberation theology methods in 1975, many of those closer to the people thought otherwise. Two-fifths of the priests (40.6 percent) and over one-third of the nuns (36.4 percent) and lay leaders (34 per-

---

[121] A survey in 1977 in Santiago of 319 women engaged in several of the more than 300 Church-related soup kitchens in shantytowns found that 55.8 percent of those with top administrative responsibilities in these soup kitchens were active in some religious activities of small base communities in the Church. Christián Vives, "La solidaridad: una forma de evangelizar y de participar en la iglesia," pp. 22–23.

[122] Katherine Ann Gilfeather, M. M. "Women and Ministry," p. 191.

cent) disagreed, and many said they were trying to combine in their parishes or base communities the teaching of religion with a critical reflection on political and economic problems. Such strategies appear to be salient among a sizable minority of priests, nuns, and lay leaders, many of whom were not necessarily sympathetic to Christians for Socialism but since the coup have become radicalized by the repression of the present regime. Ironically, the longer the military continue to impose such severe economic and political restrictions, the more likelihood that such tendencies will increase among local Church leaders and eventually this could be problematic for bishops and military alike.

Higher and lower Church leaders also disagree dramatically on the possibility of a married priesthood. Given the chronic lack of sufficient vocations to the traditional priesthood in Chile and the new emphasis on the married lay deaconate, four-fifths of local Church leaders (81.9 percent of the priests, 78.7 percent of the nuns, and 80.4 percent of the laity) in my 1975 interviews said that ordaining married men as priests was a very necessary change for the future, or at least a possibility that should be seriously studied. Sixty percent of the bishops, however, indicated that such was not a possibility applicable to Chile, or merely an interesting idea that still was not necessary to implement.

While there is not strong pressure as yet coming from the local level to promote this change, the more widespread the use of married laymen in ministerial positions the greater will be the likelihood that tensions will eventually emerge. As one bishop remarked to me in 1975, in a few more years the people themselves will begin to ask the hierarchy why married deacons cannot say Mass and hear confessions on Sunday when they are performing all other priestly functions in areas where there are no priests. He said he would not have a good theological answer to that question when it arises.[123]

A final area of difference between higher and lower leaders which forbodes trouble is the question of the incorporation of women into official

---

[123] Celibacy has been a disciplinary, although not doctrinal, requirement for Catholic clerics since the fourth century. Aside from religious reasons, there have been a number of sociological factors accounting for its perdurance in the Church. By precluding a hereditary priesthood, celibacy has helped to maintain corporate property in the hands of the Church, it has preserved universalistic recruitment patterns for the clerical office, has strengthened bureaucratic controls, and eliminated competing claims to priests' loyalties. Popes who have been the most energetic defenders of the Church's prerogatives against encroachments by secular powers (such as Pope John Paul II) have also been the ones most staunchly committed to celibacy for the clergy. Amidst Church-state conflicts (which certainly characterize contemporary Chile) celibacy has been an important means used by the hierarchy to prevent secular interests from gaining some hold over clergy through familial or social ties. Lewis A. Coser, "The Functions of Sacerdotal Celibacy," pp. 150–62; Weber, *Sociology of Religion*, p. 238.

ministerial positions. When asked if they thought that it is beneficial that participation of women in the Church continue to increase, nearly four-fifths (78.5 percent) of all the respondents in my survey said yes (including 70 percent of the bishops). Despite this approval of de facto responsibility for women, however, very few bishops (6.8 percent) were open to the possibility of women priests in the future, and nearly three-fifths (56.6 percent) actually opposed *in principle* one or several functions women are *now* performing—preaching, administering some sacraments, serving as leaders of communities in place of men. Local Church leaders were far more open to all of these roles for women in fact and principle. Over one-fifth of the priests (22.2 percent), two-fifths of the laity (43.2 percent) and one-half of the nuns (51.5 percent) also favored the ordination of women as priests, since they were already doing most of the work and not being granted formal recognition for it.

While differences in opinion on these issues by themselves are not necessarily alarming, two other factors highlight their potential explosiveness. One is the widespread lack of evaluation mechanisms throughout the Chilean Church, and the other is the absence of adequate communication between the bishops and clerical and religious personnel. These two critical weaknesses not only limit the possibility of discerning what is genuinely effective and desirable regarding needed changes, but also can hamper honest exchanges and mutual education between higher and local leaders.

There has been very little done at the national or diocesan levels to evaluate in any systematic fashion new local religious and social programs since 1973 when they have mushroomed and taken on particular vitality. Nearly three-fifths of the bishops (56.5 percent) indicated to me in 1975 that they had no trained personnel to evaluate the implementation of national guidelines in their areas. Nor did such an evaluation process exist at the national level in the central offices of the Episcopal Conference.

Mechanisms for communication are also still rather underdeveloped in many dioceses throughout the country. Most bishops rely on informal means of gathering information about pastoral needs and problems in their dioceses, such as brief visits to parishes to administer Confirmation or participate in popular religious fiestas, and casual conversations with pastors during office hours in their chanceries or over dinner in their residences. Some have established priests' senates or advisory boards, but these often are not representative of the broad spectrum of opinion that exists at the local level of their dioceses. While 70 percent of the bishops told me that they believed that there was sufficient communication between themselves and the priests in their dioceses, over one-half of the priests (51.4 percent) in my survey judged this not to be the case.

Table 9.5
The Possibility of Ordaining Married Laymen as Priests (1975)

	Bishops (N = 30)	Priests (N = 72)	Nuns (N = 33)	Laity (N = 51)	Totals (N = 186)
1. It is *not* a possibility applicable to the Chilean Church	46.7% (14) ⎱ 60.0	17.5% (9)	6.1% (2)	15.6% (8)	17.7% (33)
2. It is an interesting idea but still not necessary to implement	13.3 (4) ⎰	4.2 (3)	6.1 (2)	2.0 (1)	5.4 (10)
3. It is a possibility which should be seriously studied	33.3 (10)	58.3 (42) ⎱ 81.9	54.5 (18) ⎱ 78.7	43.1 (22) ⎱ 80.4	49.5 (92) ⎱ 73.2
4. It is one of the most necessary changes needed in the Chilean Church of the future	—	23.6 (17) ⎰	24.2 (8) ⎰	37.3 (19) ⎰	23.7 (7) ⎰
5. Other (we need to experiment more with deacons first and evalute this experience)	6.7 (2)	1.4 (1)	9.1 (3)	2.0 (1)	3.7 (7)

Table 9.6
Opinions on Women Performing Ministerial Functions (1975)
"Do you think there is any work which women should not do in the Church?"

	Bishops (N = 30)	Priests (N = 72)	Nuns (N = 33)	Laity (N = 51)	Totals (N = 186)
1. Does not oppose any work (including priesthood)	6.8% (2)	22.2% (16)	51.5% (17)	43.2% (22)	30.7% (57)
2. Opposes ordination as priests *only*	33.3 (10)	37.5 (27)	21.2 (7)	35.3 (18)	33.3 (62)
3. Opposes ordination and preaching	33.3 (10) ⎱ 56.6	18.1 (13) ⎱ 33.4	6.1 (2) ⎱ 6.1	7.8 (4) ⎱ 15.6	15.6 (29)
4. Opposes several roles for women (ordination; preaching; administering sacraments; serving as leaders when men are available)	23.3 (7) ⎰	15.3 (11) ⎰	— ⎰	7.8 (4) ⎰	11.8 (22)
5. Don't know, no answer	3.3 (1)	6.9 (5)	21.2 (7)	5.9 (3)	8.6 (16)

In addition, a national survey of 136 nuns living in poor areas that was conducted in 1976 by Centro Bellarmino discovered that 56 percent of the sisters felt that the pastoral work of the Church in catechetics, administration of the sacraments, and training of youth was still inadequate, but that they also felt that they had no effective ways of communicating this to policy-makers at the top level of the Church. In addition, 69.2 percent of the women religious in this survey felt that the position of the hierarchy regarding the ordination of women is both illogical and inadmissable. Seventy-six percent also expressed considerable frustration with the institutional Church, and 37 percent said they had no way to give an accounting of their work to official ecclesiastical leaders.[124] These women religious are seldom included as equals with priests in formal meetings with the bishops, and neither their experience nor their opinions are taken seriously enough by the hierarchy despite the fact that they are most often the ones who are responsible for the formation of small base communities and the training of lay leaders.

Hence, while the Chilean Church has made some significant headway since the coup in strengthening religious commitments among poor sectors of the population that previously had little or no contact with the Church, there are formidable issues that still remain to be resolved. Heavy reliance on laity and nuns to carry out most of the new social and religious programs sponsored by the Church among low-income groups is generating new social and religious attitudes at the base level of the institution that do not correspond with official policies at the top. Unless methods of planning and evaluation along with more adequate channels of communication are developed, serious tensions are likely to emerge between the hierarchy and local leaders especially when repression in society at large begins to abate. A new Church is clearly being formed at the grass-roots level. If the bishops are to guide it effectively in the future, they will have to face up to its vitality and its frustrations more honestly than they have done thus far.

CONCLUSIONS

(1) *Prophetic denunciations of an authoritarian state by Catholic bishops normally do not occur until the core interests of the Church are threatened, and even then have little impact on changing overall policies of repression.*

The Chilean bishops' prophetic reputation of being against repression since 1973 must be qualified. During the first three years of the military

---

[124] Gilfeather, "Women Religious, the Poor and the Institutional Church in Chile," pp. 143–44.

regime, their public statements were cautious, mutually contradictory, rarely critical, and provided the government with important early legitimacy. Despite maintaining correct relations with the Allende government, the bishops harbored private fears of Marxism. Such anxieties, coupled with the promise to restore order after a period of social chaos by an avowedly Christian group of military officers, predisposed the hierarchy at the start to be relatively understanding of the ultimate goals of the junta whatever their misgivings about some of the initial tactics used. Only after mid-1976 when the repressive apparatus of the state touched the top echelons of the Church and those close to it did they as a group issue clear condemnations of systematic abuses of power by the government.

This pattern of initial caution and gradual evolution toward a corporately prophetic position by Catholic bishops in the face of conservative authoritarian regimes has been repeated in many other contemporary third-world countries—Brazil, Bolivia, Argentina, Paraguay, El Salvador, Rhodesia, and the Philippines. While there have been some individual bishops who were openly critical during early stages of repression in these countries, the episcopacies *as a group* have followed the same ambiguous patter as the Chilean hierarchy.

Catholic bishops initially find the ideology employed by such rightwing governments (often avowedly Christian in inspiration) far less threatening to Church norms than that of leftist regimes. The former also frequently come to power in developing countries after periods of turmoil and promise to restore peace and order quickly, and this commitment also resonates with long-standing Catholic preferences for harmony in society. Moreover, when bishops believe an authoritarian situation to be emergency in nature or transitory in duration they are prone to be cautious in commiting the moral weight of their office to public denunciations of its initial performance.

In addition to these dynamics operating at the ideological level, there are structural factors in the Catholic Church that create obstacles to a prophetic role by the hierarchy. Canonical independence on the part of individual bishops (who are subject only to the pope) makes it difficult to gain a critical consensus in a national episcopal conference, especially when some prelates favor the policies of a conservative authoritarian regime. The Chilean case shows that when bishops are divided, those leaning towards a denunciatory position will sometimes compromise and accept a publicly ambiguous position endorsed by all bishops so as to prevent an authoritarian regime from exploiting their disunity for its own political purposes. While such a strategy minimizes the possibility of open schism in the Church (something that happened in the Chilean Lutheran Church), it also gives government supporters among the hierarchy a veto power over all consensus statements and leads to episcopal pronouncements that are hardly prophetic.

A more significant structural limitation on the prophetic capacities of Catholic bishops, however, is the institutional weight of the Church itself. The hierarchy perceive their first responsibility to be the preservation of Church structures so that its primary religious mission may continue—preaching the Gospel and administering the sacraments. Bishops as a whole, therefore, do not initially act as prophets under societal repression but as administrators of large bureaucracies. They are protective caretakers of their own organizations rather than outspoken guardians of public morality and human dignity.

Perhaps it is for this reason that canonically in the Catholic Church the office of bishop does not guarantee the charism of prophecy. Vatican II includes in the official responsibilities of bishops teaching, sanctifying, and governing, but not denouncing repressive secular powers.[125] In fact, in the Judeo-Christian tradition prophecy is a gift tied to no office but given to persons normally apart from administrative and priestly functions. The pattern of responses of the Chilean bishops to military rule between 1973 and 1975 confirms this truth.

Prophetic positions by episcopal conferences nevertheless emerge. When they do they are not primarily in response to brutality against ordinary people but to specific acts of violence or abuse aimed at clerical or lay elites engaged in work the hierarchy deems crucial to the institutional Church. In Chile and Argentina it was an attack on bishops personally (and in the former it included prominent Christian Democrats). In Brazil, El Salvador, Bolivia, the Philippines, and Rhodesia it was mistreatment or murder of priests. In Paraguay it was the smashing of Church-sponsored peasant leagues and small base communities. In all of these cases in recent years, the hierarchies as a group have not taken a united prophetic stance against their respective governments until the repression touched the innermost circles of Church elites.[126]

To some this pattern of defensive reaction by bishops may appear as self-serving, cowardly, and insensitive to the sufferings of those not closely associated with the Church's leadership. While the Chilean case provides evidence for such judgments in the case of some individual bishops, the concern for the institutional survival of the Church manifested by episcopal conferences as a whole permits the inauguration of many humanitarian services which otherwise would not occur if ecclesi-

---

[125] "Decree on the Bishops' Pastoral Office in the Church," no. 11, in *Documents of Vatican II*, ed. Abbott, p. 403.
[126] Smith, "Churches and Human Rights in Latin America"; Youngblood, "Church Opposition to Martial Law in the Philippines"; Windrich, "Church-State Confrontation in Rhodesia."

astical structures were smashed or severely curtailed. Probably the Chilean programs to defend legal rights or to meet basic social and economic needs of those persecuted after the coup would have encountered greater difficulties initially and experienced less freedom had the bishops strongly condemned the junta right from the start. The same is true in Paraguay, Bolivia, Brazil, and the Philippines were delayed prophetic reactions by the respective hierarchies to the escalation of terror in recent years have given lead time for local ecclesiastical structures to expand and strengthen their networks before the storm of persecution hit the Churches themselves.

Moreover, in Chile as well as in other third-world countries where Catholic bishops have eventually articulated clear and specific condemnations of human rights violations by authoritarian governments, public leaders have not significantly changed their policies. Prophetic episcopal statements may reduce pressures on the Church for a time, diminish the moral legitimacy of such regimes and discredit them further in world opinion, and revive the lost moral credibility of the bishops themselves. They do not, however, precipitate the downfall of such governments, nor effect basic changes in their structures or tactics. The moral power of the Catholic Church in comparison to the resources for physical coercion enjoyed by repressive authoritarian rulers, while not insignificant, is clearly limited.

(2) *The structures of the Catholic Church are capable of significant role expansion to perform a variety of resistance functions under authoritarian regimes, but they are vulnerable to direct and indirect restrictions by the state.*

The institutional resources of the Church are more effective than its moral voice in countering some of the effects of an authoritarian state. Third-world repressive governments that profess Christian values cannot afford to conduct an all-out attack on the Church, particularly during the period of consolidation of their power when they want moral legitimation by clergy and diplomatic recognition from Western nations. Under such circumstances, the layered organizational network of the Church survives and can take quick action. The building of communication networks, the dissemination of accurate information, the delivery of legal and economic services, and the promotion of alternate forms of social participation are roles that the institutional apparatus of the Church has been able to perform in the 1970s in Chile, Brazil, Bolivia, Paraguay, El Salvador, Guatemala, Bolivia, the Philippines, Rhodesia, and South Africa.[127]

[127] Smith, "Churches and Human Rights in Latin America"; Youngblood, "Church Opposition to Martial Law in the Philippines"; Windrich, "Church-State Confrontation in Rhodesia"; Hastings, *A History of African Christianity*, pp. 202–9, 215–17.

Such role expansion of the institutional Church is not possible in thoroughly secular authoritarian regimes or in totalitarian societies—Nazi Germany, the Soviet Union, Eastern Europe. In none of these situations do rulers need moral legitimation by Christian Churches. Moreover, in these cases, the state is more capable of orchestrating social services for its citizens and does not permit the Church to function significantly in this realm. Conversely, the bishops are more willing to reduce, or see dismantled, the outer structures of the Church peripheral to its strictly religious mission (lay organizations, youth clubs, labor unions, magazines and newspapers), because through infiltration by well-organized secular cadres, they can be taken over and act as resources for the state rather than for the Church itself.[128]

While not subject to annihilation or the same type of manipulation, ecclesiastical structures in authoritarian regimes of purported Christian inspiration are vulnerable to some forms of state pressure once they begin to oppose the objectives of the regime. The Chilean case indicates that there is a whole range of strategies such a government can employ, short of formally declaring a persecution, in order to hamper the Church's effectiveness—harassment and arrest of local leaders, threats against, and censorship of, its public channels of communication, and periodic vilification campaigns against its personnel and programs. When the pressure becomes relentless and adamant (as in the case of the Committee of Cooperation for Peace), Church leaders are likely to accede to government demands rather than risk losses in other areas, especially those that relate more directly to its religious activities.

The Church has some maneuverability to counter such tactics. The immediate creation of the Vicariate of Solidarity as successor to the Committee of Cooperation for Peace, the renewal of close ties between the bishops and *Mensaje,* the invoking of the privilege granted by its public juridical personality under law to avoid financial disclosures of COPACHI, are all examples of shrewdness on the part of Church leaders to parry attempted government restrictions on their institutional freedom. Nevertheless, when the Church is heavily dependent on the state for financial support for a critical apostolate (e.g., education), it has no effective options to resist controls. In such situations it must forego the possibility of using such a channel or program to oppose the ideology or policies of the regime.

---

[128] Lewy, *Catholic Church and Nazi Germany,* chap. 5; Bohdan R. Bociurkiw and John W. Strong, eds., *Religion and Atheism,* chaps. 10, 13, 15, 17, and 20. For a comprehensive analysis of the differences between authoritarian and totalitarian regimes, see Juan J. Linz, "Totalitarian and Authoritarian Regimes," in *Handbook of Political Science,* ed. Fred Greenstein and Nelson Polsby, 9 vols. (Menlo Park, Cal.: Addison-Wesley, 1975) 3:175–411.

Other authoritarian governments in third-world countries have exercised similar intimidation and controls against the Church in recent years. South Africa has placed legal bans on public activities of dissenting clergy. Lay deacons have been tortured in Paraguay, and priests murdered in Honduras, El Salvador, Bolivia, and Brazil. Church radio stations have also been closed in Brazil and some of its publications heavily censored. Priests and nuns have been publicly denounced as communists in the Philippines and the government has threatened to tax Church properties.[129]

While it is true that the Church cannot undermine such states or substantially alter their political economy, it is also a fact that the Church has staying power and is not easily smashed. There is a certain line beyond which most authoritarian governments will not go even when they have begun to mount an offensive against Church personnel and programs. The organizational network of the Church, therefore, can act as an important holding operation or locus of minimal resistance until other forms of domestic and international pressure can be mobilized. It cannot by itself, however, act as an effective front line of a major opposition to authoritarian regimes.

(3) *International linkages provide important resources for the Church's commitments to human rights under authoritarian regimes, but can also be exploited by governments to limit its freedom.*

In recent years, the pope, the Vatican curia, international synods of bishops, and various regional and national episcopal conferences have all publicly endorsed local Churches' efforts to defend human rights as part of their moral and religious mission. Such statements provide important legitimacy for Church-sponsored humanitarian efforts in many parts of the world, and help to discredit claims by repressive governments that such commitments are primarily political in purpose.

The most important international supports to Churches in repressive third-world countries, however, are money and materials. None of the humanitarian programs sponsored by the Chilean Catholic and Protestant Churches since the coup could have been inaugurated or sustained without massive financial assistance and food, clothing, and medicine from Western Europe and North America. Such aid, moreover, originated in both religious and governmental organizations in these wealthier countries. Hence, while Church networks in the past may have been conduits for foreign governments to counter leftist organizations in developing countries (as probably happened in Chile in the 1960s), under different circumstances they can be used by the same governments

---

[129] Smith, "Churches and Human Rights in Latin America"; Youngblood, "Church Opposition to Martial Law in the Philippines"; Hastings, *History of African Christianity,* pp. 206–9.

(especially the United States) to blunt some of the policies of conservative authoritarian regimes.[130]

The Chilean case also demonstrates that there are definite limitations on the controls which authoritarian states can impose on international financial support to Churches. Many of the authoritarian governments now in power in Asia, Africa, and Latin America are themselves heavily dependent upon public and private institutions in Western Europe and North America for loans and credits. When such governments attempt to interfere with ecclesiastical financial transactions they are tampering with the free flow of currency, and in so doing, as the IAF incident in Chile in 1978 indicated, they risk losses in loans and credits from international financial institutions that place a high value on unhampered monetary transfers on all fronts.

Hence, dependency linkages can sometimes have unforeseen positive consequences, since, in the case of economically weak authoritarian regimes, these provide a certain maneuverability which internationally supported Churches can turn to their own advantage. Such international constraints, however, are not as salient in totalitarian states that are far more economically self-contained and financially autonomous. Such regimes are less vulnerable to outside pressures when they exert controls over their own domestic institutions, including Churches.

The Chilean case also proves that even in dependent authoritarian regimes not all international economic transactions are beyond government controls, including those with Churches. The Chilean junta is learning to play the international money game without breaking the rules. Loans from private foreign banks have more than replaced the international public funds the junta has lost due to its brutal image abroad (Table 9.2). Moreover, the junta's 1980 repayment of its U.S. debts in dollars instead of pesos to the Social Progress Trust Fund may, if continued, considerably curtail the recycling of U.S. government money back into Church-sponsored human rights programs in Chile.

Moreover, personnel support from abroad to Churches in authoritarian countries is very vulnerable to immediate government control. Concordats between the Vatican and nation-states do not cover protections for foreign clergy, nor do host countries from which such priests come normally protest against the expulsion of these priests provided that their lives and physical integrity are not jeopardized in the process. Revocation of residency permits to foreign clerics by authoritarian governments can be carried out swiftly, expeditiously, and without much risk

---

[130] My own comparative study of several other Latin American Churches in the 1970s confirms this heavy dependency on foreign private and governmental assistance (much of the latter given indirectly) that has characterized Chilean Churches since 1973. Smith, "Churches and Human Rights in Latin America."

of serious repercussions from abroad since they are considered a legitimate exercise of national sovereignty. While Chile is a dramatic case of the expulsion of a large number of foreign priests after the coup, a considerable number have been sent packing in Churches in Brazil, Paraguay, Bolivia, Rhodesia, the Philippines, and South Korea, all of which depend heavily on foreign priests and have had clashes with the state over human rights violations.

If over the long term some authoritarian regimes gain sufficient political power and economic autonomy so as to take on the characteristics of totalitarian states, international Church financial linkages are likely to be reduced drastically in such societies. Under such circumstances, local Church structures that expanded rapidly in earlier crisis periods with the help of foreign aid will shrink as outside support is cut off unless autonomous local financing is generated.

(4) *While Churches offering humanitarian services under authoritarian regimes may experience an influx of new adherents, this may be of short-term duration and could be offset by the permanent loss of some influential groups. Moreover, ad hoc improvisations in pastoral responsibilities can also produce a latent rejection of traditional Catholic Church disciplinary positions by those who stay.*

When a Church in a conservative authoritarian society becomes an important source of needed social services it may have a unique opportunity to evangelize many who have never had much contact with the institution—workers, peasants, intellectuals, leftist sympathizers—all of whom are the ones most in need of the Church's protection and assistance. Furthermore, the needs of these new adherents are such that equal institutional emphasis can be given to both social action and religious evangelization, an objective central to newly announced goals in official Church documents and synods. Hence, despite all the economic and political problems in Chile since the coup, the vitality of Church life (especially among the poor) has dramatically risen, and several of the goals of Medellín and Puebla are being realized—deeper voluntary commitments, incorporation of laity into leadership positions, promotion of more communitarian styles of spirituality, and the generation of new attitudinal values combining religious faith and a commitment to justice.

As exciting and hopeful as are all of these vital signs, much of this new participation is certainly temporary crisis support. Workers, peasants, intellectuals, and leftists have no other alternatives for sustenance and solidarity besides Church-sponsored projects at the present time. Undoubtedly there is a strengthening of faith on the part of many since new catechetical, deaconate, Bible study, and prayer group programs demand more than superficial religious responses on the part of their members. One could expect, however, that once the repression subsides and other forms of social expression become viable many of the new church-goers will decrease their rate of participation in the institution's programs.

Significant withdrawals will almost certainly occur among those engaged in human rights or social action work when the economic and political crises subsides. Many leftist Catholics and nonbelievers will take with them more positive attitudes about the Church and religion, and this will further reduce the possibility of future conflicts between the Church and the Left. Very little associational identification with the Church on the part of the contemporary social activists, however, will be likely once a political opening occurs and they can achieve their goals more effectively elsewhere.

Such an outcome in no way would detract from the importance of new forms of participation in the Church at present. Involvement in its contemporary programs is clearly having an important impact on the religious, social, political, and economic lives of large numbers of citizens. There is a certain overconfidence that bishops now manifest in Chile and elsewhere, however, that the Church's vitality will continue. What is important for them to realize is that recent increases of new members may very well be a short-term phenomenon. When democracy returns to Chile (and to other authoritarian societies in the third world where lay participation in the Church has risen in recent years), ecclesiastical leaders may have to develop new motivational resources to attract members who no longer feel the same intense need for the Church as they do now.

The Chilean case also suggests that the erosion of allegiances among more traditional Christians may not be a transitory phenomenon. The self-distancing from the Catholic Church and the Lutheran Church by wealthier members and their public opposition to social programs has led to much bitterness, and in the Lutheran case has led to a permanent schism. This alienation of the rich is not a sudden change in the Catholic Church in Chile but has been steadily growing since the late 1960s. Moreover, there is no indication that official Church positions favoring social justice and small, communitarian lay-directed religious programs will be altered in the foreseeable future regardless of changes in the political system. Unless there are dramatic changes in the attitudes of upper-income Christians, one would have to expect that their alienation will continue rather than diminish.

While this group in the Catholic Church is relatively small in comparison to middle and low-income sectors (and accounts for less than 10 percent of the baptized) their role in Chilean society is very important. They cannot be written off if the Church wants to exert influence in public policy-making, in business, and in finance through its most prestigious laity. Moreover, if the Church is ever going to develop an autonomous base of financial support it will have to convince these people to shoulder much of the responsibility. Their exodus from the institution precisely at a time when it is attempting *both* to develop new lay resources for influence in society *and* to expand its services to the poor weakens the institution politically, socially, and economically.

This weakening of allegiances among upper-income Christians is not unique to the Chilean Church. Other national Catholic and Protestant Churches in third-world countries that recently have redirected their energies toward the protection of human rights and the fulfillment of basic needs of the persecuted—Brazil, Paraguay, El Salvador, the Philippines, and Rhodesia—have also experienced mounting disaffection by wealthier members. Evidence from Western Europe and North America also indicates that wealthier Christians are reluctant to accept new social emphases in their Churches that conflict with their own economic self-interest merely because they are exposed to sermons or new Church pronouncements on social morality.[131] Class interests, therefore, tend to outweigh religious motivations in shaping attitudes of believers with money and status in several different cultures, not merely in Chile.

A final critical attitudinal problem for the new Church which the Chilean case highlights pertains to the unforeseen value changes that are occurring among participants as a result of pastoral improvisations to meet emergency situations. Given the rapid inflation of both religious and social services and the necessity to incorporate nonclerical personnel into leadership positions to administer them, local attitudes about styles of evangelization and ministry are getting significantly ahead of those of the hierarchy. Ironically, some of the goals of Christians for Socialism and "the 200" which the Chilean bishops rejected are now becoming attractive to significant numbers of laity and local leaders on the basis of recent pastoral experiences—the usefulness of a liberation theology method in evangelization, the declericalization of leadership roles, the decentralization of authority, the desirability of married priests. Other objectives, such as the ordination of women, which neither the Vatican nor the episcopacy deem possible, are also growing more appealing to many Chileans as a result of their seeing nuns and laywomen competently perform several priestly functions since the coup.

The longer authoritariansm continues in Chile and other third-world

<hr/>

[131] Charles Glock and Rodney Stark, *Religion and Society,* pp. 201–6; Gerhard Lenski, *The Religious Factor* (Garden City, N.Y.: Doubleday-Anchor, 1963), p. 184; Jeffrey K. Hadden, *The Gathering Storm in the Churches* (Garden City, N.Y.: Doubleday-Anchor, 1970), p. 110. The recent upsurge in evangelical Christianity and the Moral Majority in the United States reinforces these conservative social and political tendencies among many middle and upper-class Christians.

countries where similar pastoral practices are going on with official acquiescence, the harder it will be for the hierarchy later to revise or control the resultant attitudinal and behavioral changes accompanying
them. One would expect that when societal repression subsides and
Church personnel turn their attention once again to predominantly religious concerns, the present latent differences of opinion between higher
and lower leaders on thesse issues may become overt points of conflict.

These recent attitudinal permutations (especially on women priests,
married clergy, sectarian forms of evangelization) touch more closely
some core disciplinary and doctrinal issues in Roman Catholicism than
do commitments to promote social change. Critical differences in those
areas between official policies and membership preferences could, therefore, precipitate even more serious internal problems for the institution
than the loss of recent crisis-support adherents or the alienation of
upper-income Catholics. Unless there is more effective communication,
honest evaluation, and adjustments at both the top and bottom of the
Church on these issues in the near future, bitter disillusionment or open
authority conflicts could very well characterize the next stage of the institution's evolution.

Hence, the experience of the Chilean Church since 1973 highlights
both the advantages and the problems that repressive authoritarian regimes create for the religious mission of Catholicism. Churches under
such circumstances have unique opportunities to develop new methods
of evangelization among many sectors of their nominal membership,
especially the poor and the persecuted. Given their multiclass membership allegiances, however, a weakening of their influence is almost inevitable among other baptized who dislike or fear such new commitments.
Moreover, bishops are likely to be so preoccupied with crisis demands
that they are prone to permit new ministerial patterns without sufficiently reflecting upon the long-range consequences these will have for
traditional positions the official Church is not ready to change. Whether
such challenges will result in further creative adaptations within the
Catholic Church or to painful retrenchments and disillusionment once
these crises are over will depend upon the honesty, imagination, and
courage of its leaders under the guidance of the Holy Spirit.

Selected Bibliography

Abbott, Walter M., S.J., ed. *The Documents of Vatican II.* New York: America Press, 1966.

Aldunate L., José, S.J. "Remuneraciones y costos de vida." *Mensaje* (Santiago) 23 (December 1974): 634–36.

————. "Salarios y precios: ¿cómo sigue la situación?" *Mensaje* 24 (May 1975): 186–88.

Alessandri, Arturo. *Recuerdos de gobierno.* 3 vols. Santiago: Editorial Nacimiento, 1967.

Alexander, Robert. *Arturo Alessandri: A Biography.* 2 vols. Ann Arbor: University Microfilms International, 1977.

Allende, Salvador. "Pesidente Allende y la libertad religiosa." *Iglesia de Santiago* (Santiago) 8 (November 1970): 11.

————. *Salvador Allende: su pensamiento político.* Santiago: Empresa Editora Nacional Quimantú, 1973.

Altamirano, Carlos. *Dialéctica de una derrota.* Mexico, D.F.: Siglo Veintiuno Editores, 1977.

Angell, Alan. *Politics and the Labour Movement in Chile.* London: Oxford University Press, 1972.

Apter, David E. *Choice and the Politics of Allocation: A Development Theory.* New Haven: Yale University Press, 1971.

Araneda Bravo, Fidel. *El Arzobispo Errázuriz y la evolución política y social de Chile.* Santiago: Editorial Jurídica de Chile, 1956.

Arevas, José M., S.J. "Religiosidad popular: en torno a un encuentro." *Mensaje* 23 (January–February 1974): 47–49.

Arroyo, Gonzalo, S.J. "Historia y significado de CpS." Mimeographed. Santiago, November 1972.

————. *Coup d'etat du Chili.* Paris: Editions du Cerf., 1974.

————. "The Ideological and Cultural Action of the Church." *LARU Studies* (Toronto), no. 2 (February 1977): 5–12.

Assmann, Hugo. *Theology for a Nomad Church.* Maryknoll, N.Y.: Orbis Books, 1979.

Barnes, Samuel H. "Italy: Religion and Class in Electoral Behavior." In *Electoral Behavior: A Comparative Handbook,* edited by Richard Rose, pp. 171–225. New York: The Free Press, 1974.

Berger, Suzanne, ed. *Religion and Politics in Western Europe.* London: Frank Cass, 1982.

Berlinguer, Enrico. "Cattolici e comunisti." *L'Unità* (Rome) 13 (October 1977).

Berryman, Phillip. "Popular Catholicism in Latin America." *Cross Currents* 21 (1971): 284–301.

―――. "Latin American Liberation Theology." *Theological Studies* 34 (September 1973): 357–95.

Bihlmeyer, Karl. *Church History.* Revised by Hermann Tüchle. 3 vols. Westminster, Md.: Newman Press, 1958–1966.

Binchy, D. A. *Church and State in Fascist Italy.* London: Oxford University Press, 1970.

Bitar, Sergio, ed. *Chile: liberalismo económico y dictadurs política.* Lima: Instituto de Estudios Peruanos, 1980.

Blanco, Guillermo. "Hora de decisión en la iglesia." *Mensaje* 25 (January–February 1976): 3–5.

―――. *Los incidentes de Riobamba y Pudahuel en tres diarios chilenos.* Santiago: ICHEH, 1977.

Bociurkiw, Bohdan R., and Strong, John W., eds. *Religion and Atheism in the U.S.S.R. and Eastern Europe.* Toronto: University of Toronto Press, 1975.

Bonilla, Frank, and Glazer, Myron. *Student Politics in Chile.* New York: Basic Books, 1970.

Bono, Agostino. "Five Years After Medellín: Social Action Fades in Latin America." *National Catholic Reporter,* 9 November 1973, pp. 1, 6, 11.

Bosworth, William. *Catholicism and Crisis in Modern France: French Catholic Groups at the Threshold of the Fifth Republic.* Princeton: Princeton University Press, 1962.

Bouscaren, T. Lincoln, S.J., et al. *Canon Law: A Text and Commentary.* Milwaukee: Bruce Publishing Co., 1963.

Brahm M., Louis A.; Cariola, Patricio, S.J.; and Silva U., Juan José. *Educación particular en Chile: antecedentes y dilemas.* Santiago: Centro de Investigación y Desarrollo de la Educación (CIDE), 1971.

Bruneau, Thomas C. *The Political Transformation of the Brazilian Catholic Church.* Cambridge: Cambridge University Press, 1974.

―――. "Church and State in Portugal: Crises of Cross and Sword." *Journal of Church and State* 18 (Autumn 1976): 463–90.

―――. "Basic Christian Communities in Latin America: Their Nature and Significance (especially in Brazil)." In *Churches and Politics in Latin America,* edited by Daniel H. Levine, pp. 225–37. Beverly Hills: Sage Publications, 1980.

―――. *Religiosity and Politicization in Brazil: The Church in an Authoritarian Regime.* Austin: University of Texas Press, 1981.

Calvez, Jean-Yves, S.J., and Perrin, Jacques, S.J. *The Church and Social Justice: The Social Teachings of the Popes from Leo XIII to Pius XII, 1878–1958.* Chicago: Regnery Co., 1961.

Camarero, José M. "Los 200: ¿qué son?" *Mundo '73* (Santiago), no. 63 (September 1973): 31–33.

Caporale, Rocco. *Vatican II: Last of the Councils.* Baltimore: Helicon Press, 1964.

Cariola, Julio Chaná. *Situación jurídica de la iglesia.* Santiago: Universidad de Chile, 1931.

Carrillo, Santiago. *Eurocomunismo y estado.* Barcelona: Editorial Crítica, 1977.

Cassidy, Sheila. *Audacity to Believe*. London: Collins, 1977.

Castillo Velasco, Jaime. *Las fuentes de la democracia cristiana*. 2nd edition, revised. Santiago: Editorial del Pacífico, 1963.

Castro, Fidel. *Fidel in Chile: A Symbolic Meeting between Two Historical Processes*. New York: International Publishers, 1972.

Centro Bellarmino. *Estudio de opinión pública sobre la iglesia: Santiago y Concepción*. Santiago, 1969.

Chile. *Libro Blanco del cambio de gobierno en Chile*. Santiago: Editorial Lord Cochrane, 1973.

————. *Declaración de principios del gobierno de Chile*. Santiago: Gabriela Mistral, 1974.

Chile: masacre de un pueblo. Lima: CEP, 1974.

Chonchol, Jacques. "Informe político." Mimeographed. Santiago: Comisión Coordinadora Nacional de MAPU, May 1969.

Christians for Socialism: Highlights from Chile's Religious Revolution. Washington, D.C.: EPICA, 1973.

"The Churches of Latin America in Confrontation with the State and the Ideology of National Security: The Reality and Its Causes." *Pro Mundi Vita* (Brussels), no. 7⅟ (March–April 1978): 1–36.

Coleman, John A., S.J. *The Evolution of Dutch Catholicism, 1958–1974*. Berkeley: University of California Press, 1978.

Comblin, Joseph O.P. *Teología de la revolución*. Bilbao: Editorial España, Desclèe de Brouwer, 1973.

————. *The Church and the National Security State*. Maryknoll, N.Y.: Orbis Books, 1979.

Comisión Evangélica Latinoamericana de Educación Cristiana (CELADEC). "Iglesia Argentina: ¿fidelidad a evangelio? ¿conquista del poder?" Mimeographed. Lima, March 1975.

Comité de Cooperación para la Paz en Chile. "Crónica de sus dos años de labor solidaria." Mimeographed. Santiago, December 1975.

Condamines, Carlos. "Chili: l'Eglise et la Junte." *La revue nouvelle* (Brussels) 60 (December 1974): 503–57.

Congar, Yves, O.P. "The Historical Development of Authority in the Church: Points for Christian Reflection." In *Problems of Authority,* edited by John M. Todd, pp. 119–56. Baltimore: Helicon Press, 1962.

Conseil permanent de la Conférence épiscopale espagnole. "Les chretiens et la politique." *La Documentation Catholique* (Paris), 6 March 1977, pp. 239–50.

Conseil permanent de l'Éspiscopat français. "Le marxisme, l'homme et la foi chretienne." *La Documentation Catholique,* 17 July 1977, pp. 684–90.

Considine, John J., M.M. *The Missionary's Role in Socio-Economic Betterment*. Westminster, Md.: Newman Press, 1960.

Conway, J. S. *The Nazi Persecution of the Churches, 1933–1945*. London: Weidenfeld and Nicholson, 1968.

Cooper, Norman B. *Catholicism and the Franco Regime*. Contemporary European Studies Series, no. 90–019. Beverly Hills: Sage Publications, 1975.

Coser, Lewis A. "The Functions of Sacerdotal Celibacy." In his *Greedy Institu-*

tions: Patterns of Undivided Commitment, pp. 150–62. New York: Free Press, 1974.

Crahan, Margaret E. "Religious Freedom in Cuba." *Cuba Review* 5 (September 1975): 22–27.

――――. "Salvation Through Christ or Marx: Religion in Revolutionary Cuba." *Journal of Interamerican Studies and World Affairs* 21 (February 1979): 156–84.

Cristianos latinamericanos y socialismo. Bogotá: CEDIAL, 1972.

Cristianos por el Socialismo, Secretariado Nacional. "Cómo cristianos: ¿por qué nos importan las elecciones de marzo?" Mimeographed. Santiago, January 1973.

――――. *La ENU: ¿control de las conciencias o educación liberadora?* Talca: Fundación Obispo Manuel Larraín, 1973.

Los cristianos y la revolución: un debate abierto en América Latina. Santiago: Quimantú, 1972.

Debray, Regis. *The Chilean Revolution: Conversations with Allende.* New York: Vintage, 1971.

de Kadt, Emanuel. *Catholic Radicals in Brazil.* London: Oxford University Press, 1970.

Della Cava, Ralph. "Catholicism and Society in Twentieth-Century Brazil." *Latin American Research Review* 11 (Summer 1976): 7–50.

――――. "Short-term Politics and Long-term Religion in Brazil." (with a critique by Paulo S. Krischke). Latin American Working Paper 12. Washington, D.C.: Woodrow Wilson International Center for Scholars, 1978.

de Vylder, Stefan. *Allende's Chile: The Political Economy of the Rise and Fall of the Unidad Popular.* Cambridge: Cambridge University Press, 1976.

Dewart, Leslie. *Christianity and Revolution: The Lesson of Cuba.* New York: Herder and Herder, 1963.

Diamont, Alfred. *Austrian Catholics and the First Republic.* Princeton: Princeton University Press, 1960.

Dodson, Michael. "Religious Innovation and the Politics of Argentina: A Study of the Movement of Priests for the Third World." Ph.D. dissertation, Indiana University, 1973.

――――. "Priests and Peronism: Radical Clergy in Argentine Politics." *Latin American Perspectives* 1 (Fall 1974): 58–72.

――――. "The Christian Left in Latin American Politics." *Journal of Interamerican Studies and World Affairs* 21 (February 1979): 45–68.

――――. "Liberation Theology and Christian Radicalism in Contemporary Latin America." *Journal of Latin American Studies* 11 (May 1979): 203–22.

――――. "Prophetic Politics and Political Theory." *Polity* 12 (Srping 1980): 388–408.

――――, and Montgomery, Tommie Sue. "The Churches in the Nicaraguan Revolution." In *Nicaragua in Revolution,* edited by Thomas Walker. New York: Praeger, 1981.

Dulles, Avery, S.J. *Models of the Church.* Garden City, N.Y.: Doubleday, 1974.

Dunn, Dennis J. *Detente and Papal-Communist Relations, 1962–1978.* Boulder, Colo.: Westview Press, 1979.

Durkheim, Emile. *Elementary Forms of Religious Life.* New York: Collier, 1947.

Dussel, Enrique. *History and the Theology of Liberation.* Translated by John Drury. Maryknoll, N.Y.: Orbis Books, 1976.

Eagleson, John, ed. *Christians and Socialism: Documentation of the Christians for Socialism Movement in Latin America.* Maryknoll, N.Y.: Orbis Books, 1975.

————, and Scharper, Philip, eds. *Puebla and Beyond: Documentation and Commentary.* Translated by John Drury. Maryknoll, N.Y.: Orbis Books, 1979.

Edwards Vives, Alberto, and Frei Montalva, Eduardo. *Historia de los partidos chilenos.* Santiago: Editorial del Pacífico, 1949.

Einaudi, Luigi, et al. *Latin American Institutional Development: The Changing Catholic Church.* Santa Monica: Rand Corporation, 1969.

Ellacuría, Ignacio, S.J. *Freedom Made Flesh: The Mission of Christ and His Church.* Maryknoll, N.Y.: Orbis Books, 1976.

Episcopado Chileno. "Pastoral colectiva de los obispos de Chile sobre la separación de la iglesia y el estado." (1925) In *Obras de Crescente Errázuriz,* edited by Raúl Silva Castro, 3:117–21. Santiago: Edición Zig-Zag, 1936.

————. *La veradera y única solución de la cuestión social.* Santiago: Imprenta Chile, 1932.

————. "Circular dirigida al clero y a nuestros amados diocesanos sobre la relación de la iglesia con la política." *Boletín de la Acción Católica de Chile* (Santiago) 3 (December 1935): 537–41.

————. *El justo salario.* Santiago: Splendor, 1937.

————. "Deber social de los católicos." *Política y Espíritu* (Santiago) 2 (January 1947): 42–46.

————. *Instrucción pastoral acerca a los problemas sociales.* Santiago: San Pancracio, 1949.

————. "Firmes en la fe: la masonería, el protestantismo y el comunismo, enemigos de los católicos." *Boletín de la Acción Católica Chilena* 19,2 (1951): 1–3.

————. *"La iglesia y el campesinado chileno."* *Mensaje* 11 (May 1962): 185–94A.

————. "El deber social y político en la hora presente." *Mensaje* 11 (November 1962): 577–87.

————. "Pastoral Plan of the Chilean Episcopate." *Pro Mundi Vita,* no. 1 (1964): 1–18.

————. "Chile, voluntad de ser," *Mensaje* 17 (May 1968): 190–97.

————, Comité Permanente. "Declaración episcopal sobre la situación actual del país." (December 1969) *Mensaje* 19 (January–February 1970): 77–79.

————, "Declaración de los obispos chilenos sobre la situación actual del país." (September 1970). In *Documentos del Episcopado: Chile, 1970–1973,* edited by Bishop Carlos Oviedo Cavada, pp. 28–30. Santiago: Ediciones Mundo, 1974.

————. "Evangelio, política y socialismos." (May 1971). In *Documentos del Episcopado: Chile, 1970–1973,* pp. 58–100.

————. "Declaración del Señor Cardenal y del Comité Permanente del Episcopado Chileno." (September 1973) *Mensaje* 22 (October 1973): 509.

————. Christian Faith and Political Activity." (October 1973). In *Christians and Socialism: Documentation of the Christians for Socialism Movement in Latin*

America, edited by John Eagleson, pp. 179–228. Maryknoll, N.Y.: Orbis Books, 1975.

———. "La reconciliación en Chile." (April 1974). *Mensaje* 23 (May 1974): 196–98.

———. "Sínodo de obispos, 1974: respuesta de la Conferencia Episcopal de Chile." Mimeographed. Santiago, 1974.

———, Comité Permanente. "Evangelio y paz." (September 1975). *Mensaje* 24 (October 1975).

———, Comité Permanente. "Declaración del Comité Permanente del Episcopado." (August 1976) *Mensaje* 25 (September 1976): 436–37.

———. *Guia de la iglesia en Chile, 1976.* Santiago: Ediciones Mundo, 1976.

———, Comité Permanente. "Nuestra convivencia nacional." (March 1977). *Mensaje* 26 (April 1977): 166–69.

———. "El sufrimiento del exilio." *Mensaje* 27 (January–February 1978): 84.

———, Comité Permanente. "Los detenidos desaparecidos y sus familiares en huelga de hambre." *Mensaje* 27 (July 1978): 428.

———. "Carta a los trabajadores cristianos del campo y la cuidad." *Mensaje* 28 (January–February 1979): 79–80.

———. "Declaración sobre el plebiscito." *Mensaje* 29 (September 1980): 519–20.

Erdozaín, Plácido. *Archbishop Romero: Martyr of Salvador.* Translated by John McFadden and Ruth Warner. Maryknoll, N.Y.: Orbis Books, 1981.

Esquerré, Françoise. " 'Cristianos por el Socialismo,' política y fe cristiana," *Política y Espíritu* 29 (June–July 1973): 47–53.

Fischer, Kathleen B. "Political Ideology and Educational Reform in Chile, 1964–1976." Ph.D. dissertation, University of California at Los Angeles, 1977.

Fogarty, Michael P. *Christian Democracy in Western Europe, 1820–1953.* London: Routledge and Kegan Paul, 1957.

Fontaine, Pablo, SS. CC. "El revolucionario cristiano y la fe." *Mensaje* 19 (May 1970): 165–72.

———. "Algunos aspectos de la iglesia chilena de hoy." *Mensaje* 24 (June 1975): 246–51.

Francis, Michael J. *The Allende Victory: An Analysis of the 1970 Chilean Presidential Election.* Tucson: Institute of Government Research, University of Arizona, 1973.

Freire, Paulo. *Pedagogy of the Oppressed.* Translated by Myra Bergman Ramos. New York: Herder and Herder, 1972.

———. *Education for Critical Consciousness.* New York: Seabury Press, 1973.

Fremantle, Anne, ed., *The Papal Encyclincals in Their Historical Context.* New York: New American Library, Mentor-Omega, 1963.

Gaete, Arturo, S.J. "El largo camino del diálogo cristiano-marxista." *Mensaje* 17 (June 1968): 209–19.

———. "Socialismo y comunismo: historia de una problemática condenación." *Mensaje* 20 (July 1971): 290–302.

———. "Catolicismo social y marxismo en el siglo XIX: un diálogo imposible." *Mensaje* 20 (December 1971): 588–602.

————. "Los cristianos y el marxismo: de Pio XI a Pablo VI." *Mensaje* 21 (June 1972): 328–41. (These last three articles have been translated into English and appear in *Latin Americans Discuss Marxism-Socialism,* LADOC "Keyhole Series" no. 13, pp. 16–66. Washington, D.C.: United States Catholic Conference, 1975).

Galdames, Luis. *A History of Chile.* Chapel Hill: University of North Carolina Press, 1941.

Galilea, Carmen, and Puga, Josefina. *Religiosidad y secularización en Chile.* Santiago: Centro Bellarmino, 1974.

Garaudy, Roger. *From Anathema to Dialogue: A Marxist Challenge to the Christian Churches.* New York: Herder and Herder, 1966.

————. *The Alternative Future: A Vision of Christian Marxism.* New York: Simon and Schuster, 1974.

Garces, Joan E. *1970: la pugna por la presidencia en Chile.* Santiago: Editorial Universitaria, 1971.

Gil, Federico. *The Political System of Chile.* Boston: Houghton Mifflin, 1966.

————, et al, eds. *Chile at the Turning Point: Lessons of the Socialist Years, 1970–1973.* Philadelphia: Institute for the Study of Human Issues, 1979.

Gilfeather, Katherine Ann, M.M. "Women and Ministry." *America,* 2 October 1976, pp. 191–94.

————. "Women Religious, the Poor and the Institutional Church in Chile." *Journal of Interamerican Studies and World Affairs* 21 (February 1979): 125–55.

Girardi, Giulio. *Marxism and Christianity.* New York: Macmillan, 1968.

————. *Cristianos por el socialismo: exigencias de una opción.* Montevideo: Editorial Tierra Nueva, 1973.

Glock, Charles, and Stark, Rodney. *Religion and Society in Tension.* Chicago: Rand McNally, 1965.

Gollwitzer, Helmut. *The Christian Faith and the Marxist Criticism of Religion.* New York: Scribner, 1970.

Graham, Robert, S.J. *Vatican Diplomacy: A Study of Church and State on the International Plane.* Princeton: Princeton University Press, 1959.

Grayson, George. "Chile's Christian Democratic Party: Power, Factions, and Ideology." *Review of Politics* 31 (1969): 147–71.

————. *The Chilean Christian Democratic Party: Genesis and Development.* Ann Arbor: University Microfilms, 1974.

Greeley, Andrew M. *Priests in the United States: Reflections on a Survey.* Garden City, N.Y.: Doubleday, 1972.

————. *The American Catholic: A Social Portrait.* New York: Basic Books, 1977.

————, and Rossi, Peter H. *The Education of Catholic Americans.* Chicago: Aldine, 1966.

Gremillion, Joseph, ed. *The Gospel of Peace and Justice: Catholic Social Teaching Since Pope John.* Maryknoll, N.Y.: Orbis Books, 1976.

Guerra, José Guillermo. *La Constitución de 1925.* Santiago: Balcells, 1929.

Gutiérrez, Gustavo. *A Theology of Liberation.* Translated and edited by Sister Caridad Inda and John Eagleson. Maryknoll, N.Y.: Orbis Books, 1973.

Guzmán E., Jaime. "The Church in Chile and the Political Debate." In *Chile:*

A Critical Debate, edited by Pablo Baraona Urzua, pp. 277–309. Santiago: Institute for General Studies, 1972.

Hales, E.E.Y. *Pope John and His Revolution*. Garden City, N.Y.: Doubleday, 1965.

Halperin, Ernst. *Nationalism and Communism in Chile*. Cambridge: MIT Press, 1965.

Hastings, Adrian. *A History of African Christianity, 1950–1975*. Cambridge: Cambridge University Press, 1979.

Hazelrigg, Laurence E. "Religious and Class Basis of Political Conflict in Italy." *American Journal of Sociology* 26 (1970): 496–511.

Hebblethwaite, Peter. *The Runaway Church: Post Conciliar Growth or Decline*. New York: Seabury Press, 1975.

————. *The Christian-Marxist Dialogue*. New York: Paulist Press, 1977.

Hennelly, Alfred T., S.J. *Theologies in Conflict: The Challenge of Juan Luis Segundo*. Maryknoll, N.Y.: Orbis Books, 1979.

Hollenbach, David, S.J. *Claims in Conflict: Retrieving and Renewing the Catholic Human Rights Tradition*. New York: Paulist Press, 1979.

Houtart, François, and Rousseau, André. *The Church and Revolution*. Maryknoll, N.Y.: Orbis Books, 1971.

Hübner Gallo, Jorge Iván. *Los católicos y la política*. Santiago: Empresa Editora Zig-Zag, 1959.

Hurtado, Alberto, S.J. *¿Es Chile un país católico?* Santiago: Editorial Splendor, 1941.

Husslein, Joseph, S.J., ed. *Social Wellsprings: Fourteen Epochal Documents by Pope Leo XIII*. Milwaukee: Bruce Publishing Co., 1940.

————. ed. *Social Wellsprings 2: Eighteen Encyclicals of Social Reconstruction by Pope Pius XI*. Milwaukee: Bruce Publishing Co., 1942.

"La iglesia chilena vista por Corvalán." *Qué Pasa* (Santiago), no. 323, 30 June–6 July 1977, p. 7.

Iglesia Joven. *Documentos: Movimiento Iglesia Joven, 11 Agosto 1968–11 Agosto 1969*. Santiago, 1969.

Illich, Ivan. "The Seamy Side of Charity." *America*, 21 January 1967, pp. 89–91.

Irarrázaval C., Diego. "¿Qué hacer?: cristianos en el proceso socialista." Mimeographed. Santiago, November 1972.

————. "Cristianos, compromiso revolucionario, comunidad de creyentes." *Boletín de CpS* (Santiago), 19 March 1973, pp. 6–7.

Jancar, Barbara Wolfe. "Religious Dissent in the Soviet Union." In *Dissent in the U.S.S.R.: Politics, Ideology and People*, edited by Rudolf L. Tökes, pp. 191–230. Baltimore: Johns Hopkins, 1975.

Jiménez B., Julio, S.J. "Don Crescente y la evolución político-religiosa de Chile." *Mensaje* 6 (January–February 1957): 18–28.

————. "Don Crescente y Monseñor Caro." *Mensaje* 15 (August 1966): 377–82.

John XXIII, Pope. "Mater et Magistra." (1961). In *The Gospel of Peace and Justice: Catholic Social Teaching Since Pope John*, edited by Joseph Gremillion, pp. 143–200. Maryknoll, N.Y.: Orbis Books, 1976.

————. "Pacem in Terris." (1963). In *The Gospel of Peace and Justice: Catholic Social Teaching Since Pope John*, pp. 201–41.

John Paul II, Pope. *The Redeemer of Man (Redemptor Hominis)*. Boston: Daughters of St. Paul, 1979.

————. *On Human Work (Laborem Exercens)*. Boston: Daughters of St Paul, 1981.

Johnson, Dale L., ed. *The Chilean Road to Socialism*. Garden City, N.Y.: Doubleday-Anchor, 1973.

Journal of Current Social Issues 15 (Summer 1978). Special issue dedicated to human rights in Brazil, the Philippines, South Korea, U.S.S.R., Uganda, U.S.A., and South Africa.

Kertzer, David I. *Comrades and Christians: Religion and Political Struggle in Communist Italy*. Cambridge: Cambridge University Press, 1980.

Klaiber, Jeffrey L., S.J. *Religion and Revolution in Peru, 1824–1976*. Notre Dame: University of Notre Dame Press, 1977.

Kramer, John M. "The Vatican's Ostpolitik." *Review of Politics* 42 (July 1980): 283–308.

Küng, Hans. *The Church*. New York: Sheed and Ward, 1967.

Labarca Goddard, Eduardo. *Chile invadido: reportaje a la intromisión extranjera*. Santiago: Empresa Editora Austral, 1968.

————. *Corvalán, 27 horas: el PC Chileno por fuera y por dentro*. Santiago: Empresa Editora Nacional Quimantú, 1972.

Landsberger, Henry A., ed. *The Church and Social Change in Latin America*. Notre Dame: University of Notre Dame Press, 1970.

————. "Time, Persons, Doctrine: The Modernization of the Church in Chile." In *The Church and Social Change in Latin America*, edited by Henry A. Landsberger, pp. 77–94. Notre Dame: University of Notre Dame Press, 1970.

Langton, Kenneth P., and Rapoport, Ronald. "Religion and Leftist Mobilization in Chile." *Comparative Political Studies* 9 (October 1976): 277–308.

Lara B., Hervi. *'Cristianos por el Socialismo': manifestación de crisis de fe*. Santiago: ILADES, 1977.

Larson, Oscar. *La ANEC y la democracia cristiana*. Santiago: Ediciones Rafaga, 1967.

Latin American Bishops Discuss Human Rights. LADOC "Keyhole Series" nos. 15 and 16. Washington, D.C.: U.S. Catholic Conference, 1978.

Latin American Episcopal Council (CELAM). *The Church in the Present-Day Transformation of Latin America in the Light of the Council*. 2 vols. Bogotá: General Secretariat of CELAM, 1970.

————. "Evangelization in Latin America's Present and Future." In *Puebla and Beyond*, edited by John Eagleson and Philip Scharper, pp. 113–285. Maryknoll, N.Y.: Orbis Books, 1979.

————, Comisión Episcopal del Departamento de Acción Social. "La instrumentalización política de la Iglesia en América Latina." *Política y Espíritu* 28 (April 1973): 76–77.

Latin Americans Discuss Marxism-Socialism. LADOC "Keyhole Series" no. 13. Washington, D.C.: United States Catholic Conference, 1975.

Latorre Cabal, Hugo, ed. *El pensamiento de Salvador Allende.* Mexico, D.F.: Fondo de Cultura Económica, 1974.

Lauer, Quentin, S.J., and Garaudy, Roger. *A Christian Communist Dialogue.* New York: Doubleday, 1968.

Leo XIII, Pope. "Rerum Novarum." (1891). In *Social Wellsprings: Fourteen Epochal Documents by Pope Leo XIII,* edited by Joseph Husslein, S.J., pp. 164–204. Milwaukee: Bruce Publishing Co. 1940.

Lernoux, Penny. *The Cry of the People: United States Involvement in the Rise of Fascism, Torture and Murder, and the Persecution of the Catholic Church in Latin America.* New York: Doubleday, 1980.

———. "The Latin American Church." *Latin American Research Review* 15, 2 (1980): 201–11.

Levine, Daniel H. *Conflict and Political Change in Venezuela.* Princeton: Princeton University Press, 1973.

———. "Religion and Politics: Recent Works." *Journal of Interamerican Studies and World Affairs* 16 (November 1974): 497–507.

———. "Authority in Church and Society: Latin American Models." *Comparative Studies in Society and History* 20 (October 1978): 517–44.

———. "Church Elites in Venezuela and Colombia: Context, Background and Beliefs." *Latin American Research Review* 14, 1 (1979): 51–79.

———. *Religion and Politics in Latin America: The Catholic Church in Venezuela and Colombia.* Princeton: Princeton University Press, 1981.

———. "Religion, Society and Politics: States of the Art." *Latin American Research Review* 16 (1981):185–209.

———, ed. *Churches and Politics in Latin America.* Beverly Hills: Sage Publications, 1980.

———, and Wilde, Alexander W. "The Catholic Church, 'Politics' and Violence: The Colombian Case." *Review of Politics* 39 (April 1977): 220–49.

Levy, Daniel. "Chilean University Policy Under the Junta." In *Military Rule In Chile,* edited by Arturo and J. Samuel Valenzuela. Forthcoming.

Lewy, Guenter. *The Catholic Church and Nazi Germany.* New York: McGraw-Hill, 1964.

Linz, Juan J. "The Social Bases of West German Politics." Ph.D. dissertation, Columbia University, 1959.

———. "Totalitarian and Authoritarian Regimes." In *Handbook of Political Science,* ed. Fred Greenstein and Nelson Polsby, 3:175–411. Menlo Park, Ca.: Addison-Wesley, 1975.

———. "Religion and Politics in Spain: From Conflict to Consensus above Cleavage." *Social Compass* (Brussels) 27 (1980): 255–77.

———, and Stepan, Alfred, eds. *The Breakdown of Democratic Regimes.* 4 vols. Baltimore: The Johns Hopkins University Press, 1978.

Lipset, Seymour M., and Rokkan, Stein, eds. *Party Systems and Voter Alignments: Cross-National Perspectives.* New York: Free Press, 1967.

López F., Francisco. *La crítica de la iglesia chilena al modelo autoritario liberal: discurso y praxis crítica, análisis de la experiencia.* Santiago: Academia de Humanismo Cristiano, 1980.

López Trujillo, Alfonso, Bishop. "Análisis marxista y liberación cristiana." *Tierra Nueva* (Bogotá), no. 4 (January 1973): 5–43.

Loveman, Brian. *Struggle in the Countryside: Politics and Rural Labor in Chile, 1919–1973.* Bloomington: Indiana University Press, 1976.

Macaulay, Michael Gregory. "Ideological Change and Internal Cleavages in the Peruvian Church: Change, Status Quo and the Priest; The Case of ONIS." Ph.D. dissertation, University of Notre Dame, 1972.

Magnet, Alejandro. *El Padre Hurtado.* 3rd edition, revised. Santiago: Editorial Pacífico, 1957.

Maira, Luis. "Opciones políticas para la iglesia." *Chile Hoy* (Santiago), 17–23 August 1973, p. 6.

Malinowski, Bronislaw. *Magic, Science and Religion.* Garden City, N.Y.: Doubleday, 1948.

Marchais, Georges. "Report to the 22nd Congress of the French Communist Party on Feb. 4, 1976." Excerpts translated in *On the Dictatorship of the Proletariat,* edited by Etienne Balibar, pp. 182–92. London: Unwin, 1977.

———. "Adresse aux Chretiens de France." (June 1976). In *Communistes et Chretiens,* edited by Maurice Thorez, Waldeck Rochet, and Georges Marchais, pp. 25–50. Paris: Editions Sociales, 1976.

Marins, José; Trevisan, Teolide M.; and Chanona, Carolee. *Praxis de los Padres de América Latina: documentos de las Conferencias Episcopales de Medellín a Puebla, 1968–1978.* Bogotá: Ediciones Paulinas, 1978.

Maritain, Jacques. "Catholic Action and Political Action." In his *Scholasticism and Politics,* pp. 185–211. Garden City, N.Y.: Doubleday, Image Books, 1960.

Marx, Karl. "Contribution to the Critique of Hegel's Philosophy of Right: Introduction." In *Karl Marx: Early Writings,* edited by T. B. Bottomore, pp. 43–59. New York: McGraw-Hill, 1963.

———, and Engels, Friedrich. *On Religion.* New York: Schocken Books, 1964.

McBrien, Richard P. *The Remaking of the Church: An Agenda for Reform.* New York: Harper & Row, 1973.

McGovern, Arthur F., S.J. "Chile under Allende and Christians for Socialism." In his *Marxism: An American Christian Perspective,* pp. 210–42. Maryknoll, N.Y.: Orbis Books, 1980.

McHale, Vincent E. "Religion and Electoral Politics in France: Some Recent Observations." *Canadian Journal of Political Science* 2 (1969): 292–311.

McKenzie, Robert, and Silver, Allan. *Angels in Marble: Working-Class Conservatives in Urban England.* Chicago: University of Chicago Press, 1968.

Mecham, J. Lloyd. *Church and State in Latin America: A History of Politico-Ecclesiastical Relations.* 2nd edition, revised. Chapel Hill: University of North Carolina Press, 1966.

Mensaje 11 (December 1962): 589–748. Special issue devoted to "Revolución en América Latina: visión cristiana."

Mensaje 12 (October 1963): 480–686. Special issue devoted to "Reformas revolucionarias en América Latina."

Michelat, Guy, and Simon, Michel. *Classe, religion et comportement politique.*

Paris: La Presse de la Fondation Nationale des Sciences Politiques Editions Sociales, 1977.
————. "Religion, Class and Politics." *Comparative Politics* 10 (October 1977): 159–86.
Míguez Bonino, José. *Doing Theology in a Revolutionary Situation.* Philadelphia: Fortress Press, 1975.
————. *Christians and Marxists: The Mutual Challenge to Revolution.* Grand Rapids, Mi.: William B. Eerdmans Publishing Co., 1976.
Miranda, José Porfirio. *Marx and the Bible: A Critique of the Philosophy of Repression.* Maryknoll, N.Y.: Orbis Books, 1974.
————. *Marx Against the Marxists: The Christian Humanism of Karl Marx.* Maryknoll, N.Y.: Orbis Books, 1980.
Moffitt, Michael, and Letelier, Isabel. *Human Rights, Economic Aid and Private Banks: The Case of Chile.* Washington, D.C.: Institute for Policy Studies, 1978.
Molina, Sergio, and Larraín, Hernan, S.J. "Socialismo democrático: alternativa al socialismo totalitario." *Mensaje* 20 (March-April 1971): 75–83.
Moody, Joseph N., ed. *Church and Society: Catholic Social and Political Thought and Movements, 1789–1950.* New York: Arts Inc., 1953.
Mooney, Mary Helen. "The Role of the Church in Peruvian Political Development." Master's thesis, University of Windsor, 1976.
————, and Soderlund, Walter C. "Clerical Attitudes toward Political Development in Peru." *Journal of Developing Areas* 12 (October 1977): 17–30.
Muñoz Ramirez, Humberto. *Sociología religiosa de Chile.* Santiago: Ediciones Paulinas, 1956.
————. *Memorias de un cura de campo.* Santiago: Ediciones Paulinas, 1967.
Murphy, Francis X., C.S.S.R. "Vatican Politics: Structure and Function." *World Politics* 26 (1974): 542–59.
Mutchler, David E. *The Church as a Political Factor in Latin America: With Particular Reference to Colombia and Chile.* New York: Praeger, 1971.
Nichols, Peter. *The Politics of the Vatican.* New York: Praeger, 1968.
Nordlinger, Eric A. *The Working-class Tories: Authority, Deference and Stable Democracy.* London: McGibbon and Kee, 1967.
Novitsky, Joseph. "Allende Sees Chile Finding Her Own Way to Socialism." *New York Times,* 4 October 1970, pp. 1, 24.
Nunn, Frederick M. *Chilean Politics, 1920–1931: The Honorable Mission of the Armed Forces.* Albuquerque: University of New Mexico Press, 1970.
O'Dea, Thomas F. *The Catholic Crisis.* Boston: Beacon Press, 1968.
Oestreicher, Paul, ed. *The Christian-Marxist Dialogue: An International Symposium.* London: Collier Macmillan, 1969.
Oficina Nacional de Estadística de la Acción Católica Chilena. *Estado de la iglesia en Chile.* Santiago, 1946.
Ogletree, Thomas, ed. *Openings for Marxist-Christian Dialogue.* Nashville: Abingdon Press, 1969.
Oviedo Cavada, Carlos, Bishop. "Carácter de la separación entre la iglesia y el estado en Chile." *Finis Terrae* (Santiago), no. 12 (1956): 50–56.

————, ed. *Documentos del Episcopado: Chile, 1970–1973.* Santiago: Ediciones Mundo, 1974.

Paul VI, Pope. "Populorum Progressio." (1967). In *The Gospel of Peace and Justice: Catholic Social Teaching Since Pope John,* edited by Joseph Gremillion, pp. 387–415. Maryknoll, N.Y.: Orbis Books, 1976.

————. "Octogesima Adveniens." (1971). In *The Gospel of Peace and Justice: Catholic Social Teaching Since Pope John,* pp. 485–512.

————. *On Evangelization in the Modern World (Evangelii Nuntiandi).* Washington, D.C.: United States Catholic Conference, 1976.

Petras, James. *Chilean Christian Democracy: Politics and Social Forces.* Berkeley: Institute of International Studies, University of California, 1967.

————. *Politics and Social Forces in Chilean Development.* Berkeley: University of California Press, 1969.

————. "The Working Class and Chilean Socialism." In *The Chilean Road to Socialism,* edited by Dale Johnson, pp. 240–47. Garden City, N.Y.: Doubleday, 1973.

Pike, Frederick B. *Chile and the United States, 1880–1962.* Notre Dame: University of Notre Dame Press, 1963.

————. "South America's Multi-faceted Catholicism: Glimpses of Twentieth-Century Argentina, Chile and Peru." In *The Church and Social Change in Latin America,* edited by Henry A. Landsberger, pp. 53–75. Notre Dame: University of Notre Dame Press, 1970.

Pironio, Eduardo, Bishop. "Relación sobre la evangelización del mundo de este tiempo en América Latina." *Medellín* (Bogotá) 1 (1975): 107–15. (Translated and reprinted in *Catholic Mind* 73 (March 1975): 35–44.)

Pius XI, Pope. "Quadragesimo Anno." (1931). In *Social Wellsprings 2: Eighteen Encyclicals of Social Reconstruction by Pope Pius XI,* edited by Joseph Husslein, S.J., pp. 174–234. Milwaukee: Bruce Publishing Co., 1942.

————. "Divini Redemptoris." (1937). In *Social Wellsprings 2: Eighteen Encyclicals of Social Reconstruction by Pope Pius XI,* pp. 339–74.

Poblete, Renato, S.J. *Crisis sacerdotal.* Santiago: Editorial del Pacífico, 1965.

————. "Socialist and Christian in Chile." *Worldview* 15 (April 1972): 18–23.

————. "Formas ministeriales en la iglesia de Chile." *Pro Mundi Vita,* no. 50 (1974): 36–38.

————. "Los católicos de derecha." *Mensaje* 27 (May 1978): 251–52.

————, and Garrido, Gino. *La iglesia en Chile,* Madrid: FERES, 1962.

————, et al. *El sacerdote chileno: estudio sociológico.* Santiago: Centro Bellarmino, 1971.

————; Galilea, Carmen W.; and Van Dorp P., Patricia. *Imagen de la iglesia de hoy y religiosidad de los chilenos.* Santiago: Centro Bellarmino, 1980.

Poggi, Giafranco. *Catholic Action in Italy: The Sociology of a Sponsored Organization.* Stanford: Stanford University Press, 1967.

Pomerleau, Claude, C.S.C. "The Missionary Dimension of the Latin American Church: A Study of the French Diocesan Clergy From 1963–1971." Ph.D. dissertation, University of Denver, 1975.

————. "The Changing Church in Mexico and Its Challenge to the State." *Review of Politics* 43 (October 1981): 540–59.

Pontifical Commission for Justice and Peace. "The Church and Human Rights." In *Official Catholic Teaching: Social Justice,* edited by Vincent P. Mainelli, pp. 344–93. Wilmington, N.C.: McGrath Publishing Company, 1978.

Poradowski, Miguel, ed. *El marxismo invade la iglesia.* Valparaíso: Ediciones Universitarias de Valparaíso, 1974.

"Posición política de los obispos." Editorial in *El Mercurio* (Santiago), 27 March 1977.

Protho, James W., and Chaparro, Patricio E. "Public Opinion and the Movement of the Chilean Government to the Left, 1952–1972." *Journal of Politics* 36 (February 1974): 2–43.

Puentes Oliva, Pedro. *Posición Evangélica.* Santiago: Editora Nacional Gabriela Mistral, 1975.

Pujadas, Ignacio. "Comunidades de cristianos revolucionarios: declaración de principios." *Pastoral Popular* (Santiago) 22 (March-April 1972): 48–50.

Quirk, Robert E. *The Mexican Revolution and the Catholic Church, 1910–1929.* Bloomington: Indiana University Press, 1973.

Rahner, Karl. *Shape of the Church to Come.* New York: Seabury Press, 1974.

———. *The Spirit of the Church.* New York: Seabury Press, 1979.

Ray, Philip L., and Taylor, J. Sherrod. "The Role of Nongovernmental Organizations in Implementing Human Rights in Latin America." *Georgia Journal of International Comparative Law* 7, supplement (1977): 484–89.

Remmer Karen. "Public Policy and Regime Consolidation: The First Five Years of the Chilean Junta." *Journal of Developing Areas* 13 (July 1979): 441–61.

Rhodes, Anthony. *The Vatican in the Age of Dictators, 1922–1945.* New York: Holt, Rinehart and Winston, 1974.

Richard G., J. Pablo. "Los obispos y la prédica de la pequeña burguesía." *Punto Final* (Santiago), no. 188 (1973): 26–27.

———. "La experiencia de los cristianos en Chile durante la Unidad Popular." In *Fe cristiana y revolución Sandinista en Nicaragua,* pp. 219–34. Managua: Instituto Histórico Centroamericano, 1979.

Rodríguez, José Luis. "The 'Poblador' in Chilean Society." Senior thesis, Lehman College, 1971.

Rose, Richard. *Electoral Behavior: A Comparative Handbook.* New York: Free Press, 1974.

———, and Urwin, Derek. "Social Cohesion, Political Parties and Strains in Regimes." In *European Politics: A Reader,* edited by Mattei Dogan and Richard Rose, pp. 217–37. Boston: Little, Brown and Company, 1971.

Ruiz-Tagle, Jaime. "La iglesia frente a la prensa: los ataques al Comité para la Paz." *Mensaje* 23 (July 1974): 265–67.

Sanders, Thomas G. *Protestant Concepts of Church and State.* New York: Holt, Rinehart and Winston, 1964.

———. "Catholicism and Development: The Catholic Left in Brazil." In *Churches and States: The Religious Institution and Modernization,* edited by Kalman Silvert, pp. 81–99. New York: American Universities Field Staff, 1967.

———. "The Chilean Episcopate: An Institution in Transition." *American*

Universities Field Staff Reports, West Coast South America Series no. 15 (August 1968): 1–30.

―――. *Catholic Innovation in a Changing Latin America.* Cuernavaca: CIDOC, 1969.

―――. "The Puebla Conference." *American Universities Field Staff Reports,* South America Series no. 30 (1979): 1–9.

―――. "The Catholic Church in Brazil's Political Transition." *American Universities Field Staff Reports,* South America Series no. 48 (1980): 1–17.

―――. "Popular Religion, Pastoral Renewal, and National Reconciliation in Chilean Catholicism." *American Universities Field Staff Reports,* South America Series no. 16 (1981): 1–12.

―――, and Smith, Brian H. "The Chilean Catholic Church During the Allende and Pinochet Regimes." *American Universities Field Staff Reports,* West Coast South America Series no. 23 (March 1976): 1–25.

Sani, Giacomo. "The PCI on the Threshold." *Problems in Communism* 25 (November-December 1976): 28–36.

Secretariado sacerdotal de los "80." *El compromiso político de los cristianos.* Talca: Fundación Obispo Manuel Larraín, 1971.

Segundo, Juan Luis, S.J. *La iglesia chilena ante el socialismo.* Talca: Fundación Obispo Manuel Larraín, 1971.

―――. *A Theology for Artisans of a New Humanity.* 5 vols. Maryknoll, N.Y.: Orbis Books, 1973.

―――. *The Liberation of Theology.* Maryknoll, N.Y.: Orbis Books, 1976.

―――. *The Hidden Motives of Pastoral Action: Latin American Reflections.* Maryknoll, N.Y.: Orbis Books, 1978.

Sigmund, Paul E. "Latin American Catholicism's Opening to the Left." *Review of Politics* 35 (January 1973): 61–76.

―――. *The Overthrow of Allende and the Politics of Chile, 1964–1976.* Pittsburgh: University of Pittsburgh Press, 1977.

Silva Bascuñán, Alejandro. *Una experiencia social cristiana.* Santiago: Política y Espíritu, 1949.

Silva Castro, Raúl, ed. *Obras de Crescente Errázuriz.* 3 vols. Santiago: Edición Zig-Zag, 1936.

Silva Henríquez, Raúl, Cardinal. *El pensamiento social del Cardenal Silva Henríquez.* Santiago: Ediciones Paulinas, 1976.

Silva Solar, Julio. "El integrismo católico-fascista en la ideología de la junta militar." *Chile-América* (Rome) 2 (January 1975): 1–13.

Simon, Gerhard. "The Catholic Church and the Communist State in the Soviet Union and Eastern Europe." In *Religion and Atheism in the U.S.S.R. and Eastern Europe,* edited by B. R. Bociurkiw and J. W. Strong, pp. 190–221. Toronto: University of Toronto Press, 1975.

Sínodo Pastoral. *Iglesia de Santiago: ¿qué dices de tí misma?* 2 vols. Santiago: Ediciones Paulinas, 1969.

Smith, Brian H. "Religion and Social Change: Classical Theories and New Formulations in the Context of Recent Developments in Latin America." *Latin American Research Review* 10 (Summer 1975): 3–34.

―――. "The Impact of Foreign Church Aid: The Case of Chile." In *Communi-*

cation in the Church, edited by Gregory Baum and Andrew Greeley, pp. 23–29. New York: Seabury Press, 1978.

———. "Churches and Human Rights in Latin America: Recent Trends in the Subcontinent." *Journal of Interamerican Studies and World Affairs* 21 (February 1979): 89–128.

———. "The Catholic Church and Political Change in Chile, 1920–1978." Ph.D. dissertation, Yale University, 1979.

———. "Christians and Marxists in Allende's Chile: Lessons for Western Europe." In *Religion and Politics in Western Europe,* edited by Suzanne Berger. London: Frank Cass, 1982.

———, and Rodríguez, José Luis. "Comparative Working-Class Political Behavior: Chile, France and Italy." *American Behavioral Scientist* 18 (September-October 1974): 59–96.

Smith, Donald E. *Religion and Political Development.* Boston: Little, Brown and Company, 1970.

Sobel, Lester A., ed. *Chile and Allende.* New York: Facts on File, 1974.

Social-Activist Priests: Chile. LADOC "Keyhole Series" no. 5. Washington, D.C.: United States Catholic Conference, 1974.

Social-Activist Priests: Colombia, Argentina. LADOC "Keyhole Series" no. 6. Washington, D.C.: United States Catholic Conference, 1974.

Sociedad Chilena de Defensa de la Tradición, Familia y Propiedad (TFP). "La autodemolición de la iglesia, factor de la demolición de Chile." *La Tribuna* (Santiago) 27 February 1973.

———. *La iglesia del silencio en Chile.* Santiago: Edunsa, 1976.

Sorge, Bartoloméo. "El movimiento de los 'Cristianos por el Socialismo.' " *Criterio* (Buenos Aires) 12 September 1974, pp. 488–97.

Spencer, Herbert. *The Principles of Sociology.* 3 vols. New York: D. Appleton and Co., 1896.

Stallings, Barbara. *Class Conflict and Economic Development in Chile, 1958–1973.* Stanford: Stanford University Press, 1978.

Stehle, Hansjakob. *Eastern Politics of the Vatican, 1917–1979.* Translated by Sandra Smith. Athens: Ohio University Press, 1981.

Stevenson, John Reese. *The Chilean Popular Front.* Philadelphia: University of Pennsylvania Press, 1942.

Synod of Bishops, Second General Assembly (1971). "Justice in the World." In *The Gospel of Peace and Justice: Catholic Social Teaching Since Pope John,* edited by Joseph Gremillion, pp. 513–29. Maryknoll, N.Y.: Orbis Books, 1976.

———, Third General Assembly (1974). "Evangelización y derechos humanos." *Mensaje* 23 (November 1974): 591–92.

The Theology of Liberation. LADOC "Keyhole Series" no. 2. Washington, D.C.: United States Catholic Conference, 1974.

Thorez, Maurice; Rochet, Waldeck; and Marchais, Georges. *Communistes et Chretiens.* Paris: Editions Sociales, 1976.

Tiago de Chile. "O.P.A. sur l'Eglise de Chili." *Esprit* (Paris) 43 (January 1975): 119–37.

Torres, Sergio. *El quehacer de la iglesia en Chile, 1925–1970.* Talca: Fundación Obispo Manuel Larraín, 1971.

————, and Eagleson, John, eds. *Theology in the Americas.* Maryknoll, N.Y.: Orbis Books, 1976.

————, eds. *The Challenge of Basic Christian Communities.* Maryknoll, N.Y.: Orbis Books, 1981.

Troeltsch, Ernst. *The Social Teachings of the Christian Churches.* Translated by Olive Wyon. 2 vols. New York: Macmillan, 1931.

Turner, Frederick C. *Catholicism and Political Development in Latin America.* Chapel Hill: University of North Carolina Press, 1971.

Tusell Gomez, Xavier. *Historia de la democracia cristiana en España.* 2 vols. Madrid: Editorial Cuadernos para el Diálogo, 1974.

U.S. Catholic Conference, Administrative Board. "Human Rights Violations in Chile." *National Catholic Reporter,* 22 February 1974, p. 19.

U.S. Congress, Senate, Select Committee to Study Governmental Operations with Respect to Intelligence Activities. *Alleged Assassination Plots Involving Foreign Leaders.* Report no. 94–465, 94th Congress, 1st Session, 1975.

U.S. Congress, Senate, Staff Report of the Select Committee to Study Governmental Organizations with Respect to Intelligence Activities. "Covert Action in Chile: 1963–1973." *Hearings Before the Select Committee to Study Governmental Operations with Respect to Intelligence Activities.* 94th Congress, 1st Session, 1975, vol. 7, Appendix A, pp. 144–209.

U.S. Congress, House, Subcommittee on International Organizations of the Committee on International Relations. "Prepared Statement of José Zalaquett Daher, Chief Legal Counsel, Committee of Cooperation for Peace in Chile." *Chile: The Status of Human Rights and Its Relationship to U.S. Economic Assistance Programs,* 94th Congress, 2nd Session, 1976, pp. 57–65.

Vaillancourt, Yves. "La crisis de'Ilades.' " *Víspera* (Montevideo), April 1971, pp. 18–27. Translated and reprinted in *Social Activist Priests: Chile,* LADOC "Keyhole Series" no. 5. Washington, D.C.: United States Catholic Conference, 1974, pp. 9–18.

Valenzuela, Arturo. *Chile: The Breakdown of Democratic Regimes.* Edited by Juan J. Linz and Alfred Stepan, vol. 4. Baltimore: Johns Hopkins, 1978.

————, and Valenzuela, J. Samuel, eds. *Chile: Politics and Society.* New Brunswick, N.J.: Transaction Books, 1976.

————, eds. *Military Rule in Chile.* Forthcoming.

Vallier, Ivan. "Religious Elites: Differentiation and Developments in Roman Catholicism." In *Elites in Latin America,* edited by Seymour M. Lipset and Aldo Solari, pp. 190–232. New York: Oxford University Press, 1967.

————. "Comparative Studies of Roman Catholicism: Dioceses as Strategic Units." *Social Compass* 16 (1969): 147–84.

————. *Catholicism, Social Control and Modernization in Latin America.* Englewood Cliffs, N.J.: Prentice-Hall, 1970.

————. "Extraction, Insulation and Re-entry: Toward a Theory of Religious Change." In *The Church and Social Change in Latin America,* edited by Henry A. Landsberger, pp. 9–35. Notre Dame: University of Notre Dame Press, 1970.

———. "The Roman Catholic Church: A Transnational Actor." *International Organization* 25 (1971): 479–502.

———. "Radical Priests and the Revolution." In *Changing Latin America: New Interpretations of its Politics and Society,* edited by Douglas Chalmers, pp. 15–26. New York: Academy of Political Science, 1972.

Vanderschueren, Franz, and Rojas, Jaime. "The Catholic Church of Chile: From 'Social Christianity' to 'Christians for Socialism.' " *LARU Studies* 1 (February 1977): 13–59.

Vescovi italiani. "Testimonianza concorde dei Vescovi italiani sul dovere de coerenza nelle scelte civili." *L'Osservatore Romano* (Rome), 26 May 1976, pp. 1–2.

Vicaría de la Solidaridad. *Vicaría de la Solidaridad: un año de labor.* Santiago: Arzobispado de Santiago, 1977.

———. *Vicaría de la Solidaridad: segundo año de labor.* Santiago: Arzobispado de Santiago, 1978.

———. *Vicaría de la Solidaridad: tercer año de labor.* Santiago: Arzobispado de Santiago, 1979.

———. *Vicaría de la Solidaridad: cuarto año de labor.* Santiago: Arzobispado de Santiago, 1980.

———. *Vicaría de la Solidaridad: quinto año de labor.* Santiago: Arizobispado de Santiago, 1981.

Vives, Cristián. "La solidaridad: una forma de evangelizar y de participar en la iglesia." Mimeographed. Santiago: Centro Bellarmino, May 1978.

Wayland-Smith, Giles. *The Christian Democratic Party in Chile: A Study of Political Organization and Activity with Primary Emphasis on the Local Level.* Cuernavaca: CIDOC, 1969.

Weber, Max. *The Protestant Ethic and the Spirit of Capitalism.* Translated by Talcott Parsons. New York: Scribner, 1958.

———. *The Sociology of Religion.* Translated by Ephraim Fishcoff. Boston: Beacon Press, 1963.

Weingartner, Erich, ed. *Church Within Socialism: Church and State in East European Republics.* Rome: IDOC International, 1976.

Wilde, Alexander. "The Years of Change in the Church: Puebla and the Future." *Journal of Interamerican Studies and World Affairs* 21 (August 1979): 299–312.

———. "The Contemporary Church: The Political and the Pastoral." In *The Politics of Compromise: Coalition Government in Colombia,* edited by R. Albert Berry, Ronald G. Hellman, and Mauricio Solaún, pp. 207–35. New Brunswick, N.J.: Transaction Books, 1980.

———. *Politics and the Church in Colombia.* Durham: Duke University Press, forthcoming.

Williams, Margaret Todaro. "The Politicization of the Brazilian Catholic Church: The Catholic Electoral League." *Journal of Interamerican Studies and World Affairs* 16 (August 1974): 301–25.

———. "Church and State in Vargas's Brazil: The Politics of Cooperation." *Journal of Church and State* 18 (Autumn 1976): 443–62.

Windrich, Elaine. "Church-State Confrontation in Rhodesia." *Africa Today* 24 (October-December 1977): 67–73.

Wipfler, William L. *Poder, influencia e impotencia: la iglesia como factor socio-político en República Dominicana.* Santo Domingo: Centro de Planificación y acción Ecuménica, 1980.

Wolpin, Miles D. *Cuban Foreign Policy and Chilean Politics.* Lexington, Mass.: D.C. Heath, 1972.

Youngblood, Robert. "Church Opposition to Martial Law in the Philippines." *Asian Survey* 18 (May 1978): 505–20.

Zañartu, Mario, S.J. *Desarrollo económico y moral católica.* Cuernavaca: CIDOC, 1969.

Zeitlin, Maurice, and Petras, James. "The Working-class Vote in Chile: Christian Democracy versus Marxism." *British Journal of Sociology* 21 (March 1970): 16–29.

Zerón Domínguez, Juan. "Una experiencia de trabajo ecuménico: Comité para la Paz." *Mensaje* 25 (January-February 1976): 54–56.

Index